COLERIDGE
Early Visions
RICHARD HOLMES

By the same author

ONE FOR SORROW (poems) (*Café Books*, 1970)
SHELLEY: THE PURSUIT (*Weidenfeld & Nicolson*, 1974)
GAUTIER: MY FANTOMS (translations) (*Quartet Books*, 1976)
SHELLEY ON LOVE (*Anvil Press*, 1980)
COLERIDGE (*OUP*, 1982)
NERVAL: THE CHIMERAS (with Peter Jay) (*Anvil Press*, 1985)
FOOTSTEPS: ADVENTURES OF A ROMANTIC BIOGRAPHER (*Hodder & Stoughton*, 1985)
MARY WOLLSTONECRAFT AND WILLIAM GODWIN: A SHORT RESIDENCE IN SWEDEN *AND* MEMOIRS (*Penguin Classics*, 1987)
KIPLING: SOMETHING OF MYSELF (with Robert Hampson) (*Penguin Classics*, 1987)
DE FEMINISTE EN DE FILOSOOF (Amsterdam, 1988)

COLERIDGE
Early Visions

RICHARD HOLMES

Hodder & Stoughton
LONDON SYDNEY AUCKLAND TORONTO

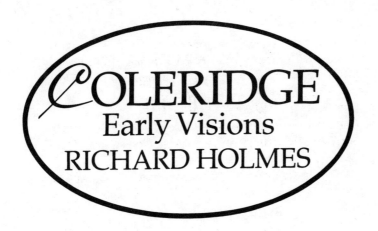

British Library Cataloguing in Publication Data

Holmes, Richard, *1945–*
The young Coleridge.
1. Poetry in English. Coleridge, Samuel Taylor,
1772–1834
I. Title
821′.7

ISBN 0-340-28335-1

First published in Great Britain 1989
Second impression 1989
Third impression 1989
Fourth impression 1990

Published by Hodder and Stoughton,
a division of Hodder and Stoughton Ltd,
Mill Road, Dunton Green, Sevenoaks, Kent TN13 2YA.
Editorial Office: 47 Bedford Square, London WC1B 3DP.

Photoset by Rowland Phototypesetting Ltd,
Bury St Edmunds, Suffolk

Printed and bound in Great Britain by
Mackays of Chatham PLC, Chatham, Kent

To Vicki

Contents

Illustrations

Engraving of Göttingen; Portraits of Friedrich Klopstock, G. E. Lessing, Friedrich Schiller and Immanuel Kant (*Mary Evans Picture Library*)

The fells above Derwent Water (*Landscape Only*); Greta Hall and Keswick Bridge (*Reproduced by Courtesy of the Trustees of the British Museum*)

Portrait of Perdita Robinson by Thomas Gainsborough, 1781–2 (*The National Trust Waddesdon Manor and The Courtauld Institute*), William Godwin, 1802 and Humphry Davy, 1803 (*National Portrait Gallery, London*)

The wanderer above the sea of mist by Caspar David Friedrich (*Kunsthalle, Hamburg*); The Maid of Buttermere, 1798 (*Carlisle Library*), Coleridge, 21st March 1804 (*The Wordsworth Trust*)

Coleridge, 1804. After a portrait by James Northcote (*The Wordsworth Trust*)

Maps

Coleridge in Germany, an original pastel 1799.
(Reproduced by kind permission of Mrs Gardner, Private Collection*)*

Preface

Anyone who presumes to write about Coleridge runs the grave risk of sounding like the person on business from Porlock, a prosaic interrupter of marvels.

But some years ago, I suggested (anonymously) in *The Oxford Companion to English Literature* that Coleridge's best work, "both poetry and prose, has the inescapable glow of the authentic visionary". This biography has become my attempt to substantiate that wild claim, and to show what sort of visionary Coleridge really was, and why – among all the English Romantics – he is worth rediscovering today.

Wordsworth called him "the most wonderful man" he had ever known; but many subsequent biographers have been sceptical. It would seem possible to write an entire book on Coleridge's opium addiction, his plagiarisms, his fecklessness in marriage, his political "apostasy", his sexual fantasies, or his radiations of mystic humbug. And indeed, all these books have been written.[1] But no biographer, since James Dykes Campbell in 1894, has tried to examine his entire life in a broad and sympathetic manner, and to ask the one vital question: what made Coleridge – for all his extravagant panoply of faults – such an extraordinary man, such an extraordinary mind?

The most radical thing about the present book – the first of two volumes – is simply that it is a defence of Coleridge in these terms. I have attempted to recapture his fascination as a man and a writer, and above all to make him live, move, talk, and "have his being". If he does not leap out of these pages – brilliant, animated, endlessly provoking – and invade your imagination (as he has done mine), then I have failed to do him justice.

The present volume takes Coleridge to the age of thirty-one, the exact halfway point in his career, and his departure for Malta in1804, the year before the Battle of Trafalgar. But it uses materials drawn from the second half of his life – notably his labyrinthine autobiography, the *Biographia Literaria* (written in Wiltshire in 1814–15), and his journalism in *The Friend*, a paper he wrote and edited in the Lake District in 1809–10. Coleridge, like many later nineteenth-century writers (Dickens, Hardy, Kipling) worked hard to reconstruct the truth of his early experiences and opinions, and this double vision, or duplicity, is an important theme from the start. It is partly for this reason that my second volume will be entitled: *Later Reflections*.

In his first thirty years Coleridge wrote much of the poetry for which he is now remembered: "Kubla Khan", *The Rime of the Ancient Mariner*, "Christabel", "Frost at Midnight", and "Dejection: an Ode". Many of these have become part of the folklore of Romanticism, and entered proverbially into the language – "an albatross", an "ancient mariner type", a journey "to Xanadu". But what is much less well-known, is that Coleridge went on rewriting, improving, and re-presenting them in later life (the most famous case being the preface to "Kubla Khan", and the highly significant arrival of that person from Porlock), and I shall have more to say about their development in volume two. His play *Osorio*, which was written in 1798 but first performed as *Remorse* in 1812, will also receive further attention. Moreover there is much major – but neglected – poetry yet to come: "To William Wordsworth" (1807), "Constancy to an Ideal Object" (1805–25), or "The Garden of Boccaccio" (1828).

Contrary to legend, Coleridge remained a poet throughout his life, and his later work – the poetry of old age and failing vision – is some of the most moving and revealing. It is impossible to understand him without reference to such works as "A Tombless Epitaph" (1811), which re-explores the symbolic caverns of his youth, as already appears in this volume.

The sequence of autobiographical verse known as the Conversation Poems, which runs from 1794 to 1807, seems to me perhaps his finest poetic achievement (without which Wordsworth would never have developed *The Prelude*). I have examined its themes closely in my narrative, suggesting that our notion of "Romanticism" itself partly grows out of them. Coleridge (and Wordsworth) used the word "Romantic" largely in a loose, eighteenth-century, topographical sense – that "deep Romantic chasm", or even on one memorable occasion that "old Romantic goat" – to denote the visually wild and sublime (sometimes comically so). But they were equally conscious of using language experimentally, and creating a revolution in taste and sensibility. So I have also freely used the term with its modern, critical implications (disputed of course) to denote that new element of imaginative power and intensity of self-expression which we now associate with the period of political and cultural revolution throughout Europe between 1780 and 1830.

But Coleridge was much more than a Romantic poet: he was also a journalist of genius, a translator, a matchless letter-writer (six volumes), an incomparable autobiographer and self-interrogator in his Notebooks (over sixty surviving between 1794 and his death), a literary critic, a spectacular lecturer, a folklorist, a philosopher, a psychologist (specialising in dreams and creativity), a playwright and dramatic critic, and – that much disputed word – a metaphysician. He was also a travel-writer, a fell-walker, and amateur naturalist with an inspired eye for movement and transformation processes – cloud structures, plant growth, animal activity, light shifts, water changes, wind effects. All these aspects I have tried to bring alive, although Coleridge scholars will know what dreadful chasms (such as English and German Idealist philosophy) I have perilously skimmed over, in this first volume at any rate.

Indeed, on the surface at least, I hope this book will read like the most traditional form of popular narrative biography. Coleridge is such a difficult subject – his personality so complex, the exact nature of his literary gift so protean, his daily life contained so much in pure ideas – that the real challenge for me has been simply to unearth his "human story", his living footsteps through the world. Even his vast array of friends, among the living and among the dead, have not been allowed to obstruct the tale unnecessarily, but find a subsidiary place in a form of *dramatis personae* listing, "Coleridge's Circle", at the end of the book.

The tendency of much recent scholarship, following the example of Professor John Livingston Lowes in *The Road to Xanadu* (1927, see Bibliography), has been to see Coleridge's whole imaginative existence as one gigantic booklist, the life of "a library cormorant" (Coleridge's own mocking phrase), alive only in annotations and influences. Instead, I have taken Coleridge into the open air. I have made the fullest use possible of the superb editorial work of E. L. Griggs on the letters, and Kathleen Coburn on the Notebooks (an epic of modern exegesis). I have emphasised Coleridge's physical presence as much as his metaphysical one (Leigh Hunt said shrewdly that he was "a mighty intellect put upon a sensual body . . . very metaphysical and very corporeal"): he seemed to learn as much from landscapes as from literature; as much from children's games as from philosophic treatises; as much from bird-flight as from theology.

Despite the traditional form of my narrative, I have tried certain biographical experiments, two of which might be mentioned. Coleridge is remembered as the greatest talker of his age – that ephemeral form most difficult to re-create in biography (unless you are James Boswell, at your subject's elbow). So I have attempted, from the very start, to set Coleridge *talking*, to tell his story through his own magnificent – and constantly humorous – flights of phrase and metaphor. I have tried to make his *voice* sound steadily through the narrative, and indeed in the end to dominate it. So what I have written is critical biography partly in the form of Romantic monologue. (As Madame de Staël once said in exasperation, "*avec Monsieur Coleridge, c'est tout à fait un monologue*".)

Secondly, I have introduced a series of footnotes – if the reader should care to pause for breath – which does not so much add information in the traditional scholarly way, as initiate another level of speculation, a third perspective – besides those of Coleridge and his narrator. They are intended as a sort of down-stage voice, reflecting on the action as it develops, and suggesting lines of exploration through some of the biographical and critical issues raised.* They are, I suppose, my humble equivalent of Coleridge's marginal "gloss" to the *Ancient Mariner*.

But it will be clear from them, as from the book as a whole, that in the subliminal battle of imagination between subject and biographer, upon which all life-writing ultimately rests, Coleridge has very properly – and wonderfully – triumphed. He is the visionary hero of my book, a hero for a self-questioning age; though whether comedy, tragedy, or romance prevail, remains to be seen.

---

*For example, no one has described the challenge facing the Coleridge biographer, better than the novelist Henry James. After reading Campbell's Life in 1894, James confided to his own notebook how he "was infinitely struck with the suggestiveness of S.T.C.'s figure – wonderful, admirable figure – for pictorial treatment. What a subject some particular cluster of its relations would make for a little story, a small vivid picture. There was a point, as I read, at which I seemed to see a little story – to have a quick glimpse of the possible drama. Would not such a drama necessarily be the question of the acceptance by someone – someone with something important at stake – of the general *responsibility* of rising to the height of accepting him for what he is, recognizing his rare, anomalous, magnificent, interesting, curious, tremendously suggestive character, vices and all, with all its imperfections on its head, and *not* being guilty of the pedantry, the stupidity, the want of imagination, of fighting him, deploring him in the details – failing to recognize that one *must* pay for him and that on the whole he is magnificently worth it." (*The Notebooks of Henry James*, edited by F. O. Matthiessen, New York, 1947, p. 152.) The result was a short story, which is one of the shrewdest things ever written on Coleridge's – what adjective has James left me? – character. (See Bibliography.)

ONE

Child of Nature

1

Coleridge was always fascinated by anything that promised poetical marvels or metaphysical peculiarities. The subject of his own childhood was no exception. "Before I was eight years old," he used to begin in his hypnotic manner, "I was a *character* – sensibility, imagination, vanity, sloth . . . were even then prominent & manifest." And then, like the Ancient Mariner, there was no stopping him.

2

In later life he talked of boyhood and schooldays with many of his closest friends, and wrote vividly about it in his poetry, his letters, his *Biographia*, and his private Notebooks. In all these records, a rich mixture of tragi-comedy, he developed the self-portrait of a precocious, highly imaginative child, driven into "exile" in the world, before he was emotionally prepared for its rigours, by the early death of his father. Cut off from the universe of nature and family affections, he saw himself as an exceptional creature, both intellectually brilliant and morally unstable. He was to make it one of the archetypes of Romantic childhood. This is the picture he presented to his brother George, a sober clergyman, in a poem written at the age of twenty-five:

> Me from the spot where first I sprang to light
> Too soon transplanted, ere my soul had fix'd
> Its first domestic loves; and hence through life
> Chasing chance-started friendships.[1]

Thirty years later, at the age of fifty-five, talking to his physician and confidant, the surgeon James Gillman, he expressed the same feelings, though now raised into the sonorous prose of his late manner. "When I was first plucked up and transplanted from my birthplace and family, at the death of my dear father, whose revered image has ever survived in my mind . . . Providence (it has often occurred to me) gave the first intimation, that it was my lot, and that it was best for me, to make or find my way of life a detached individual, a *Terrae Filius* . . ."[2] He was to be a solitary voyager, an archetypal "son of the Earth", an orphan of the storm, flung out to wander over the world in search of visions. Or so, most wonderfully, he said.

3

Samuel Taylor Coleridge first "sprang to light" in the vicarage of the small market-town of Ottery St Mary in Devon, one autumn morning on 21 October 1772. He was the youngest of ten children, an unexpected fruit of late vintage; his father, the vicar, was already fifty-three years old and his mother forty-five. They both adored him – a large, fat, greedy baby with a shock of unruly black hair, and huge grey astonishing eyes. "My Father was very fond of me, and I was my mother's darling – in consequence, I was very miserable."[3]

He was christened after his godfather, a local worthy, Mr Samuel Taylor, and always known in the family as "Sam", a name he grew to dislike with poignant intensity. Like many a youngest child he was petted and indulged, and almost his earliest memory was of being specially carried out by his nurse to hear a strolling musician playing ballads in the moonlight, during the harvest festivities.

> To hear our old Musician, blind and grey,
> (Whom stretching from my nurse's arms I kissed,)
> His Scottish tunes and warlike marches play,
> By moonshine, on the balmy summer-night . . .[4]

Nursery tradition told of his waywardness and inquisitive mischief. When "carelessly" left by his nurse, he crawled to the fire and pulled out a live coal, badly burning his hand; a Promethean incident also fondly recalled in his poem "To an Infant" (1795). When, at the age of two, he came to be inoculated, he howled when the doctors tried to cover his eyes. It was not the pain, but the concealment of the mystery which upset him. "I manifested so much obstinate indignation, that at last they removed the bandage – and unaffrighted I looked at the lancet & suffered the scratch."[5] He was to do something like that for the rest of his life.

4

The large West Country family in which he grew up was in many ways a remarkable one. Eight of them were boys (one died in infancy), and all showed talent either for soldiering or scholarship. Their father, the Reverend John Coleridge, was not only vicar of Ottery, but also headmaster of the local King's Grammar School, a man who inspired them with notions of duty and excellence which had a profound effect on their upbringing. He referred to them, with Old Testament pride, as his "tribe". All the boys were securely launched in their careers at the time of his sudden death in 1781, except for little Sam who was not quite nine. The effects of this early bereavement were to run very deep for the youngest child.

In origin the Coleridges were a stalwart and undistinguished Devon clan of yeoman farmers and small traders, from three parishes west of Exeter, which themselves sound like some sort of folksong – Dunsford, Drewsteignton, and Doddiscombsleigh.[6] If they were renowned for anything, it was for fertility. Coleridge used to say that his grandfather was a bastard brought up by the parish, and apprenticed as a woollen-draper in Crediton, where he only briefly deviated into respectability. If there was ever a *sans-culotte* revolution, he could safely deny "one drop of Gentility".[7]

Another tale he told, emphasised eccentricity. "His grandfather, a weaver, half-poet and half-madman . . . used to ask the passing beggar to dinner in Oriental phrase, 'Will my lord turn in hither, and eat with his servant?' – and washed his feet."[8]

Nevertheless, his father, the Reverend John Coleridge, was an example of the historic rise of an English middle-class family in three generations; and his grandchildren were to be a successful race of judges, bishops, and senior academics. This pressure for family success, closely associated with Sam's elder brothers, was to have a subtle and pervasive influence throughout Coleridge's literary life – a profession where "success" and respectability are delusive concepts.

The Reverend John Coleridge was born in Crediton, north of Exeter, in January 1719. He obtained an exhibition to the local grammar school, and would have gone on directly to university but for the bankruptcy of his father, the woollen-draper. The reasons for this downfall are unknown, but there is some suggestion of heavy drinking, which can often be a family inheritance. Coleridge liked to believe that John was a dreamy and unworldly man – "a perfect Parson Adams" in an oft-repeated phrase – and would tell comic anecdotes of his father's scholarly distraction, in long evening sessions with Gillman at Highgate, "till the tears ran down his face".[9] This may have been so in later life, but there is a characteristic element of myth-making in Coleridge's accounts of John's saintly simplicities. As a young man he seems to have been determined and ambitious, riding rough-shod over his various setbacks. Temporarily cheated of university, he took a schoolmastership at the nearby village of Clysthdon, married a local Crediton girl, by whom he had four daughters, and continued to study hard and somehow to save money. In 1747, at the age of twenty-eight, he was able to apply for matriculation as a mature student at Sidney Sussex, Cambridge – a triumph over his straitened circumstances.

Here he proved himself a brilliant student of classics and Hebrew, so that by 1749 he had qualified for his first major appointment as headmaster of Squire's Latin School at South Molton, and also obtained the curacy of nearby Mariansleigh. On the death of his first wife in 1751, he did not repine but promptly married Ann Bowdon, the handsome and capable daughter of an Exmoor farmer, who had all the ambition and drive of a perfect headmaster's wife.

He also began to publish – first as an "ingenious contributor" to the *Gentleman's Magazine*: and then as an author of scholarly textbooks. There followed a series of worthy productions: a Hebrew edition of the Bible (co-edited); a short grammatical textbook for schools (1759); a *Dissertation on the Book of Judges* (1768); and a *Critical Latin Grammar* (1772). In 1776, he privately printed his own political statement, *A Fast Sermon*, deploring the outbreak of the American War of Independence, in which he rather pithily observed that "you might as well imagine the Almighty to create the Sun, Moon, and Stars, and then permit them to move at random, as to create Man, and not ordain Government." One may gather from this that John Coleridge was no Anglican radical. His literary turn even reached the stage, for he adapted a Latin comedy by Terence, which he sent to Garrick at Drury Lane, under the rather tantalising title of *The Fair Barbarian*.[10]

Coleridge gently deflated his father's achievements – "the truth is, my Father was not a first-rate Genius – he was however a first-rate Christian". He suggested that his greatest contribution to scholarship was the re-naming of the ablative case in Latin grammar with the "sonorous and expressive" term of the "Quippe-quare-quale quia-quidditive Case!"[11] But the Reverend John Coleridge's works were subscribed by many West Country notables, including the local MP,

Judge Buller, and the local landowner Sir Stafford Northcote. In 1760 their patronage brought him the headmastership of the King Henry VIII Grammar School at Ottery St Mary, a remarkable achievement for the bankrupt draper's son, at the age of forty-one.

At the end of this year, on the death of the incumbent, the Reverend Richard Holmes MA (a man who has left no significant trace), John Coleridge was also appointed vicar of St Mary's, thus establishing himself as one of the leading figures in the town. His rapidly growing family soon occupied both the School House (where there were a dozen or so private pupils) and the Vicarage. These were situated in the cluster of old medieval buildings below the church in a commanding position on the top of the Cornhill of Ottery St Mary's. There is a surviving eighteenth-century aquatint showing the Vicarage, divided from the churchyard by a sunken lane. Here a stout, old-fashioned gentleman in clerical knee-breeches and broad-brimmed hat is mounting a horse. This is the Reverend John preparing for a pastoral visit.

Next door, Sir Stafford Northcote kept his town residence in the Warden House; and at the end of the sunken lane stood Chanter's House in extensive grounds, eventually to become the family home of the most successful of the tribe. By the time of little Sam's birth in 1772, the three surviving half-sisters ("my aunts") were married and living away; and the eldest boy, John, then aged eighteen, had already departed as a soldier to India. The remaining family at Ottery consisted of William, then sixteen, who would prove a scholar; James, thirteen, who would become a successful career soldier in England; Edward, twelve, destined to become a clergyman and "the wit" of the family; George, eight, who would become a headmaster like his father; Luke, seven, who would train as a doctor; Anne, five, universally loved and affectionately known as "Nancy" by all her brothers; and Francis, two, the most handsome and dashing of the boys, who would also go to India. "All my Brothers are remarkably handsome," observed Coleridge mournfully, "but they were as inferior to Francis as I am to them."[12] This question of "inferiority" was to be a recurring anxiety of the youngest, uncertain whether he was the Benjamin or the black sheep.

5

On his own evidence, Coleridge emerged cuckoo-like from his nursery in the School House, greedy, precocious, and temperamental.

His appetite for food and books appeared almost indistinguishable, expressed by an almost alarmingly large mouth which hung permanently open because he found difficulty in breathing through his nose. By the age of three he could read a chapter of the Bible, and was attending the local dame-school, which he largely remembered for the "three cakes" he was allowed to buy at the baker's shop on the way. At home he "wallowed in a beef & pudding dinner", and devoured adventure stories: "Jack the Giant Killer", *Robinson Crusoe*, "General Belisaurius", and the strange tale of *Philip Quarll, The English Hermit.* This told of "the Sufferings and Surprising Adventures of Mr Philip Quarll, who was lately discovered by Mr Dorrington, a Bristol Merchant, upon an uninhabited island in the South Sea; where he has lived above Fifty Years, without any human Assistance, still continues to reside, and will not come away." One of Quarll's adventures was the shooting of a large and beautiful sea-bird with a home-made bow, an action he immediately regrets: "I have destroyed that as was certainly made for Nature's Diversion with such a Variety of Colours . . ."[13]

6

He was petted by his sister Nancy, who used to sing him melancholy ballads on winter evenings:

> Ballad of ship-wreck'd sailor floating dead,
> Whom his own true-love buried in the sands![14]

But he was teased by the older schoolboys, and sibling rivalry soon surfaced with his daring, extrovert brother Francis. There were angry disputes for the affection of his nurse, Molly, an old family retainer, much loved by all the other boys. In the autobiographical letters written at Nether Stowey in his twenties,* Coleridge analysed this

*Five of these were written at Nether Stowey 1797–8, at the specific request of his friend Tom Poole (see Chapter 7). But Coleridge found his autobiography an inexhaustible topic, as we shall see, in later letters to John Thelwall, Sir George Beaumont, Charles Lamb, Thomas Allsop, and many others. Coleridge's friends subsequently joined in the process of analysing and mythologising his childhood and youth, notably Wordsworth in *The Prelude* (1805), Lamb in his *Essays of Elia* (1840), Leigh Hunt in his *Autobiography* (1850), and William Godwin in some unpublished notes for a biography (1799–1804). Various Romantic themes emerge from this complex collaborative portrait, especially those of the Child of Nature, the Spiritual Exile, and the Philosopher Youth or *Wünderkind.*

with his customary psychological acuity, finding in it the beginnings of his inner imaginative life, a child escaping into his fantasy world.

> Molly, who had nursed my Brother Francis, and was immoderately fond of him, hated me because my mother took more notice of me than of Frank – and Frank hated me, because my mother gave me now & then a bit of cake, when he had none . . . So I became fretful, & timorous, & a tell-tale – & the School-boys drove me from play, & were always tormenting me – & hence I took no pleasure in boyish sports – but read incessantly . . . And I used to lie by the wall, and *mope* – and my spirits used to come upon me suddenly, & in a flood – & then I was accustomed to run up and down the church-yard, and act over all I had been reading on the docks, the nettles, and the rank-grass.[15]

The church and churchyard of St Mary Ottery, immediately outside the School House across the sunken lane, became a magic world to little Sam amidst these persecutions, mopings and tantrums. He would later strongly identify with another persecuted poet, Thomas Chatterton, who created his own imaginary world in St Mary's Redcliffe church, at Bristol.

St Mary Ottery was an evocative place, a fourteenth-century foundation modelled by Bishop Grandisson on Exeter Cathedral, a collegiate building much larger than an ordinary parish church. It dominated the Cornhill and the entire town, with two huge granite bell-towers whose peals could be heard throughout the valley of the Otter.

Outside, the old gravestones stood at angles in the sunlight. Inside were many shadowy wonders: corbells in the shape of owls and elephants, a globe mounted with an heraldic eagle, and the medieval tombs of the Grandisson family. On one side of the nave, low enough for a child to climb on, was the tomb of the crusader, Sir Otho de Grandisson (died 1359), in helmet and chain-mail, holding his broadsword; on the other, that of his wife Lady Beatrix (died 1374), with her dogs at her feet.

In the gallery of the south transept hung Bishop Grandisson's enormous mechanical clock, with its square wooden face painted bright blue. It showed the time with an intriguing system of planetary symbols, based on the Ptolemaic model, with a golden sun, and silver moon, and a gilded star, moving steadily round the gleaming dial of heaven. Such images sank deeply into the child's mind, unconsciously reappearing in the great ballads written twenty years after.

The moving Moon went up the sky
And nowhere did abide:
Softly she was going up,
And a Star or two beside.[16]

In his autobiographic poetry Coleridge transformed his unhappy memories into an idyllic Romantic version of his "native home". In "Frost at Midnight", written in 1797, the bells of St Mary's are given a thrilling, other-worldly quality, far removed from his playground miseries. The endless carillons of feast-days and fair-days, when the chimes were rung for twelve hours at a stretch, are made to promise a dream-like expansion into future happiness. He was here describing his memories as a teenage schoolboy in London, long after the "exile" from Ottery had occurred, and the poetic myth of his childhood was already being prepared for his own son, Hartley.

With unclosed lids, already had I dreamt
Of my sweet birth-place, and the old church-tower,
Whose bells, the poor man's only music, rang
From morn to evening, all the hot Fair-day,
So sweetly, that they stirred and haunted me
With a wild pleasure, falling on mine ear
Most like articulate sounds of things to come![17]

There is perhaps a hint of bitterness in the slight rhythmic dip in the third line, where Coleridge may really have been thinking of the "poor *boy's* only music" at Ottery, but otherwise the verse rises with an unbroken surge of Romantic longing to the climactic outburst of syllables in the last line, "articulate sounds", which has an almost religious force. (It is a note that Wordsworth was to explore fully in *The Prelude* of 1805.)

7

In reality, for little Sam the bells brought scant release. Because of his small size and difficult temperament, he was kept on at dame-school until the age of six – not to be "trusted among my Father's School-boys".[18] By then his elder brothers, tall distant figures, were going out into the world. William left Wadham College, Oxford, and became a schoolmaster in Hackney, aged twenty-three. James – a stocky, red-faced, resolute young man – left Ottery aged sixteen, with ten guineas sewn into the back of his waistcoat, to join the ranks of the 6th Regiment of Foot; then Edward, "the Wit of the family", left for Pembroke, Oxford.[19] Coleridge significantly put down these departures to his mother's influence in family affairs. She was, he said dispassionately, "an admirable Economist, and managed exclusively".[20] "My Father . . . had so little of parental ambition in him, that he had destined his children to be Blacksmiths etc, & had accomplished his intention but for my Mother's pride & spirit of aggrandizing her family."[21]

This was almost certainly untrue of the Reverend John, whose whole career showed a headmaster's natural drive for distinction. His academic successes were renowned throughout the county. But Coleridge's feelings for his mother were to become ambiguous, and finally bitter. By comparison his father – his lost, beloved father – was to be transformed into a humorous paragon of gentleness and understanding, utterly without worldly ambitions.

During these difficult childhood years, after being the "darling" who sat, as he fondly recalled, "at my mother's side, on my little stool, to read my little book, and to listen to the talk of my elders", he clearly felt he became at first an anxiety, and then a disappointment, to her.[22] He felt this rejection as deeply as anything in his life, and at sixteen would say of the mother of a schoolfriend in London that she "taught me what it was to have a mother".[23] In later life, he often repeated this sense of looking for mother-substitutes. At twenty-nine, he told his friend Tom Poole that Mrs Poole "was the only Being whom I ever *felt* in the relation of Mother".[24] In middle age the search for a lost mother continued, with strange consequences.[25]

Exactly how this process of alienation occurred is difficult to say, for Coleridge wrote and talked more and more about his father, and less and less about his mother as he grew older. But he seems to have felt, very early on, that in her eyes by comparison with his brothers, he was already a failure by the time he left Ottery. There are no contemporary accounts of mother and son together in these early days. But some years later, when he revisited Ottery in the autumn of 1799, there was a revealing incident which was recorded by his friend, Robert Southey. "We were all a good deal amused by the old lady," – Ann Coleridge, aged seventy-two, was by then rather deaf – "she could not hear what was going on, but seeing Samuel arguing with his brothers, took it for granted that he must have been in the wrong, and cried out, 'Ah, if your poor father had been alive, he'd soon have convinced you.'"[26]

It was amusing to Southey, but not to Coleridge. In his poetry it was to produce the recurring image of a lost or rejected child, for ever attempting to return home, or recover the feelings of home, or somehow – marvellously – to reinvent them.

The pluck and determination of his older brothers was exemplified by John, who had been in Calcutta since 1771, and within five years rose to the rank of lieutenant. His courage and generosity became legendary in the family. His vivid, good-hearted letters arrived regularly at Ottery throughout Coleridge's boyhood, often bringing money. They could hardly have failed to fire Sam's imagination. In 1775 a typical missive arrived from Monghyr, on the Ganges, a hundred miles south of the Nepalese border.

> I left Calcutta about the end of April . . . You have no doubt heard of Monghyr, famous for its wild, romantic situation, and especially for its being the Montpellier of the East. About two miles from the garrison there is a Hotwell in which the water continually boils; the Natives esteem it sacred, and flock thither from all parts of the country to receive a Holy Sprinkling, as they imagine it has the Virtue of cleansing them from their sins . . .[27]

It may have been glimpses like this that first turned Coleridge towards his lifelong fascination with travel books. James came to rely on John for help in his own military career, eventually receiving from him the sum of £1,000 to purchase a commission. Francis so worshipped John that he finally contrived to join him in India at the incredibly early age of twelve. John even had a remarkable plan for Sam to join him in India as a cadet; but this was to be forestalled by his own tragic death from malaria, at Tillicherry, in January 1787. He died penniless, having sent all his money home or lent it to fellow officers.[28]

8

By the age of six, Sam's obsessive reading had reached unhealthy proportions. Coleridge again described this with a keen eye on the young prodigy in the making. He had imported "all the gilt-covered little books" from his aunt's *every-thing* shop at Crediton, and among them *The Arabian Nights*:

> one tale of which (the tale of a man who was compelled to seek for a pure virgin) made so deep an impression on me (I had read it in the evening while my mother was mending stockings) that I was haunted by spectres, whenever I was in the dark – and I distinctly remember the anxious & fearful eagerness, with which I used to watch the window, in which the books lay – & whenever the Sun lay upon them, I would seize it, carry it by the wall, & bask, & read.[29]

The childish mixture of fantasy and superstition is acutely recalled: the beautiful virgin who is also a fearful spectre; the relentless moving finger of the sun which is also a kind of benevolent, protecting power. Again, these are themes that Coleridge would carry into his adult poetry of his late twenties, in "Christabel" and the *Ancient Mariner*.

In his forties he was still recalling the impact of *The Arabian Nights* in his essays: ". . . I can never forget with what a strange mixture of obscure dread and intense desire I used to look at the volume and *watch* it, till the morning sunshine had reached and nearly covered it, when, and not before, I felt the courage given me to seize the precious treasure . . ."[30]

Coleridge also saw himself as little Sam, becoming almost comically peculiar and precocious. "So I became a *dreamer* – and acquired an indisposition to all bodily activity – and I was fretful, and inordinately passionate, and as I could not play at any thing, and was slothful, I was despised & hated by the boys; and because I could read & spell, & had, I may truly say, a memory & understanding forced into almost an unnatural ripeness, I was flattered & wondered at by all the old women."[31] Here, incidentally, is the first glimpse of Coleridge the talker, ensconced in a circle of his clucking admirers. (He later told Godwin that he was "accustomed only to the conversation of grown persons", and became "arrogant & conceited".)[32]

The Reverend John now intervened. With characteristic forthrightness he actually burnt the offending storybooks, and enrolled Sam in the King's School where he remained a pupil to the age of nine. He soon "outstripped" all of his age. His schoolboy horizons opened, and there is evidence of much wandering about the town, and down by the River Otter, and to neighbouring houses, often in the company of Francis, with whom fraternal warfare continued. "Frank had a violent love of beating me – but whenever that was superseded by any humour or circumstance, he was always very fond of me – & used to regard me with a strange mixture of admiration & contempt – strange it was not – : for he hated books, and loved climbing, fighting, playing, & robbing orchards, to distraction."[33]

One memorable trip was to the Pixies' Parlour, a mysterious sandstone cave beneath the roots of an ancient oak tree, in a field about a mile south of the town overlooking the river. It was a place of folklore – goblins, ghosts – where Sam bravely imitated his elders by carving his initials in the shadowy recess. It was a cave that re-appeared many times in his poetry, and finally became an image of his lifelong search for esoteric knowledge:

Yea, oft alone,
Piercing the long-neglected holy cave,
The haunt obscure of old Philosophy,
He bade with lifted torch its starry walls
Sparkle, as erst they sparkled to the flame
Of odorous lamps tended by Saint and Sage.[34]

As an undergraduate he was to go back to find those initials, entwined with those of his heroic brothers.*

Another visit was to Sir Stafford Northcote's new country house, the Pynes, outside Ottery. Frank had fallen in love with the baronet's daughter Maria, to whom he was later to send messages of devotion from India. But Sam was taken by a different kind of recondite beauty – the splendid, polished, Georgian spiral staircase. Years later, when trying to explain the complex structure of his essay-collection, *The Friend*, with its expanding themes and "interposed" lighter pieces of diversion, or "landing-places", he suddenly recalled his first, awesome impression of the great house.

> Before all other objects, I was most struck by the magnificent staircase, relieved at well proportioned intervals by spacious landing-places, this adorned with shewy plants, the next looking out on an extensive prospect through the stately window with its side panes of rich blues and saturated amber or orange tints: while

*The Pixies' Parlour still exists on a low, wooded, sandstone ridge, now some fifty yards from the eastern bank of the River Otter. In 1986 I crawled in and was astonished to discover the initials STC carved at the very back of the cave. It took me a moment to realise that the sandstone walls are so porous and flaky that these could not possibly be Coleridge's original graffiti, but some later act of piety. Such carvings and re-carvings of his initials, ceremoniously repeated by generation after generation of unknown memorialists, suddenly seemed to me like a symbol of the essentially cumulative process of biography itself. (See Richard Ellmann, "Literary Biography", in *Golden Codgers*, Oxford, 1973.)

from the last and highest the eye commanded the whole spiral ascent with the marbled pavement of the great hall from which it seemed to spring up as if it merely *used* the ground on which it rested. My readers will find no difficulty in translating these forms of the outward senses into their intellectual analogies . . .[35]

In fact Coleridge himself always had the greatest difficulty with the "architectural" structure of his prose books, as his readers found to their cost. They were to be less like solid Georgian staircases, and far more like the visionary, suspended, self-circling stairways of Piranesi's famous engravings. Something of this seems already foreshadowed in the childhood sense – recorded with such visual accuracy – that on looking down over the banisters from the top of Northcote's spiral stairs, the entire structure seemed independent of the ground, simply springing up above it into the air, magically and alarmingly unsupported.

Most fondly recalled of all were the endless expeditions down to the placid, rippling waters of the Otter, which meander through low red-earthed banks and shallow shingle spits, six miles down to the sea at Budleigh Salterton:

Dear native brook! where first young Poesy
Stared wildly-eager in her noontide dream![36]

Paddling, paper-boat sailing, and solemn games of ducks and drakes, are all recalled in later verse. Sam also learned to swim here, a pastime he practised at home and abroad for many years, well into his middle age. The river produced the first really accomplished poem of his youth, which he wrote at the age of twenty-one, while still at university, the sonnet "To the River Otter".

Here again, the poetic memory is far happier than those of the letters, reaching towards a more universal and perhaps more conventionally acceptable nostalgia for childhood, the Paradise lost, that the Romantics would foster. Yet it is brilliant with living detail, full of Coleridge's sensitivity to light and movement. The rapid, effortless bouncing stone enacts the freedom of the child's mind – the skips and flights of the imagination – while the glowing waters become a symbol of memory itself.

. . . What happy and what mournful hours, since last
I skimm'd the smooth thin stone along thy breast,

Numbering its light leaps! yet so deep imprest
Sink the sweet scenes of childhood, that mine eyes
  I never shut amid the sunny ray,
But straight with all their tints thy waters rise,
  Thy crossing plank, thy marge with willows grey,
And bedded sand that vein'd with various dyes
Gleam'd through thy bright transparence! . . .
  Ah! that once more I were a careless Child![37]

9

In his first year at the King's School (1779) an epidemic swept through the pupils, and both Sam and George lay dangerously ill isolated at the top of the School House with "putrid fever". This is the first time that Coleridge experienced the terrible nightmares that returned to him intermittently for the rest of his life, dreams so vivid and overmastering that he would wake whole households at Stowey, at Grasmere, and even at Highgate with his screams, and which are the subject – and indeed the inspiration – of many poems. Even as a boy he tried to keep them off with a poetic charm, the old rhyming prayer, "Four Angels round me spread, Two at my foot & two at my head . . ."

It was to give him a lifelong sympathy not only with other children suffering night terrors, but with any adult friend on a feverish sickbed, to many of whom he would prove a tender nurse. "This prayer I said nightly – & most firmly believed the truth of it. – Frequently have I, half-awake & half-asleep, my body diseased & fevered by my imagination, seen armies of ugly Things bursting in upon me, & these four angels keeping them off."[38] The suspended condition of "half-awake & half-asleep", with the mind floating and planing between the conscious and unconscious state, always fascinated him.

During this illness, Frank, with typical daring and "in spite of orders to the contrary", would steal up to read Pope's Homer to his small brother. Sam also became much closer to George, then sixteen and about to go to Oxford, a quiet, kindly, studious boy whom Coleridge would soon look on as his second father. Of the first fifty letters Coleridge is known to have written, thirty-five were to George; and the *Poems* of 1797 would be dedicated to him, with an epigraph from Horace, "notable among brothers for his paternal spirit".[39]

He later wrote – before quarrelling with him – "My Brother George is a man of reflective mind & elegant Genius. He possesses Learning in a greater degree than any of the Family, excepting myself. His manners are grave, & hued over with a tender sadness. In his moral character he approaches every way nearer to Perfection than any man I ever yet knew – indeed, he is worth the whole family in a Lump."[40]

His sister Nancy also showed great kindness at this time, and Coleridge came to idealise the brother-sister relationship: "she lov'd me dearly, and I doted on her!" To Charles Lamb, so deeply attached to his own sister Mary, he would later say in a poem of 1794 that she became his only real confidante, listening to all his "puny sorrows" and "hidden maladies", which he poured forth "As a sick Patient in a Nurse's arms".[41]*

But in these reminiscences there is an exaggerated idealising quality, that suggests that the perfection of Nancy was really a disguised form of reproach to his real mother. John, out in India, would also make a cult of his sister, whom he had never seen, while Frank in turn idealised his old nurse, "my good, my dear, and faithful Molly", to whom he sent money.[42] Perhaps they all felt certain reservations about their mother. Yet, except for Sam, they all grew up with a marked self-confidence in personal relations. Frank would cheerfully sign a letter to Nancy, "Your affectionate and handsome brother, Francis", adding a postscript asking if Maria Northcote was kept fully informed of his growing good looks.[43]

---

* For Coleridge, the act of nursing or being nursed, and the intimacy of the sickroom, eventually became an emblem of true love and understanding. Sickroom incidents are frequent in his life, and gradually begin to pass into his poetry as a major theme. Psychologically this suggests something about his "dependent" personality (of which dependency on opium was only one manifestation). For all his intellectual brilliance and daring, Coleridge was often drawn to this twilight state, in which the distinction between adult and child could be magically suspended, responsibilities waived, and physical tenderness be freely exchanged without sexual guilt. (See Chapter 12, and Charles Lamb's Elia essay, "The Convalescent", 1833.) Some of his best poetry concerns the visions of the sick, hallucinating, or fitfully dreaming hero or heroine. And in his affairs of the heart, the sickroom becomes a zone of almost erotic intensity. Though the letters of many Romantic writers – Wordsworth, Shelley, Keats – are surprisingly full of lurid details of medical complaints (anarchic bowels, treacherous lungs, seething bladders, and mutinous teeth, together with a catalogue of fevers, rheumatics, headaches, and of course consumptive fears), Coleridge outdid his friends in this as in most things. Turning the question on its head, one might also consider what the idea of "health" meant to the Romantics; and what place – if any – it had in the New Sensibility of Feeling. (See Roy and Dorothy Porter, *In Sickness and in Health: The British Experience 1650–1850*, Fourth Estate, London, 1988.)

10

In the autumn of 1779, when he was seven, a quarrel took place between Sam and Frank which throws much light on the psychology of the youngest son, and which Coleridge himself shrewdly presented as a formative event. It is given more space than any other incident in the autobiographical letters to Tom Poole, and often reappears in the poetry. It began, one October evening in the kitchen of the Vicarage, in a dispute about food – and favouritism. Sam, typically demanding, had asked his mother to prepare him some special sliced cheese for toasting. Frank stole in, and minced it up "to disappoint the favourite", and a violent fight ensued. Fifteen years later Coleridge still entered into the drama as he wrote.

> I returned, saw the exploit, and in an agony of passion flew at Frank – he pretended to have been seriously hurt by my blow, flung himself on the ground, and there lay with outstretched limbs – I hung over him moaning & in a great fright – he leaped up, & with a horse-laugh gave me a severe blow in the face – I seized a knife, and was running at him, when my Mother came in and took me by the arm – I expected a flogging – & struggling from her I ran away, to a hill at the bottom of which the Otter flows – about one mile from Ottery.[44]

The violence of this little scene is surprising – the "dreamer" is armed with a kitchen knife – and calls into question the whole poetic image of the "careless" childhood.

Sam fled down through the gardens of the Chanter's House to his old friend the river, going along the bank almost as far as Cadhay Bridge. Here he hid. "I distinctly remember my feelings when I saw a Mr Vaughan pass over the Bridge, at about a furlong's distance – and how I watched the Calves in the field beyond the river." It grew dark, and he remained there for the entire night, "a dreadful stormy night", and a long time for a boy of seven. He said his prayers, and thought "*at the same time* with inward & gloomy satisfaction, how miserable my Mother must be!" Finally he went to sleep under a mass of old thorn bush cuttings, within a few yards of the water's edge.

His mother, indeed, was "almost distracted". She sent out first to the churchyard where he still often played, then despatched boys all round the streets; and by dark raised a general alarm. By ten o'clock half the town had turned out to search for the missing child, the

Ottery town-crier was sent to the neighbouring villages, and the ponds and mill-race were dragged. The search continued throughout the night without success, and "no one went to bed". At five in the morning Sam awoke, now frozen through, and too weak to move. "I saw the Shepherds & Workmen at a distance – & cryed but so faintly, that it was impossible to hear me 30 yards off – and there I might have lain & died – for I was now almost given over." His saviour was Sir Stafford Northcote, the good old fox-hunting squire, and Coleridge relived the moment of his rescue with perhaps the deepest emotion of all his childhood reminiscences.

> By good luck Sir Stafford Northcote, who had been out all night, resolved to make one other trial, and came so near that he heard my crying – He carried me in his arms, for near a quarter of a mile; when we met my father & Sir Stafford's Servants. – I remember, & never shall forget, my father's face as he looked upon me while I lay in the servant's arms – so calm, and the tears stealing down his face: for I was the child of his old age. – My Mother, as you may suppose, was outrageous with joy . . . I was put to bed – & recovered in a day or so – but I was certainly injured – For I was weakly, & subject to the ague for many years after.[45]

Coleridge added that "neither Philosophy or Religion" would allow him to forgive a local lady who suggested that he should have been whipped for this exploit.

Its importance to him is shown by the number of times he referred to it in later life. Both Tom Poole and the Gillmans at Highgate were given detailed accounts; and it recurs in his Notebooks. Twenty-four years later, one cold summer night at Keswick, he thought he heard one of his own children moaning: "listened anxiously, found it was a Calf bellowing – instantly came on my mind that night, I slept out at Ottery – & the Calf in the Field across the river whose lowing had so deeply impressed me – Chill+Child+Calf-lowing probably the rivers Greta and Otter."[46] Other versions of the incident appear in Act III of his verse-play *Osorio*; in his "Monody on the Death of Thomas Chatterton"; in stanza seven of his great poem "Dejection"; and in the fragmentary prologue to "The Wanderings of Cain", possibly as late as 1828:

> Alone, by night, a little child,
> In place so silent and so wild –
> Has he no friend, no loving mother near?[47]

What was its significance to Coleridge? It was clearly the idea of being the abandoned and outcast child, the child "lowing" like a calf for its lost parents. The bitter rivalry with Frank, for food and affection, was merely a pretext for this much deeper sense of grievance. Coleridge never harboured a lasting grudge against his brother, but after his departure for India, even tended to hero-worship him. He wrote to George in 1793: "he was the only one of my Family, whom similarity of Ages made more peculiarly my Brother – he was the hero of all the little tales, that make the remembrance of my earliest days interesting!"[48]

For the first time in his life he had taken the fictional drama of the outcast – Robinson Crusoe, Philip Quarll – and played it out in childish reality, enacting a kind of symbolic revenge against his parents, and especially his mother. The whole point of his flight, his night of "exile", was to demand further expressions of their affection: his father's tears, his mother's "outrageous" joy. It was to be the first of many such symbolic escapes throughout his life, and his poetry, acts of flight and exile, with their undertone of "inward and gloomy satisfaction".

Yet the exploit remains a strange episode, a piece of wilful mischief by a spoilt, clever, and highly strung child determined to be the centre of attention. Little Sam was, after all, very far from being outcast or abandoned at this time. Relations with his mother may have been passionate and difficult, but the Reverend John paid much attention to the boy, encouraging him once more in his adventurous reading, and devoting long evenings to the development of his extraordinary mind.

Of the following year, 1780, Coleridge recalled with something close to idyllic happiness:

> I read every book that came in my way without distinction – and my father was very fond of me, & used to take me on his knee, and hold long conversations with me. I remember, that at eight years old I walked with him one winter evening from a farmer's house, a mile from Ottery – & he told me the names of the stars – and how Jupiter was a thousand times larger than our world – and that the other twinkling stars were Suns that had worlds rolling round them – & when I came home, he shewed me how they rolled round –. I heard him with a profound delight & admiration; but without the least mixture of wonder or incredulity. For from my

> early reading of Faery Tales, & Genii etc etc – my mind had been habituated *to the Vast*.[49]

Looking back at this early vision of the natural universe, opened up to him by his beloved father, Coleridge characteristically saw the beginnings of his own metaphysical interests even at the age of eight. He felt that his mind was naturally formed to a religious, mystical conception of the world, always reaching towards a sense of infinity and unity within the creation. Once again he was interpreting his childhood along Romantic lines, opposed to the whole analytic and rational tradition of the eighteenth-century Enlightenment education. It is interesting to compare this with John Stuart Mill's criticism of his own strictly utilitarian upbringing in his *Autobiography* (1873).

Coleridge put this to Tom Poole with what was, at twenty-five, glowing confidence in his own powers.

> I regulated all my creeds by my conceptions not by my *sight* – even at that age. Should children be permitted to read Romances, & Relations of Giants & Magicians, & Genii? – I know all that has been said against it; but I have formed my faith in the affirmative. I know no other way of giving the mind a love of "the Great", & "the Whole" . . . I have known some who have been *rationally* educated, as it is styled. They were marked by a microscopic acuteness; but when they looked at great things, all became a blank & they saw nothing . . . and uniformly put the negation of a power for the possession of a power – & called the want of imagination, Judgment, & the never being moved to Rapture Philosophy![50]

That childlike sense of reverence and wonder remained with him, almost miraculously, far into middle age.

Despite such lyrical recollections as this, it is hard to decide how happy Sam really was at Ottery. There are no more than fleeting references to him in his brothers' letters, and Coleridge's own evidence is curiously contradictory. Against the golden memories of his father's kindness, there are the tight-lipped references to his mother, and (in later letters to George) the forlorn recollections of his brothers' lack of interest. In 1804 he would write with sudden vehemence, "I was hardly used from infancy to Boyhood; & from Boyhood to Youth most, MOST cruelly," but this was at a time of general discouragement, and self-pity.[51]

In his poetry, the picture is consistently magical and dreaming, but this was part of the carefully orchestrated Romantic myth. It has to be set against the equally vivid account of the night-escape to the Otter, which might almost suggest a disturbed child. The desire to perform, to please, to claim attention, to impress his elders, is certainly very evident; and this he would carry into later life. With it came those entrancing natural powers of talk and charm which never left him. It was a charismatic gift, coupled with the effect of his extraordinary eyes, almost like that of an actor or an old-fashioned mountebank. It was confirmed by all who met him (whether approving or not), and eventually put to work professionally in a long public career as lay preacher, popular lecturer, society talker, *improvisatore*, and philosophical sage or guru. Yet against this, the solitariness of his imaginative life, with its obsessional reading, its dream-haunted inner world, its terrors and self-doubts, also established itself in these earliest days.* One of the saddest, and yet most ironic, reflections he ever made on these first years – coming from the great champion of innocent Romantic childhood – was given with a sigh to Gillman: "Alas! I had all the simplicity, all the docility of the little child, but none of the child's habits. I never thought as a child, never had the language of a child."[52]

---

*In later life, there is at times almost an impression of *physical* discontinuity between these two sides to his personality. The public Coleridge seemed to strike onlookers as large ("big as a house" said Southey), slow, genial, expansive, a sort of amiable performing bear. He took clouds of snuff, dominated every drawing-room he shuffled into, and talked ceaselessly. But the private man always seemed to retain a small, agile, childlike and secretive presence. He moved anxiously between rooms, houses, towns; he pounded over hill-tops, leaped into coaches, and (even in his fifties) hurled himself into the sea for fun; he dosed himself surreptitiously behind doors and bedcurtains with brandy and laudanum, and nipped out to chemist shops and pot-houses; he scribbed endlessly in his Notebooks far into the night. One of the acutest observers of these physical changes and disparities was that genius of natural description, Dorothy Wordsworth. Sometimes even she said he was simply "unrecognisable". (See the extraordinarily varied impressions in *Coleridge the Talker*, edited by Richard Armour and Raymond Howes, Oxford, 1940.)

TWO

Orphan of the Storm

1

Whatever the quality of Coleridge's happiness at Ottery, everything changed just before his ninth birthday, with the sudden and wholly unexpected death of his father, the Reverend John, in October 1781. The circumstances suggest considerable stress within the family.

It had been decided – perhaps because of the rivalry and battles between the two youngest brothers – to send Frank into the navy at the early age of twelve. He was signed on as a junior midshipman under Admiral Graves, a family friend, and taken to Plymouth with his small sea-chest by his father, where he joined a convoy for Bengal. It must have been a heart-breaking parting, for the Reverend John, then aged sixty-two, could not realistically expect to see the boy again.

He returned from Plymouth via Exeter on 4 October, evidently upset, and having – according to Coleridge – dreamed a strange allegorical dream, that Death "as he is commonly painted" had touched him with his dart. He drank a bowl of punch, went to bed, and died that same night of a massive heart attack. Coleridge always remembered his mother's "shriek" in the night, and his instant realisation that "Papa is dead". He may have felt some sense of childish responsibility for his father's loss (if he had quarrelled less with Frank, it might never have happened); or he may obscurely have blamed his mother for forcing one more premature departure from Ottery. Certainly in later life he came to fear his own death at night from "a fit of Apoplexy". At all events, the sense of bereavement was very strong, and henceforth he would often refer to himself as an "orphan". He was not quite nine.[1]

His life now altered rapidly. Ann Coleridge lost her position and income, and almost immediately the family moved out of the spacious Vicarage and School House, into temporary lodgings provided by Sir Stafford Northcote in the Warden's House nearby. Of the children still nominally at home, George was at Oxford, Luke at medical school, both with fees to pay. She was now largely dependent on what James, still making his way in the army, and John, far away in India, could provide. It was decided that Nancy would have to get work as a shop-assistant in a milliner's at Exeter; and Sam would have to be sent to a boarding school on a charity grant. That winter he was temporarily allowed to continue as a day scholar, without fees, at the King's School by the new headmaster Parson Warren. Sam pronounced his father's replacement to be a "booby", and picked holes in his grammar-teaching, "every detraction from his merits seemed an oblation to the memory of my Father".[2] Plans for Charterhouse fell through, and Judge Buller recommended a formal application to Christ's Hospital, London, originally founded for the sons of needy clergy, famous throughout the city as "blue-coat charity boys". It was the same uniform that Thomas Chatterton had once worn in Bristol.

On 28 March 1782, Sam's godfather Mr Samuel Taylor drew up the petition to Christ's Hospital, countersigned by the new vicar the Reverend Fulwood Smerdon MA. (The job of vicar and headmaster had now been divided, a final testimony to the Reverend John's great abilities.) Ann's financial anxieties were emphasised by the rather misleading way she was described as being left "with a Family of Eleven Children, whom she finds it difficult to maintain and educate without assistance". She also agreed to "the right of the Governors of Christ's Hospital to apprentice her son", if Sam did not prove academically promising.[3] This clause effectively put Sam's destiny in the hands of the Christ's Hospital authorities, and did indeed make him the child of an institution. Family worries about this were to be expressed most forcibly by John in India, when he later wrote from Surat enclosing a handsome £200, and urging James not to neglect Sam's education "in any respect whatever", and suggesting he seek the help of "his very good friend" General Godard. John, incidentally, also strongly objected to the plan for Nancy: "I would rather live all the rest of my days on Bread and Water than see my sister standing behind a counter where she is hourly open to the insults of every conceited young Puppy that may chance to purchase a Yard of Ribbon from her."[4]

James, however, busily seeking promotion from his captaincy, does not seem to have bothered much with Sam, content to pursue his own very successful career. He became a lieutenant-colonel in the Exmouth and Sidmouth Volunteers, married a local heiress Frances Taylor in 1788, and by 1796 was able to purchase the Chanter's

House at Ottery, thus becoming – as Coleridge said with some irony – "a respectable Man". John, on the other hand, continued to worry about his little brother up to the time of his own death. In one of his last letters from Bengal in 1785, he wrote to James: "I have been thinking these some days past of getting Sam, a couple of years hence, sent out to me as Cadet at the India House. Let me know your sentiments on this scheme . . ."[5] Thoughts of John, and Frank, far away in India were to have subtle influence on Sam's restless dreams in the future.

Frank's convoy had been met at Bombay by his brother John, who arranged for his transfer from the navy to the Indian army as a subaltern. Dashing and high-spirited ("the young dog is as fond of his sword as a girl is of a new lover," wrote John approvingly), Frank was promoted to an ensign of infantry in 1784, and served with distinction for eight years, until wounded in a night-attack on Seringapatam. His commanding officer, Lord Cornwallis, presented him with a gold watch for his gallantry. But Frank contracted a fever, and shot himself in delirium soon after, dying in 1792 aged twenty-two.

Coleridge was much impressed by this romantic military career, which came to seem a reproach for his own fecklessness at Cambridge (as his mother no doubt pointed out), and later composed a fictional sketch of Frank's upbringing in his poem "The Foster Mother's Tale", which ends with a haunting image of the young man's loss in the distant "golden lands". Characteristically, the fever and suicide is transformed into a moonlit voyage up an imaginary river. The "poor mad youth"

> . . . seized a boat,
> And all alone, set sail by silent moonlight
> Up a great river, great as any sea,
> And ne'er was heard of more: but 'tis suppos'd
> He liv'd and died among the savage men.[6]

2

Sam was accepted at Christ's Hospital (probably through the influence of Judge Buller) for the Michaelmas term of 1782, with a six-week preliminary attendance at the preparatory school at Hertford beginning in July. If Ann Coleridge did not wish to be parted from her youngest child, there is no sign of this, for she immediately despatched him to London in April to spend the spring and summer with her brother John Bowdon. The impression that she was glad to have him off her hands is increased by the remarkable fact that he was not allowed back to Ottery, during the brief Christmas and summer vacations, more than three or possibly four times over the next nine years. Significantly, Coleridge left no memory of his parting from his mother at Ottery, except in a sonnet of 1791 when he refers rather formally to how his

> weeping childhood, torn
> By early sorrow from my native seat,
> Mingled its tears with hers – my widow'd Parent lorn.[7]

Nor is there much evidence of correspondence between school and home: of his seven known schoolboy letters, only one is to his mother; another is to Luke, and the remaining five are to George, whose role as father-figure became increasingly evident.

The first three months in London with Uncle Bowdon – who kept a tobacconist's near the Stock Exchange and was also a part-time clerk for an underwriter – were recalled with immense and comic satisfaction by Coleridge. Far from grieving for the countryside of Ottery, he revelled in his first experience of the big city, and felt his wings as a talker and social being. Bowdon was a kindly, generous man but also a drinker – "a Sot" who was "fleeced unmercifully" by his servant in the shop, and bullied at home by "an ugly and an artful" daughter. Sam accompanied him on his frequent escapes to the taverns, and had his first unforgettable taste of the great talking-shop of London, the Johnsonian world of clubs and coffee-houses, with its last echoes of the elegant, rakish Augustan society of Steele and Addison.

It was all highly unsuitable for a child of nine and a half, and pleased him no end. "My Uncle was very proud of me, & used to carry me from Coffee-house to Coffee-house, and Tavern to Tavern, where I drank, & talked & disputed, as if I had been a man –. Nothing was more common than for a large party to exclaim in my hearing, that I *was a prodigy* etc etc etc – so that, while I remained at my Uncle's, I was most completely spoilt & pampered, both mind and body."[8] But this vision of forbidden, urban, adult delights – which attracted Coleridge's gregarious nature all his life – was merely a prologue to the tribal, schoolboy horrors to come.

In July he "donned the *Blue* coat & yellow stockings", and went down to the prep school at Hertford for six weeks, where he was briefly very happy – "for I had plenty to eat & drink, & pudding & vegetables almost every day". Then, in September 1782, he was delivered up to the Under Grammar School of Christ's Hospital, one small boy among 600, with his private world reduced to an iron bedstead in a "ward" or dormitory of fifteen others. For the next three years his existence was remembered with self-pity and righteous indignation: "Oh, what a change! depressed, moping, friendless, poor orphan, half starved".[9]

These early, beastly memories of Christ's Hospital have a familiar ring, and variations can be found in the schooldays of many English writers: Shelley, Dickens, or Kipling. The rising bell at 6 a.m.; the miserable food, consisting largely of bread, thin porridge, and bad beer – and "never any vegetables"; the heartless "Nurse" or dormitory matron, who scrubbed him with stinging sulphur ointment against ringworm; the ill-fitting clog shoes and the nauseous stench of the communal boot-room and lavatories; the flogging in the classrooms and the loneliness in the cloisters. He later indignantly told Godwin that he was treated with "contumely & brutality", and frequently took refuge "in a sunny corner, shutting his eyes, & imagining himself at home".[10]

There is however evidence that Coleridge, with his verbal fluency (despite the Devon accent which he retained all his life), and his powerful, moody temperament (sometimes utterly withdrawn, sometimes exuberantly outgoing and wild) stood up quite well to the ordeal. Despite the "excessive subordination" to senior boys required, there was little overt suggestion of bullying or homosexuality. Though it is true that in his adult dreams nightmares of Christ's Hospital would often surface, suggesting more subtle forms of persecution, physical humiliations and, above all, profound, almost disabling homesickness. Many of these dreams would centre on the headmaster, James Bowyer, who became a dominating figure in the later part of his schooling.

Coleridge's first known letter home, which dates from February 1785 – when he was twelve – says almost nothing of school life, but mentions a litany of Ottery friends he wishes to greet, and a careful enumeration of small presents sent to him: "two handkerchiefs and the half-a-crown from Mr. Badcock . . . a half-a-crown from Mrs Smerdon, but . . . not a word of the plumb cake . . . My aunt [Bowdon] was so kind as to accommodate me with a box". It was a stiff, schoolboy performance, with only tiny glimpses of his real life and thoughts: "I suppose my sister Anna's beauty has many admirers. My brother Luke says that Burke's Art of Speaking would be of great use to me." It is signed rather formally to his mother, "your dutiful son"; but has a revealing concession in its postscript: "P.S. Give my kind love to Molly."[11]

3

At this period Christ's Hospital was sharply distinguished from the great public schools such as Eton (attended by Shelley), Harrow (Byron) or Westminster (Southey), with their aristocratic connections, anarchic regimes, and in-built sense of class privileges. There were no riots, no underground magazines, no tutorial friendships between boys and masters, no freedoms outside school hours. It was a highly conservative institution, largely funded by philanthropists from the City of London, with spartan facilities and food, lengthy church attendances, and strictly practical aims for most of its pupils.

The main building, founded by Edward VI in 1552, on the site of a Franciscan friary, stood on Newgate Street close to the prison burnt down by the Gordon Rioters in 1780. To the south rose the dome of St Paul's, to the east was the Bank of England, to the west the Smithfield Meat Market and the Inns of Court. The boys ate together in the Great Hall with pictures of its benefactors gazing down upon them, attended the church in a special gallery above the nave, and played in a walled and cloistered courtyard. Except on leave-days they were forbidden to go out into the city streets – though there are early records of Coleridge's truancy – and there was a single long vacation of three weeks during the summer.

Of the three main school divisions, the Writing School prepared boys for commercial apprenticeships at the age of fourteen or fifteen; the Mathematical and Drawings Schools sent boys into the navy and the East India Company at the age of sixteen; and the Grammar School retained the brightest pupils for professional careers in the law, the army, or the Church. The most gifted of these, directly supervised by James Bowyer, were put into a Classical Sixth Form, known as the Deputy Grecians, and from there three or four boys a year – distinguished as the Grecians, with special uniforms and privileges – would go on to Oxford or Cambridge.

The powerful sense of intellectual hierarchy, which affected Coleridge for the rest of his life, inculcated fear and respect for all social authority. When a Grecian walked through the cloisters every other boy was expected to get out of his way. All discipline was enforced by Bowyer with savage and frequent flogging. There was great rivalry between the boys concerning the social standing of parents, and outside gifts of food and money – well reflected in Coleridge's letters. Nearly half the boys were "orphans" (usually from a widowed family), and the daily Christ's Hospital hymn referred humiliatingly to their charity status. Coleridge's frequent references to himself as an orphan, poor and neglected, partly reflect this intense consciousness of status throughout his time at Christ's Hospital.

Despite the severity of the institution – or perhaps because of it – the school did produce at this time a number of notable literary men and scholars, all from the ranks of the Grecians. Among these were Charles Lamb, Leigh Hunt, the poet George Dyer, Thomas Barnes (the future editor of *The Times*), and Thomas Middleton (a classical scholar who became the first Bishop of Calcutta). Of these, Lamb and Middleton were Coleridge's fellow pupils, the former two years junior, the latter two years senior. All retained vivid and painful memories of Christ's Hospital.

Lamb, who would later become one of Coleridge's most faithful friends and confidants, touchingly projected himself into the older boy's homesickness. In "Christs Hospital Five-and-Thirty Years Ago" (1820), Lamb – as Elia – wrote in Coleridge's imagined voice of schoolboy grief: "My parents and those who should care for me were far away . . . How, in my dreams, would my native town (far in the west) come back, with its church, and trees, and faces! How I would wake weeping, and in the anguish of my heart exclaim upon sweet Calne in Wiltshire!" Lamb altered Ottery to Calne (the Wiltshire town where Coleridge wrote his own memoirs of Christ's Hospital in the *Biographia*) to avoid upsetting the Ottery Coleridges with accusations of – perhaps romanticised – neglect.

4

Coleridge's own private recollections have a somewhat different tone. He describes himself as magnificently idle in class – until his genius was unfortunately unearthed by Bowyer. He was a down-at-heel ragamuffin in the cloisters, a frequenter of illegal bathing expeditions to the New River in the East End, and a voracious reader of extra-curricular books. These were obtained from a public lending library in nearby King Street, to which he had been given a ticket – so he said – by an unknown gentleman he bumped into in the Strand.

The story, told long after to Gillman, describes another of his epic daydreams: he was Leander swimming the Hellespont, and "thrusting his hands before him as in the act of swimming" he inadvertently struck the man's pocket on the crowded pavement, and to his bewilderment was accused of pick-pocketing. Tearful denials were followed by a vivid, breathless account of his dreaming re-enactment of Leander's adventures, all in young Coleridge's most eloquent, large-eyed manner. The gentleman "was so struck and delighted by the novelty of the thing", that he ended by subscribing him the library ticket.[12]

This odd tale, which is certainly strange enough to be true, has something curiously prophetic about it: the daydreaming poet – the sudden interruption – the accusation of (literary) theft – the hypnotic, glittering-eyed explanation. They are all emblems of the future literary man at work. The story also suggests that Coleridge was independent enough in his world of books and dreams to regularly go "skulking", school slang for breaking bounds.

The King Street Library provided him, for two or three years, with a private larder of delights, to substitute for gifts of food.

> I read *through* the catalogue, folios and all, whether I understood them, or did not understand them, running all risks to go skulking out to get the two volumes which I was entitled to have daily . . . My whole being was, with eyes closed to every object of present sense, to crumple myself up in a sunny corner, and read, read, read; fancy myself on Robinson Crusoe's island, finding a mountain of plumb-cake, and eating a room for myself, and then eating it into the shapes of tables and chairs – hunger and fancy![13]

His earliest compositions seem to have been a couple of schoolboy charms, or dog-rhymes against sickness. One was intended to ward off the dreaded "itch" that brought the sulphur treatment. The other was against morning cramps, a rhyming spell to be chanted aloud while making magic cross-marks of spittle on the seized calf muscles, "pressing the foot on the floor, and then repeating this charm with the acts configurative thereupon prescribed".[14] These were his first essays in a long line of poetical incantations.

It was the obsessive reading that first brought him to Bowyer's fatal attentions, probably in his third year, 1785, in the Grammar School. He was then still under his junior master, the easy-going Mr Field, who had conveniently assumed that he was a daydreaming dunce. Thomas Middleton, the earnest well-meaning scholar, then a Deputy Grecian, found him reading Virgil "for pleasure" in the cloisters, and mentioned this with admiration to the headmaster. Bowyer made enquiries of Field and learned with grim interest that in class the boy was "a dull and inapt scholar" who could not repeat a single rule of syntax. Coleridge was summoned, flogged, and told that he was destined to be a Grecian. Thereafter Coleridge's dreaming and carelessness "never went unpunished"; and whenever Bowyer beat him he would cruelly add an extra stroke, "for you are such an ugly fellow!".[15] But the gentle Middleton became henceforth Coleridge's "patron and protector", a significant friendship which was to continue right through to Cambridge days, and which was remembered gratefully in the *Biographia*, with an affectionate classical tag from Petronius.[16]

Coleridge's position improved as steadily as he rose out of the most tribal ranks of the junior boys. His waywardness, cleverness, and voluble charm soon made him fast friends with two other future Grecians, Robert Allen and Valentine Le Grice, who shared the attentions of Bowyer. They formed one of those schoolboy triumvirates of contrasted talents: Bob Allen the handsome extrovert, Val Le Grice the mischievous wit, and Sam Coleridge the learned eccentric.

From 1785 he also had two of his brothers within reach in London, as Luke was training at the London Hospital under Sir William Blizard, and George came down from Oxford to teach at Newcome's Academy in Hackney. Initially it was Luke who exercised the greatest influence, and Coleridge "became wild to be apprenticed to a surgeon". He launched into medical and anatomy books – "Blanchard's Medical Dictionary I had nearly by heart" – and trudged off every Saturday to attend dressings and hold plasters at the hospital. Luke's fellow medical student, the younger brother of Admiral de Saumerez, vividly remembered the "extraordinary, enthusiastic, blue-coat boy" trailing round the wards with his endless questions.[17]

Another, more hair-brained, ambition at the age of fifteen was a scheme to apprentice himself to a local shoemaker, largely because the man and his wife had been so kind to him during the lonely "leave-days". Perhaps this was a serious attempt to escape from Christ's Hospital early (apprenticeships were, after all, allowed by the statutes), and to flee back into a less demanding, domestic existence. At all events the kindly shoemaker, a Mr Crispin, was sent packing by Bowyer after a ferocious interview – "Crispin might have sustained an action in law against him for an assault" – and Coleridge was flogged again to remind him of his privileged status as a future Grecian. "Against my will," he recalled mournfully, "I was chosen by my master as one of those destined for the university." But it is difficult to believe in his reluctance to excel by this stage, and the whole incident may have been one of Coleridge's self-dramatisations – the prodigy who merely wanted to be a simple cobbler's son, a thoroughly romantic role.[18]

Soon afterwards both shoemaking and medicine gave way to "a rage for metaphysics". He read Cato on Liberty and Necessity, discovered Voltaire's *Philosophical Dictionary*, and announced that he was a theological sceptic. Bowyer proved himself quite equal to this development too: "his argument was short and forcible – 'So, sirrah, you are an infidel, are you? then I'll flog your infidelity out of you.'"[19] Coleridge often spoke of this as the severest beating of his life, though it is one of the many peculiarities of the *Biographia* that he afterwards pretended that Bowyer was a paragon of pedagogical justice. This is contradicted by all other records of Christ's Hospital, even that of its official historian, who implicitly admitted that Bowyer was a sadist. Leigh Hunt quietly recalled that Bowyer not only flogged unmercifully, but picked up boys by their earlobes until they bled, and once threw a copy of Homer at him so hard that it knocked out one of his teeth. Hunt later said that Coleridge admitted all this in private, and "said he dreamt of the master all his life, and that his dreams were horrible".[20] Many Notebook entries confirm this.[21]

Coleridge's genial retrospective attempt to pass off Bowyer's cruelties in the *Biographia* is one of the earliest, clear examples of his urge to rewrite his personal history in a comic mode that embraced the authorities he had once rebelled against. This was to show even more sharply in his political reminiscences, where the problem of authority recurs in a different but related form. Yet the deception is a complex one, for Coleridge obviously felt genuinely indebted to Bowyer for the encouragement he was soon to give him as a fledgling poet. The truth seems to be that all his life Coleridge longed to submit to figures of authority, while at the same time he secretly resented many aspects of their domination. Casting himself in a comic role provided a sort of *modus vivendi*; yet he could rarely resolve the underlying conflict in his life. He longed to assert himself and give free rein to his enormous, anarchic talents; but at the same time he needed to submit, and be petted and approved of. Throughout his life, and his writing, he fluctuated wildly between these two extremes. Only his dead father, perhaps, ever allowed him to do both.

5

In spring 1787 Luke qualified as a doctor, and returned to Devon to take up a practice at Thorverton, near Exeter, where he was soon to marry. Coleridge missed him greatly – "I have now no one, to whom I can open my heart in full confidence" – and asked him to keep up "an epistolary correspondence". In May that year he sent Luke his first serious poems, six stanzas on "Easter Holidays", and a Latin translation which was accepted by Bowyer for the Christ's Hospital "Album". This was a notable distinction at the age of fourteen and a half. The theme is loneliness and misfortune, rendered in the manner of Gray:

> Then without child or tender wife,
> To drive away each care, each sigh,
> Lonely he treads the paths of life,
> A stranger to Affection's tye . . .[22]

Bowyer promised he would be a Deputy Grecian within a year, "if I take particular care of my exercises etc". Coleridge added that the Bowdons were still very kind to him – "I dine there every Saturday" – and that George in Hackney was now his mainstay. "*He* is father, brother, and every thing to me."[23] Instead of plum cake, he now asked for a copy of Edward Young's *Night Thoughts*, the famous volume of the "Graveyard School", with its celebration of solitary musings on death and mutability. Adolescence had arrived.

Over the next two years poetry, classics and Platonic philosophy became his dominant interests, as befitted a Grecian. He also discovered his own protégé, a boy called Tom Evans, whose widowed mother lived in London with three teenage daughters, soon to be extravagantly courted by Coleridge and the dashing Bob Allen. It was a time of rapid intellectual development, with long enthusiastic talks in the cloisters, alternating with lonely hours spent up on the school leads – or flat roof. Coleridge found he could secretly climb out through a Ward window and sit gazing at the sunset and the stars, with the spires and domes of the city laid out beneath him.

The taste for roof-top contemplation was one that returned to him years later, at Greta Hall in Keswick. It was there in 1802 that he recalled the first stirrings of his poetic longing, the rich self-conscious sense of beauty and isolation in the world.

> In my first Dawn of Youth that Fancy stole
> With many secret Yearnings on my Soul.
> At eve, sky-gazing in "ecstatic fit"
> (Alas! for cloister'd in a city School
> The Sky was all, I knew, of Beautiful)
> At the barr'd window often did I sit,
> And oft upon the leaded School-roof lay . . .[24]

Coleridge often later talked of these inspired times to his friends – he described them also in "Frost at Midnight" – and it is interesting how each subtly adapted them to conform to quite different aspects of his boyhood mythology. For Wordsworth, they became the "seed-time" of a visionary poet, the "liveried schoolboy, in the depths of the huge city, on the leaded roof", who lay alone gazing upon "the clouds moving in heaven", and who closed his eyes to see by the "internal light" of imagination

> . . . trees, and meadows, and thy native Stream,
> Far distant, thus beheld from year to year
> Of thy long exile.[25]

By contrast, for Charles Lamb the genius of Coleridge was not solitary at all. He saw him already as a public figure, finding his natural audience in the gregarious cloisters of Christ's Hospital – not exiled amidst the clouds but thoroughly at home amidst a circle of admiring boys, urbane, eloquent and sociable. Lamb wrote a celebrated encomium of this schoolboy hero, a radiant figure already bursting with confidence, though perhaps comically so:

> Come back into memory, like as thy wert in the dayspring of thy fancies, with hope like a fiery column before thee – the dark pillar not yet turned – Samuel Taylor Coleridge – Logician, Metaphysician, Bard! – How I have seen the casual passer through the Cloisters stand still, entranced with admiration (while he weighed the disproportion between the *speech* and the garb of the young Mirandula), to hear thee unfold, in thy deep and sweet intonations, the mysteries of Jamblichus, or Plotinus (for even in those years thou waxedst not pale at such philosophic draughts), or reciting

Homer in his Greek, or Pindar – while the walls of the old Grey Friars re-echoed to the accents of the inspired *charity boy*![26]

This is a very different Coleridge from the Wordsworthian exile. Nor does Elia take him entirely seriously – the Neoplatonic mystics and gnostics have the air of being plucked out of a conjuror's hat, and there is a certain undercurrent of affectionate mockery. In the frequent "wit-combats" with Val Le Grice in the cloisters, Lamb added shrewdly that Coleridge was like a magnificent Spanish galleon – "far higher in Learning", but wordy and cumbersome – being harried by an English man-o'-war, quick and inventive.

6

The year 1789 was a turning point for Coleridge's whole generation. With the fall of the Bastille in July, the first tide of revolutionary excitement flooded through Europe, reaching even into the remote cloisters of Christ's Hospital. The sixteen-and-a-half-year-old Coleridge now wrote his first substantial and original poem, "The Fall of the Bastille". In it he records the "universal cry" of liberty from "Gallia's shore", and imagines the spirit of freedom reaching down even to the humble field-labourer:

> . . . mark yon peasant's raptur'd eyes;
> Secure he views his harvests rise;
> No fetter vile the mind shall know,
> And Eloquence shall fearless glow . . .[27]

The excitement was indeed universal, and a hundred such Odes filled the newspapers and magazines: "bliss was it in that dawn to be alive". Wordsworth, already at Cambridge, felt the same sudden intensification of life among the undergraduates, and planned a walking tour in France for the following summer. But perhaps Coleridge alone characteristically pointed out that language itself – "Eloquence" – had been freed.

Feeling his wings and independence for the first time, he visited Ottery during the summer, where he went through the solemn rite of recarving his initials in the Pixies' Parlour, alongside those of his distant brothers. He learned too that his beloved sister Nancy was gravely ill, and this appears in one of his earliest sonnets, "Life", dated September 1789, "musing in torpid woe a Sister's pain".[28] Another sonnet, "To the Autumnal Moon", also belongs to this period.

This quickening of the poetic impulse – he produced two more translations for Bowyer's "Album" – reflects another outside influence. Thomas Middleton, now at Pembroke College, Cambridge, sent him a copy of the second edition of William Bowles' *Sonnets.* This was one of those books, now largely forgotten, which magically captured the spirit of the times; Coleridge was so excited by it that he wrote out by hand no less than forty copies to give to friends during his last eighteen months at school.[29]

The collection, a slim octavo volume in fine bold print, consisted of twenty-one sonnets, "Written chiefly on Picturesque Spots, During a Tour", which Bowles had made through Wales, Scotland, France and Germany in the previous year, while recovering from an unhappy love-affair. It concentrates notably on the evocative, melancholy feelings of seashores and river banks – the shores of Tynemouth, Dover, Ostend; the rivers Tweed, Wenbeck, Itchin, and the Rhine. Bowles, born in the West Country and a graduate of Trinity College, Oxford, exactly ten years older than Coleridge, brilliantly captured a new Romantic sense of spiritual isolation and nostalgia for childhood, projecting into natural surroundings the image of a rootless, wandering poet at the mercy of his dreams and memories.

Coleridge could instantly recognise this aspect of himself in many of the gentle, highly musical, and nakedly emotional sonnets, with their familiar imagery, such as "The Bells, Ostend":

> . . . And hark! with lessening cadence now they fall!
> And now, along the white and level tide,
> They fling their melancholy music wide;
> Bidding me many a tender thought recall
> Of summer-days, and those delightful years
> When from an ancient tower, in life's fair prime,
> The mournful magic of their mingling chime
> First waked my wondering childhood into tears!

In discovering Bowles, Coleridge found that for the first time in his life he was reading "a contemporary"; unlike the remote classics, these poems possessed an immediate reality of circumstances for him, so as to "inspire an actual friendship as of a man for a man". They assumed "the properties of flesh and blood".[30] For the next five years, until he became aware of Wordsworth (who had also been greatly struck by Bowles, stopping to read through the entire volume while crossing London Bridge), they were the dominant influence on his own poetry, though he could only match the "austere" style – "so tender and yet so manly, so natural and real" – intermittently.

In fact throughout this period of apprenticeship there was a long struggle between the "florid diction" and epigrammatic polish and personifications of many of his longer and more formal Odes, Effusions and Monodies; and the Bowles-like plain style, expressing emotion in run-on lines, musical alliteration, and bold monosyllabic statements of personal feeling. This second style – a profound attack on eighteenth-century conventions – became particularly evident in his own shorter pieces and sonnets composed between 1789 and 1794. These included many sonnets about his own experience of change and loss, and family griefs: "To the Autumnal Moon"; "Pain"; "On Quitting School for College"; "On Receiving an Account that his only Sister's Death was Inevitable"; and his masterpiece in the Bowles' style (but wonderfully transforming it) "To the River Otter".

In the *Biographia* he well described what he was groping after, as a poetry "of the lines running into each other, instead of closing at each couplet, and of natural language, neither bookish, nor vulgar, neither redolent of the lamp, nor of the kennel [*the gutter*], such as 'I will remember thee'; instead of the same thought tricked up in the rag-fair finery of – 'Thy image on her wing/Before my Fancy's eye shall Memory bring.'"[31] He counted Bowles' poetry, along with the friendship of Tom Evans' family, as the two humanising forces in his academic life as a Grecian. Between them, they drew him out of the bookish maze of metaphysics and classical philosophy, into the living world.[32]

7

In his happier recollections Coleridge described his final period as a Grecian, between 1790 and 1791, as "the era of poetry and love". With Bob Allen and Val Le Grice he would escort the three Miss Evanses (Anne, Eliza, and Mary) home on a Saturday, from their milliner's shop in the West End to the family house at Villiers Street, off the Strand. On summer mornings they would carry "the pillage of the Flower Gardens within six miles of Town with Sonnet or Love-rhyme wrapped round the Nosegay".[33]

Even Bowyer's teaching of poetry became a pleasure and

fascination, according to Coleridge. "At the same time that we were studying the Greek Tragic Poets, he made us read Shakespeare and Milton as lessons . . . I learnt from him, that Poetry, even that of the loftiest and, seemingly, that of the wildest odes, had a logic of its own, as severe as that of science; and more difficult, because more subtle, more complex, and dependent on more, and more fugitive causes."[34]

Both Lamb and Leigh Hunt deny that Bowyer's teaching of poetry was any more than "commonplace", and that his taste in moderns reached any higher than Pope. Perhaps Coleridge responded more subtly than they; but in reality he seems to have gained this crucial insight into the structure of poetry from his own reading of Bowles and Edward Young.*

Nevertheless he claimed too that Bowyer was an early champion of the plain style: "he showed no mercy to phrase, metaphor, or image, unsupported by sound sense . . . Lute, harp, and lyre, muse, muses, and inspirations, Pegasus, Parnassus, and Hyppocrene were all abominations to him."[35] Perhaps this was so; but the fact remains that his main contribution to the Christ's Hospital "Album" for 1790 was the highly ornate "Monody on the Death of Chatterton", packed with eighteenth-century personifications, and opening with full bardic diapason: "Now prompts the Muse poetic lays" – the very style that Bowyer was meant to abominate.

The truth seems to be that he was experimenting with every kind of poetic style and pose. His worship of Chatterton was genuine, and he had copied Bowles' "Monody on the Death of Henry Headley" into his hymn-book to inspire him. But this did not prevent him from

*The emergence between 1790 and 1797 of what I have called, rather schematically, Coleridge's "plain style" is an intricate question of literary history and influence. (See Bibliography, Norman Fruman and Kelvin Everest.) It is often said that Wordsworth was mainly responsible, but my narrative shows that Coleridge's early reading of William Bowles' sonnets, William Cowper's *The Task* (one model for "Frost at Midnight"), Edward Young, and – above all – his very detailed correspondence on the subject with Charles Lamb (who insisted on "simplicity") between 1794 and 1796, were the prime sources. Bowyer's perception that even the wildest Ode had "a logic of its own", was originally credited by Coleridge to Edward Young in a letter of 1802. Young observed that there was as "profound a Logic in the most daring & dithyrambic parts of Pindar" comparable to Aristotle's prose *Organon* (Logic) (*Letters*, II p. 864). Plain style and simplicity, with its closely related concept of "sincerity" – directness "from the heart" – can also be seen emerging everywhere in the prose writing of the early Romantic period: for example in Mary Wollstonecraft's *A Short Residence in Sweden* (1796), or William Godwin's admirably daring *Memoirs* (1798). Conversely – or perversely – Coleridge's shift from the plain, leaping, vernacular prose of his early letters and prefaces, to the loaded, baroque, reticulated armorial, clanking prose (much influenced by seventeenth-century writers) has received little attention. (But see Bibliography, Marilyn Butler.)

turning the solemn enterprise on its head with an answering "Monody on a Tea-Kettle" for George:

> While Bats shall shriek and Dogs shall howling run
> The tea-kettle is spoilt and Coleridge is undone!

In March 1791 he also sent his brother a Pindaric ode on Euclid's geometry of ghastly ingenuity. His accompanying comment on learning mathematics – a thing he could never do – contains an interesting prophesy of critical debates to come: "though Reason is feasted, Imagination is starved: whilst Reason is luxuriating in its proper Paradise, Imagination is wearily travelling over a dreary desert."[36] Those images of fruitful Paradise and sterile desert were to haunt him long after.

8

Officially his career at Christ's Hospital ended in triumph. As the senior Grecian in his year, he was awarded in January 1791 a School Exhibition worth £40 to take him to Cambridge, renewable for four years; and the following month obtained a place at Jesus College, with a promise of a Rustat Scholarship of £30, especially reserved for the sons of clergymen who showed outstanding merit. Bob Allen went to Oxford without an award, and Val Le Grice did not go up for another year. These awards delighted his family – especially George – and promised to relieve them of most of his expenses, which normally would have been more than £100 per annum.

Yet throughout that last winter Coleridge was periodically ill with rheumatic fever, contracted as a result of a late autumn bathing expedition to the New River. For several months he spent long periods in the school sanatorium, dosed with opium to help him sleep, and doing little except write some striking scraps of poetry. He lay listening to the distant shouts and laughter of the boys in the cloisters, as he recorded in his sonnet "Pain". Coleridge's long history of illness – often recurring in damp climates, and during winter months – now began. The sonnet is his first vision of the feverish invalid, besieged by "the trembling sense of wan Disease", cut off from the normal, healthy daylight world around him, a theme to be powerfully developed.[37]

He also wrote a love-poem, "Genevieve", addressed to his young nurse, whose short lyrical lines contain the first hint of the ballads he would later write. They praise her tender solicitude and generous, maternal bosom in its starched apron like a swan:

When sinking low the sufferer wan
Beholds no hand outstretch'd to save,
Fair, as the bosom of the Swan
That rises graceful o'er the wave,
I've seen your breast with pity heave,
And *therefore* love I you, sweet Genevieve![38]

The close association of poetry with sickness, feverish dreams, and isolation, set against the consoling, healing presence of the beloved, was now initiated. The theme was deepened by tragic sickness in his own family. Early in 1791 came news of Luke's sudden death of a fever at Exeter; and this was quickly followed by the death of his beloved Nancy, after a long consumptive illness. Again, Coleridge turned to poetry, writing several more sonnets of deep and clumsy emotion:

Pain after pain, and woe succeeding woe –
Is my heart destin'd for another blow?
O my sweet sister! and must thou too die?[39]

Significantly, he already linked these deaths with that of his father, and the sense of being "fated to rove thro' Life" bereft of those who had been closest to him in childhood. Perhaps this also explains the intense emotion with which he finally left Christ's Hospital that summer, celebrated in his "Sonnet: On Quitting School for College" (another theme taken from Bowles). He bid "Adieu, adieu!" to the "much-lov'd cloisters pale!", and spoke in tears of his happy days there, most of which he would later say were miserable.[40]

THREE

PRODIGAL SON

1

Coleridge was just nineteen when he went up to Jesus College, Cambridge in the autumn of 1791. Though academically outstanding, there was little in his letters or adolescent poetry to suggest any real creative originality by this age (compared for example with Shelley or Keats). With characteristic acuteness, he himself later remarked on this.[1] He was widely read, marvellously articulate, noisily self-confident but lacked any driving sense of literary vocation. Outwardly gregarious, as Lamb remembered, he was also an intensely lonely young man who longed for friendship. His unhappy family background, and growing sense of being an orphan in the world, made him even more emotionally volatile and self-conscious than most students. He referred jocosely to his "fat vacuity" of face, and his frequent blushes.

In his letters to George, and especially to the Evans family, there is overwhelming evidence of his passionate desire for intimacy and acceptance. The almost hysterical intensity of this, at times, may itself have been an alienating factor for fellow students. Self-dramatising and self-mocking by turns, he was like some brilliant overgrown child, performing ceaseless exhausting parlour games for his elders, and never settling down. He danced and jumped on his own shadow – sitting scholarship exams, writing for poetry prizes, dabbling in university politics, running up disastrous debts, flirting with drink, whores, and suicide – and all the time seemed to know that the performance was somehow hollow, a dazzling demand for attention, sympathy, and recognition. Yet in the process something real and extraordinary did happen: it released the language of his imagination, at first in his letters, then gradually in his poetry.

The opening note of this *commedia* of university life was struck, very early on, with almost conscious design, in his first letter from Jesus College to Mrs Evans and her daughters, written in February 1792.

Believe me, that You and my Sisters have the very first row in the front box of my Heart's little theatre – and – God knows! *you are not crowded.* There, my dear Spectators! you shall see what you shall see – Farce, Comedy, & Tragedy – my Laughter, my Chearfulness, and my Melancholy. A thousand figures pass before you, shifting in perpetual succession – these are my Joys and my Sorrows, my Hopes and my Fears, my Good tempers, and my Peevishnesses: you will however observe two, that remain unalterably fixed – and these are Love and Gratitude. In short, my dear Mrs Evans! my whole heart shall be laid open like any sheep's heart . . . Come Ladies! will you not take your seats in this play house?[2]

2

Coleridge's first act in Cambridge was to go round to Pembroke College to see his schoolboy mentor Thomas Middleton, as soon as he got off the London coach. Middleton, who was studying hard for his finals the following summer, reasserted his old scholarly influence, and did much to shape the success of Coleridge's first year, which was otherwise lonely and unsettled. He found his own college, Jesus, bleak and unfriendly, "the very palace of winds", set on the edge of the city surrounded by the exposed parklands of Jesus Green. "Neither Lectures, or Chapel – or anything – is begun," he wrote plaintively to George. "The College very thin – and Middleton has not the least acquaintance with any of Jesus, except a very blackguardly fellow, whose phisiog: I did not like."[3]

With the return of the Master, Dr William Pearce, he was assigned rooms on the ground floor, opposite the gatehouse. They were cold and damp, and he mistakenly spent much money on credit trying to furnish them comfortably. These debts were to be the cause of growing difficulties between him and his brothers. After a bad bout of flu, when he took opium without "any disagreeable effects", he established under Middleton's guidance a strict, scholarly routine. Chapel twice a day, mathematical reading and lectures in the morning, walks in the afternoons, and long evenings of classical reading and translation work in Middleton's rooms until eleven o'clock at night, occasionally enlivened by taking pot-shots at the Pembroke College rats.

Val Le Grice sent him parcels of second-hand books from London, and he discovered manuscripts of Thomas Gray's poems in the

Pembroke Library, which he copied out as he had done Bowles'.[4] In November he reported virtuously to George, "If I were to read on as I do now – there is not the least doubt, that I should be Classical Medallist, and a very high Wrangler – but *Freshmen* always *begin* very *furiously*. I am reading Pindar, and composing Greek verse, like a mad dog. I am very fond of Greek verse, and shall try hard for the Brown's Prize ode ... There is no such thing as *discipline* at our college."[5]

A letter to Edward Coleridge, written in a "feverish state of body and mind" had a less reassuring effect, being full of "petulance and passion", complaining about the college, lack of money, and the wild behaviour of the young bloods.[6] That month, two undergraduates fought a duel at Newmarket, and one was killed. Thereafter, Coleridge was careful to edit his letters to Ottery and Hackney – they are very different from the wild accounts he sent to the Evans family – and he assured George that he was an "economist", living without invitations or wine parties, and stressed the improving friendship with Middleton.[7]

The Christmas vacation of 1791 was spent with the Evanses in Villiers Street where Coleridge passed a "potently medicinal" fortnight, eating turkey, tutoring Tom, and walking the three sisters to their milliner's shop in Jermyn Street. The sixth-form flirtation now subtly altered into a general seduction of the whole family. He liked both Anne and Mary – the former for her intelligence, the latter for her "beautiful little leg" – but the real attraction, at least initially, was the mother, who treated him with "maternal affection". He longed to be considered as one of her "*very* children", but felt that he was physically too ugly for that.[8]

Back at Cambridge for the Easter term, while he assured George that he was soberly reading Homer and Horace for the Rustat Exams, he regaled the Evans family with a more colourful version of his doings, as he had promised. He had purchased a swanskin waistcoat in the latest mode, kept a cat in his rooms, and was planning to hire an allotment garden with a fellow undergraduate, George Caldwell (later a Fellow and Tutor of Jesus). He attended wine parties, at which three or four freshmen were "deplorably drunk", and described hauling one of them out of the shallow Cambridge gutter in King's Parade. (The man insisted that he save his friend instead: "never mind me – *I* can swim.")[9]

In his rooms, he raised the ghost of Thomas Gray – this for Mary's benefit – who advised him in a hollow voice: "O Young Man . . . write no more verses – in the first place, your poetry is vile stuff: and secondly (here he sighed almost to bursting) all poets go to –ll, we are so intolerably addicted to the Vice of Lying!"[10] He sent his verses, "Odelings" and translations to Mary – also copies of Bowles, a sure mark of favour. But it was Anne he proposed as his Valentine, perhaps because she was not so dauntingly pretty. He would even have sent the drawing of a heart pierced with arrows – "But as the Gods have not made me a drawer (of any thing but corks) you must accept the will for the deed."[11]

Physical inferiority was a constant, if comic note, in these early letters: he described his bad teeth, and asked for a box of "Mr Stringer's tooth powder", and noted that a dashing literary lady had described him as "a very gentle Bear".[12] The small, dishevelled schoolboy had grown into a large, shambling young man, with a mass of long dark hair and excitable manners. The mouth was "voluptuous", the eyebrows stormy, the eyes bigger than ever. (All these features he would later enumerate with mock impartiality.) Nevertheless, he was proud of his robust energy, and described a marathon eight-hour walk round the villages of Cambridge with Middleton, ending benighted in a quagmire and pursued by footpads and Jack-o'-lanterns.

He also boated on the Cam, and fell in gloriously: "we swam to shore, and walking dripping home, like so many River Gods."[13] There was no doubt that "brother Coly" in his tragical farcical role was a grand success at Villiers Street, and when he went there again for the Easter vacation it began to feel like his adopted home. It was to be the first of many.

3

Despite, or perhaps because of, these distractions, it is clear that Coleridge worked very hard at Cambridge throughout the spring and summer of 1792. "I have been writing for all the prizes," he told George, and he submitted pieces for university awards in the Greek Sapphic Ode (Brown Medal), the Latin Ode, and the Greek Epigrams. He also found time to provide George with the text of sermons to preach at Hackney, an early example of his skill in assimilating and rehandling the writings of others, invaluable for a journalist and lecturer, but a dangerous facility for a literary man later to be much tempted by plagiarism. "I have sent you a sermon metamorphosed from an obscure publication by vamping, transposition, etc – if you like it, I can send you two more of the same kidney."[14]* Doggerel verses – "A Fragment found in a Lecture Room" – and an elegant Greek epitaph were also sent, carefully sandwiched round an urgent request for £5 or £10, "as I am at present cashless".[15]

The first academic year closed brilliantly in June 1792, when Coleridge's Greek Sapphic "Ode on the Slave Trade" was declared the winner of the Brown Gold Medal. He had chosen a subject that was politically popular – the West Indian slave trade had recently been debated both in parliament, and in the University Senate – and which showed his growing interest in public affairs, and the libertarian ideas of the French Revolution. Technically it was not quite flawless: Richard Porson, the new Professor of Greek, privately offered to show 134 examples of bad Greek in it. Since the Ode was twenty-five stanzas long, this was more than one error per line.

But for a freshman it was a triumph; he formally declaimed it before the assembled Fellows at the Encaenia on 3 July, and proudly posted an autographed copy to George, before going down to Ottery for the long vacation. George was so delighted by his youngest brother's success that he broke out into congratulatory verses earnestly praising the Sacred Fire that flowed "spontaneous from thy golden lyre".[16] For a few brief weeks, Coleridge basked in the approval of his entire family, perhaps the one time in his life that he felt he had achieved what was expected of him.

---

*The story of Coleridge's plagiarisms is complex and fascinating, and will emerge in the course of this narrative, especially in Volume two. Coleridge, Wordsworth and Southey all borrowed freely from each other (and earlier poets), while creating their individual style in the 1790s, and published work under each other's name. (Coleridge for example used a Wordsworth lyric for "Lewti", while Wordsworth used Coleridge's suggested lines to begin "We are Seven". R. L. Stevenson observed that all young writers play "the sedulous ape" before finding their own voices, and in the youthful Coleridge this is really part of his gift: an enormous reading capacity, a retentive memory, a talker's talent for conjuring and orchestrating other people's ideas, and the natural instinct of a lecturer and preacher to harvest materials wherever he found them. But real plagiarism begins in Germany in 1799 (see Chapters 9 and 12), and becomes critical in the preparation of lectures and philosophical materials ten years later. Finally this slips into a pathological dependence on stolen materials (usually translated), what Thomas McFarland has shrewdly called a kind of literary "kleptomania" (See Bibliography). Such dependence, which Coleridge found it agonising to admit even to himself, is clearly related in psychological terms to his opium dependence; and cuckoo-like invasion of other people's households. And all this, in turn, bears on the problem of what Coleridge himself called his spiritual "hollowness" – the profound Romantic identity crisis, so similar to the anxieties of modern Existentialism (See Bibliography, Thomas McFarland, Herbert Read, Rupert Christiansen and Norman Fruman).

Through July and August he made a triumphal tour of West Country relatives: Edward at Salisbury, his half-sister at Tiverton, James at Exeter, his mother at Ottery. Racy accounts flowed back to George at Hackney, now written in Latin, prose alternating with hexameters. There was much talk of events in revolutionary France – the storming of the Tuileries Palace, and Tom Paine being elected to the National Convention. Coleridge was amazed at the conservative attitudes displayed: it was thought "very sad" that Paine was "not cut to pieces at Canterbury" on his way to the Continent.[17]

In fact he was witnessing the beginning of the great wave of English reaction against France, which would harden further with the September Massacres in Paris. "King and Country" mobs would soon sweep through many of the great cities, and by December Paine would be burnt in effigy even on the Cornhill at Cambridge; and Joseph Priestley be driven out of Birmingham by rioters, who set fire to his house.

Coleridge was depressed by the narrow provincialism of his family circle, and later told George that this visitation to Devon "annihilated whatever tender ideas" he had treasured of the place. He found Edward vain and eccentric, indulging in "Punnomania, with which he at present foams". While James was cold, a stickler for appearances, and much concerned with the Sidmouth Volunteers. Coleridge could only show them "the semblance of Affection – perhaps, by persevering in appearing, I at last shall learn to be, a Brother."[18] They in turn evidently found him difficult and demanding, and it is notable that his mother forbade him to drink wine at table, "not a 'single drop'".[19]

His thoughts turned instead to Frank out in India; he wrote him an affectionate letter (which has not survived), and while walking nostalgically in the Ottery churchyard had a long talk about his "most wonderful prospects" with a relative of the Governor-General of India, who said he would recommend him. Coleridge noted, with a touch of the old rivalry, that his mother "positively drank in" such dreams of Frank's advancement. He told George, rather defensively, that he was studying Cicero hard and was determined to fulfil the expectations he had created for himself at Cambridge: "God forbid that I should perish" – this from Homer's *Iliad* – "without effort and without renown." No one in England yet knew that Frank had already committed suicide at Seringapatam.[20]

4

His second year at Jesus College was certainly an active one. Exams, university politics, drinking, debts, and a growing infatuation with Mary Evans, all swept him in a ceaseless whirlpool of pleasures and anxieties. Though later he would characteristically say: "I became a proverb to the University for Idleness."[21]

His academic targets were probably far too ambitious, particularly now that his mentor Middleton had left Pembroke (without obtaining the expected Fellowship). His fellow undergraduates at Jesus were largely taken up with the *cause célèbre* of their radical tutor William Frend, who was tried in the Senate for religious blasphemy. Coleridge became a chief organiser of the Frend faction,* and by 1793 his rooms were a renowned centre both for political and literary discussions held long into the night.

Val Le Grice's brother, Charles (the inimitable Val had lost his Exhibition because of drunkenness, evidently a Grecian weakness), decorously recalled what were obviously rowdy and undecorous sessions with Coleridge in full flow. "What evenings I have spent in those rooms! . . . when Aeschylus, and Plato, and Thucydides were pushed aside, with a pile of lexicons etc, to discuss the pamphlets of the day. Ever and anon, a pamphlet issued from the pen of Burke. There was no need of having the book before us. Coleridge had read it in the morning, and in the evening he would repeat whole pages verbatim."[22]

Vendettas were also pursued against the more conservative Jesus dons. Coleridge told Mary Evans of his taunting of Mr Newton their

*William Frend (1757–1841), mathematician and Unitarian, was the outstanding Cambridge representative of an entire generation of radical preachers, dons, lecturers and literary intellectuals whose lives were inspired (and careers often wrecked) by the idealism of the early French Revolution. History has usually treated them with irony, but biography is slowly coming to their rescue. These "English Jacobins", as they are sometimes loosely called, were men – and women – of eccentricity, courage, intelligence, and what one might call subversive vision. (See Carl B. Cone, *The English Jacobins*, New York, 1968.) Here it is sufficient to recall some of their names: the Unitarian preacher Richard Price; the political lecturer "Citizen" John Thelwall; the philosopher William Godwin; the feminist Mary Wollstonecraft; the poets George Dyer and William Blake; the playwright and novelist Thomas Holcroft; the publisher Joseph Johnson; the agitator Tom Paine. (See my appendix, "Coleridge's Circle".) Coleridge's (and Wordsworth's) shifting relations with them all are controversial throughout the 1790s, but have been ably traced by Nicolas Roe in *Wordsworth and Coleridge: the Radical Years*, Oxford (1988); and a brilliant picture of their intellectual milieu and aspirations appears in the first part of William St Clair's *The Godwins and the Shelleys*, Faber (1989).

Mathematics Tutor, even to the point of harassing the tutor's doctor who had been so unwise as to treat him for a fever that had conveniently prevented him lecturing: "six of his duteous pupils, myself as their General, sallied forth to the Apothecary's house with a fixed determination to thrash him for having performed so speedy a cure – but luckily for himself the Rascal was not at home."[23] Slogans such as "Frend and Liberty" were daubed on the college walls, and at the height of the agitation even burnt in gunpowder on the sacred turf of Trinity College quadrangle.

Amidst these stirring events, and the increasingly exciting despatches from Paris, Coleridge sat for his exams and prizes. In December he was selected by Professor Porson as one of the seventeen undergraduates in the university to take the prestigious Craven Scholarship, and by January 1793 was in the last four finalists. "We circumnavigated the Encyclopaedia – so very severe an examination was never remembered." In April he sat again for the annual Rustat Exams, and in June again competed for the Brown Medal – submitting a Greek Ode on Astronomy.

His results were not undistinguished, though clearly his family were disappointed. The Rustat Scholarship was renewed, and he came second in the Brown Medal (the winner was Keate, subsequently Shelley's headmaster at Eton, the notorious "Flogger" Keate). The Craven was given to the youngest finalist, Christopher Bethell, who later became Bishop of Bangor. But the Master of Jesus, Dr Pearce, was so pleased with Coleridge's performance that he awarded him the college "Chapel Clerk's Place", which brought him a further £33 per annum towards his expenses. It also required Coleridge – for Pearce was a shrewd man – to attend chapel at least four mornings a week, no doubt intended as a check on his nocturnal activities.

For several weeks after the effort of the Craven, he was confined to his rooms with an abscessed tooth, and wrote a teasing series of letters to Mary. One, enclosing a spirited imitation of Ossian's poetry, concluded: "Are you asleep, my dear Mary? – I have administered rather a strong Dose of Opium – : however, if in the course of your Nap you should chance to dream, that – I am with the ardour/of fraternal friendship/Your affectionate S. T. Coleridge – you will never have dreamt a truer dream in all *your born days.*"[24]

5

One thing that Coleridge did not tell Mary in his letters, or George, was of his involvement in William Frend's trial before the University Vice-Chancellor throughout the month of May 1793. Frend had published a pamphlet, *Peace and Union*, which became famous in the university that spring. Not only did it attack Anglican doctrines of faith, it also criticised the British declaration of war against France, and argued that Prime Minister Pitt was deliberately oppressing the poor weavers of the Midlands with war taxation. Deist and republican in tone, it strongly appealed to undergraduates like Coleridge who were questioning their own Christian beliefs, and who were fascinated by the egalitarian ideas of the French Revolution. The charge was a serious one, "sedition and defamation of the Church of England", and the case eventually went before the Court of King's Bench in London, that autumn, where the proceedings were recorded in the *State Trials* for that year.[25]

The atmosphere at the university had become both politicised and polarised. Not only was Tom Paine burnt in effigy; several dissenting tradesmen in the town had their business premises wrecked and were forced, like Priestley, to emigrate. A Patriotic Declaration by 112 tavern-keepers promised to report any undergraduates to the local magistrates who showed "treasonable or seditious tendencies" in their pubs and inns "by public conversation or by public reading, or circulation of any books, pamphlets, or papers".[26] The university authorities regarded Frend's trial as crucial, and the Vice-Chancellor later wrote: "I don't believe Pitt was ever aware of how much consequence the expulsion of Frend was: it was the ruin of the Jacobinical party as a *University thing* . . ."[27]

From 1793 to 1796 Coleridge would flirt with many of the ideas of the English Jacobins, as he later freely admitted in private correspondence. Yet he always denied it in his public statements after 1800, and censored his own lectures and newspaper articles accordingly when they were later republished – another clear example of his reconstructed autobiography. This flirtation began at Jesus when, as Charles Le Grice noted, Coleridge's rooms became a centre of the Frend faction, and during the trial "pamphlets swarmed from the press. Coleridge had read them all; and in the evenings, with our *negus*, we had them *viva voce* gloriously."[28]

Coleridge attended the trial in the public gallery of the Senate House, during eight days in May, and was one of the ringleaders of what the Vice-Chancellor described as "the noisy and tumultuous irregularities of conduct" which frequently interrupted the proceedings.[29] On one particular day the clapping and heckling became so bad that the Senior Proctor, Mr Farish, was sent to arrest "one man who had particularly distinguished himself", his position in the gallery having been carefully noted. This offender was in fact Coleridge; but when Farish pushed through the crowd and seized the man's shoulder, he discovered that it was an undergraduate with a deformed arm who was quite incapable of clapping. The error produced a barrage of ironic applause, "which continued for some minutes". What had actually occurred was observed by a Junior Fellow, Henry Gunning, who subsequently included the incident in a history of Cambridge life at this period.

> The name of the young man was Charnock, and his college was Clare Hall; the real culprit was S. T. Coleridge, of Jesus College, who having observed that the Proctor had noticed him, and was coming into the Gallery, turned round to the person who was standing behind him, and made an offer of changing places, which was gladly accepted by the unsuspecting man. Coleridge immediately retreated, and mixing with the crowd, entirely escaped suspicion. This conduct on the part of Coleridge, was severely censured by the Undergraduates as it was quite clear that, to escape punishment himself, he would have subjected an innocent man to rustication or expulsion.[30]

Coleridge, not surprisingly, gave rather different versions of this escapade to later friends. To his newspaper editor, Daniel Stuart, who once accompanied him on a nostalgic trip to Cambridge in 1812, he recast the incident as a piece of high farce: Charnock was a man with "an iron hook" instead of a hand, and the kindly Proctor, "well knowing" that Coleridge was the real culprit who might be expelled, deliberately picked on a man who could not possibly be blamed.[31] Later still, he told James Gillman that after Charnock's arrest, he went directly to the Proctor's office and confessed "that no innocent person should incur blame". Farish told him that he had "a narrow escape", and let him off.[32]

This may be true, though it is odd that Gunning does not mention it. Yet the pattern of extravagant behaviour, followed by remorseful confession to the authorities, is one that further emerges in 1793 and thenceforth recurs throughout Coleridge's life, and is surely significant. Gunning's only other comment is that Coleridge was by now renowned throughout the university for brilliant classical scholarship, flamboyant talk, and peculiar political views.[33]

6

There was no doubt that after Coleridge's failure to win the Craven Scholarship, his whole attitude to academic success altered. There was now little chance that he would obtain a Fellowship, and his secret religious doubts made a conventional career in the Church impossible – though George still hoped for one. It is indicative that the other three finalists either became bishops – as, also, did Middleton – or celebrated public school headmasters.

Yet this failure can be seen as an immensely liberating one: it saved Coleridge from a safe, Establishment career (as pursued by his brothers in the Church and the army), and threw him back on his inner, imaginative resources, which drew him powerfully and naturally towards poetry, religious speculation, metaphysics, and the political idealism of the time. But unable to explain these wayward longings to his brothers, it also brought intense guilt. He began to live a kind of double life at Cambridge, his wild expenditure on books, drinking, violin lessons, theatre and whoring (he later described this as the time of his "unchastities") alternating with fits of suicidal gloom and remorse. These were deepened by the news of Frank's death, which finally reached him soon after the scholarship results, and filled him with depression.[34]

The first of many plans for reform, announced to George, now significantly included his earliest scheme to publish poetry.

> I am now employing myself *omni Marte* in translating the best Lyric Poems from the Greek, and the modern Latin Writers – which I mean in about half a year's time to publish by Subscription. By means of Caldwell, Tucket, & Middleton I can ensure more than two hundred Subscribers – so that this and frugality will enable me to pay off my debts, which have corroded my Spirits greatly for some time Past. – I owe about £50 to my Tutor – and about £8 elsewhere . . . I think therefore of staying all the Summer in Cambridge . . . I have been lesson'd by the wholesome discipline of Experience.[35]

Meanwhile his letters to Mary Evans continued to describe wine parties, "swingeing Impositions" from the Dean, the radical politics of the opposition leader Charles James Fox – "quite the *political Go* at Cambridge" – and the performances of Mrs Siddons, which suggest that he was already making clandestine visits to London. "And why should *not* a man amuse himself sometimes? Vive la bagatelle!"[36]

By July, his finances were in such a state that he was forced to go down to Ottery for the vacation, to confront James and George with his debts: from £58 they had suddenly grown to the remarkable sum of £148 17s 1¼d, a figure of delusory accuracy.[37] He confessed some at least of his "follies", and after a severe family conference, fraternal cash was provided to pay off some of these at the commencement of the Michaelmas term. Meanwhile he embarked on his customary tour of relations in Salisbury, Exeter and Tiverton.

The atmosphere was now subtly different from the scholarly triumph of the previous year: there was much drinking and arguing with Edward, much flirtation with local girls, and considerably more poetry. At Salisbury he first glimpsed Bowles crossing the market-place, but did not dare to speak to him; at Exeter he attended a literary society at which a newly published poem, "An Evening Walk", by an unknown writer, William Wordsworth, was read out and praised.[38]

He wrote unguardedly to George in August: "I stayed at Tiverton about 10 days, and got no small *kudos* among the young Belles by complimentary effusions in the poetic Way . . . Do you know Fanny Nesbitt? She was my fellow-traveller in the Tiverton diligence from Exeter. – I think a very pretty Girl."[39] This suggests that he was seeking consolation for Mary Evans having already decided that his love for her was ill-starred because of his lack of academic prospects: though he had not plucked up courage to declare himself, and indeed would never do so until the very end of the affair in November 1794.[40] The poems of this summer included, besides various pieces "of the namby pamby Genius", his "Sonnet: To the River Otter", and a long sentimental Ode set in the Pixies' Parlour at Ottery, "Songs of the Pixies". Here he presents himself in the melancholy manner of Bowles, as the sorrowing, lonely, lovelorn young poet:

> Thither, while the murmuring throng
> Of wild-bees hum their drowsy song,
> By Indolence and Fancy brought,
> A youthful Bard, "unknown to Fame",
> Wooes the Queen of Solemn Thought . . .[41]

Perhaps the most striking aspect of this poem is the prose preface, which Coleridge subsequently attached to it for publication in 1796. In it he first shows his genius for mythologising the place and conditions in which his poetry was conceived. In a quiet and delicately understated way, it entwines local folklore with the magic psychology of memory and love, in a manner that points towards much later work. It was his first attempt to re-invent a poetic world of natural emblems, in which the imagination stealthily transforms the everyday into the visionary. The little sandstone cave of his childhood becomes, or half becomes, a cavern of emotions "measureless to man", haunted by a magic "damsel".

> The Pixies, in the superstition of Devonshire, are a race of beings invisibly small, and harmless or friendly to man. At a small distance from a village in that county, half-way up a wood-covered hill, is an excavation called the Pixies' Parlour. The roots of old trees form its ceiling; and on its sides are innumerable cyphers, among which the author discovered his own cypher and those of his brothers, cut by the hand of their childhood. At the foot of the hill flows the river Otter. To this place, during the summer months of the year 1793, the Author conducted a party of young ladies; one of whom, of stature elegantly small, and of complexion colourless yet clear, was proclaimed the Faery Queen.[42]

7

It was hardly surprising that Coleridge did not return to Cambridge in September 1793 in the most prosaic state of mind. In fact, he lingered in London to see Mary, and much of the money provided for his debts was squandered on unspecified entertainment. "So small a sum remained, that I could not mock my Tutor with it."[43]

By the end of October his "Embarrassments" buzzed round him "like a Nest of Hornets", and in November he gave up all attempts to get his affairs under control. Instead he abandoned himself to a whirl of drunken socialising, alternating with grim solitary resolutions to shoot himself as the final solution to bad debts, unrequited love, and academic disgrace. (The example of Frank seems to have mixed itself up with the fate of Goethe's Young Werther.) No letters survive from this traumatic month, for not even the Evans family were now in his confidence, but he subsequently gave George a lurid account.

> My Agitations were a delirium – I formed a Party, dashed to London at eleven o'clock at night, and for three days lived in all the tempest of Pleasure – resolved on my return – but I will not shock your religious feelings – I again returned to Cambridge – staid a week – such a week! – Where Vice has not annihilated Sensibility, there is little need of a Hell! On Sunday night I packed up a few things, – went off in the mail . . . still looking forwards with a kind of recklessness to the dernier resort of misery . . .[44]

This was the Sunday of 24 November.

Oddly enough, the one thing that flourished during these delirious three weeks of November was Coleridge's poetry. In a desperate attempt to recoup his debts, Coleridge had put money in an Irish lottery in London, and while awaiting the outcome he wrote an Ode "To Fortune", composed while walking from a tavern in Gray's Inn Lane, and the lottery shop in the Cornhill. He submitted it to the *Morning Chronicle*, and to his amazement it was published in the paper on 7 November, earning him a guinea (unlike the lottery). This was, ironically, his first professional publication: and the following year the same newspaper was publishing an entire sequence of his sonnets. It contains a suggestive confusion of unpaid debts with unrequited love, both exciting bitter and evidently liberating tears:

> Let the little bosom cold
> Melt only at the sunbeam ray of gold –
> My pale cheeks glow – the big drops start –
> The rebel *Feeling* riots at my heart![45]

It was this rebellious release of dammed-up, pent-up emotions – going all the way back to childhood – that was evidently so important to Coleridge throughout these catastrophic and glorious weeks.

Despite the "delirium", Coleridge was also regularly attending a newly founded Literary Society in Cambridge, formed by Charles Le Grice and a Trinity College undergraduate, Christopher Wordsworth – younger brother of William. The minutes between 5 and 13 November record a brilliant and relatively sober Coleridge, declaiming his love-poetry of the summer, "spouting" Bowles, quoting the Greek poets with crashing fluency, and studiously promising to deliver a special paper on modern poetry. His poem "To Fortune" was read from the newspaper to great applause; and there was earnest discussion of the elder Wordsworth's "Evening Walk".

The only ominous note was his failure to appear and deliver his special paper at the Society's meeting of 20 November, as arranged. But his absence was not especially remarked upon, for his inspired vagaries were obviously well-known among the undergraduates.[46]

While he should have been debating the finer points of verse at Trinity, Coleridge was probably drinking heavily in Holborn; but very little is known of this final climactic week in London at the end of November. Coleridge later embroidered such a tapestry of adventures that they became the subject of a novel by his friend Charles Lloyd, *Edmund Oliver*, published in 1798. But the absence of any reliable witness is indicated by the fact that no friend knew of his whereabouts, or succeeded in making contact with him, for the next two months, until February 1794. As on that famous night at Ottery, he simply ran away in a storm of emotion, and awaited discovery and rescue, with "inward and gloomy satisfaction".

Amid the general chaos of debts and guilt and misery, so strangely shadowed by the growing confidence in his own powers as a poet, there may have been some final, isolating horror. He might, for example, have thought that his whoring had given him a venereal disease.[47] Certainly his final resolution was not an act of rebellion at all, but a bitterly remorseful attempt to redeem his honour in the most humiliating tradition of family loyalties. Like John, like James, like Frank, he volunteered for the army.*

On 2 December 1793, he accepted the six and a half guinea bounty of a volunteer private in the 15th Light Dragoons, reporting to Colonel Gwynne's recruiting office in Chancery Lane. Two days later he was sworn in at the regimental headquarters in Reading, and was issued with leather breeches, stable jacket, riding boots, and a

*William Godwin gives an interesting account of Coleridge's days in London immediately before enlistment, together with some general observations on the nature of this crisis, in the series of unpublished manuscript Notes from Coleridge's conversation in London in 1799. (See Chapter 10.) Godwin records: "never told his love [to Mary Evans] – loose in sexual morality – spends a night in a house of ill-fame, ruminating in a chair: next morning meditates suicide, walks in the park, enlists, sleeps 12 hours on the officer's bed, and upon awaking is offered his liberty, which from a scruple of honour he refuses – marched to Reading – dinnerless on Christmas day, his pocket having been picked by a comrade." (Bodleian Ms Abinger C.604/3) Characteristically a very different, and much more highly coloured account was being written almost simultaneously in the opportunist novel, *Edmund Oliver* by Charles Lloyd (2 vols, Cottle 1798). Lloyd contrives to suggest that the whole thing took place in a haze of opium. "I have at all times a strange dreaminess about me . . . if at any time thought-troubled, I have swallowed some spirits, or had recourse to opium." (See vol. I, p. 245; and vol. II, pp. 1–11.) Neither writer quite seems to understand the family history which lay behind the event.

carbine, and began his training mucking out the stables. He gave his name, according to his initials, as Silas Tomkyn Comberbache. The outlandish surname, somehow so expressive of his total inability to ride a horse, may have been a last, muffled dactylic tribute to Frank, whose middle name was Syndercombe. He became, in his own mocking phrase, "a very indocile Equestrian".[48]

8

The Army has a way of dealing with even its most unlikely recruits. After two months' basic training at Reading, during which he did guard duty at the Reading Fair and wrote love-letters on behalf of his illiterate comrades, he was seconded to Henley on Thames as temporarily unfit to ride. He had saddle-sores and boils: "dreadfully troublesome eruptions, which so grimly constellated my Posteriors."[49]

His orders were to nurse a fellow dragoon, whose illness turned out to be smallpox, at that time usually a fatal disease. The two men were isolated in the single room of the Pest House, a low brick building in the grounds of Henley workhouse. Here, in the first fortnight of February 1794, Coleridge faithfully nursed his "poor Comrade" through fever and real delirium, amidst "the putrid smell and the fatiguing Struggles" of long, sleepless nights. Food and buckets of water were left at the door (for which Coleridge had to pay), and for eight days and nights he did not undress, bathing and feeding his comrade through the crisis.

Both men survived, but the experience of this nightmare of sickness may well have contributed something to the hallucinations of the *Ancient Mariner*, four years later. It was another intense vision of the sickroom and its peculiar intimacies. Coleridge later told many tales, to Gillman, to Bowles and others, of his military service, but most of them were comic accounts of how his real identity as a runaway Cambridge scholar was discovered. In one version, he was on guard duty, and could not prevent himself from correcting a Greek quotation from Euripedes, made by the duty officer. In another, he was found regaling his fellow dragoons with stories from Thucydides' *Peloponnesian War*. In a third, a line of Latin verse was found pencilled on the wall above his harness peg.[50] But curiously he chose to say nothing about his time in the little, claustrophobic Pest House, which affected him more deeply than any other part of his ordeal.

News of his whereabouts eventually leaked back to Cambridge via the Grecians of Christ's Hospital, some of whom must have heard of his adventures in Holborn. Once the story was out, Coleridge received several letters of support and offers of help, from Val Le Grice, Tucker, and Bob Allen. Even his old headmaster, James Bowyer, allowed it to be understood that his prize pupil had volunteered with his permission, thereby safeguarding the precious Christ's Hospital Exhibition, which would otherwise have been instantly forfeited.[51] George Coleridge was naturally distraught and, still not knowing Coleridge's regiment, persuaded his fellow Jesus College undergraduate Tucker, to forward an unaddressed letter, begging him to get in touch and saying that their mother was ill with worry.

This letter reached Coleridge at the Henley Pest House on 6 February, but he did not dare to open it for two days. His reply on 8 February was hysterical with grief and guilt. "I have been a fool even to madness. What shall I dare promise? My mind is illegible to myself – I am lost in the labyrinth, the trackless wilderness of my own bosom ... The shame and sorrow of those who loved me – the anguish of him, who protected me from my childhood upwards – the sore travail of her who bore me – intolerable Images of horror! They haunt my sleep – they enfever my Dreams!"[52] The "riot" of feeling was still running with melodramatic strength, oddly confused with the "loathsome form" of the feverish man Coleridge was still patiently nursing.

George immediately answered with a letter of great patience and kindness. "A handsome Sum shall be gotten ready for the liquidation of your College debts, if either my interest or person can procure it – and the business of your discharge commenc'd immediately – Write me as swift as wind – that I may take every step for restoring you to happiness & myself."[53] Once these communications were opened in such a manner, Coleridge was immensely relieved. He could now play the part of the prodigal son, and he proceeded to do so with something approaching gusto.

To James Coleridge, who was put in charge of the delicate and expensive business of negotiating the discharge (which was rumoured to cost more than forty guineas), he wrote that his conduct had "displayed a strange Combination of Madness, Ingratitude, & Dishonesty"; adding pitifully that recruits from his regiment were already being drafted for service abroad. (The manuscript of this letter still hangs in the Officers Mess of the 15th King's Royal Hussars, one of its most treasured memorabilia.)[54]

While to George he promised more expansively "a minute history" of all his secret thoughts and actions for the last two years at Cambridge. This emotional confession was written late one Sunday night, 23 February, after his duties at the Pest House were completed. Though it studiously omits any details about Mary Evans, Frend's trial, or his new political and literary aspirations, it does reveal much of the pent-up guilt he had felt for so long.

His new identity as Trooper Comberbache gave him, paradoxically, a chance to be himself. For the first time one can really hear the voice of the frantic young poet & intellectual, dramatising and over-dramatising himself with a lurid satisfaction that so frequently hovers on pure comedy. As so often in Coleridge's later life, the absurd disaster of his practical affairs seems almost a liberation of the spirit. His letter soars upwards out of the catastrophe it recounts, with something close to exultation. He makes the worst of everything, brilliantly.

> I laugh almost like an insane person when I cast my eye backward on the prospect of my past two years – What a gloomy *Huddle* of eccentric Actions, and dim-discovered motives! To real Happiness I bade adieu from the moment, I received my first Tutor's Bill – since that time since that period my Mind has been irradiated by Bursts only of Sunshine – at all other times gloomy with clouds, or turbulent with tempests . . . I became a proverb to the University for Idleness – the time, which I should have bestowed on the academic studies, I employed in dreaming out wild Schemes of impossible extrication. It had been better for me, if my Imagination had been less vivid – I could not with such facility have shoved aside Reflection! How many and how many hours have I stolen from the bitterness of Truth in these soul-enervating Reveries – in building magnificent Edifices of Happiness on some fleeting Shadow of Reality! My Affairs became more and more involved – I fled to Debauchery – fled from silent and solitary Anguish to all the uproar of senseless Mirth! Having, or imagining that I had, no *stock* of Happiness, to which I could look forwards, I seized the empty gratifications of the moment, and snatched at the Foam, as the Wave passed by me. – I feel a painful blush on my cheek, while I write it – but even for the Un. Scholarship, for which I affected to have read so severely, I did not read three days uninterruptedly –

for the whole six weeks, that preceded the examination, I was almost constantly intoxicated! My Brother, you shudder as you read –[55]

No doubt George was intended to shudder; but also, to forgive. Even allowing for the Wertherism and exaggeration of all this (Coleridge was deliberately dismissing any academic achievement whatever), it is interesting to find him, long before his days of opium addiction, accusing himself of "soul-enervating Reveries", and touching on the "Kubla Khan" imagery of edifices, waves and fleeting shadows.

Indeed he was beginning to define the world of his own poetic imagination; and lack of money, lack of "stock", was really a symbol of a more general lack of worldly, conventional ambitions: something his brothers would never understand. The earnestness with which they now all rallied round to get him back to Cambridge has a touching futility. Coleridge had really escaped through Comberbache. In the Henley Pest House, close to disease and death, he had glimpsed other possibilities. He would go through the motions, but he would not really "come back" again.

9

It took over six weeks to obtain his discharge. Meanwhile he was shifted on the regimental baggage cart from Henley to High Wycombe, where he was stationed in a tavern, and effortlessly made friends with the adjutant, Captain Nathaniel Ogle. Seconded to light stable duties, he shared gentlemanly bottles of wine with Ogle, took a daily newspaper, translated Casimir's poems for his intended classical anthology, and dashed off an essay on the evils of the modern novel for Bob Allen – who submitted it at Oxford for his declamation.[56] His letters to George rapidly recovered their old *élan*, and he gave an amusing account of a pot-house philosopher at the inn, who kept him up till three in the morning spinning "theories of Heaven and Hell". He added with boldly returning self-confidence: "My Memory tenacious & systematizing would enable me to write an Octavo from his Conversation."[57]

Negotiations for the discharge continued with Colonel Gwynne's office throughout March, but it proved no military formality. The problem was to find a substitute recruit. James did not pursue the matter with much alacrity (he probably felt that the army was just what his younger brother needed), but the faithful George tactfully pressed the case in a series of letters, pointing out that Coleridge needed to return to Jesus by mid-April in order to take his annual Rustat Scholarship exam. George finally went to the regimental headquarters in person. Coleridge meanwhile was drafted back to Henley, quartered at the White Hart and began further training on "an horse, young and as undisciplined as myself". It ran away with him during each parade, and he was thrown off three times in one week.[58]

To his embarrassment, several friends came to visit him, including Charles Le Grice, and George Cornish of Ottery who initially failed to recognise him in his riding breeches and powdered and pomatumed hair tied back in a military pigtail. Cornish thought him "much agitated", and half suspecting his brothers meant to punish him by the delay in discharge: "he gave me a little detail of his sufferings, but he says they are not half enough to expiate his follies." Cornish slipped him a guinea, quite shocked to see him go through "all the drudgery of a Dragoon recruit".[59]

On 30 March, still not discharged, Coleridge wrote humbly to George promising the "utmost contrivances of Economy" and speaking for the first time of his religious doubts. "Fond of the dazzle of Wit, fond of subtlety of Argument", he had read Voltaire and Helvetius, who had drawn him into "a kind of *religious Twilight*". He still loved the Jesus of the Gospels, but "my reasonings would not permit me to *worship*." This marks the beginning of his Unitarian phase, which would lead him for several years into a radical view of Christianity as a philosophy of social reform, with strong egalitarian overtones, which were evidently encouraged by his army experience. He fervently reassured George of his penitence: "believe me your severities only wound me as they awake the *Voice within* to speak ah! how more harshly! I feel gratitude and love towards you, even when I shrink and shiver –"[60]

When on 7 April definite news of his imminent discharge arrived, he cheered up again and announced he was writing the libretto for an opera.[61] The army had found its own method of dealing with the matter; after an unofficial payment from George of some twenty-five guineas, the Regimental Muster Roll recorded succinctly: "discharged S. T. Comberbache, Insane; 10 April 1794".[62]

FOUR

PANTISOCRAT

1

Coleridge returned to Cambridge on 11 April 1794, travelling up on the outside of the night mail after symbolically missing the Cambridge fly. He had booked a seat, but then went for a contemplative walk, and the fly shot by him on the road. For all his brothers' hopes, he would never again settle down at the university; his dreams were elsewhere. Outwardly he was full of good resolutions: having sat the Rustat Exam and got a credit, he would now study hard, contend "for all the Prizes", and compile his slim volume of *Imitations from the Modern Latin Poets* to pay off his debts. (It was advertised in the *Cambridge Intelligencer* for June, but never appeared.) He would "solemnly" drop all unsuitable college friends, rise at six o'clock every morning, forswear wine parties and politics, and practise a "severe Economy". "Every enjoyment – except of *necessary* comforts – I look upon as criminal." Even in his Greek verse he would now aim at "correctness & perspicuity, not *genius*". His last Ode had been so sublime that no one could understand it.[1]

He accepted the college's reprimand, a month's gating, and ninety pages of Greek translation from Demetrius Phalereus ("dry, and utterly intransferable to *modern* use") with a great show of philosophy. Though his tutor, Mr Plampin, had treated him with "exceeding and most delicate kindness", the Master, Dr Pearce, had behaved with great asperity. "All the Fellows tried to persuade the Master to greater Lenity, but in vain – without the least affectation I applaud his conduct – and think nothing of it," he told George on 1 May. "The confinement is nothing – I have the fields and Grove of the college to walk in – and what can I wish more? What do I wish more? Nothing."[2]

But of course, he now wished for everything. He played the part of the penitent prodigal with conviction, indeed he rather enjoyed it. But as Trooper Comberbache he had seen the outside world, and tasted notoriety; and guiltily he enjoyed that too. How could he return to the small existence of college honours, the remote degree (now postponed until Christmas 1795), or the narrow prospect of a clergyman's career like dear, earnest brother George? Radical politics, Unitarian theology, poetry, newspapers, the glories of nature and science, were all fizzing in his mind. He had already attracted a following among Bob Allen's circle in Oxford. At Cambridge, even cautious men like Caldwell treated him with respect and "almost fraternal affection". He had become one of the wild men of his university generation, and people waited to see what he would do next. He confided to his fellow undergraduate Samuel Butler: "There are hours in which I am inclined to think very meanly of myself, but when I call to memory the number & character of those who have honoured me with their esteem, I am almost reconciled to my follies, and again listen to the whispers of self-adulation."[3] Pride and guilt mixed in him like combustible fuel, waiting to be ignited. What he wished for was an ideal cause, a grand scheme, a mighty passion. And even deeper than this, perhaps, love and friendship. It was to come initially in the shape of Pantisocracy.

2

Like many things in Coleridge's life, it all began with a walking tour. These tours, common enough today, were then a new fashion with strong democratic overtones. Young men from the universities dressed as tramps and wandered over the countryside, staying at local inns, talking enthusiastically with "the common people", hill-climbing, swimming, star-gazing and communing with nature. William Frend had walked through France, Wordsworth had crossed the Alps into Italy, Bowles had wandered through Wales and Germany. Coleridge now planned "a pedestrian scheme" through the Wye Valley and up into North Wales, starting the moment that his gating was officially over. His practical preparations consisted largely in purchasing a curious five-foot walking-stick carved to a suitably modest design. "On one side it displays the head of an Eagle, the Eyes of which represent rising Suns, and the Ears Turkish Crescents. On the other side is the portrait of the Owner in Wood-work. Beneath the head of the Eagle is a Welch Wig – and around the neck of the Stick is a Queen Elizabeth's Ruff in Tin. All adown it waves the Line of Beauty in very ugly Carving."[4]

He chose a large, genial, fellow undergraduate, Joseph Hucks, to accompany him: "a man of cultivated, tho' not vigorous understanding", as Coleridge kindly described his Sancho Panza. Hucks subsequently published a Rousseauesque account of the tour, which leadenly omits every incident of human interest. When they met nude female bathers at Abergele, Hucks chose "to retire further up the shore". Coleridge insisted on wearing rough workmen's jackets, loose trousers, (rather than gentleman's breeches and stockings), and carrying canvas knapsacks, which Hucks thought gave them the appearance of "two pilgrims performing a journey to the tomb of some wonder-working saint". In fact they were usually mistaken for French tinkers (dangerously republican) or demobbed soldiers (dangerously drunk).

It was the first of Coleridge's many epic walks: during the serious part of the tour they covered over 500 miles in just over a month – from Gloucester to Anglesey through the Welsh hills, and back by the coast to Bristol. They departed from Cambridge at dawn on 15 June, planning a brief stop-over with Bob Allen in Oxford, before disappearing into wild Wales. Coleridge, feeling like a man released from prison, was in a state of manic enthusiasm. On the way he bought the first of many Notebooks, with a "portable Ink horn" and quills: "as I journey onward, I ever and anon pluck the wild Flowers of Poesy."[5]

They tramped into Oxford about 17 June, going straight round to Allen's rooms in University College for a memorable reunion between the two Grecians. Coleridge had brought a subscribers' list for his *Imitations* in his knapsack, and armed with this they trooped over to Balliol to meet Robert Southey, the twenty-year-old poet from Bristol who was already renowned for his extreme republican views. This meeting delayed their planned three-day stop-over for three weeks, and saw the birth of the famous "Pantisocratic" scheme.

The tall, idealistic, rather forbidding young Southey was then sporting a radical beard, studying anatomy, and finishing an epic drama, *Joan of Arc*. His rooms were next to the college lavatories, by an alley that opened on to St Giles. He was leaving Oxford that summer without a degree, destined for the Church, though he proclaimed himself an atheist and democrat with strong French Jacobin sympathies. He was profoundly depressed at his situation, and the arrival of the ebullient and voluble Coleridge took him by storm. He wrote instantly to his old school friend, Grosvenor Bedford, after their first interview: "I am delaying the pickling of my tripes again till the departure of a Cantab; one whom I very much esteem and admire tho two thirds of our conversation be spent in disputing on metaphysical subjects."[6]

Southey was a schoolboy rebel who had been expelled from Westminster for editing a magazine, the *Flagellant*, against flogging and other undemocratic practices. (Southey wrote as "St Basil", and Bedford as "Peter the Hermit".) He had come up to Oxford in 1792 with "a heart full of poetry and feeling, a head full of Rousseau and Werther, and my religious principles shaken by Gibbon". He wrote bad poetry at tremendous speed, having already burnt 10,000 lines of *Joan of Arc*, and bound up the rest in expensive marbled paper with a green silk ribbon.

Like Coleridge, he felt trapped by his home situation and lack of money. His father, a failed Bristol linen-merchant, had recently died, leaving a consumptive mother with two infant children, besides Robert and his younger brother Tom. His education had been paid for by a clerical uncle, Herbert Hill, and an eccentric aunt, Elizabeth Tyler, both of whom expected him to go into the Church. For months he had been fantasising his way out of this impasse. Southey composed long lyrical letters to Bedford, which alternately considered suicide, joining the French Revolutionary Army, and emigrating to America where he would build a farm "on ground uncultivated since the creation" and live in Rousseauesque seclusion until "cooked for a Cherokee, or oysterised by a tiger".[7] He considered British society hopelessly corrupt, and with the suspension of habeas corpus in May, expected an imminent revolution. He carried a copy of Goethe's *Werther* everywhere he went, and like Coleridge also worshipped the poetry of Bowles.

Exactly what "metaphysical subjects" they discussed with increasing wildness at Oxford, becomes clear from their subsequent letters during the summer. In sum it was Rousseau and the back to Nature movement; Godwin and the anarchist society of shared property and ideal communism; David Hartley and the psychological motivations of human action and intellectual prejudice; Joseph Priestley and the American emigration movement. (Priestley had already left for Philadelphia that April.) All these figures contributed something to the scheme which Coleridge christened at first "*Pantocracy*": that is, an experimental society, living in pastoral seclusion, sharing property, labour, and self-government equally among all its adult members, both men and women. (Coleridge created the word from the Greek roots *pan-socratia*, an all-governing-society; not of course from the Latin root *panto-mimus*, meaning a comic dumb-show.) It was, in effect, a heady cocktail of all the progressive idealism of the Romantic Age.*

As the first rapturous outlines of the scheme emerged (they were to take six months of clarifying), Southey and Coleridge became fast friends. Their enormous differences in temperament and outlook were not immediately evident. Southey confided to Bedford, in London: "Allen is with us daily, and his friend from Cambridge, Coleridge, whose poems you will oblige me by subscribing to . . . He is of the most uncommon merit, – of the strongest genius, the clearest judgement, the best heart. My friend he already is, and must hereafter be yours. It is, I fear, impossible to keep him till you come, but my efforts shall not be wanting."[8] He later added to his brother, Thomas Southey: "This Pantisocratic system has given me new life new hope new energy. All the faculties of my mind are dilated."[9]

Coleridge in turn was deeply, but differently, impressed by Southey. He saw him as a lonely dreamer like himself (he urged him to fight despondency, "I once shipwrecked my frail bark on that rock"), but far more politicised and self-disciplined – hard-working, early rising, poetically fluent, morally pure, "a Nightingale among Owls" in Oxford. He later wrote: "His Genius and acquirements are uncommonly great – yet they bear no proportion to his moral Excellence – He is truly a man of *perpendicular Virtue – a down-right upright Republican*!" (He would add, in private conversation, that Southey was a virgin, and sternly "converted" him back from sexual promiscuity.)[10]

---

*The intellectual sources for Pantisocracy perhaps belong even more to the eighteenth-century Enlightenment – the Unitarian rationalist and scientist Priestley, the associationist psychologist David Hartley – than to French revolutionary radicalism. (See "Coleridge's Circle".) But the urge to break away into some ideal, small, rural, community runs right through English literature from Shelley in Italy to D. H. Lawrence in New Mexico, and Robert Louis Stevenson in the South Seas. (See for example, *R. L. S. in the South Seas*, by Alanna Knight, Mainstream, 1986.) What perhaps distinguished these various attempts is their differing attitudes to the value of "the primitive" and "the native": Coleridge did not suppose that the Pantisocrats would rediscover "ethnic values" or tribal wisdom. They were going, like the Pilgrim Fathers, to a naked land. Coleridge's version of the emigration scheme has, at times, almost a science-fiction quality. In a stanza added to the Chatterton "Monody" between 1794–6, he imagines creating a time-warp to enable the young Bristol poet to accompany the Pantisocrats:

> O Chatterton! that thou wert yet alive!
> Sure thou would'st spread the canvass to the gale
> And love with us the tinkling team to drive
> O'er peaceful Freedom's undivided dale . . .
>
> (*P.W.*, p. 130)

As in so many of his later friendships, Coleridge was hypnotically drawn by a man of less humour and imagination than himself, but with far greater force of character and willpower. Southey was soon to replace George in his emotional esteem. There was also a sexual component to the friendship: the handsome, hawk-nosed, narcissistic Southey (he had once paraded through Bristol in women's clothes) attracted Coleridge with a physical self-confidence that he had always lacked. Southey in turn was dazzled and enchanted by Coleridge's warmth and generosity of feeling, his spectacular talk, his responsiveness, and superb imaginative flights. From the beginning he recognised an intellect far richer than his own, but chaotically undirected; and determined – like many others – to discipline it. The two young men were soon dancing round each other in mutual delight, and frequently comic misunderstanding, whirling into their scheme any bystanders they could find. It is notable that those who knew them best at that time – Allen, Hucks, Bedford, Caldwell – were never drawn in.

3

When Hucks finally dragged Coleridge off to Gloucester (by the mail) on 5 July, it had been decided that Southey would return to Bristol to canvass for Pantisocrats among his Balliol College friends George Burnett and Robert Lovell, and find others. Coleridge would proselytise in Wales, and they would perhaps meet again in Aberystwyth to plan the financing of the scheme by the sale of *Imitations*, *Joan of Arc*, and other literary work. While Southey wrote long, apocalyptic letters prophesying violent revolution in England, and urging his friends to join him in Kentucky (the first site for Pantisocracy), Coleridge adopted an altogether lighter touch. The difference in tone here was already significant, for there was always an element of humorous fantasy in Coleridge's Pantisocracy which quite escaped Southey's earnestness. Having seen a poor beggar girl ejected from their inn for begging a bit of bread and meat, Coleridge announced to Southey: "When the pure System of Pantisocracy shall have aspheterized the Bounties of Nature, these things will not be so –! I trust, you admire the word 'aspheterized' from α non, σφετεωος proprius! . . . We really *wanted* such a word – instead of travelling along the circuitous dusty, beaten high-Road of Diction, you thus cut across the soft, green pathless Field of Novelty! Similies forever! Hurra!" At the end of this letter, he gravely promised his "sturdy Republican" a more "sober & chastised Epistle" in his next. Meanwhile, "Fraternity & civic Remembrances" were conveyed to Lovell.[11]

With disconcerting swiftness, the patriot trooper and the prodigal son now gave way to the missionary Pantisocrat and republican. After long hours of foot-slogging over white, dusty roads which seemed to quiver in the summer heat through Hereford and Shropshire, Coleridge was indefatigable. At the King's Arms, Ross, he scratched democratic verses upon the window shutter, speaking of "wine-cheer'd moments" and the honest man of Ross, friend to the friendless, and "nobler than Kings or king-polluted Lords". At Llanfyllin, beyond Welshpool, he "preached Pantisocracy and Aspheterism with so much success that two great huge Fellows of Butcher like appearance, danced about the room in enthusiastic agitation". They drank seditious toasts in brandy to the King: "May he be the last".

At Bala, according to Coleridge, they almost got in a pub-room brawl when he provokingly proposed an American toast, to General Washington, in front of the local JP, the doctor, the parson, and other assembled Welsh worthies. The doctor immediately countered with: "I gives a sentiment, Gemmen! May all Republicans be *gul*lotined!" and this was answered by a Welsh democrat who proposed guillotining fools. "Thereon Rogue, Villain, Traitor flew thick in each other's faces as a hailstorm."

Coleridge claims to have finally pacified everyone by appealing to Christian brotherhood, and they all shook his hand (except for the parson) calling him "an open-speaking, honest-hearted Fellow, tho' I was a *bit* of a Democrat". Coleridge varied these accounts for comic effect, in another saying he had proposed the toast to Priestley (an even greater provocation), and caught fleas from the Welsh democrat: "I trembled, lest some discontented Citizens of the *animalcular* Republic should have emigrated."[12] Hucks says they took no part in the dispute at all, but silently withdrew.[13]

Coleridge's play-acting and high-spirited fooling was partly for Southey's benefit. It was a sort of exhibitionism with which he often dazzled and delighted new friends, a form of intellectual flirtation, a floor-show, an intense desire to please and astound. He later came to regard this as one of the great moral weaknesses of his character, and an older and wiser Southey would upbraid him for it. But it was also the result of genuine excitement and enthusiasm, the discovery of a cause which he felt would rescue him from all the confusions and disappointments of Cambridge. Eleven years after, in Malta, he soberly looked back at this "stormy time", when "for a few months America really inspired Hope, & I became an exalted Being."[14]

Writing publicly in *The Friend* in 1809, at a time of political reaction, he still acknowledged that exaltation, and saw Pantisocracy with great perception as a peculiar product of the French revolutionary excitement. More than that, he claimed it as essential to his education in human affairs. This passage is important in the light of the accusations of political apostasy, which were subsequently heaped on him by William Hazlitt and others.

> My feelings, however, and imagination did not remain unkindled in the general conflagration; and I confess I should be more inclined to be ashamed of myself, if they had! I was a sharer in the general vortex, though my little World described the path of Revolution in an orbit of its own. What I dared not expect from constitutions of Government and whole Nations, I hoped from Religion and a small Company of chosen Individuals, and formed a plan, as harmless as it was extravagant, of trying the experiment of human Perfectibility on the banks of the Susquahannah; where our little Society, in its second generation, was to have combined the innocence of the patriarchal Age with the knowledge and genuine refinements of European culture: and where I had dreamt of beholding, in the sober evening of my life, the Cottages of Independence in the *undivided* Dale of Industry . . . Strange fancies! and as vain as strange! yet to the intense interest and impassioned zeal, which called forth and strained every faculty of my intellect for the organization and defence of this Scheme, I owe much of whatever I at present possess, my clearest insight into the nature of individual Man, and my most comprehensive views of his social relations . . .[15]

It is an exculpatory statement, perhaps; yet much of it is borne out in the ideological struggle with Southey that developed over the next few months, in London and Bristol.

4

It was not just the Pantisocrat who emerged on the Welsh tour, either. Coleridge began writing poetry with much greater fluency, and for the first time showed his passionate response to wild nature, so physical and direct that he felt almost at times like a child suckling at her rocky breasts.

> From Llanvunnog we walked over the mountains to Bala – most sublimely terrible! It was scorchingly hot – I applied my mouth ever and anon to the side of the Rocks and sucked in draughts of Water cold as Ice, and clear as infant Diamonds in their embryo Dew! The rugged and stony Clefts are stupendous – and in winter must form Cataracts most astonishing . . . I slept by the side of one an hour & more. As we descended the Mountain the Sun was reflected in the River that winded thro' the valley with insufferable Brightness – it rivalled the Sky.[16]

Coleridge's physical energy exhausted Hucks. He bathed in the sacred pool at Holywell, climbed Penmaenmawr, Snowdon, Plynlimon and Cader Idris; and at Beaumaris "ordered a supper sufficient for ten aldermen". While tramping, Coleridge fuelled himself with vast supplies of bread, cheese and brandy. He insisted on climbing Penmaenmawr without a guide: they got lost, ran out of water, and were then benighted and thought they were pursued by monsters. Years later Coleridge said the discovery of water under a flat stone on the summit when they "grinned like idiots", provided an image for the *Ancient Mariner*.[17] After that, Hucks refused to go up Snowdon, and Coleridge climbed it with two other undergraduates. At Harlech, he scaled the castle walls without permission, and had to buy beer all round to pacify the town watch.[18]

Coleridge's rapturous letters to Southey, and to his Jesus College friend, Henry Martin, were full of such escapades, set against a vividly perceived Romantic landscape of rivers, waterfalls, mountains, sunsets, and ruins by moonlight. In a sense he was still seeing self-consciously through the eyes of Bowles' sonnets of travel. Yet everywhere "the sublime" was punctured by his individual sense of fun and farce. His favourite device was to adopt some Romantic pose, and then explode it with laughter. In the ruins of Denbigh Castle, he spied a melancholy young man sitting beneath the moon with a flute – "Bless thee, Man of Genius and Sensibility! I silently exclaimed" – and then appreciatively described the ludicrous effect of the "Romantic Youth" instantly striking up the bawdy drinking song of "Mrs Casey".[19] This was play-acting at being the poet, like the Pantisocrat; yet the feelings beneath were evidently deep and genuine. It was almost as if he were frightened of the intensity of his own emotions.

The most revealing of these Romantic incidents occurred at Wrexham. Standing at the window of their inn with Hucks, one Sunday morning, Coleridge was astonished to see the figures of Mary Evans and her sister coming back from church. In a flash he realised that they must have come for a summer holiday with their Welsh grandmother who lived in the town. He had not seen her since joining the dragoons and had been told that she was engaged to another man in London. All his frustrated love for her burst out: "I turned sick and all but fainted away." He hid in the inn, and then fled from Wrexham as soon as possible with Hucks. For a day he could not eat or sleep, and tried to lose himself "amid the terrible Graces of the wildwood scenery". All this he recounted for Southey's benefit with spectacular displays of lovelorn emotion. "Her Image is in the sanctuary of my Heart, and never can it be torn away but with the strings that grapple it to Life. – Southey! There are few men of whose delicacy I think so highly as to have written all this – I am glad, I have so deemed of you – We are soothed by communication."[20]

The part of the star-crossed lover was too good to keep only for Southey. A week later he gave an even more tortured and detailed account to Henry Martin of the meeting, now adding a throw-away line: "But Love is a local Anguish – I am 50 miles distant, and am not half so miserable."[21] What did he really feel about Mary Evans at this juncture? It is impossible to say, and probably Coleridge himself knew least of all, besides unaccountable longings and the old loneliness and rejection he had always felt. But it did produce a touching lyric (afterwards set to music) which marks the sudden flowering of his poetry on this tour, "The Sigh":

> . . . And though in distant climes to roam,
> A wanderer from my native home,
> I fain would soothe the sense of Care,
> And lull to sleep the Joys that were!
> Thy Image may not banish'd be –
> Still, Mary! still I sigh for thee.[22]

5

Southey never met them as arranged, on the return leg through Aberystwyth; and Hucks had had enough by the time they reached Llandovery on 2 August. So Coleridge pushed on southwards alone, catching his first glimpse of Tintern, and then hastily crossing by the Chepstow ferry to Bristol, where he arrived on 5 August, sending a note round to his "fellow Citizen", Robert Lovell.[23] Southey was agreeably surprised by Coleridge's "unexpected arrival", and spent the next ten days introducing him to his circle of friends in the city.[24]

News of Pantisocracy quickly spread through Bristol, where Southey, Lovell and Coleridge (two Oxons and one Cantab) were regarded as the three moving spirits of the enterprise. Coleridge met Joseph Cottle, a young Unitarian publisher who was already printing Southey's *Joan of Arc*, and who immediately offered to publish anything by Coleridge. "I instantly descried his intellectual character," wrote Cottle, "exhibiting as he did, an eye, a brow, and a forehead, indicative of commanding genius. Interviews succeeded and these increased the impression of respect."[25] Cottle gained the impression, from the fervour of the three, that they were considering taking ship for America from Bristol at any moment, and considered it as a noble but "epidemic delusion". This was an important introduction, and Cottle would become Coleridge's first publisher in 1796.

Southey and Lovell also introduced Coleridge to the Fricker family. They were a household of five, high-spirited, dashing girls, whose widowed mother kept a dress shop in Bristol. (There was also a son, George Fricker, who was always getting into scrapes.) Robert Lovell had just married the second daughter, Mary, who had worked as an actress; and Southey was courting the third, Edith, who was generally regarded as the sweetest-natured of the Frickers, and who worked as a milliner.

Of the remaining two of marriageable age (little Eliza was still a schoolgirl), Sara Fricker, the eldest then twenty-four, was thought to be the most handsome and hot-tempered; and Martha Fricker the most wayward and amusing. Among the Pantisocrats, George Burnett – then living in Somerset – had expressed interest in Martha, and would propose to her later that autumn. (She turned him down.) By simple mathematics, that left Sara and Coleridge, though temperamentally they were the most wildly unsuited of the couples.

Under normal circumstances it would be difficult to imagine anything more than a brief, summer holiday flirtation taking place. But circumstances were not normal, for several reasons. In the first place, the entire Fricker family was also caught up in the Pantisocratic whirlwind, and as Coleridge later observed mournfully, it was easy to mistake "the ebullience of *schematism* for affection, which a moment's reflection might have told me, is not a plant of so mushroom a growth".[26]

In the second place, Coleridge's encounter with Mary Evans at Wrexham had reminded him how avidly he craved affection, and of the lost joys of the Evans family household. The Fricker family seemed to offer an instant and almost miraculous substitute. He was – in the old phrase, which seems particularly suited to Coleridge – on the rebound, and feeling increasingly isolated from his own people at Ottery. Moreover, Southey was now aware of this volatility, as later events that autumn showed. He felt a moral duty to help Coleridge put his emotions in proper order. An alliance with Sara seemed the logical answer, which fitted so beautifully into all their plans.

Southey's own position was curiously ambiguous. There is evidence that his own attentions had first been paid to Sara until, finding her too demanding, he had turned to the more docile Edith.[27] He always retained great fondness for Sara (as life at Keswick later showed), and there may well have been some element of soothing his own guilty conscience in the brotherly rigour with which he soon pressed her suit with Coleridge.

Finally, there can be little doubt that there was considerable sexual attraction on both sides. Coleridge was generally acknowledged as the most brilliant of the Pantisocrats, a Cambridge scholar with a possibly dazzling future, which greatly appealed to the high-strung and ambitious Sara, who loved his jokes, his dark hair, and large wild eyes. While Coleridge, always susceptible to female beauty, must easily have fallen for Sara's bright animated face, her bubbling ringlets of brown hair, her quick teasing wit and generous, carefully laced figure turned out in the latest dress-shop fashions.

6

Coleridge and Southey now had much to talk about between themselves, and on 14 August they left Bristol together, on a further walking tour through Somerset to see George Burnett at Huntspill, and work out further Pantisocratic details. Accompanied by Southey's enthusiastic dog Rover (also a Pantisocrat), they climbed the Mendip Hills, visited the towering red cliffs and echoing caverns of Cheddar Gorge – and made their way to Bridgwater at the foot of the Quantocks.[28] (See map.)

They were in wild spirits. At the Cheddar Inn, the landlady insisted on locking them all into the garret room for the night (including

Rover), fearing they were footpads. They slept in the same bed, and Southey – with a revealing touch of physical distaste – found Coleridge to be "a vile bedfellow", much disturbed by dreams.[29] At Chilcompton, Coleridge dashed off a thirty-two-line poem about the village stream, describing the small boys sailing paper navies on its "milky waters cold and clear", which greatly impressed Southey.[30]

At Nether Stowey, they called in to introduce themselves to the family of Thomas Poole, the young owner of the local tannery who was well-known in Bristol for his democratic views. News of the death of Robespierre in Paris (28 July) had just reached the village, and provoked animated discussion, during which Southey dramatically announced that he had rather have heard of the death of his own father.[31] This might have lost some of its impact had anyone realised that Southey's father was already dead.

Poole's cousin, John, was shocked by their behaviour and recorded in his Latin diary for 18 August: "About one o'clock, Thomas Poole . . . and two young men, friends of his, come in. One is an undergraduate of Oxford, the other of Cambridge. Each of them was shamefully hot with Democratic Rage as regards politics, and both Infidel as to religion. I was extremely indignant."[32] But Tom Poole himself was greatly excited by the Pantisocratic scheme, and was particularly impressed by Coleridge, without taking his wild talk entirely seriously. In the course of a few hours, another fast friendship was formed which would endure for many years, and which again shows Coleridge's almost hypnotic effect on new acquaintances.

Tom Poole was then twenty-eight years old, a bachelor, much attached to his invalid and widowed mother. He had been born in Stowey, and given a practical education to prepare him for the lucrative business of the local tannery which he inherited from his father. Quiet, thoughtful, and widely read, he early dedicated himself to liberal causes and philanthropy. He founded the Stowey Book Club, which circulated the works of Paine, Franklin, and Mary Wollstonecraft. Later, in 1817, he founded the first Stowey Co-Operative Bank. He followed the events of the French Revolution closely, and often dreamed of emigrating to America. In 1790 he was the youngest delegate from the West of England to the Tanners' Conference in London, and was elected to interview Prime Minister Pitt for the conference the following year. In the summer of 1793, he dressed himself as a common workman and travelled through the Midlands to discover the conditions of working people for himself. It was said that he first heard of Coleridge in the dragoons, while at the Reading Fair at the end of that year.

From a very different class background, he shared a political idealism close to Coleridge, and was constantly criticised by his relatives for his extreme views. He fell in love with one of his cousins at Over Stowey, but she always refused him for this reason. A self-made and self-educated man, he had the highest respect for literature and science, and collected a library at Stowey in a special upstairs Book Parlour, which later attracted not only Coleridge, but also Wordsworth and Humphry Davy. Almost naïvely fascinated by those he regarded as men of intellectual genius, his letters show him as earnest, sententious, slightly humourless and yet resolutely down-to-earth. In appearance he was short and stocky (the perfect yeoman farmer, said De Quincey), with prematurely balding hair and slow, deliberate Somersetshire speech: one of nature's favourite uncles.

Poole's characteristic first reaction to Pantisocracy was this:

> Could they realise [their plan] they would, indeed, realise the age of reason; but however perfectible human nature may be, I fear it is not yet perfect enough to exist long under the regulations of such a system, particularly when the Executors of the plan are taken from a society in a high degree civilized and corrupted . . . I think a man would do well first to see the country and his future hopes, before he removes his connections or any large portion of his property, there. I could live, I think, in America, much to my satisfaction and credit, without joining such a scheme . . . though I should like well to accompany them, and see what progress they make.[33]

Poole also gave a summary of the Pantisocratic plan as it had matured by mid-August. Coleridge and Southey were talking of twelve couples, who would embark from Bristol the following April. The men would provide a capital of £125 each, and expect to labour on a common land-holding for two or three hours a day. "The produce of their industry is to be laid up in common for the use of all, and a good library of books is to be collected, and their leisure hours to be spent in study, liberal discussions, and the education of their children." Political and religious opinions would be free, but the essence of the scheme was to bring up a new generation of enlightened children untainted by corrupt values. In particular, the absence of property ownership – Coleridge's "Aspheterism" – would philosophically ensure that there were no grounds for selfish materialism. Poole added shrewdly: "the regulations relating to the females strike them as the most difficult; whether the marriage contract shall be dissolved if agreeable to one or both parties, and many other circumstances, are not yet determined."[34]

But most perceptive of all was Tom Poole's first impression of Coleridge, whom he considered "the Principal in the undertaking", and a man of "splendid abilities". He saw at once his mixture of genius and impracticality, someone struggling with themselves, a "shining scholar" bursting with ideas but almost dangerously adrift and confused in his personal life. He also sensed immediately the undercurrent of guilt.

> He speaks with much elegance and energy, and with uncommon facility, but he, as it generally happens to men of his class, feels the justice of Providence in the want of those inferior abilities which are necessary to the rational discharge of the common duties of life. His aberrations from prudence, to use his own expression, have been great; but he now promises to be as sober and rational as his most sober friends could wish. In religion he is a Unitarian, if not a Deist; in politicks a Democrat, to the utmost extent of the word.[35]

It is evident from this that even at their first meeting, Coleridge had spoken freely of himself and such matters as the dragoon episode; and that Poole was already adopting the paternal attitude that would soon make him Coleridge's "sheet-anchor". By contrast, Poole was much less impressed by Southey, whom he considered "more violent in his principles", wavering between deism and atheism, and intellectually "a mere Boy" compared to Coleridge. Already there is a touch of surprise that the two young men should be so closely associated, an acute premonition of future difficulties.

The Pantisocrats were back in Bristol by 22 August. They immediately decided to raise money by writing a topical verse-drama on the death of Robespierre, using the newspaper reports of the final struggle in the Convention between Barère, Tallien, Robespierre and St-Just. Eight hundred lines were completed in forty-eight hours of furious all-night composition. Coleridge wrote the first Act, Southey the second, and Robert Lovell was meant to write the third; but he could not keep Pantisocratic pace. Coleridge's section shows clearly his sympathies for the Girondists such as Madame Roland and

Brissot, whom Robespierre – "the *tyrant guardian* of the country's freedom" – had executed. In general it is a farrago of rhetorical bad verse, remarkable only for the swiftness of composition, though Coleridge came up with some striking scientific metaphors, comparing the power of liberty to condensed air in a glass jar,

> . . . bursting
> (Force irresistible!) from its compressure –
> To shatter the arch chemist in the explosion![36]

Even Joseph Cottle refused to publish it, but Coleridge announced confidently that he would get it printed under his own name in Cambridge that autumn. Cottle may have overlooked – or Coleridge may have later added – one outstanding passage, the Song to "Domestic Peace", which shows the rapid development of his lyric gift, already heralded in "Genevieve" and "The Sigh", and soon to overflow in a mass of sonnet-writing. Far from revolutionary in tone, it indicates perhaps better than anything the real undercurrent of his thoughts during this wild summer of scheming and romance: a wistful mixture of Pantisocratic dreams, marriage fantasies (Mary or Sara?), and magic childhood nostalgia (that small boy playing in a distant country churchyard):

> Tell me, on what holy ground
> May Domestic Peace be found?
> Halcyon daughter of the skies,
> Far on fearful wings she flies,
> From the pomp of Sceptered State,
> From the Rebel's noisy hate,
> In a cottag'd vale She dwells
> Listening to the Sabbath bells! . . .[37]

What strikes one is the Rousseauism of the entire enterprise, and Coleridge's underlying philosophical belief in the essential innocence of man once retired from corrupt European civilisation in the rural "cottag'd vale". This philosophical assumption, the absence of inherent evil in man's nature, and the possibility of retrieving some paradisial "unfallen" state, was to become a central theme in his poetry over the next four years.

Poole already understood this problem, in his practical way. But Southey, who seemed to think in political cartoons, never touched on the issue at any depth. As he wrote jauntily in Bristol: "Should the resolution of others fail, Coleridge and I will go together, and either find repose in an Indian wig-wam – or from an Indian tomahawk . . . if earthly virtue and fortitude can be relied on, I shall be happy . . . What is the origin of moral evil? Whence arise the various vices and misfortunes that disgrace human nature and destroy human happiness? From individual property."[38]

7

Coleridge left Bristol on 2 September 1794, bidding emotional farewells to the Frickers, Lovell, Burnett, and Southey. It was decided that "by this day twelve months the Pantisocratic society of Aspheterists will be settled on the banks of the Susquehanna."[39] It is not known exactly on what terms he parted from Sara Fricker, but it was certainly tenderly and flirtatiously. For Southey it was "like the losing a limb to part from him".

Coleridge was to continue the missionary work in London and Cambridge, research land-purchase deals for Pennsylvania, get *The Fall of Robespierre* published, and send back "packages" of letters and information. Meanwhile Southey pondered on his emigrant's wardrobe – "what do common blue trousers cost?" – and continued his rapturous cartooning to Bedford. "When Coleridge and I are sawing down a tree we shall discuss metaphysics: criticise poetry when hunting a buffalo, and write sonnets whilst following the plough."[40]

Southey's catalogue of pioneering delights included the full range of domestic comforts – the Fricker girls, the servants, Lovell's two sisters, and his own mother, were all of the party. "Our society will be of the most polished order . . . Our females are beautiful amiable and accomplished – and I shall then call Coleridge my brother in the real sense of the word." This last remark suggests that, for Southey at least, an engagement between Coleridge and Sara was understood; and this seems to be the clear implication of Coleridge's first letter from Cambridge just over a fortnight later, which shows the lights of Pantisocracy burning with undimmed brightness in a forest of exclamation marks.

> Sept. 18th – 10 o'clock Thursday Morning – Well, my dear Southey! I am at last arrived at Jesus. My God! how tumultous are the movements of my Heart – Since I quitted this room what and how important Events have been evolved! America! Southey! Miss

> Fricker! – Yes – Southey – you are right – Even Love is the creature of strong Motive – I certainly love her. I think of her incessantly & with unspeakable tenderness – with that inward melting away of Soul that symptomatizes it. Pantisocracy – O I shall have such a scheme of it! My head, my heart are all alive – I have drawn up my arguments in battle array – they shall have the *Tactician* excellence of the Mathematics with the Enthusiasm of the Poet.[41]

Poetry indeed was now much in evidence. They were exchanging bulging packets of verse, and this letter enclosed Coleridge's early version of the sonnet "Pantisocracy", which lyrically develops the theme of the Song to "Domestic Peace", with the prophetic addition of a ritual dance:

> . . . Sublime of Hope I seek the cottag'd Dell,
> Where Virtue calm with careless step may stray,
> And dancing to the moonlight Roundelay
> The Wizard Passions weave an holy Spell.[42]

This same dream-like evocation also includes a more darkly prophetic phrase, where Coleridge refers to the return of nightmares (one recalls the "vile bedfellow") and vividly describes waking with a start "From Precipices of distemper'd sleep".[43] But Southey does not seem to have understood this side of Coleridge either.

During the fortnight in London, Coleridge had been immensely busy on Pantisocratic business. Taking lodgings – still in his filthy tramping clothes – at a tavern near Christ's Hospital, the Salutation & Cat in Newgate Street, he sought out converts among the new generation of Grecians – the younger Le Grice, Favell – and argued with older ones like the poet George Dyer (author of *The Complaints of the Poor People of England*). "He was enraptured – pronounced it impregnable – He is intimate with Dr Priestley."[44]

An attempt to convert the rather starchy Grosvenor Bedford – to whom Southey had provided a heady introduction – was less successful, foundering (thought Coleridge) on the "anti-genteel" appearance of his clothes and Newgate Street address, altogether too democratic. Bedford observed that he was "sorry, very sorry" about the whole scheme; a sentiment soon to be echoed by Coleridge's own family.

Undeterred, Coleridge now began to research the whole subject in the bookshops, rediscovering on the way his old childhood passion for adventures and travel-writing. He read Brissot's *Travels in the United States* (one of Poole's favoured books), Thomas Cooper's *Some Information Respecting America* (just published), and the stimulating book by Mary Wollstonecraft's American lover, Gilbert Imlay, *A Topographical Description of North America* (1792).

Cooper's book seems to have particularly attracted him. It gave details of land prices, farming methods, climate, and local resources such as wildfowl and bison, as well as painting a seductive picture of an idyllic Pennsylvanian hinterland: "At this distance, you look down upon the Susquehannah about three or four miles off, a river about half a mile broad, running at the foot of bold and steep mountains, through a valley . . . rich, beautiful and variagated."[45]

Coleridge also made contact with a young American land-agent (ex-Christ's Hospital) who had spent the last five years there and who enthusiastically drank punch in the Salutation & Cat, descanting on mosquitoes, Indians, bison, diet ("the Women's *teeth* are bad there"), and the practicalities of twelve men clearing 300 acres in five months. Like Cooper, he also recommended the Susquehanna for its "excessive Beauty, & its security from hostile Indians".[46]

One of Coleridge's surprisingly practical conclusions was that after so much "academic" indolence, they should all spend the winter getting their bodies into "full tone and strength" and learn the "theory and practice of agriculture and carpentry".[47] He intended to write a short treatise on the whole subject, also outlining their political creed of aspheterism.

At Cambridge during this autumn term of 1794, which was to be Coleridge's last, Pantisocracy became the talk of the whole university, and not only among the undergraduates. Coleridge argued out his ideas with his tutors, with Dr Pearce, with young dons like Francis Wrangham, as well as with friends like Caldwell. "Caldwell the most excellent, the most pantisocratic of Aristocrats, has been laughing at me – Up I arose terrible in Reasoning – he fled from me – because 'he could not answer for his own Sanity sitting so near a madman of Genius!'"[48]

One debate, with the theologian Dr Thomas Edwards and a local councillor Mr Lushington ("A Democrat – and a man of most powerful and Briarean Intellect") lasted for six hours over the tea cups, and Coleridge came back to Jesus at one in the morning triumphant, feeling that he had "exhibited closer argument in more elegant and appropriate Language, than I had ever conceived myself capable of".[49]

The verse-drama, *The Fall of Robespierre*, was published by Benjamin Flower in October in an edition of 500 copies, and gave further publicity to the cause, circulating widely in Cambridge, London and Bath.[50] Coleridge became a fashionable figure among the undergraduates, and conducted a public flirtation with a popular young actress, Elizabeth Brunton. But he was also reading and writing hard, composing many sonnets, adding a Pantisocratic section to his "Monody on the Death of Chatterton", and beginning a long philosophic poem, "Religious Musings", which dramatised his thoughts about the French Revolution, and the political significance of English radicals like Priestley, "Patriot and Sage".

Long and furiously argued letters about poetry and Pantisocracy passed between him and Southey throughout these months. How should the children be educated? What status should servants have? (Coleridge thought they should evidently be equal.) What religious beliefs should be taught? How should the women be freed from domestic drudgery? Time and again Coleridge revealed himself as both the most radical, and the most visionary, of the two. "Let the married Women do only what is absolutely convenient and customary for pregnant Women or nurses. – Let the Husbands do *all* the Rest – and what will that all be – ?Washing with a Machine and cleaning the House. One Hour's addition to our daily Labor – and *Pantisocracy* in its most perfect Sense is practicable."[51]

While pressing the philosophic basis for the scheme, he also emphasised the need for a total revolution in their daily lives, often phrasing his arguments with striking and poetic force.

> The leading Idea of Pantisocracy is to make men *necessarily* virtuous by removing all Motives to Evil – all possible Temptations . . . It is each Individual's *duty* to be Just, *because* it is in his *Interest*. To perceive this and assent to it as an abstract proposition – is easy – but it requires the most wakeful attentions of the most reflective minds in all moments to bring it into practice. – It is not enough, that we have once swallowed it – The *Heart* should have *fed* upon the *truth*, as Insects on a Leaf – till it be tinged with the colour, and show its food in every the minutest fibre.[52]

8

Yet despite the high, optimistic tone of these exchanges, privately all was not well with the two Pantisocrats. In Bristol, Southey had been ejected from Aunt Tyler's house because of the scheme, and threatened with disinheritance. He feared for his engagement with Edith Fricker, and even more he feared that Coleridge – now apparently flourishing in Cambridge – was allowing his own commitment to Sara to slide conveniently away.

Coleridge himself was once again in deep family difficulties. His brothers, George and James, had now discovered the emigration plan – worse even than the dragoons – and had written letters of "remonstrance, and Anguish", suggesting that he was "deranged", and threatening to cut off his finances. They proposed that he should leave Cambridge, and study law at the Temple.

Worse still, at the beginning of October, an unsigned letter from Mary Evans arrived at Jesus College, also begging him to abandon his "absurd and extravagant" scheme, and repeating the suggestion that his was a noble mind "o'erthrown" (like Hamlet). Brother George may have instigated this appeal as a stratagem, through Mrs Evans; for it held out the tantalising possibility of renewal of their friendship should Coleridge abandon his mad Bristol friends. "There is an Eagerness in your Nature," Mary wrote gently, "which is ever hurrying you into the sad Extreme . . . I often reflect on the happy hours we spent together, and regret the loss of your Society. I cannot easily forget those whom I once loved . . ."[53]

Coleridge was now in "a waking Night-mare of Spirits", with his thoughts "floating about in a most Chaotic State".[54] Torn between Mary Evans and Sara Fricker, and berated by both Southey and George for disloyalty, it was difficult to know which way to turn. He wrote an agonised sonnet beginning, "Thou bleedest, my poor Heart! . . ."; but added drily: "When a Man is unhappy, he writes damned bad Poetry, I find."[55]

In fact his sonnet-writing, if nothing else, continued to flourish and improve under these pressures, and he composed a fine Gothic piece to Schiller, after reading his verse-drama *The Robbers* at one o'clock in the morning, in a delicious state of terror that brought obvious relief from his own problems. "My God! Southey! Who is this Schiller? This Convulser of the Heart? Did he write his tragedy amid the yelling of Fiends? . . . I tremble like an Aspen Leaf."[56] His desperation also brought excitement and exhilaration.

In November, he did his best to grapple with his affairs, writing long explanatory letters to both Mary Evans and George, and going for a week to London in an attempt to sort out matters. He travelled down stylishly in a friend's phaeton. To George he insisted that he was neither a mad democrat nor an atheist, but that Pantisocracy was a serious plan. "After a diligent, I *may* say, an intense study of Locke, Hartley and others who have written most wisely on the Nature of Man – I appear to myself to see the point of *possible* perfection at which the World may perhaps be destined to arrive."

He went through the usual gestures of self-recrimination, which were becoming habitual in his relations with George, this time describing himself as a poor fluttering creature escaping from a "birdlimed thorn-bush" of his follies.[57]* George does not appear to have been mollified, failing perhaps to acknowledge the Coleridgean spirit of adventure that had taken John and Frank to India. It must have struck Coleridge very painfully that while Southey's mother and younger brother so actively supported Pantisocracy, his own family simply regarded the whole thing as an aberration.

To Mary Evans he wrote with passionate sincerity, describing his four years of "ardent attachment" to her, asking whether or no she was actually engaged to another suitor, Fryer Todd, and begging her to say outright whether she felt any more than sisterly affection for him. "Restore me to *Reality*, however gloomy."[58] Several other letters and poems seem to have passed between them at this period, but Mary's final response was to be delayed until the end of December, leaving Coleridge in an agony of indecision. They do not appear to have met face to face, and this uncertainty accounts for much of the confusion in his arrangements with Southey. An immediate plan to make a flying visit to Bath was postponed.

---

*This is one of Coleridge's earliest uses of a whole series of bird-images and figures, which come to fill his letters and his poetry. Some of the birds that one can find include the albatross, the starling, the ostrich, vulture, nightingale, bustard, sea-mew, cormorant, canary, parrot, eagle, sparrow, thrush, dove, duck, linnet, lark, tom-tit, king-fisher, rook, and swan. Often these birds provide an image of the imagination at work: either flying freely, or else trapped and caged. Flight is itself ambiguous – either a piece of virtuoso self-expression (as also in Shelley's "To a Skylark"), or else a form of escape from reality or responsibility. The tenderness of mother-birds was also significant to Coleridge. Finally, as we shall see, birds provided a sort of self-image of his own fluttering, vibrating, uncertain identity. It is possible that Charles Baudelaire was thinking of Coleridge, when in 1859 he published his poem *L'Albatros*, which ends:

> Le Poëte est semblable au prince des nuées
> Qui hante la tempête et se rit de l'archer;
> Exilé sur le sol au milieu des huées
> Ses ailes géant l'empêchent de marcher.

(The Poet is like this Prince of the Clouds, who flourishes in the storm and mocks the bowman below; but exiled on the earth amidst cries of derision, his huge wings prevent him from walking.) (See Bibliography.)

Instead Coleridge used the time in London to follow the Treason Trials of Hardy, Tooke, Thelwall and Holcroft which were then taking place at the Old Bailey. Lovell too was in London, and actually visited Holcroft in Newgate Gaol, where he received a blessing upon the Pantisocratic scheme. Then Coleridge hurried back to Cambridge, where he remained until the end of the academic term in mid-December.

Still determinedly seeking literary publicity, he proposed a whole series of sonnets on "Eminent Contemporaries" to the *Morning Chronicle*, and these began to appear on 1 December. His twelve subjects were carefully chosen among the distinguished reformers and liberal figures among the arts; they included Joseph Priestley, Lord Stanhope and William Godwin; Thomas Erskine, the lawyer who had defended Hardy and earlier Tom Paine; the politician and philosopher Edmund Burke; the French statesman Lafayette and the Polish nationalist, General Kosciusko; and his poetical master William Bowles. His theatrical interests were represented by the actress, Mrs Siddons, and the playwright R. B. Sheridan; while Southey was also honoured. One last sonnnet daringly attacked the Prime Minister, William Pitt, as eminent "fiend" and warmonger.

These were all essentially ideological pieces, which caused a considerable stir in the city and made Coleridge's name generally known for the first time. As verse, they were clumsy and laboured, but Coleridge was aware of this, telling Southey: "I cannot write without a *body* of *thought* – hence my *Poetry* is crowded and sweats beneath a heavy burthen of Ideas and Imagery! It has seldom Ease . . ." But this was soon to come.[59]

9

Throughout this time letters continued to fly between Cambridge and Bath (where Southey was now living with his mother), hammering out the details of Pantisocracy. Because of the emotional drama over Sara Fricker and Mary Evans (which always ended in Coleridge grimly promising to do his "Duty"), it is easy to overlook the brilliant coherence with which Coleridge developed the concepts behind the emigration scheme. He never wrote the promised treatise on Pantisocracy, but it is possible to summarise the body of ideas which emerges from the letters between October and December 1794. Several of them were to shape Coleridge's writing for the rest of his life. Far from being an aberration, or – as is often suggested – a temporary fit of youthful idealism, they form the intellectual basis of many of the speculative questions which Coleridge carried into his major poetry and later critical prose.

Behind the broad, rather Godwinian notion of a small, self-governing community of friends (with its Quaker overtones), lay several Coleridgean ideas about the nature of man and his relations to the physical world. First was "Aspheterism", a word coinage of memorable unpleasantness, which implied not simply the common ownership of land and stock, but the abolition of the idea of ownership itself: "non proprius". Coleridge would later specifically deny that he intended the abolition of private property as the basis for national government, as opposed to a small community.[60] But the notion that the land, and particularly the countryside, could never be "owned" in the ordinary way, that it was a common heritage belonging to all, remains in his thought. It was, so to speak, a national trust.

Second, and closely related to this, is a characteristically poetic and humorous notion of the brotherhood of man and animals, as belonging to a common nature. The Pantisocrats would befriend the natural world, and live harmoniously as part of it. This fraternal idea first appears in a splendid signing-off passage in a letter of 24 October to Francis Wrangham.

> If there be any whom I deem worthy of remembrance – I am their Brother. I call even my Cat Sister in the Fraternity of universal Nature. Owls I respect & Jack Asses I love: for Alderman & Hogs, Bishops & Royston Crows, I have not particular partiality –; they are my Cousins however, at least by Courtesy. But Kings, Wolves, Tygers, Generals, Ministers, & Hyaenas, I renounce them all . . . May the Almighty Pantisocratizer of Souls pantisocratize the Earth, and bless you and S.T. Coleridge.[61]

As often with Coleridge, one of his most serious and even mystical ideas begins as a flight of extravagant fancy, a poetical joke, in which humour and imagination are inextricably entwined. Two weeks later he had developed the ideas into a deliberately provoking little poem, "Address to a Young Jack Ass", inspired by an animal he had noticed tethered on Jesus Green, a "poor little Foal of an oppressed Race". Here the fraternal idea is directly presented with a mixture of comic bathos and polemic defiance, with coat-trailing, "democratic" references to poverty, the "fellowship of woe", and a "scoundrel monarch". He daringly submitted it to the *Morning Chronicle* where it appeared on 9 December, the first public allusion to Pantisocracy in print:

> Innocent Foal! thou poor despis'd Forlorn! –
> I hail thee Brother, spite of the Fool's Scorn!
> And fain I'd take thee with me in the Dell
> Of high-soul'd Pantisocracy to dwell . . .[62]

It was, of course, a gift to satirists: five years later Coleridge appeared as a braying jack-ass in a famous cartoon against the British radicals which appears in the *Anti-Jacobin*: and Byron would long after recall this jibe in *English Bards and Scotch Renewers*. Coleridge was in this sense as innocent as his foal. Yet the idea of the fraternal community in nature, the "One Life", was to be crucial to him.

A third, shaping idea that grew out of his reflection on Pantisocracy, was the notion of the "child of Nature". Throughout the letters he emphasises again and again to Southey the need to bring up children outside the old, transmitted "prejudications" of corrupt society.[63] Thoughtless fathers, uneducated mothers, and even older schoolfellows, could unwittingly pass on the "Fear and Selfishness" which warps the infant mind in an unreformed state of civilisation. Even religious doctrines could be dangerous – "How can we ensure their silence concerning God etc?" – when these were not allowed to develop naturally and directly from personal reverence for the creation. It was nature herself who must be the great teacher, and the essential role of education – and by extension, poetry and philosophy itself – must be as an affectionate interpreter of man's place in the natural world. In the countryside the images of divine beauty and goodness "are miniatured on the mind of the beholder, as a Landscape on a Convex Mirror".[64]

10

Coleridge was back in London for the Christmas vacation by 11 December, where he was to remain for a month, lodging at the Salutation & Cat, furiously writing letters and poetry, and trying to decide if he should really leave the university. In theory the Pantisocratic expedition was still scheduled for March or April 1795, but none of the £2,000 capital had been raised, and various alternatives had to be considered.

Southey, still demanding his immediate presence in Bath, proposed with Lovell a preliminary scheme to go shares in a Welsh farm where they could learn agricultural skills before departing. He was also arguing that they should take servants to do the manual labour, and that the women should have exclusive charge of the children and domestic work. Coleridge described all these compromises succinctly as "nonsense", and continued the debate of first principles.[65] But having still not settled matters with Mary Evans, he was in a growing panic about Sara Fricker, and felt he had written to her "like an hypocrite". For the time being it was arranged that Southey would return with him to Cambridge in the New Year, to argue out the Welsh scheme, and help raise money from his *Imitations*.[66] Meanwhile Burnett and Lovell would prospect for farms in Caernarvonshire or Merioneth.

But London now presented all sorts of exciting opportunities for Coleridge. With his sonnets being published, he met Perry, the editor of the *Morning Chronicle*, and discussed a future in journalism. He spent lively evenings with William Godwin and Thomas Holcroft, the leading radical writers, who cross-questioned him about Pantisocracy.

Godwin, then thirty-eight, was at the height of his fame, having followed *Political Justice* (1793) with his intellectual gothic thriller *Caleb Williams* (1794), which became a bestseller. He was still advocating atheism and anti-matrimonialism (he had not yet formed his liaison with Mary Wollstonecraft), and this deeply shocked Coleridge. But the celebrated philosopher and the wild young poet fiercely argued the merits of atheism and Unitarian belief, and a close friendship was later to form that Godwin would describe as one of the most influential in his life.[67] Holcroft – "he absolutely infests you with *Atheism*" – outraged Coleridge by his "*Blasphemy* against the divinity of *a Bowles*!" It is clear that the Pantisocrat was not in the mood to be overawed by these distinguished introductions: "my great coolness and command of impressive Language certainly *did him over*."

Meanwhile George Dyer, perhaps attempting some gentle delaying tactics to keep Coleridge in England, came up with a possible post for him as a family tutor to the Earl of Buchan.[68] On top of all this, brother George was still assiduously making "liberal proposals" for financing a career at the Bar. Coleridge, as so often in his later life, found himself drifting among an embarrassment of siren possibilities, vaguely and good-naturedly trying to please and charm everybody, but at heart deeply confused and temperamentally incapable of imposing himself decisively upon events. Pantisocracy and poetry were still his real passions. But he was discovering his genius for prevarication.

One advantage of this was the easy and undemanding friendship which now developed with schoolfellow and junior Grecian, Charles Lamb. Lamb was living nearby at the Inner Temple with his aged parents and invalid elder sister, Mary, whom he adored. He had taken a clerkship at the East India Office to support them all, and dedicated his evenings to literature and drinking. His fine pixieish wit and cultivated, bookish eccentricity were enhanced by a nervous stutter and inexhaustible supply of puns. Tall, shy and depressive, with one eye blue and one eye brown, he was drawn like a moth to the spinning, phosphorescent conversations that took place each night at the Salutation & Cat. His gentle hero-worship was exactly what Coleridge needed at this juncture. Long, alcoholic evenings passed effortlessly away in the tavern snug, fuelled by egg-flip and heady clouds of oronoko tobacco, while they exchanged new sonnets and emotional intimacies of their tortured love-lives.

A revealing topic that emerged in common – among all the high talk of philosophy, religion, and Pantisocracy – was a shared attachment for their sisters. Charles talked fondly of Mary, Coleridge reminisced lyrically about the Evans sisters and about his own dear, dead sister Nancy Coleridge. This depth of curious, asexual, but genuinely fraternal feeling tells as much of Coleridge's struggles between Mary Evans and Sara Fricker (both essentially part of sisterly families) as any of his melodramatic outpourings to Southey.

Moreover, it produced one of Coleridge's most striking early poems in the "Conversational" mode which was later to become so important in his work: an intimate, low-key, blank verse style very close to his most personal letters. Back in September he had written a touching and unexpected note to Edith Fricker (rather than Sara), in which he fondly recalled Nancy: "I *had* a Sister – an only Sister. Most tenderly did I love her! Yea, I have woke at midnight, and wept – because *she was not* . . . My Sister, like you, was beautiful and accomplished – like you, she was lowly of Heart . . . I know, and *feel*, that I am *your Brother*."[69]

He now versified these sentiments to Lamb, finding a new naturalness of phrase and grace of rhythm, which has the startling inevitability of a completely original, spontaneous kind of Romantic self-declaration. It is a landmark in his work.

In Fancy, well I know,
Thou creepest round a dear-lov'd Sister's Bed
With noiseless step, and watchest the faint Look
Soothing each Pang with fond Solicitudes
And tenderest Tones medicinal of Love.
I too a Sister *had* – an only Sister –
She loved me dearly – and I doted on her –
On her soft Bosom I repos'd my Cares,
And gaind' for every wound an healing Tear.
To her I pour'd forth all my puny Sorrows,
(As a sick Patient in his Nurse's arms)
And of the Heart those hidden Maladies
That shrink asham'd from even Friendship's Eye.
O! I have woke at midnight, and have wept
Because she was not! . . .[70]

Love here expresses itself as tenderness, confidentiality, and – once again – as maternal nursing. Charles Lamb nurses, and Coleridge – in his careful parenthesis – is nursed. Love is a form of healing, for both of them.

The intimacy of the poem is a great advance on most of the public sonnets, and allowed Coleridge even to allude amusingly to Lamb's fondness for puns, describing Mary's polished wit "as mild as *lambent* Glories/That play around an holy Infant's head". Coleridge gave him the poem together with an early manuscript draft of "Religious Musings" (dated Christmas Eve, 1794), the long philosophic piece which he here dismissed as "Elaborate & swelling – but the Heart / Not owns it". This, too, indicates his own sense of breaking through to a more powerful and direct verse form, in which spontaneity of feeling and simplicity of expression become important new values.

Coleridge admired and even envied the relationship between Lamb and his sister ("Her mind is elegantly stored – her Heart feeling"), as he would later be attracted by the relationship between Wordsworth and Dorothy. And it was probably this kind of closeness and love that he wished, above all, from Mary Evans.

But it was not to be. On 24 December he finally received a letter confirming Mary Evans' engagement. He wrote a short, concluding note in reply, honourably free of all reproach: "To love you Habit has made unalterable. This passion however, divested, as it now is, of all Shadow of Hope, will lose its disquieting power. Far distant from you I shall journey thro' the vale of Men in calmness . . . I have burnt your

Letters – forget mine – and that I have pained you, forgive me! May God infinitely love you."[71]

On 29 December he informed Southey of this outcome. But he was now almost brutally frank about his dilemma over Sara Fricker in a letter which acknowledges the disturbing element of sexual enticement he felt: "to marry a woman whom I do *not* love – to degrade her, whom I call my Wife, by making her the Instrument of low Desire – and on the removal of a desultory Appetite, to be perhaps not displeased with her Absence! – Enough! These Refinements are the wildering Fires that lead me into Vice. Mark you, Southey! – *I will do my Duty.*"[72]

11

But what *was* his duty now? London, Cambridge, Bath, Wales, America – in which direction should he go? How could he best pursue the Pantisocratic dream? Coleridge sat on in the snug at the Salutation & Cat, smoking and drinking and talking with Lamb, in a haze of indecision, into the New Year 1795. Southey, sweeping aside delicacies, insisted that he must come to Bath immediately. Coleridge replied, in a fantastical letter, that he would come down "helter skelter" on a local farm cart, the two-mile-an-hour "Flying Wagon", wrapped up in hay, "fraternizing" with the calves, and well supplied with gin and oronoko. "I shall be with you by Wednesday [7th January], I suppose."[73]

Southey took this proposal literally, and was full of amazed indignation when, having walked to Marlborough with Lovell to intercept the Flying Wagon, it failed to deliver its Pantisocratic contents. By 11 January he was himself in London, "to reclaim his stray", who even then proved elusive. "I went to the Salutation and Cat – a most foul stye – no Coleridge," he told Edith Fricker. "I went to Christ's Hospital . . . where is Coleridge?" Finally he was located with Lamb in the Unitarian Chapel, seeking divine guidance. They had a difficult dinner together.

"Coleridge objected to Wales and thought it best to find some situation in London till we could prosecute our original plan. He talks of tutorage – a public office – a newspaper one for me. I went to bed in dirty sheets – and tost and turned, cold, weary and heart sick till seven in the morning."[74] It was a low moment for Pantisocracy. Southey's letter shows how much he counted on Coleridge's support, increasingly anxious about his own marriage to Edith, his retreating work prospects, and the financial difficulties at Bath. It was this appeal to Coleridge's generosity and easy good nature, as much as any bullying over Sara Fricker, that finally convinced Coleridge that his Pantisocratic "duty" lay in the West Country. By the end of January 1795 his university degree, his career at the Bar, his London journalism were all abandoned. The three Pantisocrats – Coleridge, Southey and Burnett – were established in their first commune, a cramped apartment at 25 College Green, Bristol.

FIVE

Watchman

1

The story of the ensuing ten months in Bristol has been told (notably by Coleridge himself) in terms of the inevitable and comic collapse of naïve Pantisocratic ideals when exposed to the mundane realities of human nature. Family pressures, financial difficulties, temperamental differences between Coleridge and Southey and Lovell, can all be seen as the inescapable emergence of the Old Adam in such unworldly dreams. It was what Tom Poole had already foreseen at Stowey: and what Coleridge himself revealed in a long, bitter, retrospective letter to Southey of November 1795, in which he referred contemptuously to "the Mouse of which the Mountain Pantisocracy was at last safely delivered!"[1] But this is far from being the whole story, or the whole truth.

In the first place, the Susquehanna scheme did become a reality in other hands, and had considerable influence on radical thinking in England at this time. In January 1795 the *British Critic* carried a long article on the rival emigration schemes for the Susquehanna and for Kentucky, which were being promoted by Thomas Cooper and Gilbert Imlay. Though it mocked them as "two rival auctioneers, or rather show-men, stationed for the allurement of incautious passengers", it acknowledged the growing popularity of such expeditions among Quakers, Unitarians, and other idealistic freethinkers. By 1796 it was calculated that some 2,000 people had set out, though many returned disillusioned.[2]

The most distinguished of these pioneers was Joseph Priestley, who set up a scientific academy at Northumberland, Pennsylvania, and remained there until his death in 1804. His *Memoirs* clearly indicate that Coleridge's Pantisocracy was part of a larger, undefined movement among "the friends of liberty" to settle on the Susquehanna.

> At the time of my leaving England (April 1794), my son in conjunction with Mr Cooper, and other English emigrants, had a scheme for a large settlement for the friends of liberty in general near the head of the Susquehannah in Pennsylvania. And taking it for granted that it would be carried into effect, after landing at New York, I went to Philadelphia, and thence came to Northumberland (in July 1794), a town nearest the proposed settlement, thinking to reside there until some progress had been made in it.[3]

Priestley's son, who was in partnership with Thomas Cooper, explains that this was to be a substantial settlement of 300,000 acres, situated in the "forks" or confluence of the north-east and Western branches of the Susquehanna, some 150 miles west of Philadelphia, and fifty miles from Northumberland.[4]

The promised English settlers never arrived in any numbers, but interestingly a French colony of exiled Girondists and royalist émigrés did successfully settle near the Susquehanna at Frenchtown, as was reported in the *Gentleman's Magazine* for June 1795. One of them, La Rochefoucauld-Liancourt, left a vivid sketch of Priestley's Northumberland: a one-horse town of log-cabins, five bars, and no sidewalks, in which the eminent doctor provided the focus of civilisation, refusing to be tempted back even by the offer of a professorship at Philadelphia. Thomas Cooper, the most determined of the settlers, ended his career as President of South Carolina College, and was described by the American President Adams as "a learned, ingenious, scientific, and talented madcap".[5] It is not impossible to imagine Coleridge, in some alternative life, flourishing among these original Susquehanna pioneers, and making his own distinctive contribution to the history of the Wild West.

Certainly Joseph Cottle's story, repeated by Gillman, that the Susquehanna scheme was wholly invented by Coleridge on the sole ground that the name was "pretty and metrical", emerges as one of his many humorous smoke-screens. It was propagated in later life by Coleridge himself to disguise the seriousness of his disputes with Southey.[6]

Moreover, if Pantisocracy did not produce an actual settlement in America, it still shaped Coleridge's career in England. It forced him to start to earn his living as a writer. In Bristol this spring he began to give lectures, to assemble poems for Joseph Cottle, and to keep the first of his surviving Notebooks (known as the Gutch Memorandum

Book).* He read and studied hard at the Bristol Library (the list of his extensive borrowings has survived), and he began to pursue his highly original investigations into travel-writing, philosophy, theology and the world of poetic myth. The long poems of this time, "Religious Musings" and "The Destiny of Nations: A Vision", are in effect huge, rag-bag anthologies of his reading, speculations, and enthusiasms, all released by the debate over Pantisocracy.

The arguments with Southey, increasingly fierce and personalised, were an intellectual and emotional education in themselves. The relationship with Sara Fricker, which had begun in the "ebullience of schematism" and sexual excitement, did surprisingly mature into a genuine love-affair which – though fraught with difficulties and tensions from the start – released real passion on both sides, and greatly concentrated the youthful Coleridge's wild personality. This becomes especially evident in the development of the Conversation Poems.

Pantisocracy, in other words, gave him his first sense of vocation, of having a spiritual task in the world. And the dream of some form of communal life, of living among close friends and working for a common objective, in some "happy valley" or "magic dell" of inspiration, became a permanent feature of his imagination. It certainly haunted the whole next decade of his life – in Bristol, at Stowey, in the Lakes – and was never entirely abandoned. Paradoxically, it was the very visionary quality of Pantisocracy that first made him grapple with the realities of life. As he wrote angrily of Southey's own waverings over a career in August: "Southey! Pantisocracy is

---

*Though Coleridge first mentions keeping a Notebook on his Welsh tour with Hucks, the Bristol Notebook (B.M. Add. Mss. 27901) – which came into the keeping of his friend J. M. Gutch – is the first of some sixty to have survived, covering the period 1794–1834. (See Bibliography.) They are unique in the annals of Romantic autobiography, and have profoundly altered and deepened our view of his personality since editing was undertaken by Kathleen Coburn in the 1940s, a task which has proved a lifetime's labour of love and scholarship. (Previously only a short selection was available as *Anima Poetae*, 1895.) They cover every aspect of Coleridge's life – his travels, reading, dreams, nature studies, self-confession and self-analysis, philosophical theories, friendships, sexual fantasies, lecture notes, observations of his children, literary schemes, brewing recipes, opium addiction, horrors, puns, prayers. For the biographer they also pose a profound problem of interpretation: how "sincere" is a private Notebook? how "true" is a confession? how "historical" is a memory? One thing is certain: Coleridge dramatised himself in his most solitary moments (as we all, on reflection, do); and his Notebooks can never be accepted as the last word on anything (least of all as the last word from Coleridge). Coleridge was a man who could confess spiritual despair at midday; and dine out brilliantly at midnight. (See Kathleen Coburn, *The Self-Conscious Imagination*, Oxford, 1974.)

not the Question – it's realization is distant – perhaps a miraculous Millenium – What you have seen, or think, that you have seen of the human heart, may render the formation even of a pantisocratic *seminary* improbable to you – but this is not the question."[7] Defining the question, the way forward, became the real story of these months.

2

Bristol was an immensely stimulating place to be in the 1790s, much improved from the backwater of commercial dullards and "Damn'd narrow notions" experienced by Thomas Chatterton twenty-five years before, where there was "no credit" for the Muses.[8] The second city, and the first port in the kingdom, it had a thriving community of Unitarian businessmen who acted as an intellectual leaven among the rich commercial clan of merchants, ship-owners, lawyers, manufacturers and shopkeepers. The public life of the city was sustained by several newspapers, publishing houses, theatres, Assembly Rooms, lecture halls in the Corn Market, a large municipal lending library, and research bodies like Dr Beddoes' Pneumatic Institute. Great national issues like the war with France, the slave trade, the breach with the American colonies, Pitt's increasingly draconian legislation against "English Jacobins", and the questions of free speech and habeas corpus, were regarded as the personal responsibilities of the Bristol citizens. But lacking its own university, the city was an ideal arena for men from Oxford and Cambridge to attract immediate attention, and the Pantisocrats – who revealed a flair for publicity – were rapidly drawn to the centre of public affairs, in a way that would never have happened so quickly in London. A Bristolian writing many years later in the *Monthly Magazine*, and discreetly signing himself "Q", described Coleridge's arrival as "like a comet or meteor in our horizon".[9]

Looking urgently for sources of income, Coleridge was encouraged to embark on a career of public speaking, and with the example of John Thelwall's controversial political lectures in London, he immediately announced a series of three "Moral and Political Lectures" in rooms above the Corn Market, with entrance tickets at a shilling each. These took place in late January and early February, arousing such passions that the last had to be moved to a private house in Castle Green. Drawing on his endless daylong and night-long discussions with Southey, he took as his theme a radical analysis of the various zealous "Advocates of Freedom" – Paine, Godwin,

Tooke, Gerrald – attempting "to evince the necessity of *bottoming* on fixed Principles, that so we may not be the unstable Patriots of Passion or Accident, or hurried away by names of which we have not sifted the meaning, and by tenets of which we have not examined the consequences."[10]

The combination of wild enthusiasm and "flame-coloured epithets", with a strongly religious emphasis against revolutionary violence is the characteristic of these early speeches: "The annals of the French Revolution have recorded in Letters of Blood, that the Knowledge of the Few cannot counteract the Ignorance of the Many." They left his hearers (and perhaps himself) deeply confused as to his exact ideological position: at one moment a fiery democrat, at the next an unworldly Unitarian idealist preaching universal benevolence.

Coleridge's talent for public speaking, and gift for projecting an intense, Romantic persona, were however at once evident. Cottle records the enthusiasm of his audiences, and his instinctive gift for dealing with hecklers. When assailed on one occasion by jeers and hisses, he responded with a majestic smile: "I am not at all surprised, when the red hot prejudices of aristocrats are suddenly plunged into the cool waters of reason, that they should go off with a hiss!"[11]

He revealed, too, a power of poetic imagery, which reached out directly to his listeners with sometimes magical effect. Standing at the window of the Corn Market Rooms, which overlooked the clusters of ships' masts along the Bristol quay, he opened his first lecture with a skilful maritime analogy.

> When the Wind is fair and the planks of the vessel sound, we may safely trust everything to the management of professional Mariners; but in a Tempest and on board a crazy Bark, all must contribute their Quota of Exertion. The Stripling is not exempted from it by his Youth, nor the Passenger by his Inexperience. Even so in the present agitations of the public mind, every one ought to consider his intellectual faculties as in a *state of requisition*.[12]

One can hear both the poet and the lay preacher in this.

The reporter "Q", who attended this lecture, gained the impression that Coleridge was "a favourer of revolution", and that his views were "positively and decidedly democratic".[13] To prove that his views were not, however, Jacobin or treasonable, Coleridge was "obliged" to publish his text, which he did in a sixpenny pamphlet by

"ST Coleridge of Jesus College", with a superscription from Akenside: "'To calm and guide / The swelling democratic tide'." He told George Dyer that the whole thing had been concocted at one sitting between midnight and breakfast, on the morning on which it was delivered.[14]

After the third lecture, when the house was surrounded by a small crowd complaining of the "damn'd Jacobin . . . jawing away", Coleridge received death-threats and was advised to desist; he did not speak publicly again until May. He seems rather to have enjoyed his notoriety, all the same. "Mobs and Mayors, Blockheads and Brickbats, Placards and Press gangs have leagued in horrible conspiracy against me – The Democrats are as sturdy in the support of me – but their number is comparatively small."

He remained deeply angry about the practical effects of Pitt's pro-war policies, which encouraged every kind of "patriotic" fanaticism, and contradicted everything that Pantisocracy stood for. One of his first Gutch Notebook entries read: "People starved into War. – over an enlisting place in Bristol a quarter of Lamb and piece of Beef hung up."[15]

3

At 25 College Street, Southey was ecstatic about their commune. "Coleridge is writing at the same table," he told Bedford, "our names are written in the book of destiny on the same page." Arguments about the Welsh scheme modulated into the practicalities of earning rent money. They both planned further lecture series, and considered applying for reporting posts on the *Telegraph*. Cottle advanced thirty guineas to each of them, for the publication of future poems.

Much time was spent with the Frickers, and though no correspondence has survived between Sara and Coleridge from this period, he began to write a number of increasingly affectionate poems to her during the spring and summer. The pressure of the impetuous "engagement" had evidently relaxed: Lovell, and Sara's relations, were actually advising her against the match; and Sara herself was considering another suitor, though as Coleridge observed with a touch of pique, he was "a man whom she strongly dislikes, in spite of his fortune and solicitous attentions to her."[16]

He still felt that Southey did not understand with what an effort he had broken off his love for Mary Evans, "as if it had been a Sinew of my Heart"; and this was to remain a bitter point between them. But it is clear that Coleridge now courted Sara with growing ardour, responsive as before to her immediate and seductive physical presence, and throwing all caution to the winds. Southey cannot be held responsible for this. As Coleridge told him frankly in his otherwise accusatory letter of November: "I returned to Bristol, and my addresses to Sara, which I at first payed from Principle not Feeling, from Feeling & from Principle I renewed: and I met a reward more than proportionate to the greatness of the Effort. I love and I am beloved, and I am happy!"[17]

This is certainly the evidence of his beautiful Conversation Poem, "The Eolian Harp", which hints at the physical delights of their courtship that summer, and is dated 20 August, some six weeks before their actual marriage:

> And that simplest Lute,
> Placed length-ways in the clasping casement, hark!
> How by the desultory breeze caress'd,
> Like some coy maid half yielding to her lover,
> It pours such sweet upbraiding, as must needs
> Tempt to repeat the wrong![18]

By the end of March, Southey gives the impression of a definitely amended Pantisocratic plan, with Coleridge having yielded to the Welsh scheme, and the Fricker sisters committed to join them, once the financing was assured. "If Coleridge and I can get 150 pounds a year between us," he told his brother Thomas, "we purpose marrying, and retiring into the country, as our literary business can be carried on there, and practising agriculture till we can raise money for America – still the grand object in view."[19] It was in fact Southey's anxieties about money, and his own difficulties in marrying Edith against family opposition, which were to prove the destruction of the Pantisocratic brotherhood.

They soon renewed their lecturing, Southey completing a bi-weekly series on the historical background to the French Revolution on 28 April; and Coleridge returning to the fray at the Assembly Coffeehouse, Bristol Quay, on 19 May. His subject appeared suitably esoteric: "Six Lectures on Revealed Religion" according to the well-advertised prospectus, but containing the sting in its subtitle: "Its Corruptions and Political Views".

This series was now officially under the patronage of several leading Bristol citizens, of Unitarian or liberal persuasion, who were to become lifelong supporters of Coleridge. They included Joseph Cottle and his brother; John Prior Estlin, an influential Unitarian preacher; and the Morgans, a wealthy family of wine-shippers, whose son John was later to look after Coleridge in the very worst days of his opium addiction, one of the most striking examples of the loyalty which Coleridge so frequently inspired.* This group of supporters were also responsible for commissioning the fine and charismatic portrait of Coleridge by Peter Vandyke (1795) which now hangs in the National Portrait Gallery. The bright top-coat and high white silk stock are in the latest fashion of the French Directory, and the radiant face of the young lecturer, with parted lips, glows with "sensibility" and inspiration.

The patrons seem to have got their money's worth, and there was no further talk of the "damn'd Jacobin", though Coleridge's central theme was the relevance of the "essential beliefs" of Christianity to the poor and oppressed. But he also attacked the atheism of the radicals – especially Holcroft and Godwin – while weaving a brilliant path through current theological debate: Mosaic history, primitive Christianity, Newton's scientific philosophy, Paley's argument "from design", Priestley's deism, and the psychological "associationism" of Hartley (which was one of the planks of Pantisocracy).

Much of this material, in true undergraduate fashion, was in fact cannibalised more or less directly from commentaries borrowed (usually the day before) from the Bristol Library. But Coleridge

*The Unitarians, who believed in a Divine Creator based on the theological argument from Design, but who did not subscribe to the 39 Articles of the Anglican Establishment, represented the backbone of the Dissenting tradition in England. Forbidden from holding official state offices by the Test Act of 1673, Dissenters had developed an alternative, radical culture, strongly influenced by the ideas of the European Enlightenment, with an emphasis of the physical sciences, experiment and political reform. Every city had its Dissenting society or reading group, the most famous being the Lunar Society of Birmingham (so-called because it met on the Monday night closest to the full moon), which included among its members, Joseph Priestley, James Watt, Dr Erasmus Darwin, the Wedgwoods, and Dr Thomas Beddoes; they also owned many leading newspapers, journals and publishing houses (like the Cottle brothers); and regarded themselves, with some justice, as the progressive intellectual elite of the nation. (See "Coleridge's Circle".) Unitarians were particularly associated with four public causes: repeals of the Test and Corporation Acts; parliamentary reform; abolition of the slave trade; and freedom of the press. The local Unitarian congregations employed ministers, and welcomed visiting lay preachers to speak on public issues, rather like modern colleges welcoming visiting lecturers. Though Coleridge's own background was Anglican, the whole Unitarian ethos strongly appealed to him and suited him (much more so than the atheistical English Jacobins of London). It also fostered his talents as a charismatic public speaker. His later reputation in America was strongly fostered by Unitarian writers such as Ralph Waldo Emerson.

always added his own distinctive touch, opening lecture one for example with an elaborate allegorical dream: "It was towards Morning when the Brain begins to reassume its waking state, and our dreams approach to the regular trains of Reality, that I found myself in a vast Plain . . ."

Lecture six contained "the Fable of the Maddening Rain", an anti-Pantisocratic or distopian parable, describing how a single sane man fails to maintain his intellectual independence and reason in a community driven collectively mad, gradually sinking from "hopeless Conformity into active Guilt". This, he argued, was the fate of many erstwhile reformers like Pitt or Edmund Burke, in the national reaction against the Revolution.[20]

One thing that emerges from these lectures is the profoundly religious impulse behind all Coleridge's Pantisocratic radicalism. Unlike Paine or Godwin, he never appeals to "the Rights of Man", but always to a fundamentalist view of "Christ's teaching" about wealth, property, temporal power, and the brotherhood of man. He also begins his restless worrying at the problem of the "origins of Evil". Even in his earliest theories of "material necessity", based on a crude mechanistic interpretation of David Hartley's concepts of mental association, he is never content with the Rousseauist optimism about human nature. He acknowledges that an imperfect physical environment (such as the great cities of poverty and sickness) produces human evil. "But whence proceeds this moral Evil? Why was not Man formed without the capability of it?"[21] This question would soon become a central theme in his poetry.

Coleridge completed this second series of lectures on a high, combative note, delivering a rumbustious seventh address "On the Slave Trade" on 16 June. As Bristol was the unchallenged centre of the trade in England, this was a daring attack and very different from penning a Greek Ode on the subject in the hallowed courts of Cambridge. The Bristol *Observer* noted impartially that it was "a proof of the detestation in which he holds that infamous traffic".

His distinctive radical views were now very generally known in the city – anti-war, anti-Pitt, anti-slave trade, and professing some vision of an ideal, fraternal society halfway between a democratic "bloodless Revolution" and a hot-gospelling Christian millennium. As the *Critical Review* put it on the publication of his first lecture, in April, it was essentially the production of "a young man who possesses a poetical imagination". The address was "spirited and often brilliant, and the sentiments manly and generous . . . We also think our young political lecturer leaves his auditors abruptly, and that he has not stated, in a form sufficiently scientific and determinate, those principles to which, as he expresses it, he now proceeds as the most *important point.*"[22]

4

It was an ideological confusion that was becoming increasingly evident at College Street. Under the pressure of producing their lectures, Coleridge and Southey found fraternity difficult to sustain, and financial worries increasing. Notes to Cottle show them borrowing rent money, and even begging food for their suppers. Southey found Coleridge's endless talk, dilatory methods of composition, and general "indolence" as maddening as the fabled rain.

When Coleridge promised to stand in for the last of Southey's "Historical Lectures", and then failed to appear in the lecture hall, Southey was shocked into doubts about their whole partnership. Meticulous in his own habits, and obsessively precise in his working timetable, Southey felt that the Pantisocrats were let down by Coleridge's chaotic approach to life. Even the *Observer* contrasted Southey's precise style and presentation with Coleridge's dreamy speech and "slovenly" appearance, advising him to appear "with cleaner stockings in public" and his long black hair better "combed out".

Coleridge in turn felt that Southey was concentrating more and more on his own career, and his marriage with Edith. Having abandoned all hope of support from his own family, he was hypersensitive to the least sign of emotional betrayal from the person to whom – far more than Sara Fricker – he had committed himself at this point.

As he wrote retrospectively in November:

> We commenced lecturing. Shortly after, you began to recede in your conversation from those broad Principles, in which Pantisocracy originated. I opposed you with vehemence . . . And once (it was just before we went in to Bed) you confessed to me that you had acted wrong. But you relapsed: your manners became cold and gloomy: and pleaded with increased pertinacity for the Wisdom of making Self an undiverging Center.[23]

This has something of the overtone of a lovers' quarrel: and later, before the final breach, there were certainly tearful scenes.*

During that summer they went for several long walking expeditions together, trying to argue out their differences. Over thirty-five years later, in a Notebook of 1827, Coleridge fondly recalled the absurd intensity of one such tramp with Southey, "on a desperate hot summerday from Bath to Bristol with a Goose, 2 vls of Baxter *On the Immortality of the Soul*, and the Giblets, in my hand."[24]

In June they went on a tour to see Tintern Abbey and the Wye Valley, this time accompanied by Joseph Cottle (trying to smooth matters over between his two poets), and Edith and Sara. They lost their way, were benighted, and then had a row at the inn. The Fricker girls each supported their own fiancés. Again, Coleridge recalled the incident with painful precision.

> You had left the Table and we were standing at the Window. Then darted into my mind the Dread, that you were meditating a Separation. At *Chepstow* your conduct renewed my Suspicion: and I was greatly agitated even to many Tears. But in Percefield Walks you assured me that my Suspicions were altogether unfounded, that our differences were merely speculative, and that you would certainly go into Wales. I was glad and satisfied. For my Heart was never bent from you but by violent strength – and heaven knows, how it leapt back to esteem and love you.[25]

*The intensity – and volatility – of Coleridge's male friendships throughout his life inevitably raises for the modern reader the question of homosexuality, overt or suppressed. In the course of the narrative many young men – Tom Evans, Southey, Poole, Lloyd, Davy, Hazlitt, and Tom Wedgwood, among others – are drawn hypnotically to the Coleridgean flame. (See "Coleridge's Circle".) And in later Notebooks, through dreams and self-analysis, Coleridge himself touches on certain puzzling aspects of his emotional relations (not least, of course, with Wordsworth). Yet it must not be forgotten that this was the Age of Sensibility, of the New Man of Feeling, when open expression of emotion was valued and respected, and friendship was consciously cultivated. Men wrote each other long, passionate letters; wept freely in each other's company; talked, quarrelled, and confessed, at great length; met, dined, philosophised and drank, with domestic regularity and loyalty. In the literary world, such friendships (and their ruptures) were famous and honoured: Charles Lamb with Hazlitt, William Godwin with Thomas Holcroft, Coleridge with Wordsworth. (It is also a simple domestic fact that in cramped housing, or when staying at inns, beds were shared as a matter of course – men with men, women with women – well into the nineteenth century.) The real question with Coleridge is why his friendships were so unstable: characteristically producing among his followers a period of hero-worship followed by one of sharp disillusion. One might think that he devoured his friends, moving rapidly from one to the next, as he devoured his books, leaving them only with annotations.

It may also have been, in such scenes as this, that Coleridge began to discover his deeper feelings for Sara. George Burnett was also drawn into the embarrassing disputes, while Lovell became increasingly distanced from the whole enterprise. By July, Coleridge was convinced that there was "a plot of Separation", as he called it, and the knowledge "scorched my throat".[26]

For Southey, the problem of how he could finance his marriage to Edith Fricker had gradually overtaken everything else, including Pantisocracy, the French Revolution, and Coleridge. His Aunt Tyler, and his Uncle Herbert Hill (a chaplain returned from Portugal) had brought family influence to bear far more successfully than George and James in their negotiations with Coleridge. First they proposed that he take holy orders; then that he return to Oxford to take a law degree; and finally that he spend six months at Lisbon under Uncle Herbert's wing before making any irrevocable decision. On top of this, his wealthy friend Charles Winn promised him an annuity of £100 to begin the following year.

Coleridge fought each of these proposals with diminishing effect, until Southey announced he would rejoin Pantisocracy "in about fourteen years". They then quarrelled irrevocably, and Southey left College Street on 1 September to return to his mother's house in Bath. In the last analysis, Southey would always prove the more worldly – or prudent – of the two.

For Coleridge this was a profound shock. He had lost the friend whom he had come to regard as his "Sheet Anchor".[27] He wrote with sudden hysteria of Southey's "Catalogue of lies", and his "low, dirty, gutter-grubbing" compromise with the world. In fact it was probably this intense emotional clinging, as well as his "indolence", which finally repelled Southey and convinced him that a Pantisocratic partnership – even farming in Wales – would never work. Moreover the separation was probably beneficial for Coleridge, for it finally forced him to take his own initiative and abandon his prolonged form of undergraduate existence in Bristol.

With surprising alacrity he shouldered his new responsibilities as the last of the true Pantisocrats: he found a house in the country, he set the date for his marriage, and he set about making his professional writing career in poetry and journalism.

5

He had already found an idyllic cottage in August, by the sea at Clevedon overlooking the Bristol Channel. He now proposed to take Sara there after their marriage in October, while he completed work on his first collection of *Poems* for Cottle, and made plans to edit his own newspaper, the *Watchman.* He was busy throughout September, cultivating new friends like the Morgans, and another influential Unitarian businessman, Josiah Wade. He also met for the first time a poet he had admired since Cambridge days, and the discussions at Trinity College Literary Society, William Wordsworth. The meeting took place at 7 Great George Street, the town house of John Pinney, a rich West Indies sugar merchant. Coleridge was in the role of literary lion, and did not bother to record his impressions of the tall, silent north country man. But Wordsworth was much struck by this first, brief encounter. "Coleridge was at Bristol part of the time I was there, I saw but little of him. I wished indeed to have seen more – his talent appears to me very great."[28]

Coleridge also visited Tom Poole again at Stowey, pouring out all his plans and hopes. Poole responded with a clumsy but eloquent poem, praising his "various powers" and songs "of love and liberty", and noting how passionately his "eyeballs rolled" and "lips trembled" as he recited his work. Poole's beloved cousin, Charlotte, added crisply: "a young man of brilliant understanding, great eloquence, desperate fortune, democratick principles, and entirely led away by the feelings of the moment."[29]

Coleridge walked alone along the coast near Bridgwater, and wrote a love-poem to Sara, the "Lines Written at Shurton Bars", full of precise natural observations – the dark red earth of the Somerset cliffs, the skylarks in the corn, and the navigational watchfire, "like a sullen star". One stanza paid a prophetic compliment to Wordsworth's fresh and original poetic style:

> . . . now with curious sight
> I mark the glow-worm, as I pass,
> Move with "green radiance" through the grass,
> An emerald of light.[30]

When he published this piece in his *Poems* of 1796, Coleridge carefully identified this quotation. "The expression 'green radiance' is borrowed from Mr. Wordsworth, a Poet whose versification is occasionally harsh and his diction too frequently obscure; but whom I deem unrivalled among the writers of the day in manly sentiment, novel imagery, and vivid colouring."[31] It was almost as if Southey's abrupt departure through one door of Coleridge's imagination had instantly opened another to reveal Wordsworth already striding towards him. The house of Pantisocratic brotherhood would not be vacant for long.

6

The marriage of Samuel Taylor Coleridge and Sara Fricker took place on 4 October 1795, with proper literary overtones, at St Mary Redcliffe, Bristol, Chatterton's church where the poet's "Rowley manuscripts" had been discovered in the huge muniment room in the bell tower. "The thought," wrote Coleridge to Poole, "gave me a tinge of melancholy to the solemn Joy, which I felt – united to the woman, whom I love best of all created Beings."[32] No member of Coleridge's family attended, not even George; and Sara was not introduced at Ottery for a year. This marks the beginning of a decisive social alienation between Coleridge and his brothers.

Coleridge was evidently swept off his feet by new-found happiness. A huge list of domestic articles he had forgotten to take to the Clevedon cottage – slippers, spices, dustpan, tea kettle, even a Bible – was overwhelmed by an ecstatic sense of well-being. "The prospect around us is perhaps more *various* than any in the kingdom – Mine Eye gluttonizes. – The Sea – the distant Islands! – the opposite Coasts! – I shall assuredly write Rhymes – let the nine Muses prevent it, if they can."[33]

The honeymoon lasted six weeks, a period of Indian summer, the sea-air mild and the cottage windows shrouded in late roses, myrtle and jasmine. They walked together, clambered along the coast – Coleridge impetuously bathed – and discussed literary plans. Cottle and George Burnett visited them, and Tom Poole wrote a warming letter of solemn congratulation and good counsel.

> Providence has been pleased, if I may so express myself, to drop you on this globe as a meteor from the clouds, the track of which is undetermined. But you have now, by marrying, in some sense fixed yourself. You have created a rallying point. It is the threshold of your life. It is the epocha from which you must date every subsequent action . . . *original* works of genius are your

> forte . . . you should set yourself about some work of consequence, which may give you a reputation, whether it be in poetry or prose . . .[34]

After all the upheavals of life with Southey, these first brief weeks of domestic calm and intimacy were poetically very rich for Coleridge. Even Sara produced part of a poem, "The Silver Thimble". The idyllic "Cot", his love for Sara, and his half-playful, half-serious philosophic meditations on the landscape of their walks, form the central themes of both "The Eolian Harp" (now completed) and the "Reflections on having left a Place of Retirement", two major developments of the Conversational mode. The countryside round Clevedon is brought vividly to life – the evening scent of a bean field, the flash of white sails in the Bristol Channel, the "Dim coasts, and cloud-like hills, and shoreless Ocean". Coleridge's own voice now comes recognisably through the verse, advancing from phrase to phrase with rapid asides, speculations, and self-questionings. We see the landscape, and we hear the man.

In the first poem he celebrates the mysterious, magical life force in "animated nature"; in the second, he questions his own right to enjoy it so luxuriously, "while my unnumbered bretheren toil'd and bled". Both poems have a distinctive play or tension between Coleridge's physical relish in the natural world, and his tendency to drift away into exciting intellectual fantasies about its abstract meaning: "And what if all of animated nature / Be but organic Harps diversely fram'd, / That tremble into thought . . . ?"[35] A similar tension emerges between sensual enjoyment (with delicate sexual overtones) and Coleridge's strong sense of social duty.

In doing so they give a touching impression of the young husband and wife together: Coleridge spirited, enthusiastic, talkative, and wild; Sara seductive, teasing, outspoken, and already quite capable of delivering the "mild reproof" that her husband frequently deserved. It is a loving, humorous and realistic picture of domestic happiness together, rather than a rosily idealised one.

Charles Lamb (who was to prove one of Coleridge's most acute and sympathetic critics) immediately pounced on this when he read the poems in the spring, as something original and "exquisite". "They made my sister & self smile, as conveying a pleasure picture of Mrs C. checking your wild wanderings, which we were so fond of hearing you indulge when among us. It has endeared us more than anything to your good Lady; and your own *self-reproof* that follows delighted us."[36]

Philosophically, too, these poems mark a new stage in Coleridge's exploration of the sacred relations between man and nature, which gradually become more serious and impassioned as they carry increasingly theological implications behind his Romanticism.

It is not clear how long Coleridge and Sara had intended to stay at Clevedon – the rent was only £5 per annum, but the onset of winter, and literary affairs in Bristol, inevitably drew him back to the city. Coleridge continued to rent the cottage until the following March, but in practice he was rarely there with Sara for more than a few days at a time after November. His fellow Pantisocrat George Burnett kept her company; as well as Mrs Fricker and her youngest son. Coleridge soon found he had taken on financial responsibility for all of them.

In his poems he only recalls Clevedon alone with Sara, during the summer and late autumn. In his Notebooks, he urges himself "not to adulterize my time by absenting myself from my wife"; and wishes to "glide down the rivulet of quiet Life, a Trout!"[37] But in "Reflections", he describes how he was gradually "constrained" to quit the cottage, feeling it wrong to rest in the "delicious solitude" of their love, and that his duty was to prosecute "the bloodless fight / Of Science, Freedom, and the Truth in Christ".

This fundamentalist note genuinely reflects his plunge back into public controversy, journalism and lecturing in Bristol during the winter. But the poem actually ends with a quiet passage of bucolic regret, a backward glance of a kind that Wordsworth would later make celebrated:

> Yet oft after honourable toil
> Rests the tir'd mind, and waking loves to dream,
> My spirit shall revisit thee, dear Cot!
> Thy Jasmin and thy window-peeping Rose,
> And Myrtles fearless of the mild sea-air.
> And I shall sigh fond wishes – sweet Abode!
> Ah! – had none greater! And that all had such!
> It might be so – but the time is not yet.
> Speed it, O Father! Let thy Kingdom come![38]

This blessed image of the peaceful cottage in the country, a direct offspring of Pantisocracy, would call to Coleridge throughout the coming year of struggles and upheavals, and draw him finally to Stowey, and a "Susquehanna" of the mind.

7

He burst back into Bristol in November, with the publication of *Conciones ad Populum*, a pamphlet reprinting his first two political lectures – on the English Jacobins, and on the "Present War" against France – under the combative motto, "For Truth should be spoken at all times, but more especially at those times, when to speak Truth is dangerous".

This pamphlet was regarded as sailing fairly close to the wind, containing as it did a reference to the "Liberty Tree" (which became a *prima facie* case for prosecution as a seditious libel), and much other democratic coat-trailing. He attacked the military recruitment drive (which he knew something about) in the following satirical manner: "the Poor are not to be pitied, however great their necessities: for if they be out of employ, the KING wants men! – They may be shipped off to the Slaughterhouse abroad, if they wish to escape a Prison at home! – Fools! to commit Robberies, and get hung, when they might MURDER with impunity – yea – and have Sixpence into the bargain!" He then covered himself against sedition by impudently entering an erratum note: "Page 61, for MURDER read Fight for his King and Country".[39]

The whole pamphlet is full of such provocations. Pitt's speeches are described as "Mystery concealing Meanness, as steam-clouds envelope a dunghill". But Coleridge's concept of the "bloodless fight" did carefully eschew all incitement to a violent revolution.[40]

It is the poetic devices which remain most memorable, such as the opening essay which was headed "A Letter from Liberty to Her dear Friend Famine". It began: "Dear Famine, you will doubtless be surprised at receiving a petitionary Letter from a Perfect Stranger. But . . . all whom I once supposed my unalterable friends, I have found unable or unwilling to assist me."[41] It is notable that all Coleridge's moderate friends – Cottle, Poole, Lamb – approved of the pamphlet; though Poole as usual put his sage finger on the crucial point: "You can shock – you can charm – but the wise physician and friend of human nature will prefer that Prescription which all his patients will swallow."[42]

On the day after publication, 17 November, Coleridge attended a large public meeting at the Bristol Guildhall to petition the King "for a speedy Termination of the Present War". Coleridge was in his most seductive democratic form, as the *Star* reported:

> After a considerable time spent in fruitlessly calling "Mr Mayor! Mr Mayor!" in a tone of voice, and with that sweetness of emphasis which would have fascinated the attention even of a Robespierre; Mr Coleridge began the most elegant, the most pathetic, and the most sublime address that was ever heard, perhaps, within the walls of that building . . . Mr C contended that the poorest subjects had the most at stake, they had "their all". "Though the war," said he, "may take much from the property of the rich, it left them much: but a PENNY taken from the pocket of a poor man might deprive him of a dinner." Here he was authoritatively stopped, by the countenance of some person on the Bench . . .[43]

But not for long. On 26 November, he delivered his own lecture "On the Two Bills" with which Pitt intended to suppress seditious meetings and publications; and this was published in a pamphlet the following day, with the challenging title, *The Plot Discovered, or an Address to the People against Ministerial Treason.*

It was probably the reception of these works that decided Coleridge in December, with Cottle's help, to create a rallying point for the Unitarians and moderate democrats in a radical Christian journal, to be called the *Watchman.* For the next five months he dedicated himself to this cause – "Science, Freedom, and the Truth in Christ" – and severely disrupted his domestic life in the process. This decision to return to public affairs must also explain much of the high-principled bitterness with which he greeted Southey's secret marriage to Edith Fricker, and immediate departure (the same day) for Lisbon. Southey he felt had abandoned every duty – political, Pantisocratic, fraternal – and left him to fight alone. On New Year's Eve, 1796, Coleridge went to a Bristol Card Club with his supporters and got drunk, an effect produced, he claimed, by two "very small wine glasses" of punch.[44]

8

The *Watchman* was a considerable undertaking, not to say a quixotic one, and shows a new element emerging in Coleridge's character after his marriage: a willingness to take risks and, despite all "indolence", produce formidable bursts of concentrated activity. The paper was to be published on every eighth day (thus avoiding the government's weekly stamp-tax), running to thirty-two octavo pages per issue. It was to be financed by a 1,000-name subscription list that Coleridge calculated he could assemble within approximately one month. Two-thirds of the paper would be given over to parliamentary reports, political coverage, and foreign news (especially from France); the remaining third would be dedicated to a long leading article or essay, book reviews, short pieces of social or philosophical commentary, and some poetry. The broad stance of the paper would be "anti-Ministerial": a polemic watchdog.

All this editorial work was to be done single-handed by Coleridge, with paper and printing facilities provided by Cottle, and some sub-editing by George Burnett (who in the event proved hopeless). A "flaming Prospectus" was produced in January 1796, announcing the motto, "That all might know the Truth, and that the Truth might make us Free". When told that this itself was a "Seditious beginning", Coleridge triumphantly replied that it was quoted from the eighth chapter of St John's Gospel.

On 9 January 1796 Coleridge left Bristol for a hectic five-week subscription-gathering tour of the larger Midland towns and cities, including Worcester, Birmingham, Derby and Sheffield. It was here he reckoned that his natural readership lay, as he stated in the first issue: among the Dissenting communities (Unitarian, Methodist and Quaker); among the reading groups of skilled workers in the manufactories; among book clubs; and among all those who had felt the direct impact of Pitt's war measures and taxes. How far he could find a unified support and following among these diverse groups became the crucial factor on which the success of the paper depended. It would also raise a broader and permanent issue: as a journalist and poet, for whom was he writing?

It is not clear how far Sara Coleridge was involved, on Pantisocratic lines, in the enterprise. She never seems to have taken part in the subscription or editorial work, and this divorce from Coleridge's professional interests from the very beginning was not auspicious. Certainly they had discussed various alternative schemes together: a full-time journalistic post in London; a private school in Bristol; even a return to Cambridge to finish the "great work of *Imitations* in 2 vols".[45] Such alternative plans would recur constantly throughout the coming two years.

In the *Watchman* (number three) Coleridge would refer to the ideal of wives as the "free and equal companions" of their husbands, and the feminist views of Mary Wollstonecraft. But Sara evidently valued traditional domesticity from the start: she adored the Clevedon cottage, she remained close to her mother and sisters, and she knew she was pregnant by January. Family responsibilities were crowding in rapidly on Coleridge, bringing financial anxieties with which he proved little able to cope. His heroic and frantic activities throughout 1796 to establish himself also give the impression that he was using his work (and illness brought on by overwork) to escape from ordinary domesticity with Sara.

Pantisocracy always implied an extended household: George Burnett, and later a new protégé, Charles Lloyd, kept this dream curiously alive, while also producing practical discomforts and burdens, especially for Sara. Coleridge, like many young writers, was restless and ambitious, driven by an uncertain vocation to which he would sacrifice much of his marriage, perhaps without fully realising what he was doing. He loved Sara, and especially after the birth of their first child, felt growing tenderness and loyalty towards her (as witnessed again in his poetry): but temperamentally a real working partnership did not emerge. He laboured on the *Watchman* alone.

Throughout his Midlands tour, Coleridge wrote constantly to Josiah Wade, the businessman who had agreed to help advertise the *Watchman* in Bristol and London and who became Coleridge's financial backer. His letters to Wade are rumbustious in the style of the Welsh tour. Direct canvassing for subscriptions proved farcically ineffective. Coleridge discovered this after spending an entire morning subjecting a Birmingham tallow-chandler to his *spiel*, including a spirited recitation of "Religious Musings". He then failed to place a single copy.[46] Much time was also dissipated in picaresque adventures: "I enquired my road at a Cottage – and on lifting up the latch beheld a tall old Hag, whose soul-gelding Ugliness would chill to eternal chastity a cantharidized Satyr – However an Angel of Light could not have been more civil."[47]

Everywhere Coleridge found himself invited to preach to mixed Dissenting congregations, and this proved a better means of publicity. His reputation as a public speaker had preceded him. Wearing blue top-coat and white waistcoat, and with long unpowdered hair, he sprang up into pulpits in Birmingham, Sheffield, Nottingham, and Manchester, to deliver brilliantly extempore sermons "*precociously peppered with Politics*".[48]

These sermons gave the *Watchman* immense and unexpected publicity – at Birmingham the congregation was numbered at 1,400 people. They led to several influential introductions, most notably to the aging Dr Erasmus Darwin at Derby, whom Coleridge counted as one of the great "curiosities" of the city. He also viewed the cotton manufactories, the silk mills, and the painter Joseph Wright. Coleridge thought Darwin the "most inventive philosophical man" in Europe, except on the subject of his atheism, where the good Doctor's arguments against revealed religion would have startled him at fifteen but only raised a smile at twenty.[49]

Coleridge attended a public dinner in honour of Charles James Fox, and got among "all the first families in Nottingham" where he was "marvellously caressed", and danced at a ball with the most handsome women. Despite this he claimed to be homesick, and longing for his "comfortable little cottage", and wrote two sentimental lyrics on a first primrose, and an early almond blossom, for Sara. News reached him in early February of his wife's sickness: she suspected a miscarriage, and had moved back from the Clevedon cottage to Mrs Fricker's house on Redcliffe Hill in Bristol. But he continued his triumphant progress for a further ten days as far north as Manchester. There he finally cut short a further expedition to Liverpool, and raced back on the coach, having obtained what he calculated as 1,000 subscriptions not including London.

Years later, in the *Biographia*, Coleridge was to give an extended and comically detailed account of this whole trip, which he presented as his first essay into the career of "Author by Trade". He chose, however, to omit almost all mention of the Bristol lectures that had gone before, preferring by then to present himself as a literary tyro rather than as a political enthusiast. Yet it is clear that his actual reputation at this time was that of a radical Unitarian with strong democratic sympathies, and he admitted to Wade that his sermons were of "so political a tendency" that he had to be careful of shocking "a multitude of prejudices" even among the Dissenters, and he risked being branded as "a political Lecturer in his pulpit".[50] His actual political views, still rapidly developing, were to be further worked out in the *Watchman* itself.

After the excitement and the lionising, Coleridge was suddenly depressed by his prospects on return to Bristol. The cottage had to be abandoned, and life, packed into his mother-in-law's house with an ailing Sara, and an idle George Burnett, was far from Pantisocratic. He was still working on the proofs and preface of his *Poems* for Cottle, and the first issue of the newspaper was due on 1 March.

He unburdened himself to his publisher. "So I am forced to write for bread – write the high flights of poetic enthusiasm, when every minute I am hearing a groan of pain from my Wife – groans, and complaints & sickness! – The present hour, I am in a quickset hedge of embarrassments, and whichever way I turn, a thorn runs into me."[51] The poetry referred to here is the final version of "Religious Musings" which was to form the centrepiece of the *Poems*, and to appear in extract in the *Watchman*, and upon which Coleridge rested all his "poetical credit".[52] Cottle responded as a publisher should, by inviting him to "a good dinner".

The first issue of the *Watchman* appeared as planned on 1 March 1796, opening with a long "Introductory Essay" on the diffusion of political knowledge among his readers. It then offered a brilliant and caustic review of Edmund Burke; parliamentary reports, and foreign and domestic news items; and an adaption of a poem on the French Revolution, "To a Young Lady", originally written at Cambridge and now altered so as to dedicate the whole enterprise in a Pantisocratic manner to his wife:

> Nor, Sara! thou these early Flowers refuse –
> Ne'er lurk'd the snake beneath their simple hues;
> No purple bloom the Child of Nature brings
> From Flattery's night-shade: as he feels he sings.[53]

The paper continued to appear regularly for the next nine issues, until 13 May, a spectacular proof of Coleridge's determination to gain "a *bread-and-cheesish* profit" for his family.

9

But the editor of the *Watchman* was now leading a life far different from the child of nature. March and April 1796 were months of exhausting struggle. Coleridge moved house to Kingsdown, Bristol, where he nursed his wife, and later his brother-in-law, Robert Lovell, who was also dangerously ill. He edited, corrected, packed and despatched each issue from Cottle's shop; and he saw his *Poems* through the press to be published on 16 April. "My wife, my wife's Mother, & little Brother, & George Burnet – five mouths opening & shutting as I pull the string!"[54]

Sara's threatened miscarriage upset him more deeply than had at first appeared.

> I think the subject of Pregnancy the most obscure of all God's dispensations – it seems coercive against Immaterialism – it starts uneasy doubts respecting Immortality, & the pangs which the

> Woman suffers, seem inexplicable in the system of optimism – Other pains are only friendly admonitions that we are not acting as Nature requires – but here are pains most horrible in consequence of having obeyed Nature.[55]

This was, once again, the problem of evil within the world nagging at Coleridge.

Sara soon recovered, but now Coleridge himself, plagued by deadlines and printer's blunders and anxiety about the *Poems*, caught an agonising eye infection. For two weeks he took laudanum, "almost every night" to sleep, and this recourse to the medicament of his schooldays – which he now discovered soothed both physical pain and mental worry – set a sinister precedent for future times of trouble. Contemporary medical opinion, as in Samuel Crumpe's *An Inquiry into the Nature and Properties of Opium* (1793), had no concept of addiction. But Coleridge's private doubts perhaps appeared in an article he ran in the *Watchman* number four, which gives an interesting account of a case at the Stafford Assizes, in which the great Thomas Erskine prosecuted an apothecary who had fraudulently benefited from a dying man's will, by befuddling him with opium treatment.

Coleridge laboured on through the spring: "I am in stirrups all day, yea, and sleep in my Spurs."[56] Issue number two carried a satirical "Essay on Fasts", which began with Isaiah – "Wherefore my Bowels shall sound like a Harp" – and which caused great offence among his more conservative readers. In number three there was a polemic squib on "Modern Patriotism" which caused equal offence among the radicals, as it attacked Godwin. Having set both wings of his readership in uproar, Coleridge then tried to establish common ground in number four, with a splendidly timed and argued essay against his old enemy "The Slave Trade". Wilberforce's Bill was then being debated in parliament (where it would be defeated), and this was real campaigning journalism, which attracted wide notice. To it he added, for good measure, a fiery extract from "Religious Musings".

By early April it looked as if the paper would succeed, and in number five Coleridge opened his columns to an article by Tom Poole and sonnets by Robert Lovell, thus trying to establish a broader editorial content. He received much correspondence, mostly anonymous and much of it critical. A characteristic letter read: "Sir! I detest your principles, your prose I think very so so –; but your poetry is exquisitely beautiful, so gorgeously sublime, that I take in your Watchman solely on account of it – In Justice therefore to me & some others of my stamp I intreat you to give us more Verse & less democratic scurrility."[57] But it is possible that this was one of the ones that the editor wrote himself.

It was at this apposite moment that his first volume of *Poems* appeared, with an immediate and generous royalty from Cottle of thirty guineas.[58] Presentation copies were lavishly dispersed all over England: to the London reviews; to his old editor, Benjamin Flower in Cambridge; to the poetess Mrs Barbauld; to Dr Beddoes, Tom Poole, Charles Lamb and brother George Coleridge at Ottery (a delayed peace-offering); to old university friends like Francis Wrangham who wrote for the journals; and to political figures. The most notable of these was John Thelwall, who was to become a significant correspondent during the summer. To Thelwall, he wrote: "I beg your acceptance of my Poems – you will find much to blame in them – much effeminacy of sentiment, much faulty glitter of expression. I build all my poetic pretentions on the Religious Musings – which you will read with a POET's Eye . . ."[59]

10

Poems on Various Subjects by S. T. Coleridge, "Late of Jesus College, Cambridge", was a slim volume of fifty-one pieces, nearly half of which were sonnets, and most of which had been written since his last year at university. Weight, in every sense, was provided by the opening "Monody on the Death of Chatterton", and the closing "Religious Musings", both of them elaborate formal poems which belied the true originality of the collection. Thirty-six of the pieces were lushly classed as "Effusions" (including the sonnets), a term which Charles Lamb was gently to abominate, but which Coleridge chose defiantly to indicate a new emphasis on spontaneous and personal emotions.

The sensibility of Bowles is very evident throughout, though Coleridge defended himself against a charge of "querulous egotism" in his preface. He argued that the melancholy tone of many of the poems was essential to their personal appeal: "the communicativeness of our nature leads us to describe our own sorrows." He also pointed out that several of the verses "allude to an intended emigration to America on the scheme of an abandonment of individual property".

A vision of his life. Frontispiece to the *Ancient Mariner*, engraving by Gustave Doré, 1877.

OLD COLLEGE BVILDINGS IN THE LATTER HALF OF THE 18TH CENTVRY, FROM A CONTEMPORARY WATERCOLOVR: IN THE FOREGROVND IS THE REV. JOHN COLERIDGE MOVNTING HIS HORSE :

Coleridge's Birthplace

The vicarage Ottery St Mary. Line drawing by Edmund New, 1914.

View of St Mary, Ottery, Devon. (*British Tourist Authority*)

The cloisters Christ's Hospital, Newgate Street, where the young Coleridge was discovered reading Virgil and later haranguing his schoolmates on the Neo Platonists. (Note the leads – flat roof above – where Coleridge climbed out and contemplated the Universe.) (*The British Museum*)

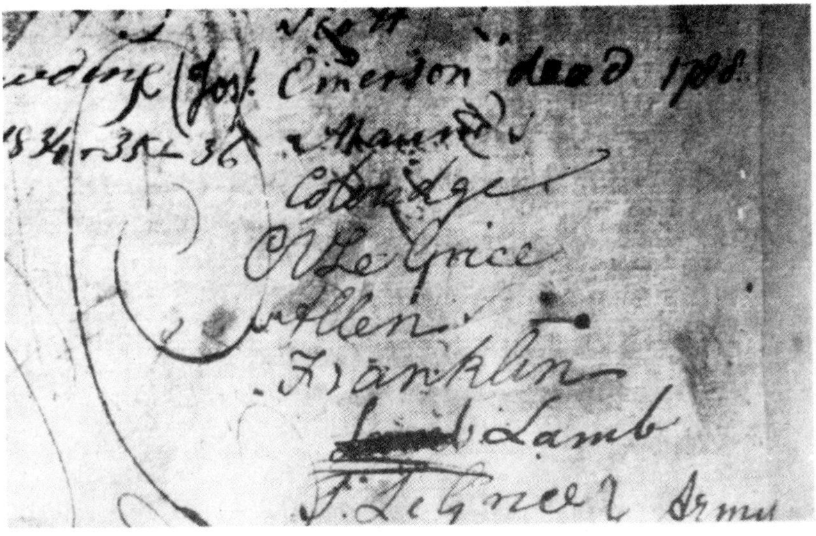

Schoolboy name-entries of Coleridge, Charles Valentine Le Grice, Bob Allen and Charles Lamb in the front of a shared copy of Homer's *Iliad*.

Jesus College Cambridge showing Jesus Green, where Coleridge saw the "young ass", and proclaimed it his Pantisocratic brother. (*The British Museum*)

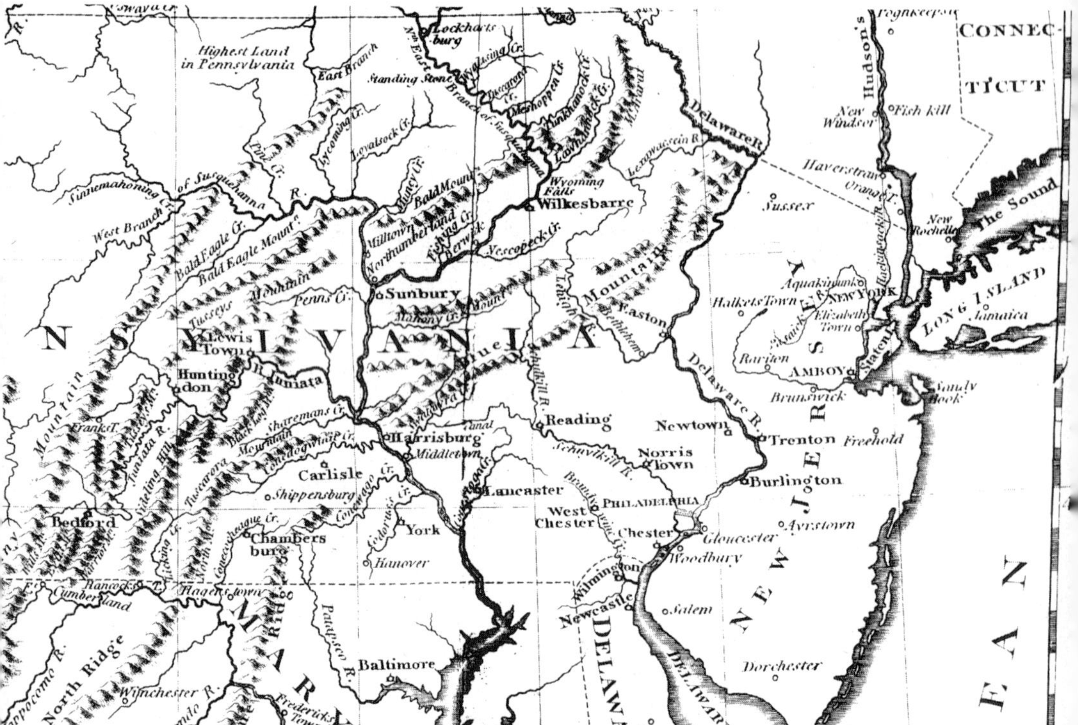

Original map of American settlements drawn for Frontispiece of Thomas Cooper's *Some Information Respecting America*, 1794. Two branches of the Susquehanna river, long dreamt of by Pantisocrats, can be seen at the top centre left of map, joining at Northumberland (near Sunbury, Pennsylvania), where Joseph Priestley actually settled.

Sara Coleridge. Miniature by Matilda Betham, 1809. (*Hulton-Deutsch Collection*)

Coleridge, 1796. Pencil and wash drawing by Robert Hancock. (*National Portrait Gallery, London*)

Robert Southey, 1796. Pencil and wash drawing by Robert Hancock. (*National Portrait Gallery, London*)

Charles Lamb, 1798. Pencil and wash drawing by Robert Hancock. (*National Portrait Gallery, London*)

Dorothy Wordsworth, silhouette c. 1798. (*The Wordsworth Trust*)

William Wordsworth, 1798. Pencil an wash drawing by Robert Hancocl (*National Portrait Gallery, London*)

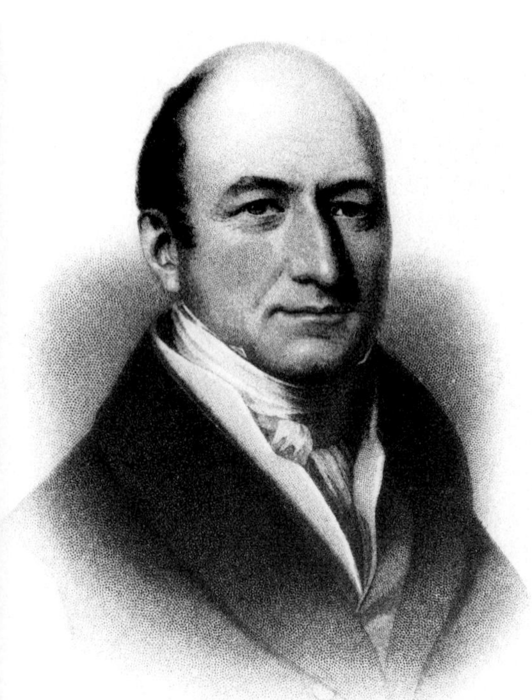

The only known portrait of Tom Poole, from frontispiece of his *Life*, 1888.

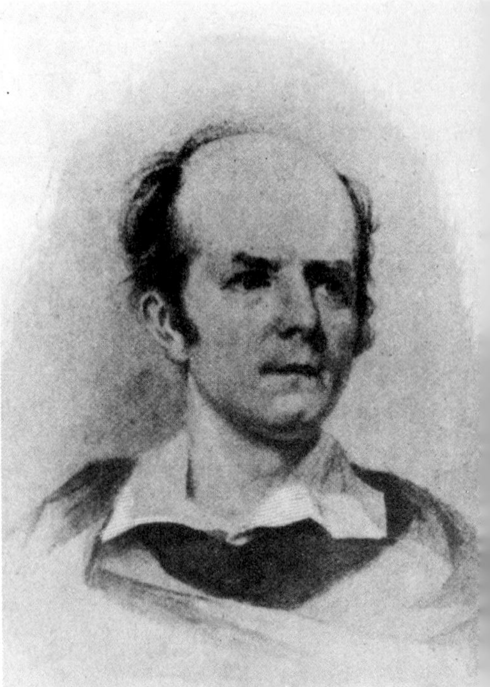

Joseph Cottle, after a contempora miniature by N. Branwhite. (*Natior Portrait Gallery, London*)

"The New Morality", 1798, cartoon in the *Anti-Jacobin* showing Coleridge with long ass's ears (centre) proclaiming his "Dactylics"; and various other contemporaries. *Left to right*: Charles James Fox obese Leader of the Opposition; Citizen Thelwall; Lamb and Lloyd (as toad and frog); Southey (kneeling ass). Also some significant publications: Daniel Stuart's newspapers, the *Morning Post* and *Courier* (evening paper burning); Mary Wollstonecraft's *The Wrongs of Women*; and Erasmus Darwin's *Zoonomia*. On altar at right, the French Trinity of revolutionary harridans etc. (*The British Museum*)

William Pitt the Younger, Prime Minister. Political sketch by James Gillray, 1789. (*National Portrait Gallery, London*)

Coleridge by Pieter van Dyke, 1795. The young radical lecturer and poet in Bristol. (*National Portrait Gallery, London*)

But there is no real evidence of a Romantic manifesto in the preface. Coleridge did not yet distinguish between the high, outmoded, Miltonic style of the longer poems, and the vividly fresh and direct language of the Conversational pieces. The best poem of the collection, "The Eolian Harp" simply appears as "Effusion 35, written at Clevedon", while the admirable poem to Lamb about their sisters is grouped with two other blank verse pieces, "To the Nightingale" and "Lines: Composed while climbing the Left Ascent of Brockley Coomb" (a meditative topographical poem written during his expedition to Somerset the previous May). Yet it is these poems that show the direction in which his work would now rapidly develop. Several lyrics touchingly declare his love for Sara, but "The Sigh" also appears still addressed to Mary Evans. The poem which had the most popular impact remained the controversial "To a Young Jack Ass".

There is a slight mystery about the absence of two of his finest early poems: the sonnet "To the River Otter", and the "Retirement" poem about leaving the Clevedon cottage. Both would appear in the next edition in 1797, and were presumably already drafted in some form (the latter was published in the *Monthly Magazine* for October 1796). But this indicates significantly how Coleridge would often hold over, and meticulously rework, several poems that would later be presented as "spontaneous" productions belonging to specific dates – the sonnet to 1793, the "Retirement" poem to the winter of 1795.

Indeed, such reworking becomes characteristic of almost all Coleridge's major poems: "The Eolian Harp" had material added as late as 1817, the superb passage containing an apparently Pantisocratic view of the "One Life" which binds man to nature. Only the past tense of the meditation ("it should have been impossible") subtly suggests a remembered vision from long after the Clevedon days:

> O! the one Life within us and abroad,
> Which meets all motion and becomes its soul,
> A light in sound, a sound-like power in light,
> Rhythm in all thought, and joyance every where –
> Methinks, it should have been impossible
> Not to love all things in a world so fill'd;
> Where the breeze warbles, and the mute still air
> Is Music slumbering on her instrument.[60]

For a first collection, published when Coleridge was not yet twenty-four, the book received wide and prompt attention in five of the leading London reviews: most notably the *Analytical*, the *Critical* and the *Monthly*. But inevitably it was the Miltonic pieces – "Chatterton", "Religious Musings", and "The Songs of the Pixies" – which drew most comment, much of it favourable. But the praise was polite rather than perceptive; no reviewer was prepared to tackle the apocalyptic mixture of religion and politics in "Religious Musings"; only one picked up the original touches in "Shurton Bars", described as "a very striking sea-piece"; and "The Eolian Harp" was not mentioned. There was some criticism of "turgid" style and "bombast". Though four of the poems made reference to Pantisocracy – most effectively perhaps, in the newly composed last stanzas of "Chatterton", which suggest something of the lyric trance and "wizard spells" of "Kubla Khan" – this theme was not picked up either. However, Coleridge's unusual fraternal gesture of including four love-poems by Charles Lamb "of East India House", was cordially noted.

Coleridge adopted a line of amused indifference to Tom Poole. "The *Monthly* has *cataracted* panegyric on me – the *Critical cascaded* it – & the *Analytical dribbled* it with civility: as to the British Critic, they *durst not* condemn and they would not praise."[61]

The *Poems* and the *Watchman* (advertised at the back) have one powerful element in common: Coleridge's attempt to bring radical religious feeling in line with his changing political vision of the French Revolution. Drawing much of his imagery from the Book of Revelations, a shorthand version of this ideology appears in the preliminary "Argument" placed at the head of "Religious Musings". It is an early version of the inward debate which would later appear in his major poem, "France: an Ode" in 1798. But already the possibilities of a political Golden Age are removed to "the odorous groves of earth reparadis'd", in a distant future millennium foreseen by Milton, and by Priestley, whom Coleridge imagines "retired" to the Susquehanna and musing "expectant on these promis'd years". The "Argument" reads succinctly: "Introduction. Person of Christ. His prayer on the Cross. The process of his Doctrines on the mind of the Individual. Character of the Elect. Superstition. Digression to the present War. Origin and Uses of Government and Property. The present State of Society. French Revolution. Millenium. Universal Redemption. Conclusion."[62]

The best criticism of the *Poems* as a whole came from Charles

Lamb, in long affectionate letters in May and June, going minutely through the text, discussing individual lines in detail, and suggesting changes to make the style "more compress'd & I think energetic".[63] Though he praised "Chatterton" and "Religious Musings" as "superlatively excellent", he was instinctively drawn to the more personal of the Effusions, and wrote for example, of "The Sigh": "I think I hear *you* again. I image to myself the little smoky room at the Salutation & Cat, where we have sat together thro' the winter nights, beguiling the cares of life with Poesy."[64]

Lamb's natural taste and perception was to be crucial in the maturing of Coleridge's verse during this year, well before he came under the personal influence of Wordsworth. It was summed up in his response to a sonnet given that November: "Cultivate simplicity, Coleridge, or rather, I should say, banish elaborateness; for simplicity springs spontaneous from the heart, and carries into daylight its own modest buds and genuine, sweet, and clear flowers of expression. I allow no hot-beds in the gardens of Parnassus."[65]

This, both in imagery and argument, must count as an early declaration of the Romantic sensibility in poetry. But seeing his own poems in print already convinced Coleridge that such simplifying and chastening of his style would be necessary. Besides the false "glitter of expression" he had acknowledged to Thelwall, he now frankly admitted to Poole that there were many instances of "vicious affectation of phraseology", picking out the memorable compound double-negative from "Religious Musings" – "'Unshudder'd, unaghasted"'.[66] Clearly there was much banishing to be done.

11

But the immediate task was keeping the *Watchman* afloat. Subscriptions failed to materialise in April (his London bookseller, Parsons, failed to pay a single return on either the paper or the *Poems*), and by the end of the month Coleridge faced growing debts. Politically, one of his main editorial positions – an end to the war with France – was destroyed when the French Directory, under Bonaparte's influence, rebuffed a tentative series of peace proposals from Pitt's government. A further setback came with the rejection of Wilberforce's Anti-Slave Trade Bill. The Whig coalition between Grey and Fox, with which the paper identified, was steadily losing ground to the forces of patriotic reaction. In issue number eight, Coleridge led with a bitter essay, "Remonstrance to the French

Legislators", in which he was forced to accuse the French revolutionary powers of naked imperialism: "Will your soldiers fight with the same enthusiasm for Ambition, as they have done for Liberty . . . ?"

These political disappointments were overshadowed by a tragic personal blow, when on 3 May Robert Lovell, the last of the original Pantisocrats, finally succumbed to fever. Coleridge sat up with the dying man, gently trying to bring some form of Christian consolation to the declared atheist as he moaned and hallucinated. Then he took Mary Lovell into his own overcrowded house. Coleridge never forgot this experience. "It was, you know, a very windy night – but his loud, deep, unintermitted groans mingled audibly with the wind, & whenever the wind dropt, they were very horrible to hear, & drove my poor young sister-in-law frantic."[67]

Two days later he decided to close down the *Watchman*. He was in debt by some £80, and his affairs were as bad "as the most Trinitarian Anathemizer, or rampant Philo-despot could wish in the moment of cursing".[68] On 13 May 1796 he brought out number ten, the last issue, advising his readers to turn to Flower's *Intelligencer* or the *New Monthly Magazine* to continue the struggle for "Rational Liberty". He explained in a final editorial that "the Work does not pay its expenses", and that he had not succeeded in finding the liberal audience that he hoped for. But he went down with a last, ironic flourish: "It must be attributed to defect of ability, not of inclination or effort, if the words of the Prophet be altogether applicable to me, 'O Watchman! thou hast watched in vain!'"

This was the end of more than a year's continuous activity in public and political affairs, the direct offspring of Pantisocracy, which had produced a remarkable series of publications: the political pamphlets, the *Poems*, and the newspaper. But Coleridge had now had enough: "I have accordingly snapped my squeaking baby-trumpet of sedition, and have hung up its fragments in the chamber of Penitences."[69] He felt that "domestic Sorrows & external disappointments" had depressed him below "*writing-point* in the thermometer of mind".[70] He took himself and Sara off immediately for a fortnight's holiday with Tom Poole in Stowey, where much time was spent in the large garden behind the house drinking local cider and reciting poetry in the stone arbour under the May-time blossoms.

SIX

Prodigal Father

1

In May 1796 Coleridge told Poole that he had two possible life-plans, "the first impracticable – the second not likely to succeed".

Either he would go with Sara to Germany, to study and translate the works of Schiller at the University of Jena. (Jena was then the centre of the German Romantic school, where the Schlegel brothers, Ludwig Tieck, and Novalis were also at work.)* Or else he would stay in Bristol and become "a Dissenting Parson & abjure Politics & carnal literature".[1]

In both plans he had a vague idea that he would also finance himself by starting a school for a dozen or so young men, based on his own highly original three-part curriculum: "1. Man as Animal: including the complete knowledge of Anatomy, Chemistry, Mechanics & Optics ... 2. Man as an *Intellectual* Being: including the ancient Metaphysics, the systems of Locke & Hartley, – of the Scotch Philosophers – & the new Kantian System ... 3. Man as a Religious Being: including an historic summary of all Religions ..." For the next six months he tried to find a practical basis for some such scheme,

*The shift of interest from France to Germany also marks a move away from political radicalism to more purely intellectual interests. The German universities were coming to be regarded as the research-centres of Europe, making rapid advances especially in three areas: natural sciences, biblical criticism, and idealist philosophy. German theatre, much influenced by the new Romantic reading of Shakespeare was also being revived (See Henri Brunschwig, *Enlightenment and Romanticism in Eighteenth Century Prussia*, Paris 1947, London 1974). Moreover the strong German interest in mystical religious experience, vividly illustrated in the rediscovery of the Gnostic philosophy of Jakob Boehme (1575–1624), and the visionary painting of Caspar David Friedrich (1774–1840) and Philipp Otto Runge (1777–1810), naturally appealed to Coleridge, and indicates the beginnings of a profound spiritual reaction against the rationalism of the French Enlightenment. (See "Coleridge's Circle".) For Coleridge these movements would eventually be summarised in the work of four figures, who came to shape his whole idea of intellectual endeavour: Lessing, Schiller, A. W. Schlegel, and Immanuel Kant. Curiously, the productions of Goethe did not have their full impact in England until the generation of Byron, Shelley, Thomas De Quincey, and Henry Crabb Robinson.

though the Pantisocratic dream of a retired life in the countryside with friends still shaped his decisions, and ultimately prevailed at the end of the year. "Bright Bubbles of the aye-ebullient brain!"[2]

Though Coleridge now abjured public affairs, it was ironic that his reputation in Bristol as an extreme democrat was now permanently formed and would remain in the public mind for the next twenty years, leading frequently to the retrospective charge of Jacobinism. His increasing anxiety about this later became something of an obsession, appearing in private correspondence with his aristocratic friend Sir George Beaumont in 1803; in the early issues of his later newspaper *The Friend* in 1809; and many defensive and disingenuous passages in the *Biographia* in 1817. Southey would remark acidly: "If he was not a Jacobine, in the common acceptation of the name, I wonder who the Devil was."[3] But the publications of 1795–6, as we have seen, do not allow such a simplistic view; and the long, brilliantly argued letters to a real Jacobin, "Citizen" John Thelwall, which Coleridge began this summer, also clearly show the peculiarities of Coleridge's radicalism and his ideological distance from the revolutionary atheism of the Godwin-Holcroft circle.

Coleridge's "trumpet of sedition" had certainly demonstrated intense sympathies with the poor and oppressed. He violently opposed Pitt's ministry, the war with France, the slave trade, and the political intolerance of the two Acts. His Christian radicalism had millennial overtones, especially in such poems as "Religious Musings", and his Pantisocratic ideal of a "brotherhood in Nature" was visionary and remained one of the strongest features in his future writing. Yet his practical politics were no more subversive than those of the Foxite-Whig opposition, and even in the *Watchman* he showed "patriotic" tendencies which soon became, in the face of the growing French imperialism under Bonaparte, positively nationalistic. His emphasis on personal philanthropy, and the sacredness of family life (both of which challenged, and finally converted, William Godwin) were permanent elements in his philosophy.

Perhaps the public, like Poole's cousin, could not be expected to make these distinctions. The "Jacobin" brush tarred broadly, bringing "guilty by association" in the increasingly reactionary world of British politics during the Napoleonic Wars. Certainly Coleridge came bitterly to regret his "flame-coloured epithets", which clung to his name like the burning shirt of Nessus. Yet there was more than a little justification in the pained righteousness with which he declared in 1809, of these early days: "With the exception of one solitary sonnet . . . I may safely defy my worst enemy to show, in any of my few writings, the least bias to Irreligion, Immorality, or Jacobinism."[4] Yet many would take up this challenge. (And one wonders which sonnet Coleridge had in mind?)

Returning from Stowey at the end of May, when parliamentary elections were due, Coleridge found hustings erected in the deserted morning square at Bridgwater, and thought dismissively of the corrupt political world: "I mounted & pacing the boards mused on Bribery, False Swearing, and other *foibles* of Election Times." He then wandered along the quayside of River Parrett, noting the merchant ships unloading their expensive cargoes, and the swirling, muddy waters that looked "as filthy as if all the Parrots in the House of Commons has been washing their consciences therein". He consoled himself with a breakfast of three boiled eggs, and a small mountain of bread and butter.

Already he was longing to return to the arcadia of Poole's house, and the pure rural tinkling of the stream from the Quantocks. "Were I transported to Italian Plains, and lay by the side of a streamlet that murmured thro' an Orange-Grove, I would think of thee, dear Gutter of Stowy!"[5] The sound of running water, with its promise of life, seemed much in his mind as he sought for a new form of existence with Sara and the coming baby. He entered in his Notebook a prophetic image: "There is not a new or strange opinion – Truth returned from banishment – a river run under ground."[6]

2

The immediate problem of finances solved itself in a miraculous manner that Coleridge – a Micawber before his time – was only too happy to rely on. First Poole announced that he had arranged for a £40 honorarium to be paid annually, from the contributions of various admiring friends, including himself, Estlin, Wade, Morgan, and Lord Egremont's land-agent at Stowey, John Cruikshank. Then Coleridge's friend in London, the poet George Dyer, volunteered to pay off all the outstanding printer's bills on the *Watchman*.[7] Finally, an unexpected donation of ten guineas arrived from the Royal Literary Fund for needy authors. For the first time, Coleridge felt himself truly valued: his efforts had been recognised and appreciated. He wrote in revealing holiday mood to Estlin: "I am with you in spirit: – and almost feel 'the sea-breeze lift my youthful locks.' – I would write Odes & Sonnets Morning & Evening – & metaphysicize at Noon – and of rainy days I would overwhelm you with an Avalanche of Puns & Conundrums loosened by sudden thaw from the Alps of my Imagination."[8]

After the debilitating struggles with the *Watchman*, Coleridge bounced back with innumerable plans and schemes during the summer of 1796. His Notebooks, in between recipes for Lancashire Hot Pot and home-made ginger wine, were full of long lists of the works he planned to write. These included essays on Bowles, Godwin ("Strictures"), Pantisocracy, marriage ("in opposition to French Principles"), the mystic Jakob Boehme, and the "Reveries" of Swedenborg; as well as an opera, a tragedy, and an epic poem on "The Origin of Evil".[9] All sorts of shorter poems were also envisaged, and though none of these was ever completed in its original form, they indicate the direction in which his mind was working: a "Wild Poem on Maniac", six hymns "to the Sun, the Moon, and the Elements", something called "Egomist, a metaphysical Rhapsody", and "Escapes from Misery, a Poem" with this expressive notation – "Halo round the Candle – Sigh visible".[10]*

He was also in correspondence about poetry with William Wordsworth. After the Bristol meeting in autumn 1795, Wordsworth had sent him the manuscript of "Salisbury Plain" from Racedown, in Dorset, where he had settled with his sister, Dorothy, in the country house owned by John Pinney. It was delivered by Pinney's brother with a request that Coleridge make any comment before handing it on to Cottle for publication. Pinney told Wordsworth on 26 March

*This is the first of many such tantalising lists of projected works – both in the Notebooks and his letters – the vast majority of which were never fulfilled. (Hazlitt would later ironically praise Coleridge as the past master of the Prospectus.) In later life, some of these subjects are so often repeated – "Christabel", "The Men and the Times", "The Fall of Jerusalem", the "Opus Maximum" – that they take on the quality of a threnody, a ritual chorus of non-fulfilment. They exasperated many of Coleridge's editors, friends (and biographers) beyond endurance. Yet such visionary lists have their own interest, and indeed it could be argued that they are almost a literary form in their own right (see Thomas McFarland, *Romanticism and the Forms of Ruin: Wordsworth, Coleridge and Modalities of Fragmentation*, Princeton 1981). A projected work – a few stanzas, a single line, even a title alone – can have an immense power of suggestion (like an artist's sketch), opening up vistas. (The reader will find that image of the candle mysteriously recurring in the Lake District writings.) Moreover, Coleridge himself wrote with brilliant effect on the subject of unfinished poems in several of his prefaces, opening up the whole question of the creative impulse in startling new ways: the preface to "Kubla Khan" becomes indeed almost as fascinating as the poem itself (See Chapter 7). Finally, there is the point which Coleridge himself made with some justification in the *Biographia*: "By what I *have* effected, am I to be judged by my fellow men, what I *could* have done, is a question for my own conscience." (*Biographia*, I, p. 151.)

1796: "This Coleridge appears to have done with considerable attention, for I understand he has interleaved it with white paper to mark down whatever may strike him as worthy of your notice and intends forwarding it to you in that form." This was the first example of Coleridge adopting the role of Wordsworth's critical advisor.[11]

By April Wordsworth was in turn reading Coleridge's *Poems*. There is no suggestion that, like Lamb, he was recommending a simplification of Coleridge's style. On the contrary, he picked out the millennial close to "Religious Musings" as the best lines in the volume, where the "massy gates of Paradise" are thrown open, releasing "sweet echoes and unearthly melodies" which are heard by the favoured good man "in his lonely walk", so his silent spirit "drinks Strange bliss."[12] It was perhaps this image of the solitary meditator that appealed to Wordsworth amidst the transcendental sublimities, for he was, thought Coleridge, "a Republican & at least a *Semi*-atheist". Coleridge now knew something of Wordsworth's early sojourn in revolutionary Paris, and his Godwinian politics, which he distrusted; but he valued his literary opinion, for he already suspected that Wordsworth was "the best poet of the age".[13] From now on, the two poets were very much aware of each other's work, though close personal contact was not yet established.

By July, various professional posts were being offered to Coleridge. In London, Perry of the *Morning Chronicle*, evidently impressed by his *Watchman* journalism (and on the recommendation of Dr Beddoes), proposed an associate editorship. In Derby, a certain Dr Crompton and a rich widow, Mrs Evans, were both anxious to discuss separate plans for Coleridge to set up private schools in the Midlands. While as far afield as Liverpool, another proposal came from William Roscoe, the friend and patron of Mary Wollstonecraft, for a "comfortable situation" as a lay preacher.

Coleridge's reputation as a journalist, lecturer and preacher had already spread wide, but it was difficult to choose between these conflicting careers. The London newspaper offer was superficially the most tempting, but its rejection revealed Coleridge's stubborn new sense of his own independence. He wrote to Poole: "I love Bristol & I do not love London – & besides, local and temporary politics have become my aversion. They narrow the Understanding, and at least *acidulate* the Heart: – but those two Giants, yclept BREAD & CHEESE, bend me into compliance. I must do something. If I go, farewell Philosophy! Farewell, the Muse! Farewell, my literary Fame!" In the event, with the support of Poole and Wade, he rejected the temptations of Fleet Street. Lamb regretted it, considering London "the only fostering soil for *Genius*".[14]

Sometime in July Coleridge visited Ottery, the first occasion since his marriage. He claimed to have been received "by my mother with transport, and by my Brother George with joy & tenderness, and by my other Brothers with affectionate civility".[15] But even if this is true, it is surely more significant – and indeed astonishing – that he did not take Sara with him to meet her new in-laws at this time. Instead, Coleridge took Sara north to explore the schools proposals, and the young couple completely captivated the benevolent Mrs Evans, who swept them both off on a picturesque carriage-tour of Matlock and the surrounding valleys which lasted into August. Coleridge particularly enjoyed picnicking on cold meats at Dove Dale, "in a cavern at the head of a divine little fountain", and returned to Mrs Evans' abode in Darley, "quite worn out with the succession of sweet Sensations".[16] However, the trustees did not sanction Coleridge's tutorial post, a disappointment which Mrs Evans softened with an impetuous gift of £95, and a mass of fine lace-work baby clothes for Sara.[17] This money represented almost a year's income, and is further testimony to the extraordinary effect of Coleridge's company.

He went on to Birmingham to preach – the possibility of joining the Unitarian ministry was also being pressed on him – while Sara returned to Bristol. By September, yet another proposal materialised in the form of a private tutorship for the twenty-one-year-old son of a rich Quaker banking family, Charles Lloyd. The youth was clever, but mentally unstable and subject to epileptic fits, and the suggestion was that he be taken on as Coleridge's personal pupil and private house-guest. Charles had heard Coleridge preach and had fallen completely under his spell, and begged his father to obtain the pupilship at the extravagant fee of £80 per annum.

This time the interview, with Lloyd senior, proved satisfactory, but hardly was it complete when news arrived at Birmingham of the sudden birth of Sara's child, some two weeks premature. Coleridge's arrangements had been so chaotic that not even a midwife had been present, and Sara had delivered the baby herself. "The Nurse just came in time to take away the after-birth"; but both mother and son were "uncommonly well".[18]

3

It seems ominous that Coleridge was a hundred miles away for this signal event. He explained that "Sara had strangely miscalculated" her dates. He left for Bristol the next day, in the grip of powerful but conflicting feelings, which he put into three vividly expressive sonnets, the first written on the coach home.

As in the case of his first Conversation Poem to Lamb, these initially emerged as prose in a long letter of 24 September, containing many of the phrases that he was shaping into poetry. He wrote to Poole:

> I was quite annihilated by the suddenness of the information – and retired to my room to address myself to my Maker – but I could only offer up to him the silence of stupified Feelings. – I hastened home & Charles Lloyd returned with me. – When I first saw the Child, I did not feel that thrill & overflowing of affection which I expected – I looked on it with a melancholy gaze – my mind intensely contemplative & my heart only sad. – But when two hours after, I saw it at the bosom of it's Mother; on her arm; and her eye tearful & watching it's little features, then I was thrilled & melted, & gave it the Kiss of a FATHER.[19]

The baffled and touching honesty with which he admits that he did not immediately experience the conventional "joy of fatherhood", seems immensely revealing. As a man, he was shaken by his new responsibility, but as a poet he was fascinated by the ambiguity of his reactions. Each of the three sonnets explores a different stage in this developing pattern of feeling, to form a study of domestic emotion which is highly original of its kind. Instead of the lover, it is the father who speaks, slowly recognising a complex change of attitudes to his wife, and to his own sense of identity in time, which emerges as fundamentally religious. In an experience common to many fathers, the final full acceptance of the child's physical existence – both as part of himself, and as utterly "other" – brings a confirmation of reality, and a new acceptance of his marriage.

In the first sonnet, "On Receiving a Letter Informing Me of the Birth of A Son", he explores "the unquiet silence of confused thought / And shapeless feeling". In the second, "Composed on a Journey Homeward" (an early glance at the theme of homecoming, to be so central in the Conversation Poems) he reflects on the sudden fears for his child's life, as if the very tentativeness of his feelings might somehow bring about its death – "I think that I should struggle to believe / Thou wert a spirit".

And in the beautiful third sonnet, "To A Friend Who Asked, How I Felt When The Nurse Presented My Infant To Me", he records the final swelling and bursting through of glowing paternal emotions – pride for the child, love for the mother, in a major chord of grateful acceptance. It is this sonnet which comes closest to the wording of the letter, and first touches on many of the concerns of "Frost at Midnight" (the friend addressed may have been Charles Lloyd, or perhaps Charles Lamb):

> Charles! my slow heart was only sad, when first
> I scann'd that face of feeble infancy:
> For dimly on my thoughtful spirit burst
> All I had been, and all my child might be!
> But when I saw it on its mother's arm,
> And hanging at her bosom (she the while
> Bent o'er its features with a tearful smile)
> Then I was thrill'd and melted, and most warm
> Impress'd a father's kiss: and all beguil'd
> Of dark remembrance and presageful fear,
> I seem'd to see an angel-form appear –
> 'Twas even thine, belovéd woman mild!
> So for the mother's sake the child was dear,
> And dearer was the mother for the child.[20]

The baby – whom the old nurse insisted was the image of its father ("no great compliment to me") – was named David Hartley Coleridge, after the "great Master of Christian Philosophy". Perhaps only Coleridge would have named a child after a metaphysician. Hartley was to remain his father's lifelong favourite, the source of great pleasure and great anxiety, and some of his best poetry. The child brought the parents together more closely than they would ever be again, for a magically happy period of some two years, despite all domestic difficulties.

4

It was the birth of Hartley that finally decided Coleridge against all his teaching and preaching plans in Derbyshire and Birmingham. Instead he announced his "rustic scheme": a cottage near Poole in the

Quantocks, where he could live simply on Pantisocratic lines, and devote his energies to writing. "I am anxious that my children should be bred up from earliest infancy in the simplicity of peasants," he grandly told Charles Lloyd's father; "their food, dress and habits completely rustic. I never shall, and I never will, have any fortune to leave them: I will leave them therefore hearts that desire little, heads that know how little is to be desired, and hands and arms accustomed to earn that little."[21] He had determined to "retire once for all and utterly from cities and towns".

Poole would instruct him in "the toils of the Garden and the Field". His house would be tucked away in the tiny farming valley of Adscombe, nestling into the hills, two miles above Nether Stowey, where the streams come down from Seven Wells Wood in the heart of the Quantocks. Here he would cultivate half a dozen acres, near a ruined medieval chantry among the trees along the river, on land rented from Lord Egremont. In fact this first idyllic version of the scheme fell through, as Coleridge realised in early November: "I am frightened at not hearing from Cruikshanks – Has Lord Thing a my bob – I forget the animal's name – refused *him* – or has Cruikshanks forgotten *me?*"[22]

Though Lloyd senior thought the scheme "monastic rather than Christian", his son Charles was enraptured by the prospect and began producing his own sonnets about the overflowings of his "restless Heart". "He is assuredly a man of great Genius," thought Coleridge. The two shared a bed, while Sara was nursing the baby.[23] Not only was space now very restricted in the Bristol house, but Coleridge felt increasingly harassed by the presence of Sara's mother, and the rustic scheme would emphatically not include her. The malign influence of a mother-in-law would appear in the first of Coleridge's ballads the following summer, "The Three Graves".

Coleridge's growing intimacy with and reliance on Poole also encouraged an intense cultivation of male friendships and "sensibility" in their letters. He was anxious to introduce Charles Lloyd to Poole, while also sending his love to Poole's new apprentice (and later business partner) Thomas Ward, "that young Man with the soul-beaming Face".[24] The freedom with which Coleridge expressed emotion to Poole at this period – "Friend! Beloved! Brother!" – is disconcerting precisely because it contains no homosexual implication, or at least is utterly innocent of any such awareness. Friendship itself has become part of his Romantic creed, vividly expressed in the ideal of an intimate masculine circle sharing thoughts and feelings and confidences which stretch across or beyond domestic boundaries. The constant exchange of each other's poetry was central to this.

In October, while at Cottle's publishing shop – "having some *paper* at the Printer's which I could employ no other way" – Coleridge suddenly concocted a little pamphlet, *Sonnets by Various Authors*, of which he ran off 200 copies privately, bringing together such an ideal, literary circle. It contained twenty-eight poems, of which four each were by Lamb, Lloyd, Southey (a great act of magnanimity), and himself, as well as others by admired older writers such as Bowles, William Sotheby, Thomas Warton, and Henry Brooks.[25]

He also wrote a preface, outlining the historical development of the sonnet form from the "cold glitter" of Petrarch's "metaphysical abstractions", to the intense intimacy and almost prayer-like power of the modern English form.

> Such compositions generate a habit of thought highly favourable to delicacy of character. They create a sweet and indissoluble union between the intellectual and the material world. Easily remembered from their briefness, and interesting alike to the eye and the affections, these are poems which we can "lay up in our heart, and our soul," and repeat them "when we walk by the way, and when we lie down, and when we rise up."[26]

One member of this circle was struck by a terrible domestic crisis in the autumn. On 22 September Mary Lamb, in a fit of insanity, attacked and killed her mother. It was the defining crisis of Charles Lamb's early life, which shaped his whole future. Coleridge responded to Lamb's grief and horror in a whole series of consoling religious letters of passionate intensity. "In storms like these, that shake the dwelling and make the heart tremble, there is no middle way between despair and the yielding up of the whole spirit unto the guidance of faith." There was a good deal of the Unitarian preacher in these exhortations, Coleridge adopting the unctious language and vocabulary of the pulpit with somewhat disconcerting ease. "It is sweet to be roused from a frightful dream by the song of birds and the gladsome rays of the morning." But Lamb had asked him to write "as religious a letter as possible", and not to mention poetry, and he seemed to be satisfied by these high sentiments, which he regarded as "an inestimable treasure".[27]

Having saved Mary from a manslaughter charge, and established her safely in a private madhouse at £60 a year (Coleridge offered money, which was immediately refused) Lamb showed his rapidly returning grip on affairs by beginning to worry, in turn, about Coleridge. He wrote on 17 October:

> My dearest friend, I grieve from my very soul to observe you in your plans of life, veering about from this hope to the other, & settling nowhere. Is it an untoward fatality (speaking humanly) that does this for you? . . . or lies the fault, as I fear it does, in your *own* mind? You seem to be taking up splendid schemes of fortune only to lay them down again, & your fortunes are in ignis fatuus . . . would to God the dancing demon *may* conduct you at last in peace & comfort to the "life & labors of a cottager".[28]

He sent tenderest remembrances to Sara, and praised him again for the Hartley birth sonnets, especially the last: "I love you for those simple, tender, heart-flowing lines." It was perhaps Lamb's quiet way of giving advice.

5

In November there was a domestic crisis in his own household at Bristol, which produced Coleridge's first deliberate piece of composition under the influence of opium. First Coleridge was struck by excruciating neuralgia down the right-hand side of his face, from eye socket to the base of the jaw: the worst pain he had ever experienced, as if he was "under the focus of some invisible Burning-Glass, which concentrated all the Rays of a Tartarean Sun". For a week he dosed himself on twenty-five drops of opium every five hours, sometimes increasing the dose to seventy drops. He ran round the house naked, in a frenzy of pain and delirium.[29]

Then, in the second week of November Charles Lloyd began to have fits, as if in sympathy. These were even more frightening, appearing to be epileptic in origin: "his distemper (which may with equal propriety be named either Somnambulism, or frightful Reverie, or *Epilepsy from accumulated feelings*) is alarming. He falls all at once into a kind of Night-mair; and all the Realities round him mingle with, and form part of, the strange Dream."[30]

To Sara, it must have seemed like Bedlam. But Coleridge was fascinated both by his own, and by Charles' symptoms, and described them vividly and at length to Poole, reaching inspired heights of hyperbole about his own sufferings: "with a shower of arrowy Death-pangs he transpierced me, & then he became a Wolf and lay gnawing my bones." He also freely admitted that his own doctor put the neuralgia down to nervous origins, overwork and anxiety; though without explaining what might have been the cause of *these*. "My beloved Poole! in excessive anxiety, I believe, it might originate!"[31]

The fantasy element in both diseases evidently excited him, and his prose gathers a manic energy and allusiveness in describing it. His letter of 5 November 1796 was "flighty", under "the immediate inspiration of Laudanum", and yet one "most accurately descriptive both of facts & feeling". In this letter he rises above his epic pains to sing a kind of psalm of deliverance to Poole, mingling the language of poetry, biblical preaching, "Sensibility", and prophetic derangement. It is also done with great good humour.

Coleridge intoned to the astonished Poole, late that Saturday night:

> To live in a beautiful country & to inure myself as much as possible to the labors of the field, have been for this year past my dream of the day, my Sigh at midnight – but to enjoy these blessings *near you*, to see you daily, to tell you all my thoughts in their first birth, and to hear your's, to be mingling identities with you, as it were; – the vision-weaving Fancy has indeed often pictured such things, but Hope never dared whisper a promise! ... Stern Pioneer of Happiness! – Thou has been '*the Cloud*' before me from the day that I left the flesh-pots of Egypt & was led thro' the way of a wilderness – the *cloud*, that hast been guiding me to a land flowing with milk & honey – the milk of Innocence, the honey of Friendship![32]

This vision of the promised land in the Quantocks, with its misty premonitions of the honey-dew and paradise-milk of "Kubla Khan", no doubt surprised Poole who found himself cast in an increasingly patriarchal role. Lamb, subject to the same enthusiasms, warned Coleridge gently: "Remember, you are not in Arcadia when you are in the West of England."[33] He also tactfully suggested that he "cultivate the filial feelings" for his real family, at Ottery St Mary.

For Sara, it was the first clear sight of her young husband's hysterical temperament, violent swings of mood, and sudden fluctuations from despair to manic elation. Yet Coleridge's humour still seemed miraculously to encompass everything. He ended his wild opium letter with a request that Poole's rich cousin William might be able to provide temporary accommodation at Marshmills, if Adscombe fell through, but added: "you know, I would not wish to touch with the edge of the Nail of my great toe the line which should be but half a barley corn out of the circle of the most trembling Delicacy!"[34] The picture is so delightful and ludicrous (and again with its hint of the dancing, weaving magic circle of "Kubla Khan"), that it somehow disarms all criticism.

6

Throughout this winter, though "anxieties eat me up", Coleridge continued working in the crowded Bristol house. Poems and reviews were sent to the *New Monthly Magazine* and the *Critical Review*;[35] a long political piece, "Ode to the Departing Year", was prepared for Flower's *Cambridge Intelligencer*; and he wrote several poems of advice to Charles Lloyd.

He also embarked on a detailed philosophical correspondence with John Thelwall, hammering out their differences in matters of religion, politics, and the nature of poetry. These letters, often covering more than a dozen sheets, were written frequently on Saturday nights long into the early hours of the morning, when the rest of the house was asleep. Coleridge argued that his disappointment with French revolutionary politics had led him to turn away from journalism, lecturing and public controversy: "I am not *fit* for *public* Life; yet the Light shall stream to a far distance from the taper in my cottage window. Meantime, do *you* uplift the *torch* dreadlessly, and show to mankind the face of the Idol, which they have worshipped in Darkness!"[36]

In his letter of Saturday 19 November, he drew a famous and mocking self-portrait of his physical appearance and temperament.[37] It is much at variance with the striking good looks of actual portraits painted in 1796 and 1799 – the thick dark hair, the large eyes, the dramatic forehead and eyebrows. But he was drawing a psychological self-study, in which inner weaknesses and eccentricity are deliberately made to predominate. This was not so much modesty, as a Romantic sense of his own peculiarities, which was soon to emerge further in his autobiographical letters to Tom Poole of the following spring.

To Thelwall he wrote:

> My face, unless when animated by immediate eloquence, expresses great Sloth, & great, indeed almost ideotic, good nature. 'Tis a mere carcase of a face: . . . my gait is awkward, & the walk, & the *Whole man* indicates *indolence capable of energies* . . . [I] have read almost every thing – a library-cormorant – I am *deep* in all out of the way books . . . Metaphysics, & Poetry, & 'Facts of mind' – (ie. Accounts of all the strange phantasms that ever possessed your philosophy-dreamers from Thoth, the Egyptian to Taylor, the English Pagan) are my darling Studies . . . Of useful knowledge, I am a so-so chemist, & I love chemistry – all else is *blank*, – but I *will* be (please God) an Horticulturist & a Farmer. I compose very little – & I absolutely hate composition. Such is my dislike, that even a sense of Duty is sometimes too weak to overpower it. I cannot breathe thro' my nose – so my mouth, with sensual thick lips, is almost always open. In conversation I am impassioned, and oppose what I deem error with an eagerness, which is often mistaken for personal asperity – but I am ever so swallowed up in the *thing*, that I perfectly forget my opponent. Such am I.[38]

The acuteness and humour of the description at all points – from the cormorant (which dives lengthily beneath the sea to find its prey), to the adenoidal mouth-gaping (which suggests a sort of permanent, fledglingly, beak-open greed) – is remarkable.

A month later, on Saturday 17 December, an even longer letter to Thelwall launched into the characteristics of Christianity as a "religion for Democrats", and attacked the cheap atheism of Godwin (against whom he still intended to write a "six shilling Octavo"). Coleridge considered that radical Christianity "certainly teaches in the most explicit terms the rights of Man, his right to Wisdom, his right to an equal share in all the blessings of Nature; it commands it's disciples to go every where, & every where to preach these rights . . ."[39] He suspected that Thelwall had never actually reread his Testament "since your Understanding was matured".

Despite their ideological differences, and his accusations of "self-contradiction" and Jacobin "bigotry", he felt drawn to Thelwall and his young wife Stella: he felt they should meet and become friends. He sent his own poems, and a presentation copy of Bowles to Stella, and offered "the hearty Grasp of Friendship".

Thelwall had himself published poetry, some of it written while imprisoned for the Treason Trials of 1794, and this led easily from politics to "a little sparring about Poetry". Coleridge argued that "mystical" philosophy could still make "very intelligible poetry"; and that sense often lay in the musical structure of the language. "As to Bowles, I affirm, that the manner of his accentuation in the words 'broad day-light' (three long Syllables) is a beauty, as it admirably expresses the Captive's *dwelling* on the sight of Noon – with rapture & a kind of Wonder."[40] He was soon to use these kind of suspended rhythmic devices with brilliant effect in his ballads.

He also began to discuss, for the first time, what he saw as the crucial balance between emotional passion of expression – "Poetry to have its highest relish must be impassioned!" – and the treatment of "lofty & abstract truths" in verse. His instinct was that these should be combined in a new directness of language, which did not deviate from "nature and simplicity", but he was still feeling his way among his models.

> . . . Tho' my poetry has in general a *hue* of tenderness, or Passion over it, yet it seldom exhibits unmixed & simple tenderness or Passion. My philosophical opinions are blended with, or deduced from, my feelings: & this, I think, peculiarizes my style of Writing. And like every thing else, it is sometimes a beauty, and sometimes a fault. But do not let us introduce an act of Uniformity against Poets – I have room enough in *my* brain to admire, aye & almost equally, the *head* and fancy of Akenside, and the *heart* and fancy of Bowles, the solemn Lordliness of Milton, & the divine Chit chat of Cowper . . .[41]

He added in his letter of 31 December that he thought a quite admirable poet could be made by "amalgamating" himself and Southey: "I *think* too much for a *Poet*; he too little for a *great* Poet." (Southey had returned from Lisbon to Bristol, and they were now "reconciled", though not intimate.) Further learned talk of Dr Beddoes, Dr Darwin, and Plato – "his dear *gorgeous* Nonsense!" – and an increasingly teasing exchange about religion, melted all further reserves: "Joking apart, I would to God we could sit by a fireside & joke vivâ voce, face to face – Stella & Sara, Jack Thelwall, & I."[42]

The entire exchange shows very well how Coleridge, through his mixture of charm, brilliance, intelligence and self-mockery, could rapidly insinuate himself into the good graces of someone as notoriously touchy as Thelwall. He made their profound political and religious differences appear as nothing more than the subject for a fireside chat between Sam and Jack. It was essentially a chameleon gift, a gift for fluent adaption and vivid response, that was remarkably close to Coleridge's own creative powers. He could project himself so sympathetically, powerfully and instinctively into another personality, another position, and make it appear almost indistinguishable from his own. But perhaps his own inner identity suffered thereby; and in the affairs of the world, would he eventually begin to seem like all things to all men?

Coleridge claimed that he and Thelwall ran "on the same ground, but we drive different Horses."[43] But he was always ready to minimise these differences, by turning a joke at his own expense. "My dear fellow! I laugh more, & talk more nonsense in a week, than most other people do in a year . . ."[44] Even in his most frontal attacks on Thelwall's atheism and political demagoguery, he had a characteristic way of softening the blow with a little deflection of flattery.

> I write these things not with any expectation of making you a Christian – I should smile at my own folly, if I conceived it even in a friendly day-dream. But I do wish to see a progression in your *moral* character, & I *hope* to see it – for while you so frequently appeal to the passions of Terror, & Ill nature & Disgust, in your popular writings, I must be blind not to perceive that you present in your daily and hourly practice the *feelings of universal Love.*[45]

7

By mid-December the "rustic scheme" had suffered a "severe process of simplification".[46] Charles Lloyd had been sent back to recover with his Papa at Birmingham; all hope of the beautiful riverside cottage at Adscombe had been abandoned; and Coleridge now planned to settle simply with Sara and the child, in a tiny semi-derelict thatched house – "the hovel" – at the north end of Lime Street in Nether Stowey itself.

He had seen it for sale on his last visit to Poole (who had suggested it as a remote possibility). It was hardly Arcadian: the last house in the village, close to the poorhouse and the baker's shop, with an open street gutter in front and a long strip of very rough vegetable garden at the back, and views up to the Quantocks southwards. Its main attraction was that the garden backed on to Poole's extensive orchard stretching from the tanning yard behind Castle Street.

Here Coleridge now planned the most primitive kind of life: no elegant further education for Lloyd, no servant for Sara, no preaching stipend for himself. It would be a spartan routine of cultivating vegetables, keeping a pig, and writing £40 of journalism a year for the *Monthly* and the *Critical*. With a low meat diet, no "strong Liquors", firewood cut and collected by himself, Sara reckoned that the three of them could live on sixteen shillings a week.[47]

Coleridge told Poole on 11 December: "I mean to work *very hard* – as Cook, Butler, Scullion, Shoe-cleaner, occasional Nurse, Gardener, Hind, Pig-protector, Chaplain, Secretary, Poet, Reviewer, and omnibotherum shilling-scavenger – in other words, I shall keep no Servant, and will cultivate my Land-acre, and my wise-acres, as well as I can."[48] Or, as he put it in the last stanza of "Ode to the Departing Year":

> Away, my soul, away!
> I unpartaking of the evil thing,
> With daily prayer and daily toil
> Soliciting for food my scanty soil . . .
> Now I recentre my immortal mind
> In the deep Sabbath of meek self-content . . .[49]

Lloyd's father (much aware of Coleridge's influence over his son), objected on practical grounds that he was shutting himself away in a remote country hamlet without companions or intellectual stimulation. Coleridge replied with fervour: "I shall have six companions – My Sara, my Babe, my own shaping and disquisitive Mind, my Books, my beloved Friend, Thomas Poole, & lastly, Nature, looking at me with a thousand looks of Beauty, and speaking to me in a thousand melodies of Love."[50] It was what he now passionately believed, and he pushed through the scheme despite all practical difficulties. These included an almost total lack of furniture, and the necessity of providing a £20 annuity for Mrs Fricker left behind in Bristol. He made the actual move, in a farm wagon, on the last day of the year.

The final hurdle was raised, quite unexpectedly, by Poole himself who suddenly announced on 13 December that he thought the cottage too small, damp, and uncomfortable. His real objections – as Coleridge sensed – were more personal: he probably thought that the Stowey villagers would be hostile to Coleridge's reputation as a wild Jacobin lecturer from Bristol, and no doubt he also realised with some misgivings the commitment he himself was taking on as the "beloved" friend.

Coleridge overwhelmed him with two long, empassioned letters of skilfully controlled hysteria, written that night and the following morning. He summoned "the Ghosts of Otway & Chatterton, & the phantasms of a Wife broken-hearted, & a hunger-bitten Baby!"; urged practicalities – "only two rooms – & two people ... our Washing we should put out . . . my evenings to Literature"; deployed influence – "Mr & Mrs Estlin approved, admired, & applauded the scheme"; and issued ultimatums – "I can accept no place in State, Church, or Dissenting Meeting. Nothing remains possible, but a School, or Writer to a Newspaper, or my present plan." Finally, he challenged the reality of their friendship: "*But if any circumstances have occurred that have lessened your Love, or Esteem, or Confidence* . . ." Poole yielded, instantly and gracefully, to this Coleridgean barrage.[51]

When all was smoothed over again by 18 December, Coleridge made a revealing apology. "I wrote to you with improper impetuosity; but I had been dwelling so long on the circumstance of living near you, that my mind was thrown by your letter into the feelings of those distressful Dreams, where we imagine ourselves falling from precipices. I seemed falling from the summit of my fondest Desires; whirled from the height, just as I had reached it."[52] Sometimes his whole life would seem like a series of such dreamlike ascents, and whirling descents into the abyss. But for now the talk settled firmly on fire-grates, green cloth wallpaper, book-chests, and bed-linen. A cheerful letter was sent to Southey, thanking him for his poems, just after Christmas; and then they rolled down in the wagon to Stowey in the bitter cold, Coleridge's face monstrously swollen – "my recondite Eye sits quaintly behind the flesh-hill; and looks as little, as a Tomtit's."[53]

But the eye was already noticing new things, and gathering them into his Notebooks: waterdrops dripping from the miller's mossy wheel, a wild colt running along the brow of Quantock, the "subtle snow" rising upwards in the wind "like pillars of cottage smoke".[54] He sent an early invitation to Poole to join them for a rustic dinner of meat and potato pie; it was written in rhyme on the back of one of the old Prospectuses for his lectures on the French Revolution.[55] He said he was "plucking flowers from the Galaxy".

SEVEN

Kubla Coleridge

1

The move to Stowey of 1797 was a deliberate rejection of any conventional career in literature or journalism. "I saw plainly, that literature was not a profession by which I could expect to live."[1] This was symbolised for Coleridge when he found Nanny (he had relented on the question of a servant-girl for Sara) laying the early morning fires with extravagant quantities of torn-up copies of the *Watchman* to make the kindling.

Though he was reviewing regularly, and preparing a new edition of his *Poems* for Cottle, he was seeking a form of self-sufficiency which would allow him time for inward growth and philosophical reflexion, in tune with the natural seasons, and genuinely involved in village life. It was indeed close to the monastic idea of a "retreat", combining hard physical labour with profound spiritual self-examination. The first fruits of this in the early spring were to be his series of brilliant autobiographical letters of childhood to Poole, and his next Conversation Poem, "To the Rev. George Coleridge", analysing his family upbringing.

The digging of his own garden was both literal and metaphorical. As he wrote to Poole in February: "I could inform the dullest author how he might write an interesting book – let him relate the events of his own Life with honesty, not disguising the feelings that accompanied them. – I never yet read even a Methodist's 'Experience' in the Gospel Magazine without receiving instruction & amusement . . . To me the task will be a useful one; it will renew and deepen *my* reflections on the past . . ."[2]

At one level, the life was perfectly domestic and humdrum, divided between garden, study and kitchen. He kept pigs, ducks, and geese; chopped firewood, dug potatoes, and sowed corn; helped with the cooking (they had no oven, and pies had to be taken across to the baker); and submitted to the drying of Hartley's endless nappies. He also took himself and Sara into village life, joining the Stowey

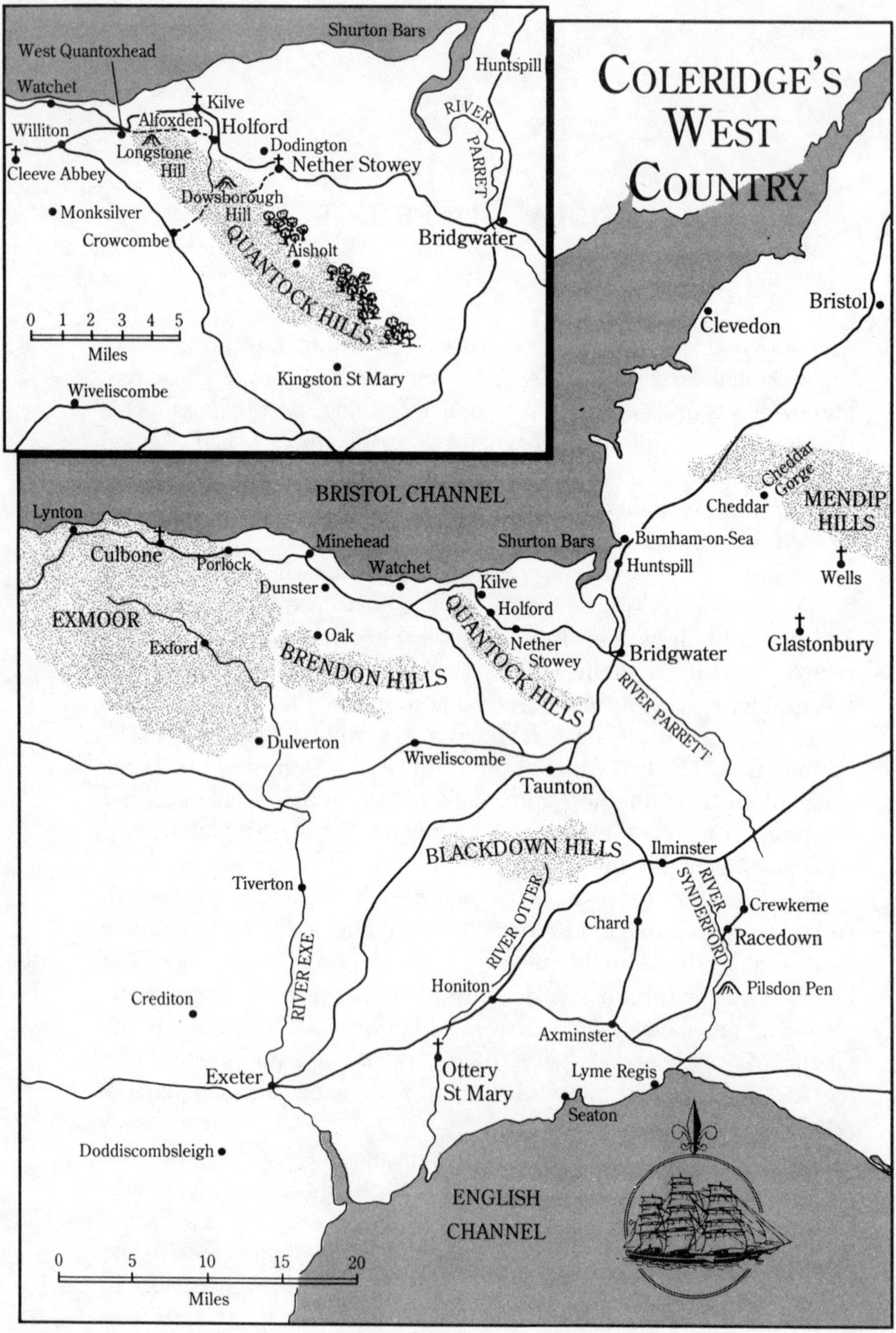
COLERIDGE'S WEST COUNTRY
Shurton Bars
West Quantoxhead
Huntspill
Watchet
Kilve
Alfoxden
Holford
Williton
RIVER PARRET
Longstone Hill
Dodington
Nether Stowey
Cleeve Abbey
Dowsborough Hill
Monksilver
Crowcombe
Bridgwater
Aisholt
QUANTOCK HILLS
0 1 2 3 4 5
Miles
Kingston St Mary
Wiveliscombe
Bristol
Clevedon
Cheddar Gorge
BRISTOL CHANNEL
Cheddar
MENDIP HILLS
Lynton
Burnham-on-Sea
Culbone
Minehead
Shurton Bars
Porlock
Huntspill
Wells
Watchet
Kilve
Dunster
Holford
EXMOOR
Glastonbury
Oak
Nether Stowey
Exford
Bridgwater
BRENDON HILLS
QUANTOCK HILLS
RIVER PARRETT
Dulverton
Wiveliscombe
Taunton
BLACKDOWN HILLS
Ilminster
RIVER SYNDERFORD
Tiverton
Crewkerne
Chard
RIVER OTTER
Racedown
RIVER EXE
Honiton
Pilsdon Pen
Crediton
Axminster
Ottery St Mary
Lyme Regis
Exeter
Seaton
Doddiscombsleigh
ENGLISH CHANNEL
0 5 10 15 20
Miles

musical society, playing his part in Poole's Reading Club, visiting the young Cruikshank family (who had a little girl of Hartley's age), and carefully dispelling any notion of some sinister Jacobin intellectual.

He described his routine after some five weeks to Thelwall.

> I never go to Bristol – from seven to half past eight I work in my garden; from breakfast till 12 I read and compose; then work again – feed the pigs, poultry, etc, till two o'clock – after dinner work again till Tea – from Tea till supper *review*. So jogs the day; & I am happy. I have society – my *friend*, T. Poole and as many acquaintances as I can dispense with – there are a large number of very pretty young women in Stowey, all musical – & I am an immense favorite: for I pun, conundrumize, *listen* & dance. The last is a recent acquirement –. We are *very* happy.[3]

The most literary character in the village was the carter-postman, whose name was Milton.

Hartley was growing strong and healthy – "a sweet boy" – and provided a snug domestic focus in the evenings – the baby, the firelight, the wind outside – which was already associated in Coleridge's mind with poetry. "You would smile to see my eye rolling up to the ceiling in a Lyric fury, and on my knee a *Diaper*, pinned, to warm."[4] This was to be exactly the setting of "Frost at Midnight", a year later.

But at a different and deeper level, Coleridge was reading hard, and reflecting on the foundations of his beliefs. "I now devoted myself to poetry and to the study of ethics and psychology . . ."[5] He was already privately sending his work in progress to Wordsworth in Dorset, and continuing to send it to Lamb, "whose *taste & judgement* I see reason to think more correct & philosophical than my own, which yet I place pretty high".[6] He was engaged on what he came to see as a spiritual voyage, in imagery that already hints at that of the *Ancient Mariner*. In December he had written to Poole a striking phrase: "I shall be again afloat on the wide sea unpiloted & unprovisioned."[7]

Looking back at this early Stowey period, some seventeen years later in the *Biographia*, the connection between the cottager and the Mariner, between the little house and the voyaging boat (or ark) of knowledge is made explicitly.

> I retired to a cottage in Somersetshire at the foot of Quantock, and devoted my thoughts and studies to the foundations of religion and

> morals. Here I found myself all afloat. Doubts rushed in; broke upon me "from the fountains of the great deep," and fell "from the windows of heaven". The fontal truths of nature religion and the books of Revelation alike contributed to the flood, and it was long ere my ark touched on an Ararat, and rested.[8]

Those "fontal" truths were to come from Coleridge's explorations of childhood – both his own and Hartley's; and from the stream-gushing combes of the Quantock Hills where he walked. Seas, rivers, streams, springs, fountains, brooks, were the literal sources of so much of his poetry and philosophical thought at this time, besides the endless travel books, philosophical treatises and anthropological studies he brought in from the Bristol Library, care of Milton. Even the "dear gutter" of Stowey seemed to represent this, and he could write to Estlin as if so much water was part of the blessing on their new life. "We are all remarkably well – & the child grows fat & strong . . . Before our door a clear brook runs of very soft water; and in the back yard is a nice *Well* of fine spring water."[9]

2

The cottage life was not altogether easy, especially in those first cold months. Poole made a gate in the connecting wall through to his orchard, and often came over to help – he supplied milk, fixed a sliding glass window in Coleridge's study, and admired the gardener's calloused hands. The fires in the two tiny ground floor parlours had to be constantly stoked, and Sara had to cook and dry washing over an open hearth in the back kitchen. The three little bedrooms above were adequate, until Coleridge decided to have Charles Lloyd back at the end of February.

But first there was damp, and then there were mice. Coleridge, with his fraternal attitude to animals, found himself in a ludicrous quandary, which curiously bears on the symbolism he would later apply to the shooting of the albatross. To kill the mice would be to betray them. A domestic joke here contains the seed of metaphysical drama.

"The mice play the very devil with us. It irks me to set a trap. By all the whiskers of all the pussies that have mewed plaintively, or amorously, since the days of Whittington, it is not fair," he solemnly informed Cottle. " 'Tis telling a lie. 'Tis as if you said, 'Here is a bit of toasted cheese; come little mice! I invite you!' – when, oh, foul breach of the rites of hospitality! I mean to assassinate my too credulous guests!"[10] A roar of laughter, much working of the dark eyebrows, and a sudden "rolling up" of the large eyes evidently accompanied this.

Yet at the same time, in some quieter place, an idea clicked home among his studies of "ethics and psychology". He would write in his preface to the great and mysterious sea-ballad, that the story showed "how the Ancient Mariner cruelly and in contempt of the laws of hospitality killed a Sea-bird . . ."[11] The notion of *hospitalitas*, of making the pilgrim or stranger welcome and at home, is central to both: and it reflects Coleridge's own fragile sense of home-making at this time.

There is one further odd level of correspondence. It is in the autobiographical letters to Poole that Coleridge now told the childhood tale of his quarrel with Frank about the "*crumbly* cheese" for toasting, which led to his traumatic night by the River Otter. Perhaps he felt some real kinship with his devilish mice cheated of their cheese. The first of these letters were written in February and March, with fluent recall and good humour, and posted through the orchard gate.

The poetry was more troublesome. Coleridge was trying to force his way through another formal philosophic piece, "The Destiny of Nations. A vision.", in an epic style that he had exhausted in "Religious Musings". It was intended as the grand opening to the new edition of his *Poems*; but Lamb, who was writing him regular pages of criticism and encouragement, attacked it without mercy. "I will enumerate some woeful blemishes, some of 'em sad deviations from that simplicity which was your aim . . ."

He felt that Coleridge had not yet found the right subject for a longer poem, but had some interesting suggestions to make.

> I have a dim recollection, that when in town you were talking of the *Origin of Evil* as a most prolific subject for a Long Poem – why not adopt it, Coleridge? there would be *room* for imagination. Or the description (from a vision or dream, suppose) of an Utopia in one of the planets (the Moon for instance). Or a five days' dream, which shall illustrate in sensible imagery, Hartley's 5 motives to conduct – sensation, imagination, ambition, sympathy, Theopathy.[12]

Coleridge struggled to turn in the copy promptly for Cottle by mid-February, but it went more and more slowly: "for I torture the poem, and myself, with corrections; and what I write in an hour, I sometimes take two or three days in correcting."[13] Finally he announced that he had "not the heart to finish the poem", and substituted the "Ode to the Departing Year" instead.

The 474 lines of "The Destiny of Nations", a series of unfinished Epic fragments, was not actually published until 1817 in *Sibylline Leaves*. Yet it contains many premonitory visions of some desolate polar sea (drawn partly from Crantz's *History of Greenland*), which seem to experiment with figures and imagery for the *Mariner*. There is the Giant Bird Vuokho, "of whose rushing wings the noise is Tempest";[14] there is the frozen desolation where "The white bear, drifting on a field of ice, / Howls to her sundered cubs with piteous rage";[15] and there are the two opposed spirits of the ocean, whom he vividly annotated in a suggestive prose footnote.

> They call the Good Spirit, Torngarsuck. The other great but malignant spirit is a nameless female; she dwells under the sea in a great house where she can detain in captivity all the animals of the ocean by her magic power. When a dearth befalls the Greenlanders, an Angekok or Magician must undertake a journey thither: he passes through the kingdom of souls, over an horrible abyss into the palace of this phantom, and by his enchantments causes the captive creatures to ascend directly to the surface of the ocean.[16]

Here is the first shadowy outline of the ritual drama of the Mariner himself, part Explorer and part Magician, who makes his sea-journey through an other-worldly kingdom of hallucinations, releasing "captive creatures" of the mental ocean, and doing battle with a "malignant" revenging Spirit of the Deep which pursues his ship. Such symbolic rituals – on the borderlines between folklore and psychology – and such Magus figures, were to haunt Coleridge's poetry in the Quantocks.

One passage in particular (drawn from another travel book, Captain James Cook's *Voyage to the Pacific*, 1784) foresees the central moment of the drama, when the Mariner's ship is becalmed in the tropics on a burning sea amidst "a thousand thousand slimy things".[17] In "The Destiny of Nations" Coleridge already imagines this state of "pestful calms" and the blessed moment of release from it, which comes like a fresh, stiffening wind, in a maritime image of renewed potency and creative power:

. . . When Love rose glittering, and his gorgeous wings
Over the abyss fluttered with such glad noise,
As what time after long and pestful calms,
With slimy shapes and miscreated life
Poisoning the vast Pacific, the fresh breeze
Wakens the merchant-sail uprising.[18]

Coleridge sensed that he was grappling with a major theme, though the elements were still confused. The allegorical bird-wing and actual sea-breeze melt into each other in an uneasy mixture of Miltonic simile and scientific observation, in which the "miscreated life" has ambiguous meaning. He noted brusquely on the manuscript: "These are very fine Lines, tho' I say it, that should not: but, hang me, if I know or ever did know the meaning of them, tho' my own composition."[19]

The implication of this apparently throw-away gesture is significant, however; for the first time he is suggesting that poetry may be written from somewhere outside conscious control.

3

On 22 February, Charles Lloyd – who had been staying with Lamb in London – returned to continue his improving life with the Coleridges. He took up residence in the third bedroom of the cottage, and spread himself into the parlour below. He brought a selection of his own and Lamb's poems, which Coleridge generously offered to have printed as an appendix to the new edition, on fraternal principles, and also shrewdly hoping for an increased sale in the Midlands where Lloyd *père* had influence.[20] Cottle was by now "clamorous" about completed copy for the new edition.

However, Lloyd's return soon disrupted the cottage routine and work-rhythms. Coleridge had just received through Bowles a valuable commission to write a verse tragedy for Richard Brinsley Sheridan, which he promised to "introduce on Drury Lane Theatre with every possible advantage".[21] Coleridge needed to concentrate all his efforts, and immediately set about a "sketch" for the play, which was to be a Spanish melodrama, "romantic & wild & somewhat terrible", with Mrs Siddons and the famous tragic actor, John Kemble, in mind.[22]

But Lloyd, as everyone should have surely realised by now, was a highly unstable young man with a difficult father-relationship and, over-excited by Coleridge's whirling presence, he almost immediately began having epileptic seizures again. By 16 March he had produced five fits in ten days, "all of them followed by a continued and agonizing Delirium of five or six hours".[23] Coleridge sat up through the nights, soothing the patient with endless talk, and physically restraining him when he became violent. Often he did not get to bed before dawn, "with aching temples & a feeble frame"; it was like his army days in the Pest House all over again. It was hopeless for writing, though it may have provided a different kind of imaginative stimulation. He thought Lloyd's "nervous complaint" was the result of the death of a woman he had idolised: "his affection for her was almost too great."[24]

Lloyd was eventually despatched back to the Midlands, where he was put under the care of Dr Erasmus Darwin in a sanatorium at Lichfield, the best treatment that money could buy. His eventual recovery was aided by the writing of a mischievous and not unreadable novel, *Edmund Oliver*, in which he recorded his adventures among the *literati* by drawing lightly disguised portraits of William Godwin, Mary Wollstonecraft, and Coleridge himself – who appears as an opium-hazed hero volunteering for the dragoons. Coleridge was to feel understandably bitter about this return for his kindness. Lloyd was perhaps the least successful of all his long line of protégés.*

---

* Charles Lloyd's later vengefulness against Coleridge (a premonition of Hazlitt's) is difficult to understand, and there may be aspects of the relationship at Bristol and Stowey which will always remain obscure. It was certainly intense, and Coleridge wrote him several poems of counsel, including, "Addressed to a Young Man of Fortune Who Abandoned Himself To an Indolent and Causeless Melancholy", and a sonnet in which he refers to Charles as "the soaring Youth with slacken'd Wing". There is also a long topographical poem describing them climbing together in the hills around Bristol, which contains this passage:

> Together thus, the world's vain turmoil left,
> Stretch'd on the crag, and shadow'd by the pine,
> And bending o'er the clear delicious fount,
> Ah! dearest youth! it were a lot divine
> To cheat our noons in moralising mood,
> While west-winds fann'd our temples toil-bedew'd.
> (*P.W.*, p. 156)

Coleridge attracted ardent, youthful, admirers, often at some crisis point in their lives, encouraging confessions and confidences; but he did not have the equanimity or emotional detachment to become a fatherly mentor or tranquil friend, until much later. Indeed one might suggest that part of Coleridge's genius was for wholly disrupting the lives and expectations of most of those who came in close contact with him. (See Bibliography, Henry James.)

4

For the first time that year, Coleridge left Stowey at the end of March to visit Cottle in Bristol, breaking off his autobiographical letters to Poole, and leaving his dramatic sketch in a state "too chaotic to be transmitted at present". He was depressed by his financial situation and discouraged with his reviewing, which had consisted largely of the popular gothic novels then in high fashion – M. G. Lewis' *The Monk*, Ann Radcliffe's *The Italian* – and which seemed increasingly hollow to him. "Indeed I am almost weary of the Terrible . . . dungeons, and old castles, & solitary Houses by the Sea Side, & Caverns, & Woods, & extraordinary characters, & all the tribe of Horror & Mystery, have crowded on me – even to surfeiting."[25]

He felt that "every mode of life which has promised me bread and cheese" had been torn from him, one after another. He solaced himself by borrowing two volumes of Brucker's *Critical History of Philosophy*, (in Greek and Latin) from the Bristol Library, and going for a long walk across the Somerset Levels to see George Burnett at Huntspill, who was ill with jaundice. On the road back to Stowey, he fell in with a garrulous old woman who confided that young Burnett had been led astray by "a vile Jacobin villain" from Bristol, someone apparently called Coleridge. She heaped "every name of abuse that the parish of Billingsgate could supply" on the miscreant. Coleridge listened politely, "exclaiming, 'dear me!' two or three times". Having entirely won the woman's heart by his civilities, he had not courage enough "to undeceive her".[26]

He still felt "depression too dreadful to be described" on his return to Stowey, and apologised to Cottle for his low spirits. The one thing that cheered him was a brief, unexpected visit from William Wordsworth (probably encouraged by Cottle) who was walking back from Bristol to Racedown in Dorset, and made a detour to call in at Stowey in early April. Wordsworth was also writing a verse play, *The Borderers*, and they discussed the possibilities of actually getting their work produced in London. Since they had already been exchanging manuscripts, it seems likely that they agreed to read the finished dramas together later in the summer.

They also grumbled together about Southey's irritating fluency in producing verse, which would certainly make "literature more *profitable to him*"; and Coleridge seems to have been amused at Wordsworth's solemn but just complaint that "Southey writes *too much at his ease* – that he seldom 'feels his burthened breast – Heaving beneath th' incumbent Deity.'"[27] He told Cottle: "Wordsworth's conversation, etc roused me somewhat." Years later he would also recall the "sudden effect" of hearing Wordsworth read from his manuscript of "Salisbury Plain", the rich and powerful northern voice bringing the "union of deep feeling with profound thought", that stirred Coleridge profoundly.[28]

The coming of spring to the Quantocks, the lengthening days, the seductive trails of wild flowers leading up into the combes above Stowey, must also have stimulated him. Coleridge buckled down to his work again, and by 10 May had written 1,500 lines of his Spanish tragedy, to be called *Osorio.* "T. Poole is in extacies with it – he says, it has passion, well-conducted plot, stage effect, & the spirit of poetic language without the technicalities."[29]

During this period Coleridge must have been producing something like fifty lines of blank verse a day, and a tremendous sense of liberation came over him. From the mundane problems of "bread and cheese", his eyes lifted to the hills of the Quantocks and his imagination soared towards immortal works. It was at this time that he produced a celebrated description of how a modern Epic poem should be produced, with massive preparatory labours worthy of some intellectual Hercules. The subject had perhaps arisen in the conversation with Wordsworth. There is a perceptible undertone of self-parody so characteristic of Coleridge, since it was a definition given to his publisher Cottle who had been waiting so patiently, week after week, for the poet to finish his proof corrections.

> Observe the march of Milton – his severe application, his laborious polish, his deep metaphysical researches, his prayers to God before he began his great poem, all that could lift and swell his intellect, became his daily food. I should not think of devoting less than 20 years to an Epic Poem. Ten to collect materials and warm my mind with universal science. I would be a tolerable Mathematician, I would thoroughly know Mechanics, Hydrostatics, Optics, and Astronomy, Botany, Metallurgy, Fossilism, Chemistry, Geology, Anatomy, Medicine – then the *mind of man* – then the *minds of men* in all Travels, Voyages and Histories. So I would spend ten years – the next five to the composition of the poem – and the five last to the correction of it. So I would write haply not unhearing of that divine and rightly-whispering Voice, which speaks to mighty minds of predestined Garlands, starry and unwithering.[30]

Coleridge was writing at a time when the possibilities of such a Renaissance scope of universal knowledge were just beginning to foreclose; and it is this awareness as much as anything which gives the passage its curious mixture of nobility and self-mockery. Already the great polymaths like Darwin and Priestley were beginning to seem like men of a former age, "curiosities". But there is also the sense that such huge, leisured, deployments of time were no longer possible for a literary man.

Ironically, Coleridge received in early May a library demand for the immediate return of the Brucker volumes. He replied acidly that he supposed that the "learned & ingenuous" Library Committee might well read 2,400 pages of "*close printed Greek & Latin*" in three weeks, but that he himself pretended to "no such intenseness of application or rapidity of Genius".[31]

Yet his instinct that the modern Epic subject must now centre on "the mind of man", through "travels, voyages and histories", shows a shift of poetic focus characteristic of the new Romantic age. The Epic could no longer draw on classical or religious mythology for the framework of its action. It must become contemporary with the world of scientific, anthropological, and psychological exploration: it must centre in some way on the drama of self-knowledge, on the growth of consciousness and civilisation.

It was these great themes that he would begin to press steadily upon Wordsworth in the coming months and years, and which would profoundly affect Coleridge's own poetry and reflective prose. It was these "foundations" that he had set about exploring in his retreat from conventional politics and literature at Nether Stowey.

5

Coleridge laboured on throughout May, working on *Osorio* and completing the proof corrections to the *Poems*. Lamb heard nothing from him until early June, but learning of Lloyd's breakdown, wrote anxiously for news: "God bless us all, and shield us from insanity, which is 'the sorest malady of all'."[32] Poole provided steady support, and it was now that Coleridge began his regular visits through the orchard gate, under the lime trees, and up the iron outdoor staircase that led to Poole's "book parlour". This was a low vaulted chamber at the back of the house, with fireplace and well-stocked shelves, which provided Coleridge with an invaluable study where he could isolate himself from the bustle of the cottage.

It was perhaps Poole too, who, musing on the autobiographical letters, inspired Cottle to ask for a dedicatory piece for the new edition. Cottle later recalled shrewdly of his author:

> He appeared like a being dropt from the clouds, without tie or connexion on earth; and during the years in which I knew him, he never once visited (that I could learn) any one of his relations, nor exchanged a letter with them. It used to fill myself and others with concern, and the deepest astonishment, that such a man should, apparently, be abandoned. On some occasions, I urged him to break through all impediments, and go and visit his friends, but this his high spirits could not brook. I then pressed him to dedicate his Poems to one of his relatives, his brother George, of whom he occasionally spoke with peculiar kindness.[33]

In fact Coleridge had visited Ottery St Mary the previous summer, but both Cottle and Poole correctly divined the painful division in the family and Coleridge's deepening sense of being "abandoned". After several days of thoughtful silence, Coleridge agreed to Cottle's suggestion, and wrote the subtle and reflective Conversation poem "To the Rev. George Coleridge", which he dated Nether Stowey, 26 May 1797.[34]

Arising directly from his autobiographical letters to Poole which describe his childhood, the poem explores his sense of being "too soon transplanted" from Ottery, and his feeling "still most a stranger, most with naked heart / At mine own home and birth-place." He hints at the mistakes and storms of his adolescence, and the various false friends (among whom one may assume Southey) who led him astray. His poetic development is now given central significance from the "wild firstling-lays" of his schooldays, to the "deeper notes" that have been tuned "to these tumultuous times". He dedicates all these to George, while apologising in advance for any that may strike "discordant" on his brother's "milder mind". He repeatedly calls George his "earliest Friend", and the whole tone is grateful and conciliatory.

Coleridge also celebrates his new life at Stowey, in what he calls with a touch of impious humour his "lowly shed", where he is blessed as both husband and father, and has "one Friend" (Poole) "beneath the impervious cover of one oak". The tree is here both symbol of protection, and of family continuity, of being rooted into his destiny at Stowey in a way he never achieved at Ottery. (One thinks of Gainsborough's picture of "Mr and Mrs Robert Andrews".)

His growing ambitions as a poet and writer are also expressed, once again in words very close to those used at the end of his letter on Epic poetry to Cottle:

> . . . not unhearing
> Of that divine and nightly-whispering Voice,
> Which from my childhood to maturer years
> Spake to me of predestinated wreaths,
> Bright with no fading colours![35]

This shows an increasing confidence in his powers, despite the wistful humour that still plays about the heroic phrasing.

The picture which he now draws of his life with Sara and Poole at the Lime Street cottage and in the adjoining orchard, is full of tender delight. The homely cottage scenes he had described the previous year at Clevedon are given an added dimension by drawing in the seasonal imagery of the Quantocks for the first time. In a way this is the heart of the new Conversation Poem. The passage is alive with immediate domestic detail, and yet given psychological depth by the extended family awareness which reaches towards the absent George. It is, says Coleridge, in reflecting on George's kind influence on his lonely childhood that he most feels the new richness of his family life. The past irradiates the present and gives his long-dreamt "rustic scheme" new meaning and happiness in Stowey. Though he does not explicitly mention Hartley, the imagery of "Frost at Midnight" is again steadily forming, and the terms of a new Romantic Pastoral are vividly set in place, which can contain both winter and springtime:

> Oh! 'tis to me an ever new delight,
> To talk of thee and thine: or when the blast
> Of the shrill winter, rattling our rude sash,
> Endears the cleanly hearth and social bowl;
> Or when, as now, on some delicious eve,
> We in our sweet sequester'd orchard-plot
> Sit on the tree crook'd earth-ward; whose old boughs,
> That hang above us in an arborous roof,
> Stirr'd by the faint gale of departing May,
> Send their loose blossoms slanting o'er our heads![36]

That stream of white blossoms gains a quiet metaphorical force, like the stream of their talk, whirling outwards through time, and spreading over the whole countryside. It somehow manages to suggest more poetry, and more friendships, to come.

Many years later, Coleridge made a sad note on his copy of the *Poems* that the book displeased his brother George, who thought "his character endangered by the Dedication".[37] Whether this was for political reasons, or because he felt Coleridge had spoken too openly of his unhappy childhood (or had retrospectively invented it) is not clear.

Coleridge was delighted with the completion of the volume in July, though characteristically he sent a vast list of errata to Cottle when the sheets were already bound, blithely suggesting that his publisher "might employ a boy for sixpence or a shilling to go thro' them & with a fine pen, and dainty ink, make the alterations in each volume". The collection finally appeared on 28 October 1797. The reviewers noted the efforts he had made to simplify his style, and purge his "double-epithets" (as described in his new preface). The *Critical Review*, already sensing his new poetic direction and authority, especially picked out for praise the dedicatory poem to George, the "Sonnet: To the River Otter", and the "Reflections on having left a Place of Retirement", an extremely perceptive choice.[38]

6

Almost the moment he had delivered the final copy for the *Poems* to Bristol, Coleridge set out on a long summer walk through the Vale of Taunton and over the Black Down Hills to visit Wordsworth at Racedown. He carried with him the completed first draft of *Osorio*, as he had promised. He preached at the Unitarian chapel at Bridgwater on Sunday 4 June, and then pounded the forty-odd miles southwards in a day and a half, reaching the road going down from Crewkerne on the early evening of 5 June.

Here, at a field gate that still exists, he paused to look over the little valley of the River Synderford, from the hillside near Pilsdon Pen. Below him, across a field of corn, he could see the square, brick Georgian façade of Racedown Lodge among a little grove of beech trees, with a woman's figure working in the vegetable garden behind. She looked up, and he vaulted the gate and hurried down through corn towards her.

Dorothy Wordsworth, then twenty-five, never forgot this apparition; nor did Wordsworth. "We both have a distinct remembrance of his arrival," he said forty years later; "he did not keep to the high road, but leaped over a gate and bounded down a pathless field by which he cut off an angle."[39] His impetuosity seemed a portent. Coleridge remained at Racedown for a fortnight, during which two of the greatest friendships of his life were formed irrevocably, for good and ill.

They began by immediately reading each other's plays, out loud. Both were impressed by what they heard, and Coleridge sent an ecstatic report to Cottle on 8 June.

> Wordsworth admires my Tragedy – which gives me great hopes. Wordsworth has written a Tragedy himself. I speak with heart-felt sincerity & (I think) unblinded judgement, when I tell you, that I feel myself a *little man by his* side; & yet do not think myself the less man, than I formerly thought myself. – His Drama is absolutely wonderful . . . There are in the piece those *profound* touches of the human heart, which I find three or four times in "The Robbers" of Schiller, & often in Shakespeare – but in Wordsworth there are no *inequalities*.[40]

In a way, such enthusiasm was common currency for Coleridge; he had spoken in similar terms on first meeting Southey. But he seemed genuinely unaware of the equally dazzling effect he produced on the Wordsworths, a much rarer reaction for them. Dorothy expressed this in an intimate letter to her friend Mary Hutchinson, who had just left Racedown. For her – and the clear implication is, for Wordsworth also – Coleridge seemed a sort of incarnation of the Romantic poetic personality. His impact was physical as much as intellectual. It was not merely his writing: it was his talk, his face, his darting intelligence, his eyes, his warmth, his supreme attention and response to everything around him. For the quietly observant Dorothy, he was like some astonishing natural phenomenon.

> You had a great loss in not seeing Coleridge. He is a wonderful man. His conversation teems with soul, mind and spirit. Then he is so benevolent, so good tempered and cheerful, and, like William, interests himself so much about every little trifle.
>
> At first I thought him very plain, that is, for about three minutes;

> he is pale and thin, has a wide mouth, thick lips, and not very good teeth, longish loose-growing half-curling rough black hair. But if you hear him speak for five minutes you think no more of them.
>
> His eye is large and full, not dark but grey; such an eye as would receive from a heavy soul the dullest expression; but it speaks every emotion of his animated mind; it has more of the "poet's eye in a fine frenzy rolling" than I ever witnessed. He has fine dark eye-brows and an overhanging forehead.[41]

The distinguishing word here is "wonderful". It is a word used repeatedly by both Dorothy and William of Coleridge, and not used lightly by either of them. Dorothy also catches what no painted portrait could ever do, Coleridge's movement and animation, his quickness of response – to "every little trifle" – and the mobility of his face and eyes which *acted out* his emotions, as in the reference to Hamlet. It is interesting that both descriptions use a Shakespearean standard: for Coleridge, Wordsworth *writes* like Shakespeare; for Dorothy, Coleridge *behaves* like a Shakespearean vision of the poet.

Dorothy perceives too that subtle principle of contradiction in him, expressed by the large heavy mouth with its "not very good" teeth, and the contrasting eyes with their extraordinary life and power. Her instinctive tenderness towards him is unconsciously revealed in the curious impression that the large, and ebullient Coleridge was somehow "pale and thin", at their first meeting.

These initial impressions at Racedown are most fascinating for the light they throw on the way the friendship would develop in the early years: Coleridge would give Wordsworth unstinting critical admiration for his work, and greatly influence its direction; while the Wordsworths would support Coleridge emotionally, by confirming his fluctuating and uncertain sense of his own identity and genius. Wordsworth wanted above all else to be a great poet, and Coleridge told him he was; Coleridge wanted above all else to be poetically wonderful and intellectually inspiring, and the Wordsworths showed him this was true. Each gave the other his ideal self; it was the essence of Romantic friendship.

This friendship became, in terms of literary influence, the most important of both their lives; and as a combined force it would prove the most powerful in the history of English Romanticism. Over the next fifteen years it went through many changes. To start with, though Coleridge was the younger man (Wordsworth being then twenty-seven), he was intellectually the dominant partner. He quickly exploded, for example, Wordsworth's naïve political radicalism and faith in Godwinian theories of social progress. But within three years this domination would alter decisively.

The friendship was based on an attraction of temperamental opposites: Coleridge was fleshy, rumbustious, excitable, overflowing with talk and animal sympathies; while Wordsworth was tall, bony, taciturn, and powerfully self-sufficient. From the beginning there was a form of power-struggle, with each asserting different kinds of creative force. Intellectually the two men were markedly opposed in type and background. Coleridge, with his enormous reading, his scholarship, his religious enthusiasm, his knowledge of classical and European literatures, his scientific interests, his emotional approach to politics, was a man of speculation, restless enquiry and self-questioning. While Wordsworth, with his intense childhood loyalties, his harrowing experiences in revolutionary Paris, his love-affair with Annette Vallon in Blois and Orléans (which had produced an illegitimate child), and his passionate responses to the natural world, was a man of physical experience and steadily accumulating moral certainties by which ideas might be judged and settled. Intellectually, Coleridge was a huge river; while Wordsworth was a mighty rock.

In these early days they excited and stimulated each other by these very contrasts; and Dorothy held them together. As a threesome they immediately found many pleasures in common – reading poetry aloud, walking and scrambling through the countryside, picnicking, talking long into the night, and matching (as only friends can) the sublime against the ridiculous. Though real intimacy only came later, towards the end of this first summer, within the first few days Coleridge had done enough to bring Wordsworth's self-imposed isolation in Dorset to an end.

The remainder of the fortnight at Racedown was spent tramping over the escarpment of the Black Down Hills, from where they could glimpse the sea, reading poetry in the candle-lit parlour, and doing further work on their plays. Coleridge fired off delighted reports in all directions – "this is a lovely country – & Wordsworth a great man" – and was seized with a new vision of a Pantisocratic circle of his friends in the Quantocks.[42] Suddenly invitations were flying to every quarter: Charles and Mary Lamb must come to Stowey, John and Stella Thelwall must come to Stowey, above all William and Dorothy must come to Stowey. By July, in the face of every domestic impracticality, he had enticed most of them into the Quantocks.

He even made a throw at Southey: "so divine and wild is the

country that I am sure it would increase your stock of images ... Edith Southey & Sara may not have another opportunity of seeing each other – & Wordsworth is very solicitous to know you – & Miss Wordsworth is a most exquisite young woman in her mind, & heart."[43]

Coleridge had little difficulty in sweeping away the Wordsworths from Dorset with his impetuosity. On 28 June he was back in Lime Street with William, explaining his plan to Sara, and installing his guest in the third bedroom. By 2 July he had hired a trap, driven back to Racedown, collected Dorothy and their books and luggage, and returned over "forty miles of execrable road ... [I] am now no inexpert whip."[44] On 7 July Charles Lamb arrived as well, and the cottage bulged with makeshift beds, and the chaos of picnic meals.*

Poole was persuaded to look for a property for Wordsworth to rent, and within a week had lighted upon the country house of Alfoxden, (owned by the absent St Aubin family) at Holford, four miles west of Stowey. It was a fine, three-storey mansion set in a deer park high on the edge of the Quantocks above Hodder's Combe, where the old coach road climbs through a beautiful beech hanger up Longstone Hill. Meanwhile the party made long rambles over Quantock from Stowey, exploring all the courses of the streams that run from the ancient Stone Age fort on Dowsborough Hill, with their enchanting names – Five Lords Combe, Butterfly Combe, Seven Wells Wood.

By mid-July, Coleridge wrote in triumph: "I brought [Wordsworth] and his Sister back with me & here I have *settled them* –. By a combination of curious circumstances a gentleman's seat, with a park & woods, elegantly & completely *furnished* – with 9 *lodging rooms*, three parlours & a Hall – in a most beautiful & romantic situation by the sea side – 4 miles from Stowey – this we have got for Wordsworth at the rent of *£23 a year, taxes included!!*"[45] Dorothy echoed this delight: "There is everything here: sea, woods wild as fancy ever

---

*Mary Lamb, now legally released from her asylum under her brother's care and power of attorney, was not sufficiently recovered to accompany Charles on such a visit. Lamb's reiterated refusal to bring her to Stowey on another occasion, in January 1798, throws a revealing side-light on the effect of Coleridge's ebullient company in these Quantock months: "your invitation went to my very heart – but you have a power of exciting interest, of leading all hearts captive, too forcible to admit of Mary's being with you –. I consider her perpetually on the brink of madness –. I think, you would almost make her dance within an inch of the precipice – she must be with duller fancies, & cooler intellects." (*Lamb*, I, p. 127)

painted, brooks clear and pebbly as in Cumberland, villages so romantic . . . Walks extend for miles over the hill-tops; the great beauty of which is their wild simplicity . . ."[46] But the "principal inducement" in settling there, she told Mary Hutchinson, was "Coleridge's society". By 17 July, John Thelwall had also arrived in Coleridge's kingdom.

7

This sudden influx of friends in the summer of 1797, and the new open-air existence of hill-walking, eating together, and talking poetry long into the night, had a profound effect on Coleridge's imaginative life and brought new energy into his writing. It also affected his relations with Sara. Two domestic incidents are suggestive of this turmoil. On 4 July, in the chaotic bustle of the cottage, Sara accidently emptied a skillet of boiling milk over Coleridge's foot, laming him for several days. Then, towards the end of the month, Sara had a miscarriage – "in so early a stage, that it occasioned but little pain, one day's indisposition, and no confinement." Coleridge's anxiety about this is expressed obliquely in his comment to Josiah Wade: "Indeed, the circumstance is quite unknown, except to me. My little Hartley grows a beautiful child."[47]

It was while sitting in Poole's arbour under the lime trees, recuperating from his burn, that Coleridge wrote his next Conversation Poem, "This Lime-Tree Bower My Prison", during a day when Lamb, Sara, and the Wordsworths were out on the Quantocks. The poem, which imagines their walk in a brilliant series of topographical reflections, was originally addressed to all of them: "my gentle-hearted Charles . . . My Sara and my Friends".[48] But later, he dropped Sara's name from the published text, as if she had ceased to share in the experience.

Yet a deepening sense of the beauty and fragility of life now entered steadily into both his letters and poetry. Surrounded by these friends, and especially the Wordsworths, he was happier and more expansive than ever before. His imagination began to take on a heightened responsiveness, almost as if the Wordsworths were willing him to become more fully himself. Something of this shows in his famous description of Dorothy, given to Cottle in early July. He takes three lines from his unpublished "Destiny of Nations", and gives them a sudden human relevance (far greater than in the original poem).

Coleridge wrote of Dorothy: "She is a woman indeed! – in mind, I mean, & heart . . . her manners are simple, ardent, impressive –

> In every motion her most innocent soul
> Outbeams so brightly, that who saw would say,
> Guilt was a thing impossible in her. –

Her information various – her eye watchful in minutest observation of nature – and her taste a perfect electrometer – it bends, protrudes, and draws in, at subtlest beauties & most recondite faults."[49] Is this simply Dorothy, or some half-projected image of the poet as child of nature? A shadow even of the future Christabel? Coleridge's image of the electrometer (which he also later used in a letter to Thelwall) is always associated with the action of the imagination: a tiny piece of exquisite gold foil in a glass vacuum, responding to minute fluctuations of an external electrical charge. Years later, he also recalled how Dorothy's response to his "devilish clever" reviewing, made him feel he was cheapening his own literary gifts.

The same heightened directness of response appears in the new poem, which draws more powerfully than ever on the Quantocks imagery. It vividly evokes the bare "springy" heath of the upper hills, the damp "ferny" dark of Holford Combe and its waterfall, the "deep radiance" of the evening sunlight on Poole's garden of limes, walnut trees and ancient ivy. Coleridge sees these both through his own eyes, and those of Charles Lamb, who "hast pined / And hunger'd after Nature, many a year, / In the great City pent": as they both had done in his romantic mythology of childhood. (Lamb allowed this myth-making – though in reality he loved the "great City" above everything – but violently objected to the term "gentle-hearted Charles", suggesting instead "drunken-dog, ragged head, seld-shaven, odd-ey'd, stuttering, or any other epithet which truly and properly belongs".)[50]

The subtlety of the poem lies in the constant series of transpositions between the "prison" of Poole's lime-tree arbour, down in the village, where Coleridge is marooned; and the panoramic freedom of the wild Quantocks above, where his friends are walking, and enjoying the wide landscape, "silent with swimming sense". By imagining his friends' feelings, and drawing on his own solitary experience of the hills, Coleridge gradually brings a powerful sense of unity to their shared delight in nature. He is freed from his "prison", and finds the "One Life" of nature embraces all of them.

The slow coming of twilight produces a sense of calm and blessing, the sacred pastoral, which is captured in the small, glowing details of the final movement of the poem, which has moved in a carefully arranged time-sequence from midday to dusk:

> . . . now the bat
> Wheels silent by, and not a swallow twitters,
> Yet still the solitary humble-bee
> Sings in the bean-flower![51]

Here the bee is an emblem of the poet himself, a continuing point of activity in the slumbering harmony that falls across the world. And the sense of homecoming and completion is also imaged in a "last rook" which flies across the "dilated glory" of the setting sun, and passes with "creaking" wings overhead. For Coleridge, and his friends, "no sound is dissonant which tells of Life". The poem closes with undertones of prayer and music like an Evensong.

Coleridge was now more conscious of these blank verse Conversation Poems forming a new development in his poetry. He told Southey in July that he was "pleased" with "This Lime-Tree Bower", and that "To the Rev. George Coleridge" was "dear" to him: "in point of *taste* I place it next to 'Low was our pretty cot', which I think the best of my poems."[52] This shows him thinking of the Conversation Poems as a group for the first time, and marks a decisive shift away from the importance he had attached to "Religious Musings" only six months before.

8

John Thelwall's arrival at Stowey caused a considerable stir in the district, and convinced many local people that some sort of Jacobin colony was being set up at Alfoxden. Charlotte Poole's diary was a faithful record of local suspicions: "We are shocked to hear that Mr Thelwall has spent some time at Stowey this week with Mr Coleridge, and consequently with Tom Poole. Alfoxden house is taken by another of the fraternity . . . To what are we coming?"[53]

At a time when there were naval mutinies in the Channel ports, and much talk of a French invasion fleet off Fishguard, this alarm was not surprising; and in August the Home Office sent down a special agent to enquire into their activities. In fact Thelwall was in headlong retreat from radical politics, having had his latest lectures broken up by "patriot" gangs, his life threatened, papers seized, and his teaching career destroyed in London. Looking for some peaceful form of subsistence farming, he immediately fell under the spell of the "rural scheme". He wrote to his wife on 18 July:

> Everything but my Stella and my babes are now banished from my mind by the enchanting retreat (the Academus of Stowey) from which I write this, and by the delightful society of Coleridge and of Wordsworth, the present occupier of Allfox Den [*sic*]. We have been having a delightful ramble today among the plantations, and along a wild, romantic dell in these grounds, through which a foaming, rushing, murmuring torrent of water winds its long artless course.[54]

It is striking that even Thelwall immediately began to write in the language of Xanadu, and use the word "Romantic". He remained for ten days.

A dinner was held at Alfoxden, at which Cottle and Wordsworth's friend, the young lawyer Basil Montagu, were also present. According to Thelwall they "passed sentence on the productions and characters of the age, burst forth in poetical flights of enthusiasm, and philosophised our minds into a state of tranquillity."[55] Another and rather different account of this literary banquet was later obtained by the Home Office agent, from a local serving man, Thomas Jones. The report read: ". . . The Sunday after Wordsworth came, he Jones was desired to wait at table, that there were fourteen persons at dinner. Poole and Coldridge [*sic*] were there, and there was a little stout man with dark cropt hair and wore a White Hat and Glasses [Thelwall] who after dinner got up and talked so loud and was in such a passion that Jones was frightened and did not like to go near them since."[56]

It is ironic that Coleridge, far from being converted by Thelwall's Jacobin rhetoric, only had his view confirmed as to the gulf that now separated him from the extreme English radicals. He liked Thelwall as much as he disliked his politics, and explained this paradox in a crisp letter to Josiah Wade on 1 August.

> John Thelwall is a very warm hearted honest man – and disagreeing, as we do, on almost every point of religion, of morals, of politics, and of philosophy; we like each other uncommonly well –

> He is a great favorite with Sara. *Energetic Activity*, of *mind* and of *heart*, is his Master-feature ... he is intrepid, eloquent, and – honest. – Perhaps the only *acting* Democrat, that *is* honest for the *Patriots* are ragged cattle – a most execrable herd – arrogant because they are ignorant, and boastful of the strength of reason, because they have never tried it enough to know its *weakness*. – O my poor Country! The Clouds cover thee ...[57]

It was feelings like these that would shape the complex self-examination of his political loyalties the following spring, in "Fears in Solitude".

Sara approved much of Thelwall: it was his "energetic activity" more than his politics that doubtless attracted her; and also perhaps a touch of gallantry, for he enjoyed chatting to her over the washtub and admired her figure.[58] Perhaps she thought he would put her husband on his mettle. Thelwall always afterwards entertained the most idyllic memories of Stowey and Alfoxden, describing them in glowing Pantisocratic terms in a surprisingly good blank verse poem, evidently inspired by Coleridge, "Lines written at Bridgwater" on 27 July, which draws a vivid picture of the rural retreat which he longs to join.

He imagines the "sequester'd dell" where he might build a "low cot" next to Coleridge's ("My Samuel!"), sharing the cultivation of their "little garden plots", and long hours of evening talk:

> Ah! 'twould be sweet, beneath the neighbouring thatch
> In philosophic amity to dwell ...
> To share our frugal viands, and the bowl
> Sparkling with home-brew'd beverage: – by our sides
> Thy Sara, and my Susan; and perchance,
> All foxden's musing tenant, and the maid
> Of ardent eye, who, with fraternal love,
> Sweetens his solitude. With these should join
> Arcadian Poole ... O it would be
> A Golden Age reviv'd![59]

There is some indication that Coleridge, for his part, rather teased the great seditionist. "We were once sitting in a beautiful recess in the Quantocks, when I said to him, 'Citizen John, this is a fine place to talk treason in!' – 'Nay! Citizen Samuel,' replied he, 'it is rather a place to make a man forget that there is any necessity for treason!'"[60]* Wordsworth also recalled this incident taking place in the glen at Alfoxden.[61]

On another occasion, Coleridge wittily attacked Thelwall's idea that a child should be brought up as an agnostic until it reached an age of discretion to choose between religion and atheism. "I showed him my garden, and told him it was my botanical garden. 'How so?' said he, 'it is covered with weeds.' – 'Oh,' I replied, '*that* is only because it has not yet come to its age of discretion and choice. The weeds, you see, have taken the liberty to grow, and I thought it unfair in me to *prejudice* the soil towards roses and strawberries.'"[62] This story Coleridge retold so often in later life, improving it with each retelling, that it may have ended up as largely a fiction; if so, it was because the ideal of imaginatively "cultivating" the mind had become central to his objections to pure "rationalism". It does however suggest that his actual gardening routine at the cottage had rather lapsed since May. But it was the image, and the concept, that he had harvested; rather than the fruits and flowers.

Thelwall left the Quantocks at the end of July, to prospect in Wales; but throughout August he begged Coleridge to obtain him a permanent cottage in the Quantocks area, so he could join the circle. Coleridge made great efforts to help him, on one occasion walking forty-one miles back from Bristol where he had intercepted Thelwall's mislaid trunk; on another, writing an empassioned letter to John Chubb, a magistrate and leading merchant in Bridgwater, begging him to obtain Thelwall a cottage "*anywhere* 5 or 6 miles round Stowey." He argued that "Truth & Liberty" made it their duty

*Some twenty years later Thelwall revoked all his Arcadian fantasies and bitterly attacked Coleridge for his political apostasy. He angrily and minutely annotated Coleridge's account of the Stowey months in a copy of the *Biographia* (which has survived) and accused him of backsliding and humbug. At Stowey, Thelwall claims to have "found him a decided Leveller – abusing the democrats for their hypocritical moderatism", and preaching "equality of property – or rather abolition of all property". This could well be the Coleridge of 1794, but does not sound like the Quantocks poet of 1797, nor indeed like the cultivator of little private garden plots next to whom Thelwall wished to dwell in "philosophic amity". He also excoriated Coleridge for saying that his principles were "opposite" to those of Jacobinism or democracy, by that time. "Mr. C. was indeed far from Democracy, because he was far beyond it, I well remember – for he was a down right zealous leveller & indeed in one of the worst senses of the word he was a Jacobin, a man of blood. – Does he forget the letters he wrote to me (& which I believe I yet have) acknowledging the justice of my castigation of him for the violence, and sanguinary tendency of some of his doctrines. –" (Bulletin of the New York Public Library, XXX, 1970.) We do have those letters, but they do not bear Thelwall out. Nevertheless, exaggerating and unreliable as Thelwall was, his sense that Coleridge had shifted ground and evaded awkward questions in the *Biographia* is certainly true. (See Bibliography, E. P. Thompson.)

despite "odium & inconvenience" to find him a home. Coleridge evidently saw his Quantocks community as a place for political discussion and re-education as far as Jacobin radicals like Thelwall were concerned. If revolution – "the day of darkness & tempest" – should come, then Thelwall, with his acknowledged influence on the "lower classes", could be taught "tolerance" and "disciplined into patience" first. In the Quantocks he would find "the society of men equal to himself in talents, & probably superior in acquired knowledge," to perform this essential act of political enlightenment.[63] Here it is possible to feel that Coleridge was hedging his political bets.

Yet the situation was extremely delicate at Stowey, and even Arcadian Poole was under investigation by the Home Office, particularly with regards to his Poor Man Benefit Club, a group he had set up for the unemployed. When Coleridge wrote to Thelwall at Swansea on 21 August, he was not being alarmist.

> Very great odium T. Poole incurred by bringing *me* here – my peaceable manners & known attachment to Christianity had almost worn it away – when Wordsworth came & he likewise by T. Poole's agency settled here – You cannot conceive the tumult, calumnies, & apparatus of threatened persecutions which this event has occasioned round about us. If *you* too should come, I am afraid, that even riots & dangerous riots might be the consequence . . . what can it be less than plot & damned conspiracy – a school for the propagation of demagogy & atheism?"[64]

The special agent's report of 15 August referred to rumours in the Globe Inn that they were "people that will do as much harm, as All the French can do"; and described them as "a mischievous gang of disaffected Englishmen". The following day he reported that "the inhabitants of Alfoxton House are a Sett of violent Democrats".[65] Coleridge had some knowledge of this investigation, though years later in the *Biographia* he deliberately chose to describe it comically as the tale of "Spy Nozy", based on the agent's misunderstanding of his discussion with Wordsworth of the philosopher Spinoza. But the comedy was a characteristic cover-up, and the matter at the time was wholly serious.

In the end no house was obtained for Thelwall, and Coleridge was reduced to advising him to temporise until the situation had calmed down. "When the *monstrosity* of the thing is gone off, & the people shall have begun to consider you, as a man whose mouth won't eat them – & whose pocket is better adapted for a bundle of sonnets than the transportation or ambush-place of a French army – then you may take a *house*."[66] In the event, Thelwall settled with his family in Wales the following year, and was much persecuted even there.

9

Throughout the long summer days, and moonlit nights, of August and September 1797, Coleridge, Wordsworth and Dorothy continued their exploration of the Quantocks. (Lamb had returned to London, and Sara seemed reluctant to venture forth on the hills since her miscarriage, though she sometimes walked over with Hartley to Alfoxden for meals.) One of their favourite pursuits was tracking the converging course of the streams from Dowsborough Hill, and following them down to the sea at Kilve. They began to work like *plein-air* painters, taking elaborate notes of the varied effects of light on the landscape, of plants and water, of wind and cloud and starlight. Night walks were as frequent as daylight ones, and Dorothy's Journal (which begins in January1798) shows that this continued into the winter.[67]

There was one wonderful glimpse of this process in the Home Office report for 11 August, which is particularly vivid precisely because the special agent completely misinterpreted what had been seen and overheard. It is a classic description of Romantic poets at work, because it is recorded in absolute ignorance – or innocence – of the literary significance of what was being done.

Describing Wordsworth and Dorothy as "an emigrant family", the report engagingly presents their nefarious activities with Coleridge.

> The man has Camp Stools, which he and his visitors take with them when they go about the country upon their nocturnal or diurnal excursions, and have also a Portfolio in which they enter their observations, which they have been heard to say were almost finished. They have been heard to say that they should be rewarded for them, and were very attentive to the River near them – probably the River coming within a mile or two of Alfoxton from Bridgwater. These people may *possibly* be under Agents to some principal at Bristol.[68]

An additional report has them asking whether the Holford stream was navigable, and "examining the Brook quite down to the Sea". The agent clearly thought they were fifth columnists.

Coleridge could never have seen these reports in his lifetime, though he recounts in the *Biographia* how it was his own landlord at the Globe who finally disabused the agent, after poor "Spy Nozy" had spent hours listening to their conversations on the sea bank ("our favourite seat") at Kilve. The landlord confided to the agent: "Why, folks do say, your honor! as how he is a *Poet*, and that he is going to put Quantock and all about her in print."[69] In fact the long poem Coleridge was planning that summer was to be called "The Brook", and his preparations were remarkably close to those observed by the agent.

"My walks therefore were almost daily on the top of Quantock, and among its sloping combes. With my pencil and memorandum book in my hand, I was *making studies*, as the artists call them, and often moulding my thoughts into verse, with the objects and imagery immediately before my senses."[70] This process was revolutionary in a quite different sense from that supposed by the spy. For Coleridge was now deliberately exploring the technique of making immediate notations made from nature, which he had begun in the early Conversation Poems, and which was now steadily intensifying the quality of his vision.

Coleridge's poem "The Brook" was never written in the form he planned. But the controlling image of the river or stream occupied him throughout these months, and eventually emerged in "Kubla Khan". Initially he had thought of a lengthy reflective poem, not unlike Cowper's "The Task", which would use the evolution of the Holford stream to provide development and transitions which would not be "abrupt and arbitrary". He described this idea with marvellous clarity in the *Biographia*, in a passage that itself approaches the condition of poetry, and shows how deeply the idea had entered his mind so that it was still clear to him nearly fifteen years later.

> I sought for a subject, that should give equal room and freedom for description, incident, and impassioned reflections on men, nature, and society, yet supply in itself a natural connection to the parts, and unity to the whole. Such a subject I conceived myself to have found in a stream, traced from its source in the hills among the yellow-red moss and conical glass-shaped tufts of bent, to the first break or fall, where its drops become audible, and it begins to form a channel; thence to the peat and turf barn, itself built of the same dark squares as it sheltered; to the sheepfold; to the first cultivated plot of ground; to the lonely cottage and its bleak garden won from

> the heath; to the hamlet, the villages, the market-town, the manufactories, and the seaport.[71]

He adds, with gentle irony, that had he written it he would have dedicated it to the Home Office, "to our then Committee of Public Safety as containing the charts and maps, with which I was to have supplied the French Government in aid of their plans of invasion."

10

Coleridge was busy with these preparations for "The Brook" and working on *Osorio*, throughout August and September, and he wrote few letters. On 9 October he recommenced his autobiographical notes to Poole, remarking "from March to October – a long silence! but as it is possible, that I may have been preparing materials for future letters, the time cannot be considered as altogether subtracted from you." Between that date and 14 October he was absent for some five days from Stowey, and on his return he wrote to Bowles on the 16th that his tragedy was now "complete and neatly transcribed", but had caused him endless difficulties and much depression.[72]

It was some time during this first fortnight in October 1797 that he probably went for a long solitary walk along the coast to Lynton, exhausted from his labours, and, taken ill on his return journey, stopped off at Ash Farm above Culbone Church, where he wrote "Kubla Khan".

This, at any rate, is the implication of the circumstantial note he wrote on the earliest known manuscript of the poem (the Crewe Ms, now in the British Museum, which is reproduced in full on the end-papers of this volume). "This fragment with a good deal more, not recoverable, composed, in a sort of Reverie brought on by two grains of Opium taken to check a dysentry, at a Farm House between Porlock & Linton, a quarter of a mile from Culbone Church, in the fall of the year, 1797."

The coastal path, which runs for fifteen miles above the cliffs and woods between Porlock Bay and Lynton, is very remote at this point. On the many occasions Coleridge made this journey in 1797–8 (with the Wordsworths, with Hazlitt, and alone), he must frequently have sought food and shelter at one of the two solitary farms along the way: Ash Farm, immediately at the head of Culbone Combe; and Broomstreet Farm, some two miles west by Yenworthy Common. Either would be a natural place to break a walk from Quantock, being about thirty miles across the hills from Stowey, and it is possible he sometimes spent the night at one or other of the farms.

But Ash Farm seems the most likely setting for the composition of "Kubla Khan" since it is the closest to Culbone Church (a field path runs directly down from the farmyard into the combe) and the view from its seaward windows is perfectly described at the opening of Act V of *Osorio*, which he was working on until the middle of October.[73] In a speech given to his heroine, Alhadra, he evokes a wooded countryside near the seashore, "on the coast of Granada". But the original setting is clearly that of the Quantock Hills, and the woods running down to the Bristol Channel at Culbone, as he observed them that autumn at sunset, just as the moon began to rise above the lonely farmhouse:

> *Alhadra (alone)*
>
> The hanging woods, that touch'd by autumn seem'd
> As they were blossoming hues of fire and gold,
> The hanging woods, most lovely in decay,
> The many clouds, the sea, the rock, the sands,
> Lay in the silent moonshine; and the owl,
> (Strange! very strange!) the scritch owl only wak'd
> Sole voice, sole eye of all that world of beauty![74]

In his preface to "Kubla Khan" of 1816, Coleridge drew attention to the opening two sentences from Book 4, Chapter 13, of Purchas' *Pilgrimage* which had launched him into his opium dream at "the lonely farmhouse between Porlock and Linton".

The *Pilgrimage* (1614) is a vast anthology of travel-stories and folk-myths, covering each continent in nine separate books, an early seventeenth-century work of anthropology, which he had borrowed, perhaps from Southey who owned a copy. There are several references to it in his Notebooks of this period up to 1804[75] and Coleridge was reading it constantly – exactly the kind of work he had told Thelwall that he most favoured. In the preface Coleridge did not give the entire paragraph concerning Kubla in Xanadu. But this throws interesting light on the sacrificial drama of the final poem.

> In *Xanada* did *Cublai Can* build a stately Pallace, encompassing sixteene miles of plaine ground with a wall, wherein are fertile Meddows, pleasant Springs, delightful Streames, and all sorts of beasts of chase and game, and in the midst thereof a sumptuous house of pleasure, which may be removed from place to place.

> Here he doth abide in the months of June, July, and August, on the eight and twentieth day whereof, he departeth thence to another place to do sacrifice in this manner: He hath a Herd or Drove of Horses and Mares, about ten thousand, as white as snow; of the milke whereof none may taste, except he be of the blood of *Cingis Can*. Yea, the Tartars do these beasts great reverence, nor dare any cross their way, or go before them. According to the directions of his Astrologers or Magicians, he on the eight and twentieth day of August aforesaid, spendeth and poureth forth with his owne hands the milke of these Mares in the aire, and on the earth, to give drink to the spirits and Idols which they worship, that they may preserve the men, women, beasts, birds, corne, and other things growing on the earth.[76]

It seems clear from this beautiful passage that Coleridge's immediate source refers not only to a magic, walled, summer kingdom; but also to a form of harvest festival, or fertility sacrifice (with its repeated emphasis on milk) which is performed there in the autumn. Of course Coleridge added many other elements – the demon lover, the River Alph, the caves of ice, the Abyssinian maid. But this two-fold structure remains firmly behind the form of "Kubla Khan": the joyful construction of the summer kingdom, followed by the ritual fertility offering. His myth of creativity contains both these elements, which like Shelley's "Ode to the West Wind", implies both destruction and preservation of a poetic paradise.*

---

*Although Coleridge gave only Samuel Purchas as his inspiration, "Kubla Khan" has been endowed with more bibliographical sources than any other poem in the English language. Among the more convincing are: Milton's *Paradise Lost*; Plato's *Phaedrus and Ion*; James Bruce's *Travels to Discover the Source of the Nile*; William Bartram's *Travels through North and South Carolina*; Thomas Burnet's *Sacred Theory of the Earth*; Samuel Johnson's *Rasselas*; Chatterton's *"African Eclogues"*; Mary Wollstonecraft's *A Short Residence in Sweden* . . . (See for example J. L. Lowes, *The Road to Xanadu*, 1927, and Picador 1978; and Elisabeth Schneider, *Coleridge, Opium and 'Kubla Khan'*, Chicago 1953.) But any footwalker can still discover the most striking topographical "source" for themselves: it lies in what might be called the erotic, magical geography of Culbone Combe seen from Ash Farm. Between the smooth curved flanks of the coastal hills, a thickly wooded gulley runs down to the sea (the "romantic chasm"), enclosing a hidden stream which gushes beneath the tiny medieval chapel of Culbone, a plague-church and "sacred site" since Anglo-Saxon and possibly pre-Christian times. The place is as remote and mysterious as ever, and even in modern times has attracted "healing" communities such as that run by the West Country potters, Wastel and Joan Cooper in the 1970s. In the late eighteenth century this mystical character of the combe was already recognised, when the family at Ash Farm donated an iron market-cross erected there in 1770 (see *Culbone: A Spiritual History*, 1977, by Joan Cooper). But the search for "sources" is itself suggestive of a restless curiosity about the poem's meaning, which does not seem entirely "enclosed" by the text alone.

11

It is perhaps the repeated use of Ash Farm during these months which explains Coleridge's evident uncertainty about the exact date of the poem's composition. In a Notebook entry of 1810, he seems to consign the "retirement between Linton & Porlock ... the first occasion of my having recourse to Opium" to the spring of 1798 shortly after the upsetting publication of Charles Lloyd's novel.[77] Though he does not mention "Kubla Khan" in this context, which is almost as surprising as his claim to having "first" taken opium at this time. (Yet he probably means first using it as a supportive drug, rather than as a medicinal pain-killer – having "recourse" to it.) Again, in the even more detailed preface to the poem of 1816, which first mentions the inspiration he found in Samuel Purchas' book, and his famous interruption by "a person on business from Porlock", the composition is placed in "the summer of 1797". It could thus have been written any time between, say, August 1797 and May 1798.

Stranger than this, at a period when he frequently mentions his poetry in progress in his letters to friends, and even quotes it, there is no word of "Kubla Khan". Indeed, the first known reference to the poem at all occurs in a joking remark made by Dorothy in her Journal for October 1798 (in Germany), where she mentions carrying "*Kubla*" – i.e. a water-can – "to a fountain". But perhaps this simply suggests that by then the poem was often recited by Coleridge and had become proverbial among them, even if "unfinished". Another clear reference to such recitation occurs in some complimentary verse to Coleridge, written by Perdita Robinson (a poetess he met in London) in December 1800:

> I'll mark thy "sunny dome", and view
> Thy "caves of ice", thy "fields of dew" . . .[78]

All this seems to imply that Coleridge kept back the poem as one of his "wonderful" enchantments, known by heart, and chanted in private company, but never considered for publication. Indeed the intricate rhyming of the piece, and haunting cadences, are strongly contrasted with the blank verse he was mostly writing at this time. If there is any parallel, in musical form, it is with the "Song" he wrote for the third Act of *Osorio*, which begins:

Hear, sweet spirit! hear the spell
Lest a blacker charm compell!
So shall the midnight breezes swell
With thy deep long-lingering knell . . .[79]

Yet the imagery of the poem, quite apart from its source in Purchas, is strongly connected with that first autumn in the Quantocks. The sacred river, the deep romantic chasm, the threats of war, the weaving dance of the poet in his magic dell, are all prophesied in the poetry he had been recently writing. While the "caverns measureless to man" go back to his visit to Cheddar Gorge with Southey in 1794, and even perhaps to the mysterious "Pixies' Parlour" of his childhood.

Moreover the idea of the Quantocks themselves as his magic kingdom, the land of "milk and honey" he had longed for in his first opium letter to Tom Poole of winter 1796, pervades the whole vision. "Xanadu" is both the fabled domain of the Tartar Emperor Kubla, and the ideal world of poetry he was creating in his wanderings with the Wordsworths.

For the central subject of the poem, however it is interpreted in detail, is the creative and imaginative power itself. Like the hymns he had been considering to the sun and moon[80] "Kubla Khan" is a pagan celebration of creative force in the universe, which the poet shares in the moment – perhaps irrecoverable – of trance-like inspiration. In the sudden release of unconscious images, which Coleridge credited to his opium "reverie", the poet becomes both the controlling magus of this power, and also perhaps its sacrificial victim.

The haunting, almost proverbial, Romantic folk-myth which the poem seems to embody, takes much of its memorable force from the uncertainty about the poet's own fate. Does the power finally anoint him as an emperor of the Imagination, or destroy him as its slave and sacrifice?

12

One further fact connects "Kubla Khan" with Coleridge's absence from Stowey in early October 1797. On the 14th, "having been absent for a day or two", Coleridge wrote a long letter to Thelwall, very different in style from anything in their previous correspondence. Quoting the visionary passage from "This Lime-Tree Bower" about the Quantock landscape, "a Living Thing / Which acts upon the mind", and also from Alhadra's soliloquy "in the *fall of the* year", he launched into a strange dreamlike evocation of Oriental philosophy. "I should much wish, like the Indian Vishna, to float about along an infinite ocean cradled in the flower of the Lotos, & wake once in a million years for a few minutes – just to know I was going to sleep a million years more."[81] This strongly suggests the atmosphere of Purchas' book, and the opium "reveries" of Ash Farm. He also summons up a mystical view of nature, or rather, the longing to attain it, which suggests a crisis in his imaginative powers beyond anything yet examined in the Conversation Poems.

> I can *at times* feel strongly the beauties, you describe, in themselves, & for themselves – but more frequently *all things* appear little – all the knowledge, that can be acquired, child's play – the universe itself – what but an immense heap of *little* things? . . . My mind feels as if it ached to behold & know something *great* – something *one* & *indivisible* – and it is only in the faith of this that rocks or waterfalls, mountains or caverns give me the sense of sublimity or majesty![82]

This "aching" of the mind for faith seems to bear closely on the longing for creative power expressed towards the close of "Kubla Khan":

> Could I revive within me
> Her symphony and song,
> To such a deep delight 'twould win me,
> That with music loud and long,
> I would build that dome in air,
> That sunny dome! those caves of ice![83]

Most scholars now date the composition of "Kubla Khan" to October 1797, based on the evidence of the Crewe Ms and this letter to Thelwall of 14 October 1797. But there are many anomalies in the evidence, not least the strong sense of a *reprise* in the second part of the text ("A damsel with a dulcimer / In a vision once I saw") which feels very much like a conscious addition at some later period. This would be confirmed by Coleridge's almost invariable habit of giving his major poems specific dates of composition, and subsequently editing and revising them, often years afterwards.

Both May 1798 and October 1799 are alternative possibilities, when Coleridge was in the Porlock area. The latter date is particularly interesting, since he had been with Southey in Exeter, reading Southey's drafts of *Thalaba*, a poem which has many images and prose notes drawn from Purchas' *Pilgrimage.* In a letter of 15 October 1799, he refers to rheumatic illness and implies opium dosing, and adds: ". . . it leaves my sensitive Frame *so* sensitive! My enjoyments are so deep, of the fire, of the Candle, of the thought I am thinking, of the old Folio I am reading – and the silence of the silent House is so *most* & very delightful."[84]

Perhaps Coleridge actually worked further on the poem at these dates. Certainly there is one vivid verbal echo of the "Abyssinian maid" in a stanza (later cut) from "Lines Composed in a Concert Room", published in the *Morning Post* in September 1799:

> Dear Maid! whose form in solitude I seek,
> Such songs in such a mood to hear thee sing,
> It were a deep delight! . . .[85]

Nevertheless, there is no reason to disbelieve the basic truth of Coleridge's wonderful story of the "lonely farmhouse", the opium, and the old folio. And the poem is indissolubly linked with his Quantock days of walking, writing, and dreaming.

EIGHT

Mariner

1

All that autumn of 1797, Coleridge had been discussing the revival of the ballad form with Wordsworth, as the next project after the completion of *Osorio* and *The Borderers*. He was fascinated by the narrative mode, and indeed "Kubla Khan" in the form in which he originally dreamed it, as a poem of "two to three hundred lines", was perhaps a lost vision of one of his earliest ballad tales.

He had already been trying out at least two other narrative ideas, before the *Ancient Mariner* emerged. One was based on an unfinished manuscript that Wordsworth had brought from Racedown, concerning a rural tale of cottage witchcraft, "The Three Graves", which Coleridge rewrote and added two further sections to, but without completing it.[1] It is clear that he could not fully identify with the materials (sexual jealousy within a realistic domestic setting), though he would later publish it with an acute psychological commentary in *The Friend*. The other was based on a biblical story, "The Wanderings of Cain", which they had intended to write in collaboration, and which contained the significant themes of spiritual guilt and lonely exile. Here it was Coleridge who initiated the idea, though with no greater success.

Coleridge later gave a wry account of the first collaborative effort on "The Wanderings of Cain", which he and Wordsworth were to write simultaneously at Stowey and Alfoxden.

> My partner undertook the first canto: I the second: and which ever had *done first*, was to set about the third . . . Methinks I see his grand and noble countenance as at the moment when having despatched my own portion of the task at full-finger speed, I hastened to him with my manuscript – that look of humorous despondency fixed on his almost blank sheet of paper, and then its silent mock-piteous admission of failure struggling with the sense of the exceeding ridiculousness of the whole scheme – which broke up in a laugh: and the Ancient Mariner was written instead.[2]

It was now Coleridge, not Wordsworth, who was driving ahead with new poetry "at full-finger speed"; and indeed Wordsworth would write little sustained verse until the following spring.[3] Even "The Wanderings of Cain" produced, besides a long prose summary of one canto (which suggests his theme of "The Origin of Evil" and a landscape setting drawn from the desolate Valley of Rocks at Lynton), another haunting verse "fragment". Its tight rhyming and musical form is strongly reminiscent of the "Kubla Khan" style, together with phrases that begin to suggest the resonant archaicisms of the *Mariner*.* The material however has a different kind of autobiographical overtone, going back to his childhood days at Ottery, which he had been describing in his letters to Poole:

> Encinctured with a twine of leaves,
> That leafy twine his only dress!
> A lovely Boy was plucking fruits,
> By moonlight, in a wilderness.
> The moon was bright, the air was free,
> And fruits and flowers together grew
> On many a shrub and many a tree . . .
> Alone, by night, a little child,
> In place so silent and so wild –
> Has he no friend, no loving mother near?[4]

---

*As with "Kubla Khan", publication was held back by Coleridge for many years: the verse first appeared as a footnote to his theological work, *Aids to Reflection* (p. 383) in 1825, as a description of Enos, the Child of Cain, finding his way by chance "to an Oasis or natural Garden" in the desert, "from a Ms Poem". The prose canto was first published in the *Bijou* magazine for 1828. In 1829 Coleridge added the explanatory preface to the whole fragment, which in places recalls the fatal interruption of the composition of "Kubla Khan", though here there is no "person on business from Porlock", but a maritime metaphor – "adverse gales drove my bark off the 'Fortunate Isles' of the Muses" – followed by an interesting analogy from archaeology: "I have tried in vain to recover the lines from the palimpsest tablet of my memory . . ." (A palimpsest is a paper, parchment, or tablet, written over two or more times, the original being wholly or partially deleted by each subsequent rewriting.) In all these explanations of the interruption, fragmentation, or loss of literary work, Coleridge was drawing attention to the highly critical conditions of the creative act itself, and the circumstances which surround the actual composition of a poem. This critical and biographical framing of the circumstances of poetry was to be one of his original contributions to the Romantic theory of imagination, and our modern ideas of how poets actually write – in what sense they are "inspired" – are still powerfully shaped by his psychological accounts. The whole "Porlock complex", and Coleridge's myth of poetic failure, will be further examined in volume two. (See Bibliography, Stevie Smith.)

2

According to Dorothy's letters, the *Ancient Mariner* was first conceived on a long winter walk over Quantoxhead to Watchet and Dulverton, beginning on 13 November at about four o'clock when the sun was just setting over Longstone Hill.[5] This walk, deliberately started at a time when they could watch the transition from sunlight to moonlight over the sea, lasted for several days. Sara Coleridge did not accompany them. Wordsworth later gave a long account of the expedition, with many "droll-enough recollections" of their adventures along the coast, and at country inns, while the ballad of the Mariner was talked into life.

It was originally conceived, like "The Wanderings of Cain", as a collaboration in the gothic style of G. A. Bürger and Monk Lewis, then immensely popular. (Translations of Bürger's *Lenore* were appearing in the *Monthly Magazine*, and Wordsworth expected the *Mariner* to be sent there to earn guineas "to defray the expenses of their November tour".)[6] Wordsworth said he soon found that their "respective manners proved so widely different" that it would have been "presumptuous" for him to continue. He contributed two characteristic images, of the Wedding Guest listening "like a three years' child", and of the Mariner looking "long and lank and brown / As is the ribbed sea-sand". He would have known of Coleridge's long-standing interest in exotic sea-voyages, and spirits of the deep (as witnessed in "Religious Musing"), and he brilliantly focused this potential imaginative world for his friend, by several specific plot suggestions.

> Much the greatest part of the story was Mr Coleridge's invention; but certain parts I myself suggested, for example, some crime was to be committed which should bring upon the Old Navigator, as Coleridge afterwards delighted to call him, the spectral persecution, as a consequence of that crime, and his own wanderings. I had been reading in Shelvock's *Voyages* a day or two before that while doubling Cape Horn they frequently saw Albatrosses in that latitude . . . "Suppose," I said, "you represent him as having killed one of these birds on entering the South Sea, and that the tutelary Spirits of these regions take upon them to avenge the crime." The incident was thought fit for the purpose and adopted accordingly. I also suggested the navigation of the ship by the dead men, but do

> not recall that I had anything more to do with the scheme of the poem . . .[7]

What Wordsworth could not have known was how long Coleridge had been unconsciously gathering the incidents and images for the poem in his own life, from earliest childhood. The ballads heard in his nurse's arms; the sea-bird shot by Philip Quarll; the moving sun and moon on the Ottery church clock; the "grinning" thirst experienced on his Welsh undergraduate tour; the hallucinations of the dragoon in the Henley Pest House and the seizures of Charles Lloyd; the sea-boats and sailors along the quayside at Bristol; the idea of the spiritual sea-voyage in his cottage at Stowey; and even the laws of hospitality protecting the little mice: all found their place magically in the ballad. No one could have given him those.

Coleridge also added that his Stowey friend, John Cruikshank, had recently had a vivid nightmare of a spectre ship, and this too concentrated his mind with extraordinary force.

The central drama of the ballad, of the outcast sailor, the violated natural laws of "hospitality", and the purgatorial period of drifting and hallucinations, was thus given a firm narrative structure of a kind he had lacked in the previous experiments.

Wordsworth's recollections suggest, perhaps unconsciously, that the ballad was quickly composed in his company during that single walk. In fact Coleridge laboured immensely hard on the poem for nearly five months. Though an early draft of 300 lines – about half the final text – was in existence by the end of November[8], Dorothy's Journal shows that the completed work was not brought over to Alfoxden for reading until 23 March 1798.

The transformation of the ballad from its crude gothic beginnings, as the tale of a nightmare journey in a pastiche style in the manner of Bürger's *Lenore* (a night ride with the devil), cost Coleridge infinite pains. He refined the traditional four-line, four-stress ballad stanza into a flexible and astonishingly musical unit of breath and phrasing, expanding and contracting between four-, five-, and six-line variations, with immensely subtle plays of alliteration, pause, repetition and internal rhyme.

> Down dropt the breeze, the sails dropt down,
> 'Twas sad as sad could be;
> And we did speak only to break
> The silence of the Sea![9]

He gradually fitted the purely gothic elements of the plot – the actual shooting of the albatross, the scenes of becalment and drought, the appearance of the spectre ship, the resurrection of the dead crew, the horrific return to harbour – into a beautifully observed and naturalistic world of shifting seascapes and weather, which reflect and intensify the spiritual experiences of the Mariner.

Above all he seized narrative control of the action, by introducing a complex time-scheme of story-telling, divided between the compulsive recollections of the Mariner and the reactions of the Wedding Guest who listens, hypnotised, to the tale. This, he knew, was his own drama.

As he worked on the poem with increasing excitement, it began to absorb many of his deepest philosophic concerns – the themes of exile and homecoming, the problematic relationship between man and nature, and his psychological fascination with states of madness, dream, and hallucination which encroach upon the normal, waking world.

Underlying all this, he also found that the Mariner's story enabled him to explore for the first time in poetry his concern with the origins of evil (his old Epic subject) and the sense of guilt and spiritual anxiety which always obsessed him. In the symbolic killing of the albatross, he found what might be called a "green parable", the idea of man's destructive effect on the natural world, so that human moral blindness inadvertently introduces evil into the benign systems of nature, releasing uncontrollable forces that take terrible revenge. The *Mariner* was thus slowly developed from a sea-yarn out of an old folio into a metaphysical allegory of the Fall, a transformation that Coleridge alone could have accomplished.*

---

*A full interpretation of the *Ancient Mariner* might make a third volume to this book (projected in the Coleridge manner). The work of Professor Lowes; an essay by Robert Penn Warren, "A Poem of Pure Imagination" (in *Selected Essays*, 1964); and the invigorating account by William Empson (in *Coleridge's Verse: A Selection*, 1972) seem to me indispensable as starting points. Modern research has suggested how far three historical voyages – those of Captain Cook, of Captain William Bligh of the *Bounty* (1789), and of John Davies of the *Desire* (1593) – may have influenced Coleridge. A brilliant speculation on Davies' voyage, and its connection with Coleridge's albatross, appears with haunting force in Bruce Chatwin's *In Patagonia* (1977). I have myself looked briefly at the different approaches – biographical, sacramental, and aesthetic (the nineteenth-century concept of the *poète maudit*) – in *Coleridge* (1982); and I think the notion of the "green parable" deserves further exploration. As a biographer I have tried to show how deeply and instinctively the image of the lonely sea-voyage runs through all Coleridge's thought, which is curious when one considers that his only maritime experience up to 1798 was his crossing on the Chepstow ferry. (Coleridge himself becomes aware of this during his voyage to Malta in 1804, which, as we shall see, eventually produced his brilliant

footnote continued overleaf

3

While steadily working on his ballad, at Stowey, Coleridge was still immensely busy with other labours. He continued his gardening, and frequently preached at the Unitarian chapels in Bridgwater and Taunton. Having left off his reviewing, he sent three mock sonnets to the *Monthly Magazine*, satirising his own early poetic style and that of Lamb and Lloyd: "in ridicule of that affectation of unaffectedness, of jumping and misplaced accent on common-place epithets, flat lines forced into poetry by Italics (signifying how well & *mouthishly* the Author would read them) puny pathos etc etc."[10] One of these, "On a Ruined House in a Romantic Country", a parody of the nursery rhyme of "The House that Jack Built", was a brilliant farewell to his own juvenile manner. The sonnets were impishly signed Nehemiah Higgingbottom, and were to cause wholly unexpected offence among his friends.

He was also studying French and German, and working on a translation of Wieland's *Oberon*.[11] News that his tragedy of *Osorio* had been ill-received by Sheridan and Kemble at Drury Lane, which reached him in early December, again turned his attention to the continuing problem of bread and cheese for his little household. Once more he was being forced towards journalism or teaching.

Help was at hand in an important contact he had made through Cottle during the summer. This was with the rich and influential dissenting family of the Wedgwoods, who had made a fortune through their pottery business at Etruria. The two elder sons, Thomas and Josiah, took the greatest philanthropic interest in the intellectual movements of the time, and the family had already shown kindly attentions to Mary Wollstonecraft and William Godwin. In September, Tom Wedgwood had visited Wordsworth at Alfoxden, and had rapidly fallen under Coleridge's spell.

Tom was an extraordinary figure, amateur scientist and philosopher, hypochondriac and manic-depressive, whose interests

---

footnote continued

framing device of the marginal, prose "gloss" to the poem.) The whole idea of a writer's life as a perilous, solitary, oceanic expedition passes powerfully into nineteenth-century poetry – in Shelley, Baudelaire, Rimbaud, for example. It still affects our responses to such modern works as the novels of William Golding, the accounts of solo circumnavigations by Sir Francis Chichester (and many others) and such a maverick, masterpiece as *The Strange Voyage of Donald Crowhurst*, by Nicholas Tomalin, 1970. As a Romantic legend – for that is what it has become – the *Ancient Mariner* would make a superb opera, or even modern ballet, as Michael Bogdanov's stage-experiments have shown.

ranged from educational methods to some of the earliest experiments in photography that have been recorded in England. He was also fascinated by various forms of hallucinogenic drugs, including hashish and opium.[12] His gift for spotting talented young men led him to introduce the young Cornish chemist, Humphry Davy, to Dr Beddoes in Bristol, where the Pneumatic Institute for chemical experiments was opened in 1798.

In December, Coleridge was invited to the Wedgwoods' country estate, Cote House at Westbury, near Bristol, and this led to a series of introductions to London literary figures, including the philosopher and historian James Mackintosh. Coleridge performed in his accustomed firework manner, and Mackintosh, impressed by his "extraordinary power", recommended him to the new editor of the *Morning Post*, Daniel Stuart. He was invited to contribute regular "verses or political essays" to the *Post*, with a retainer of a guinea a week.[13]

One of the first of these was his remarkable war eclogue, "Fire, Famine and Slaughter" which appeared on 8 January 1798. Based on a pastiche of the demonic talk of *Macbeth*'s witches, it was a political satire on Pitt's war policies, set in France, on "a desolated Tract in La Vendée". It also attacked the British campaign of anti-rebel reprisals in Ireland. The sinister nightmare dialogue which Fire and Slaughter hold over the prostrate body of Famine echoes the talk of the demonic voices over the swooning Mariner in Part VI of the ballad:

> And all the souls, that damnéd be,
> Leaped up at once in anarchy,
> Clapped their hands and danced for glee . . .[14]

Coleridge's reputation was now such that national editors were prepared to commission poetry and articles, rather than mere book reviews. The *Morning Post* was a liberal, anti-government paper, but in no sense Jacobin. Mackintosh observed flatteringly: "The political tone is such as cannot be disagreeable to your feelings or repugnant to your Principles. The Proprietor, who is no stranger to your Character & talents is ashamed of offering you so small a pittance . . ."[15]

This was the beginning of a long professional connection and friendship with Stuart, whom Coleridge would follow from the *Post* to the *Courier*, contributing both as freelance and as staff-writer, over the next fourteen years. His talent as a journalist, as well as his natural gifts as a lecturer, made him – almost against his will – a professional man of letters, and this sharply distinguished him from Wordsworth. He often complained about it, like most freelancers, yet there was something in his ebullient temperament, his exuberance and exhibitionism, which perfectly suited both métiers. His gift for preaching stemmed from the same qualities.

Journalism would also eventually draw him back towards London – again, partly against his will – and this tension between a poetic existence in the provinces, and a journalistic one in the metropolis (already shrewdly sensed by Lamb), was to shape a great deal of his career.

The financial considerations were important. A retainer of a guinea a week (Stuart immediately held out the possibility of "gladly increasing the salary" later) would cover about half his annual expenses, which he recalculated in January 1798 as "£100 a year – or but little more, even including the annual £20, for which my wife's mother has a necessity".[16] Together with the £40 annuity arranged by Poole in 1796, journalism could keep him afloat. At this time, Treasury tax-figures show, for example, that a skilled worker such as a printer earned approximately £90 a year, while a gentleman with a small household and a servant in London could live comfortably on £200 a year.[17] Coleridge's target for bread and cheese was thus a very modest competency by contemporary standards, but probably rather less than Sara hoped for.

Throughout this early part of his life, anything less than £100 per annum threatened misery, and anything more meant relative happiness. Wordsworth, incidentally, had assured his own finances early on by accepting a handsome legacy of £900 from his friend Raisley Calvert in 1795, which he was able to invest through Basil Montagu (though this only yielded £50 in the first three years).[18] It was not unusual for writers at this time, when there were few public grants or prizes, to accept private patronage of this kind, and of course Southey had already benefited in this way through his uncle Herbert Hill and his friend Wynn.

Evidently some thoughts and calculations such as these were passing through the minds of Tom and Josiah Wedgwood at Cote House that winter. On Christmas Day, they sent Coleridge a magnificent gift of £100, which he immediately and gratefully accepted, as giving him "the leisure and tranquillity of independence for the next two years", added to the income from the *Morning Post* work as well. However, the same evening, he also received the offer of a position as the Unitarian minister at Shrewsbury, with a salary of £120 and a good house worth £30 in rent. This put him in an extraordinary dilemma – torn, as he put it, between the press and the pulpit. It also implied the break-up of his life in the Quantocks with the Wordsworths, and the perhaps permanent suspension of their experiments in poetry, for even the *Mariner* was not yet finished.

The decision he came to was surprising, and underlines not only his financial anxieties, but also his sense of family responsibilities. After agonised discussions with Sara, with Poole, and with his old friend the Reverend Estlin, he chose the Unitarian ministry. On 5 January he returned the draft for £100 to the Wedgwoods, and on 13 January set out to preach an inaugural sermon at Shrewsbury. (It is perhaps significant that Wordsworth was away in London at this time.)

His long and diplomatic covering letter to Josiah Wedgwood vividly describes his domestic anxieties for the future ("it is probable my children will come fast on me"), his doubts about being hired as "a paragraph-scribbler", and his feeling that the security of the religious ministry would be both honourable and yet still allow him "motives, even of a pecuniary kind, for literary exertion". He added, on a more practical note, that the ministry would exempt him from threatened military service (those "ancestral voices prophesying war", perhaps); and in the event of his death, provide some sort of congregational pension for his family.[19]

But it is the end of this letter which is most revealing. Having acted so decisively, he then admitted all his indecision to Wedgwood, and in the process subtly left the door ajar for further negotiation. How far he was conscious of doing this is problematic; but the well-timed confession of weakness is reminiscent of many early letters to brother George. The ambiguity of it – both disarming, and yet machiavellian – is pure Coleridge.

> I do not wish to conceal from you that I have suffered more from fluctuation of mind on this than any former occasion: and even now I have scarcely courage to decide absolutely . . . I leave a lovely country, and one friend so eminently near to my affections that his society has almost been consolidated with my ideas of happiness. However I shall go to Shrewsbury, remain a little while amongst the congregation: if no new argument arises against the ministerial office . . . there I shall *certainly* pitch my *tents*, & *probably* shall build up my permanent Dwelling . . . a permanent income not

> inconsistent with my religious or political creeds, I find necessary to my quietness – without it I should be a prey to anxiety, and Anxiety, with me, always induces Sickliness, and too often Sloth . . . You will let me know of the arrival of the Bill: and it would give me very great pleasure to hear, that I had not forfeited your esteem by first accepting, & now returning it.[20]

If indeed this was Coleridge's form of asking for more, it was wholly successful. On the Tuesday after his first sermon at Shrewsbury, while breakfasting with the Unitarian minister of nearby Wem, Coleridge received his reply from Cote House: "an annuity of £150 for life, legally secured to me, *no condition whatever being annexed*". It was a proposal which, if accepted, would transform his life.

4

The sermon of 14 January 1798 had been a great success with the discerning congregation of Shrewsbury. He had entered the dark panelled chapel with a flourish, and climbed into the huge central pulpit that dominated the packed rows of box-pews. (See illustration.) The scene was remembered ardently many years later by the shy, intellectual, seventeen-year-old son of the minister of Wem.

> When I got there, the organ was playing the 100th Psalm, and when it was done Mr Coleridge rose and gave out his text, "And he went up into the mountain to pray, HIMSELF, ALONE." As he gave out this text, his voice "rose like a steam of rich distilled perfumes"; and when he came to the two last words, which he pronounced loud, deep, and distinct, it seemed to me, who was then young, as if the sounds had echoed from the bottom of the human heart, and as if that prayer might have floated in solemn silence through the universe . . . The sermon was upon peace and war; upon church and state – not their alliance, but their separation; on the spirit of the world and the spirit of Christianity . . .[21]

These recollections belong to William Hazlitt, whose meeting with Coleridge formed the turning point of his adolescence. Like so many others, he fell instantly under the spell: "I could not have been more delighted if I had heard the music of the spheres. Poetry and Philosophy had met together." Hazlitt actually describes something like a conversion-experience: up to that moment he had felt "dumb, inarticulate, helpless, like a worm by the wayside", but Coleridge turned him towards literature, gave him hope for a new world, and encouraged him to express his innermost thoughts.

This makes his witness in this essay, "On My First Acquaintance with Poets", peculiarly penetrating and poignant, with living details – such as the first meal they shared together "Welsh mutton and turnips" – engraved upon his memory. As he said in a rare moment of self-revelation: "My soul has indeed remained in its original bondage, dark, obscure, with longings infinite and unsatisfied . . . but that my understanding also did not remain dumb and brutish, or at length found a language to express itself, I owe to Coleridge."*

Two days after the Shrewsbury sermon, Coleridge came to spend the night at Wem with Hazlitt's father. The teenage boy remained tongue-tied through most of the dinner-time conversation, but recalled each topic in detail: Mary Wollstonecraft's influence over Godwin ("one instance of the ascendancy which people of imagination exercised over those of mere intellect"); Edmund Burke's superiority as a philosopher over James Mackintosh ("Burke was a metaphysician, Mackintosh a mere logician"); and Holcroft's limitations as a linguistic philosopher, requiring reductive definitions for every concept ("barricading the road to truth . . . setting up a turn-pike gate at every step we took"). It is one of the rare occasions when the *subject* of Coleridge's conversation was remembered as well as its style.

Hazlitt also memorably recalled an incident next morning. "When I came down to breakfast, I found that he had just received a letter from his friend, T. Wedgwood, making him a offer of £150 a year if he chose to waive his present pursuit, and devote himself entirely to the study of poetry and philosophy. Coleridge seemed to make up his

---

*Within five years Hazlitt's enthusiasm for Coleridge was already moderating (see Chapter 14). By 1816, when he was entering into his powers as a radical journalist for Leigh Hunt's *Examiner*, he would become one of Coleridge's most virulent, acute, and relentless critics. (This is a reaction also characteristic of charismatic conversions.) Political apostasy, intellectual sloth, and mystic humbug, were his main charges ("he merely haunts the public imagination with obscure noises . . . the Cock-lane Ghost of midday"). But Hazlitt's deeper motivation may be questioned. Hazlitt seemed to associate Coleridge with many of the political and emotional disappointments he had experienced in his own adult life, and he attacked the older man with a personal vindictiveness that suggests he was unconsciously attacking something in himself. This gives all his writing on Coleridge – but most notably in *The Spirit of the Age* (1825) – a brilliant surface of satire, with a deep undernote of passionate elegy. It is the tone that a biographer might aspire to. (See Bibliography, William Hazlitt and A. C. Swinburne.)

mind to close with this proposal in the act of trying on one of his shoes." It is interesting that neither the young Hazlitt saw, nor the older Hazlitt chose to interpolate, the overwhelming emotions that must have been covered by this tiny gesture.[22]

But Hazlitt did see Coleridge's physiognomy. He was training himself as a painter, and he interpreted what he saw retrospectively with all his customary acuteness and partiality. His impressions are fascinating to compare with Dorothy's. First there was a general impact of something wild and strange: unstable energy, "dusky obscurity", a large figure in ill-fitting clothes (Coleridge had recently borrowed a coat from Poole). Then there was a mass of full black glossy hair "peculiar to enthusiasts"; and something – thought young Hazlitt – "traditionally inseparable . . . from the pictures of Christ". Closer to, there was the florid "bloom" of a face suggesting introspection, "as we see it in the pale, thoughtful complexions of the Spanish portrait-painters, Murillo and Velasquez".

Then, almost hypnotically, all attention was drawn to the mobile, expressive features so full of heroic life and disturbing contradictions. "His forehead was broad and high, light as if built of ivory, with large projecting eyebrows, and his eyes rolling beneath them, like a sea with darkened lustre . . . His mouth was gross, voluptuous, open, eloquent; his chin good-humoured and round; but his nose, the rudder of his face, the index of the will, was small, feeble, nothing – like what he has done."

Here Hazlitt sought for a symbol of all his subsequent bitterness and disappointment, and found it with curious irony in the image of a mariner. "It might seem that the genius of his face as from a height surveyed and projected him (with sufficient capacity and huge aspiration) into the unknown world of thought and imagination, with nothing to support and guide his veering purpose, as if Columbus had launched his adventurous course for the New World in a scallop, without oars or compass. So, at least, I comment after the event."

The intensity of Hazlitt's gaze, focused as it were through a backward lense of twenty-five years, shows something of the passionate response that Coleridge would always evoke in him. Like Dorothy, like Wordsworth, he could never forget the first encounter; and it might seem that all of them were looking, in their own way, for the prophet of their youthful hopes.

Coleridge returned to Shrewsbury on 16 January. Hazlitt walked with him six miles through the frosty morning, again recording the conversation in which he now plucked up the courage to join: it was of theology and metaphysics, Hume, Berkeley, Butler and Paley. He noticed that Coleridge floated effortlessly from subject to subject, seeming "to slide on ice". He also drifted unconsciously from side to side of the muddy footpath. "This struck me as an odd movement; but I did not at that time connect it with any instability of purpose or involuntary change of principle, as I have done since."

To his delight, Coleridge wrote his Stowey address on a small card, and invited Hazlitt to pay a visit to see him and Wordsworth later in the year. This final act of encouragement to the awkward and frowning young man seemed inexplicably wonderful to Hazlitt. "During those months ... the golden sunsets, the silver star of evening, lighted me on my way to new hopes and prospects. *I was to visit Coleridge in the spring.*"[23] Aware of Hazlitt's shyness, Coleridge would tactfully renew this invitation in the middle of March, although by then he had much else to occupy him.[24]

5

From Shrewsbury, Coleridge wrote to Josiah Wedgwood on 17 January 1798 accepting the annuity, in a short, heartfelt letter of thanks. Such benevolence had "filled his eyes with tears". He dedicated himself to "honourable effort" in the future, to prove all their good intentions justified.[25] He withdrew from the Shrewsbury ministry, and returned in triumph to Bristol on 30 January, where he stayed a week at Cote House, finally reaching Stowey on 9 February.[26]

A fleet of delighted but curiously subdued letters preceded him, each characteristically tailored to its recipient. To Poole, he said that he felt as if he were dreaming: "my heart has not yet felt any of the swell & glow of personal feelings."[27] To Thelwall, he said he was "astonished, agitated".[28] To Estlin, who had disapproved of the Wedgwoods' intervention, he announced solemnly: "if I wish to acquire knowledge as a philosopher and fame as a poet, I pray for grace that I may continue to feel what I now feel, that my greatest reason for wishing the one & the other, is that I may be enabled . . . to defend Religion ably."[29] This motive should never be discounted with Coleridge.

To Wordsworth, still in London, he first touched upon a lighter note: "I accepted it on the presumption that I had talents, honesty, & propensities to perseverant effort ... But dismissing severer thoughts, believe me, my dear fellow! that of the pleasant ideas, which accompanied this unexpected event, it was not the least pleasant . . . that I should at least be able to trace the spring & early summer of Alfoxden with you."

In this same letter he begins to talk again of ballad-writing, mentioning the border ballad of "Sir Cauline" collected by Percy, in which he had found a significant name – "fayre Christabelle".[30] Indeed this letter makes it clear that without Wedgwood's extraordinary generosity, there would have been no *Lyrical Ballads*. Wordsworth's reaction, incidentally, was somewhat dry: "I hope the fruit will be good as the seed is noble."[31]

6

After all the anxieties, a period of great domestic happiness now settled over the little household at Stowey. Bills were sorted out in an unaccustomed flurry of efficiency. They were not large: £15 to Estlin; £5 to his printer Biggs, and Mrs Fricker's quarterly £5 was due. Sara was pregnant again, and a new tranquillity reigned.[32] She and Coleridge took great pleasure in the sharp, bright wintry weather, walking in the snowy orchard, showing Hartley the moon and the icicles, and keeping good large fires at night. It was during this month of February 1798 that "Frost at Midnight" was written in the little front parlour.

Coleridge had been making detailed notes about Hartley's development, and his Notebook has a page headed "Infancy & Infants". Among the observations and reflections he recorded, were:

> 1. The first smile – what kind of *reason* it displays . . . 2. Asleep with the polyanthus fast in its hand, its bells drooping over the rosy face . . . 3. Stretching after the stars . . . 5. Sports of infants – their incessant activity, the *means* being the end. – Nature how lovely a school-mistress – A blank-verse, moral poem . . . 9. mother directing a Baby's hand. Hartley's love to Papa – scrawls pothooks, & reads what he *meant* by them . . . 14. The wisdom & graciousness of God in the infancy of the human species – its beauty, long continuance etc etc. Children in the wind – hair floating, tossing, a miniature of the agitated Trees, below which they play'd . . .[33]

Coleridge also recommenced his autobiographical letters to Poole in February. These two strands of reflection, from his own and Hartley's childhood, coalesced in this most tender and perhaps most perfect of his Conversation Poems. For this, too, the Wedgwoods were indirectly responsible.

"Frost at Midnight" opens with Coleridge sitting in front of the fire in the Stowey parlour late at night, "the inmates of my cottage, all at rest", and the owl calling outside through the freezing dark. The poem appears at first an almost artless night-monologue of memories and reflections. In fact, it is one of the most intricately structured of all the Conversation Poems, performing a characteristic "outward and return" movement through time and space. From the Stowey cottage the poem moves backwards to Coleridge's own childhood at Christ's Hospital and Ottery (the bells remembered as themselves a memory of schooldays), and then forwards again to Hartley's imagined boyhood in the future. This curve of memory and prophesy gives the poem a rich emotional resonance – sadness, poignancy, hope, joy – held in exquisite tension:

For I was reared,
In the great city, pent 'mid cloisters dim,
And saw nought lovely but the sky and stars.
But *thou*, my babe! shalt wander like a breeze
By lakes and sandy shores, beneath the crags
Of ancient mountain, and beneath the clouds . . .[34]

The visionary joys of nature, celebrated in "This Lime-Tree Bower" are now developed into a philosophy of emotional education. Coleridge dedicates Hartley as a "child of Nature", who will gain religious awareness through the beauties of the natural world. This is of course another version of the *Mariner* theme, but conceived pastorally, as an education without guilt or "penance". The child finds nature already "hospitable".

These passages are often described as "Wordsworthian" (and indeed Hartley's boyhood already seems imagined in the Lake District rather than the Quantocks). But Coleridge's pastoral world is explicitly "sacred", and the Creator's presence is felt in a tradition of Christian mysticism which Wordsworth never espoused in even his most transcendental moments. Nature is the direct expression of God's Word, the divine articulation in physical form:

so shalt thou see and hear
The lovely shapes and sounds intelligible
Of that eternal language, which thy God
Utters . . .[35]

This mystical theme is sustained throughout the poem by images of light and radiance, the fire and the frost, the sun on the snow-covered thatch which steams like natural incense (an image already carefully collected in the Notebooks)[36] which are brought to a magic, trance-like climax in the final lines. Here the "secret ministry" of the frost (the powers to bless, purify, consecrate and forgive all contained in its whiteness) performs a natural miracle with the melting snow, the drops from the eaves hung up for contemplation

in silent icicles,
Quietly shining to the quiet moon.

Coleridge clearly associated his own imaginative powers, at some level, with this "secret ministry": not the official ministry that he had just escaped – but that of the religious poet and philosopher. The repeated emphasis on "quiet" – which arises out of fluctuating movements of the poem (the fire is the "sole unquiet thing") and finally settles in the reverential stillness of the "shining" icicles beneath the moon – itself carries strong, mystical implications.

Any reader feels this intuitively, but it is confirmed by Coleridge's reference at this time in the Notebooks to the natural revelation of God as understood by the Neoplatonists.[37] Later, in the *Biographia* he quoted a favourite passage from Plotinus, the third-century Greek Christian mystic, whose *Enneads* were the source of Neoplatonism, and whose remarks about "divine knowledge" clearly bear on this passage in the poem. "So that we ought not to pursue it with a view of detecting its secret source, but to watch in quiet till it suddenly shines upon us . . ."[38]

Coleridge made many alterations and refinements in the poem over the next ten years. His sense of the "curving" form of the verse meditation was so demanding that he was eventually prepared to delete an entire verse paragraph – marvellously describing Hartley – in order to achieve the visionary closing effect. As he put it in a note on the manuscript, the original ending destroyed "the rondo, and return upon itself of the Poem".[39]

Aesthetically, his decision was undoubtedly right; but it is worth recalling that first ending of 1798, because it is rarely now printed, and gives a most touching picture of the child in Sara's arms that winter at Stowey. It reads:

Or whether the secret ministry of cold
Shall hang them up in silent icicles,
Quietly shining to the quiet moon,
Like those, my babe! which ere tomorrow's warmth
Have capp'd their sharp keen points with pendulous drops,
Will catch thine eye, and with their novelty
Suspend thy little soul; then make thee shout,
And stretch and flutter from thy mother's arms
As thou wouldst fly for very eagerness.[40]

7

Dorothy's Journal shows that Coleridge, occasionally accompanied by Sara, was up at Alfoxden most days in February and March. Thereafter long walks were again impractical for Sara because of her pregnancy. Coleridge continued to come alone, and there is an increasing impression of him disappearing for days at a time into the Quantock Hills with the Wordsworths, throughout the spring of 1798. Dorothy also records night-walks, lying in the fields, and studying the moonlight. Coleridge had returned to work on the *Mariner* (finished on 23 March), and was beginning his new ballad, "Christabel", which shares several phrases of natural observations with Dorothy's journal.

In mid-March he was very ill with an abscessed tooth, and deeply upset by a quarrel with Lamb and Lloyd which had been precipitated by the satirical "Higginbottom" sonnets, and threatened to deepen with the imminent publication of Lloyd's novel, *Edmund Oliver.* He dosed himself heavily with opium for a short while. Both Coleridge and Sara stayed at Alfoxden for ten days while he was recovering, and it was at this time that a plan to go into Germany in the autumn was first discussed.

During this period of convalescence, Coleridge also attempted to re-establish friendly relations with the family at Ottery. On 10 March he wrote to George a long letter describing both his recent illness and the future literary work he hoped to undertake. Of the first, he wrote in terms that again tantalisingly conjure up the visions of "Kubla Khan": "Laudanum gave me repose, not sleep: but YOU, I believe, know how divine that repose is – what a spot of inchantment, a green spot of fountains, & flowers & trees, in the very heart of a waste of Sands! – God be praised . . . I am now recovering apace, and enjoy that *newness* of sensation from the fields, the air, & the Sun, which makes convalescence almost repay one for disease."[41]

As far as work was concerned, he denied all further interest in radical politics, though he regretfully admitted that many still deemed him to be "a Democrat & a Seditionist". In fact, at this very time, he was tracing out his disenchantment with the French Revolution in another major poem, to be contributed to Stuart's *Morning Post* in April under the title, "The Recantation: an Ode".

George already knew of the Wedgwood annuity, and Coleridge now explained how he intended to use it.

> I devote myself to such works as encroach not on the antisocial passions – in poetry, to elevate the imagination & set the affections in right tune by the beauty of the inanimate impregnated, as with a living soul, by the presence of Life – in prose, to the seeking with patience, & a slow, very slow mind . . . What our faculties are & what they are capable of becoming. – I love fields & woods & mountains with almost a visionary fondness – and because I have found benevolence & quietness growing within me as that fondness increased, therefore I should wish to be the means of implanting it in others.[42]

George may have found these noble aims rather too elevated as a work programme, but they were Coleridge's description of the imaginative philosophy which would shape the *Lyrical Ballads.*

8

The idea of a collaborative volume with Wordsworth emerged much more suddenly in these Quantock months than is often thought. Wordsworth himself, in the last Book (XIV) of *The Prelude*, afterwards gave the impression of a permanent paradisal summer, in which their poetry poured forth in lazy and instinctive harmony:

> . . . That summer, under whose indulgent skies,
> Upon smooth Quantock's airy ridge we roved
> Unchecked, or loitered 'mid her sylvan combs,
> Thou in bewitching words, with happy heart,
> Did chant the vision of that Ancient Man,
> The bright-eyed Mariner, and rueful woes
> Didst utter of the Lady Christabel;
> And I, associate with such labour, steeped
> In soft forgetfulness the livelong hours,

Murmuring of him who, joyous hap, was found,
After perils of his moonlight ride,
Near the loud waterfall; or her who sate
In misery near the miserable Thorn . . .[43]

But the idea for the *Lyrical Ballads* was not conceived until late March 1798, and the completed text – except for "The Nightingale" and "Tintern Abbey" – was with Cottle by early June.[44]

Coleridge's letters to Cottle show that on 18 February he was carefully considering publishing the *Mariner* in a third edition of his own *Poems*. Even on 13 March he was still concentrating all his efforts on this edition, which he would "utterly" transform by the omission of "near one half" of the old materials ("a sacrifice to pitch-black Oblivion"), and the banishment of what he now considered juvenile poems (including the "Chatterton" Monody), to the back of the volume.[45] Most significantly of all, he would now add "three blank verse poems" to the new ballad, which would be drawn from the recent Conversation Poems.[46] Lamb and Lloyd were withdrawing their own poems from the collection. Coleridge thus planned to appear with all this new work, under his own name, "a volume worthy of me" in about "ten weeks" time – that is, towards the middle of June 1798.[47] One can only speculate on how differently his reputation might have developed, had a single volume containing the *Ancient Mariner*, "This Lime-Tree Bower", and "Frost at Midnight" been published under his own name at this time. As it was, these two strands of his work were not to be united for nineteen years until *Sibylline Leaves*.

Nevertheless, the decision to embark on a joint "experiment", taken at Alfoxden in mid-March, was a momentous one in the history of English poetry. It began modestly as a way of earning money for the proposed German tour, and first emerged as a proposal to Cottle to publish their two tragedies, *Osorio* and *The Borderers* together.[48] By early April, the joint volume of ballads and poems had appeared as the alternative possibility, to raise the required sum of thirty guineas. Coleridge was deliberately matter-of-fact about these details – "I write to you now merely as a bookseller" – but something of his excitement appears in his pressing invitation to Cottle to join them in the Quantocks for a broad discussion of the whole scheme. "At all events, come down, Cottle, as soon as you can, but before Mid-summer, and we will procure a horse easy as thy own soul, and we will go on a roam to Linton and Lynmouth, which, if thou comest in

May, will be in all their pride of woods and waterfalls, not to speak of its august cliffs, and the green ocean, and the vast valley of stones . . ."[49]

Cottle did come in late May, and at this meeting many of the poems were read aloud "under the old trees of the park" above Alfoxden.[50] The first details of the contents page and typographical layout were considered.[51] Coleridge rejected the idea of a dedication to the Wedgwoods as unsuitable: "if after 4 or 5 years I shall have finished some work of some importance, which could not have been written but in unanxious seclusion, to them I will dedicate it . . ."[52] He also insisted, perhaps unwisely, on strict anonymity of the joint authorship: "Wordsworth's name is nothing – to a large number of persons mine *stinks.*"

But both poets were aware of the provocative nature of the work they were assembling. It was challenging in its subject-matter – combining rural low-life with figures on the edge of fantasy and madness; and in the daring plainness of its style and forms. Together these constituted what can be called the aggressive simplicity of the entire volume; and this was faithfully mirrored in Cottle's beautiful bold typesetting, with only twenty verse lines to the printed page and extravagant margins.

The nature of the challenge was made abundantly clear in the downright terms of the short "Advertisement" which Wordsworth wrote, with Coleridge's agreement, as a preface.

> The majority of the following poems are to be considered as experiments. They were written chiefly with a view to ascertain how far the language of conversation in the middle and lower classes of society is adapted to the purposes of poetic pleasure. Readers accustomed to the gaudiness and inane phraseology of many modern writers, if they persist in reading this book to its conclusion, will perhaps frequently have to struggle with feelings of strangeness and awkwardness ... but ... they should ask themselves if it contains a natural delineation of human passions, human characters, and human incidents . . .[53]

The keyword here was "natural": a term which the *Lyrical Ballads* was designed to revolutionise in both a literary and, by implication, a political way. It was, as Hazlitt later observed, a "levelling" volume, which drew its ultimate inspiration from the complex response of both authors to the French Revolution. It could be said to enfranchise a whole new class of poetical subjects.

It is remarkable that while Wordsworth produced virtually all his contributions to the collection in the three spring months of 1798, Coleridge drew on work that dated back to the beginning of 1797 (two extracts from *Osorio*), and was hoping to include work – notably "Christabel" – that was still under way in July.[54] The original idea for their compositions forming "a balance" of themes – as Coleridge described in the *Biographia* – was thus overturned by Wordsworth's speed of composition, and natural tendency to impose his own views on their collaboration.

Their original conversations had turned "on the two cardinal points of poetry, the power of exciting the sympathy of the reader by a faithful adherence to the truth of nature, and the power of giving the interest of novelty by the modifying colours of imagination." This suggested a natural division of subject-matter, according to the two distinctive and opposite poles of their imaginative interests. For Coleridge, "the incidents and agents were to be, in part at least, supernatural"; for Wordsworth, "subjects were to be chosen from ordinary life . . . such, as will be found in every village and its vicinity."[55]

This inspired combination of themes attacked the received eighteenth-century idea of a moderate, rational, upper-class nature: in effect a poetry of the well-to-do city class and landed gentry, who still composed the vast majority of potential readers. Four long, major poems were originally to represent this balanced division. From Coleridge, the *Ancient Mariner* and "Christabel"; from Wordsworth, "The Idiot Boy" and "The Thorn". In the event, of the twenty-three poems finally included, nineteen were Wordsworth's, and four were Coleridge's, only one of which was a ballad. As Coleridge later put it: "my compositions, instead of forming a balance, appeared rather an interpolation of heterogeneous matter."[56]

Yet this final, unsatisfactory mixture did allow a significant third element to enter the collection at a late stage: the intimate, blank verse nature meditations which produced two of the finest individual poems – Coleridge's "The Nightingale" and Wordsworth's "Tintern Abbey".

These three themes – which one can class as the Supernatural (psychology of the irrational); the Rural (social realism); and the Reflective (philosophy of the One Life) – do give the *Lyrical Ballads* a powerful unity, despite the apparent imbalance. To contemporary readers, this would have appeared in many startling ways.

First, the collection concentrated on the experience of "marginal" figures who had not previously received much attention from poets: very old people, very young children, mad people, and various forms of social outcasts (a convict, an abandoned Indian woman, an infanticide). Secondly, overwhelming emphasis was given to verse narrative – whether in the form of a ballad, folk tale, village gossip, or simply as domestic incident (a child telling a lie). There are probably only five poems in the entire collection which one can class as Romantic "lyrics", or what Coleridge once called "effusions". Finally, almost pedagogic importance was given to nature as a moral and educative force, so that the "child of nature" – whether young or old – becomes in some sense the human ideal of the collection. This aspect has a political dimension, and many of the poems suggest implicit alternatives to Jacobin, or specifically Godwinian, doctrines of social improvement, in which one recognises Coleridge's influence over Wordsworth.[57]

Wordworth's formulation of this counter-ideology in "The Tables Turned" became celebrated; and can be almost quoted as a piece of Romantic catechism: "One impulse from a vernal wood / May teach you more of man; Of moral evil and of good, / Than all the sages can". But it was Coleridge who expressed it in most extreme and uncompromising form in his poem "The Dungeon" (an extract from *Osorio*). Here he argued that even a condemned criminal could be reformed most effectively, not by imprisonment in a cell, but by releasing him into the countryside and treating him as "a distempered child" to be healed by nature's "ministrations":

> Thou pourest on him thy soft influences,
> Thy sunny hues, fair forms, and breathing sweets,
> Thy melodies of woods, and winds, and waters,
> Till he relent, and can no more endure
> To be a jarring and a dissonant thing,
> Amid this general dance and minstrelsy . . .[58]

In this one can recognise a body of ideas and images which not only links his treatment of the Mariner with that of the baby Hartley, but also suggests Wordsworth's much later response to daffodils.

9

The collaborative work on the volume deepened the friendship between Coleridge, Wordsworth and Dorothy, which evidently took on new intimacy this spring. For the first time, Coleridge's emotional reliance on Tom Poole was challenged, and Alfoxden began to represent an alternative household to Stowey. Moreover, for Sara there was no corresponding intimacy with Dorothy, whose "rustic" ways she found disruptive (Dorothy borrowed her clothes on one disastrous occasion after a walk in the rain) and whose enthusiasm for her husband's company threatened domestic harmony at the cottage. When Sara's second child, Berkeley, was born on 14 May, there were no more celebratory sonnets.

Coleridge's customary praise of "The Giant Wordsworth – God love him!"[59] took on a more deliberate and reflective note. They disagreed on religious matters – "we found our data dissimilar"; and their critical theories of poetry already showed a difference of emphasis which would sharpen in the second edition of the *Lyrical Ballads* in 1800. But these differences, like their temperamental ones, were wonderfully fruitful as this stage.

Coleridge wrote to Estlin on 18 May: "I have now known him a year & some months, and my admiration, I might say, my awe of his intellectual powers has increased even to this hour – & (what is of more importance) he is a tried good man ... His genius is most *apparent* in poetry – and rarely, except to me in tête à tête, breaks forth in conversational eloquence."[60] This intimate, almost proprietorial note, was new.

Dorothy's friendship was also increasingly stimulating to Coleridge: many of her Journal entries describing the Quantocks landscape, and especially effects of sun and moonlight, are mirrored by phrases in Coleridge's ballads, though it is impossible to tell who was influencing whom. The haunting female figures of "Christabel" – a quite new departure in Coleridge's poetry – must at some level have drawn inspiration from Dorothy's gypsy-like presence, especially on their night-walks, among the woodlands round Holford.

This friendship with the Wordsworths was the subject of Coleridge's next Conversation Poem, "The Nightingale", probably written at Alfoxden towards the end of April. Addressed to them both – "My Friend, and thou our Sister!" – it described a night expedition to listen to the nightingales in a grove of trees near Dodington Hall, just north of Holford-Stowey coaching road. The song of these birds, which only sing for a few weeks each spring, is exquisitely mimicked in the patterning of the verse, which forms a sort of magic chorus to their own quick talk:

> . . . far and near,
> In wood and thicket, over the wide grove,
> They answer and provoke each other's song,
> With skirmish and capricious passagings,
> And murmurs musical and swift jug jug,
> And one low piping sound more sweet than all . . .[61]

Their own discussion begins in a literary fashion, dismissing the traditional poetic idea (from Milton's "Il Penseroso") of the nightingale as a "melancholy" bird. They have learnt a "different lore", that "In Nature there is nothing melancholy", and that the nightingales really express an instinctive joy in which they can share. Later in the poem, Coleridge introduces into this companionable moonlit world a flitting female figure, who seems partly a premonition of Christabel, and partly a Romantic portrait of Dorothy herself, touched in with a hint of amorous humour (as if she had stepped out of a gothic tale, or indeed, was about to step into his own ballad):

> A most gentle Maid,
> Who dwelleth in her hospitable home
> Hard by the castle, and at latest eve
> (Even like a Lady vowed and dedicate
> To something more than Nature in the grove)
> Glides through the pathways; she knows all their notes . . .[62]

The notable absentee from this expedition, and from the poem, is Sara Coleridge. Her presence, either explicit or implied (her maternal arms in "Frost at Midnight"), is otherwise remarkably consistent throughout the Conversation Poems, at least in their earliest versions. Yet even here, Coleridge follows the curve of their talk and their wanderings to achieve a domestic "return", which poignantly includes the cottage life of Stowey.

During the spring he had carefully recorded in his Notebooks a little incident when Hartley had been crying. "Hartley fell down and hurt himself – I caught him up crying & screaming – & ran out of doors with him. – The Moon caught his eye – he ceased crying immediately – & his eyes & the tears in them, how they glittered in the Moonlight!"[63] Coleridge instantly saw this as one of those "ministrations" of nature, central to the doctrine of the *Lyrical*

Ballads. (There is also a most curious hint of the Mariner's glittering eye, which suggests all sorts of parallels between these two "children of nature", one innocent and one guilty.)

He now lifted this incident into verse, to form a beautiful home-coming and conclusion: first recalling how his "dear babe" would listen to the nightingales, himself unable to talk, but with "his hand beside his ear, / His little hand, the small forefinger up"; and then bringing the entire poem to focus on nature's powers of healing and enchantment, both for the father and for the child. Here again he announced a great Romantic theme, normally associated with Wordsworth alone:

. . . I deem it wise
To make him Nature's play-mate. He knows well
The evening-star; and once, when he awoke
In most distressful mood (some inward pain
Had made up that strange thing, an infant's dream –)
I hurried with him to our orchard-plot,
And he beheld the moon, and, hushed at once,
Suspends his sobs, and laughs most silently,
While his fair eyes, that swam with undropped tears,
Did glitter in the yellow moon-beam! Well! –
It is a father's tale: But if that Heaven
Should give me life, his childhood shall grow up
Familiar with these songs, that with the night
He may associate joy. – Once more, farewell,
Sweet Nightingale! once more, my friends! farewell.[64]*

---

* Something of the quick humour excited between Coleridge and Wordsworth, that sense of the ridiculous within the sublime (which is so difficult to recapture biographically), is splendidly expressed in the doggerel note which accompanied the manuscript of this poem, when Coleridge sent it up for inspection to Alfoxden. This note, dated 10 May 1798, begins:

In stale blank verse a subject stale
I send *per post* my *Nightingale*;
And like an honest bard, dear Wordsworth,
You'll tell me what you think, my Bird's worth.
My own opinion's briefly this –
His *bill* he opens not amiss;
And when he has sung a stave or so,
His breast, & some small space below,
So throbs & swells, that you might swear
No vulgar music's working there.
So far, so good; but then, 'od rot him!
There's something falls off at his bottom . . .

(*Letters*, I, p. 406)

footnote continued overleaf.

10

Such expeditions continued throughout May and June, as the collection was being prepared. The long, light evenings took them frequently right along the coast to Lynton, and this became their favourite extended walk, upon which all visitors were expected to route-march as well: Cottle did it with some reluctance, Hazlitt (who now arrived for his three-week stay at Alfoxden) with energetic delight. Coleridge was indefatigable – once completing the ninety-mile round trip in two consecutive days – and also making journeys to Bristol and Cheddar (in an attempt to settle the dispute with Lloyd), and walking over Quantock to preach at Taunton.

All the time he was working on his other ballads – "Christabel", "The Dark Ladie" – and sending poems to the *Morning Post* (including "Lewti", "France: an Ode", and "The Old Man of the Alps"). He was also preparing one of the most difficult of his Conversation Poems, with a political theme, "Fears in Solitude", which he described as "written in April 1798, during the alarm of an Invasion" by the French. This would be published separately, in a quarto pamphlet with two other poems, in London during the autumn. It is psychologically interesting that, years later in the *Biographia*, he would refer mournfully to Wordsworth's much greater "industry" at this time.

Hazlitt recalled his sojourn, the long walks, the frugal meals, the reading of poetry aloud in sunshine and moonlight, with a kind of ecstasy that rarely entered into his mature writing. He was fascinated to observe the intimacy between the two poets, commenting shrewdly upon it as one summer day slipped into the next.

> That morning, as soon as breakfast was over, we strolled out into the park, and seating ourselves on the trunk of an old ash-tree that stretched along the ground, Coleridge read aloud with a sonorous voice [Wordsworth's] ballad of "Betty Foy" . . . Coleridge and myself walked back to Stowey that evening, and his voice sounded

---

footnote continued.

One might recall Hazlitt's observation, which often puzzled later witnesses, that at this time in Coleridge's company, there was in Wordsworth "a convulsive inclination to laughter about the mouth, a good deal at variance with the solemn, stately expression of the rest of his face". (See Bibliography.)

high "Of Providence, foreknowledge, will and fate, / Fix'd fate, free-will, foreknowledge absolute," as we passed through echoing grove, by fairy stream or waterfall, gleaming in the summer moonlight! He lamented that Wordsworth was not prone enough to believe in the traditional superstitions of the place, and that there was something corporeal, a *matter-of-factness*, a clinging to the petty, in his poetry, in consequence . . .

I got into a metaphysical argument with Wordsworth, while Coleridge was explaining the different notes of the nightingale to his sister . . . We walked for miles on dark brown heaths overlooking the Channel, with the Welsh hills beyond . . . At Linton . . . a thunderstorm came on while we were at the inn, and Coleridge was running out bareheaded to enjoy the commotion of the elements in the Valley of Rocks . . .

He spoke of Cowper as the best modern poet. He said the "Lyrical Ballads" were an experiment about to be tried by him and Wordsworth . . . He spoke with contempt of Gray, and with intolerance of Pope . . . A fisherman gave Coleridge an account of a boy that had been drowned the day before, and that they had tried to save him at the risk of their lives. He said "he did not know how it was that they ventured, but, sir, we have a *nature* towards one another." This expression, Coleridge remarked to me, was a fine illustration . . . We returned on the third morning, and Coleridge remarked the silent cottage-smoke curling up the valleys where, a few evenings before, we had seen the lights gleaming through the dark.[65]

Hazlitt captured the atmosphere of those last summer months on the Quantocks better, perhaps, than any other witness except the poets themselves in their poems. He saw vividly how the tiny daily details of their lives rose so rapidly and continuously towards the surface of their writing. He even spotted a ship on the horizon, "within the red-orbed disc of the setting sun", which was exactly like Coleridge's spectre-ship in the *Mariner.*

He listened intently to their different voices, and watched their contrasted physical movements, with an acuteness that revealed much about not only their temperaments, but even their literary style. He saw their poetry as almost physically embodied in their figures – the animated, quicksilver darting and drifting of Coleridge; the grave, steady, striding watchfulness of Wordsworth.

> There is a *chaunt* in the recitation both of Coleridge and Wordsworth, which acts as a spell upon the hearer, and disarms judgement . . . Coleridge's manner is more full, animated, and varied; Wordsworth's more equable, sustained, and internal. The one might be termed more *dramatic*, the other more *lyrical*. Coleridge has told me that he himself liked to compose in walking over uneven ground, or breaking through the straggling branches of a copse-wood; whereas Wordsworth always wrote (if he could) walking up and down a straight gravel-walk . . .[66]

The slight, almost comic, unexpectedness of this last contrast is easy to overlook. It was Coleridge who so often clambered up into the hills alone, or plunged like a Red Indian (a comparison he would later use himself) into the woods, with his Notebooks. Wordsworth's expeditions were usually undertaken with Dorothy, and his composing was done in the smooth walks and parklands of Alfoxden. While Coleridge's poetry of these months brings the entire Quantocks landscape alive – the heath, the combes, the woodlands, the dells, the waterfalls, the hidden streams, Wordsworth's imagined countryside more often returns to the Lake District of his childhood. It was Coleridge alone who established the Quantocks as his poetic kingdom.

11

But now, like Kubla Khan, he was intending to depart. The plan for Germany arose from several considerations, but primarily because Coleridge wished to use the "munificent patronage" of the Wedgwoods to "finish his education" in philosophy, science and theology at a European university.[67] He had dreamed of such a visit since 1796. The lectures of Blumenbach, the plays of Schiller, the metaphysics of Kant, the ballads of Bürger, all drew him like a magnet towards Germany, which was now regarded – with the "loss" of France to liberty – as the intellectual outpost of Europe. The French invasion of Switzerland in February 1798, which forms the central lament in "France: an Ode", gave the matter urgency: Germany was "unsettled" and threatened like England herself with invasion, and the whole Continent might soon be closed to English visitors. Coleridge even expected that he and Wordsworth might soon be drafted into the army.

He found no difficulty in sweeping Wordsworth and Dorothy into this next plan, since the St Aubin family had refused to renew the lease on Alfoxden after June, for reasons that were evidently connected with Spy Nozy's investigations, and the continuing local suspicions of their literary circle.[68] Initially, Coleridge also intended to take Sara and his children with him, planning only for a "3 or 4 months sojourn" at Hamburg and Jena. But Berkeley's delicate health and "the uncertainty of our happiness, comfort, cheap living etc in Germany" gradually called this part of the scheme into question.

At Stowey Tom Poole now began to voice his anxieties about Wordsworth's unsettling influence on Coleridge. His growing doubts of the whole plan were echoed by many of Coleridge's old Bristol friends. But the Wedgwoods seemed satisfied with the high ambition of the undertaking – a working knowledge of German seemed indispensable to the great literary and philosophical work Coleridge talked about – and Tom Wedgwood, as restless and enquiring as Coleridge himself, was particularly enthusiastic.

In London, Coleridge's newspaper editor Daniel Stuart was also delighted to see the man whom he had marked out as a major future contributor to the *Morning Post* – a potential leader-writer as well as poet – breaking out of what he must have regarded as a provincial backwater. His idea of Coleridge as a significant former of public opinion was shown very clearly by the vigorous editorial he attached to the publication of "France: an Ode" in April.

> It is very satisfactory to find so zealous and steady an advocate of Freedom as MR. COLERIDGE concur with us in condemning the conduct of France towards the Swiss Cantons. Indeed his concurrence is not singular; we know of no Friend to Liberty who is not of his opinion. What we most admire is the *avowal* of his sentiments, and public censure of the unprincipled and atrocious conduct of France. The Poem itself is written with great energy.[69]

In June, Coleridge spent several days with the Wedgwoods discussing his plans at their new house at Cobham in Surrey. "The Wedgwoods received me with joy & affection. I have been metaphysicizing so long & so closely with T. Wedgwood, that I am a caput mortuum, mere lees & residuum." But he tried to temper his growing philosophical excitements with a soothing bucolic to Poole: "This place is a noble large house, in a rich pleasant country; but the little Toe of Quantock is better than the head and shoulders of Surrey & Middlesex."[70]

In July, the Wordsworths took leave of Alfoxden, staying for a week at Stowey, before disappearing for a summer tour up the Wye Valley, when "Tintern Abbey" – the last poem in the *Lyrical Ballads* – was written. (In this poem, Wordsworth developed some themes of "Frost at Midnight", applying the Hartley passage to Dorothy: "Therefore let the moon / Shine on thee in thy solitary walk . . .") It was also decided to print "The Nightingale" instead of "Lewti", as an apt memorial to their last Quantock days together. In the final setting of the volume, Coleridge's poems – opening with the *Mariner* – thus occupied virtually the first seventy pages of the collection (out of a total of two hundred and ten), setting a distinctive tone of Romantic strangeness, which afterwards was much deprecated by his friend.

Departure for Hamburg was scheduled for mid-September 1798. It was finally arranged that Poole would keep a fatherly eye on Sara and the children at Stowey, while Coleridge took as a travelling companion, John Chester, a young farmer who wished to study German agriculture, and whom Hazlitt remembered as frequently accompanying them on their Quantock walks – usually speechless in admiration at all the learned talk, and "attracted to Coleridge's discourse as flies are to honey".

Coleridge's decision to go without Sara was justified on practical grounds. The trip was to be one of strict "intellectual utility" and economy; and Coleridge promised to keep in touch with Stowey by long, twice-weekly travel-letters (to Sara and Poole alternately). But Sara, at first acquiescent, came to feel the separation keenly, and finally with great bitterness. Indeed Coleridge was already much absent from Stowey that summer even before departure. He was in Bristol during August, and made a "sudden dart into Wales" with the Wordsworths for a week, to see John Thelwall at his farm at Llyswen.[71] By early September he was in London with Chester, renewing contacts with Godwin, and cultivating Wordsworth's radical publisher at St Paul's Churchyard, Joseph Johnson.

From Germany he would write with intense affection to Sara, and with growing signs of homesickness for their life at Stowey. Yet the sense of some rupture in his family life is apparent. Poole came to play a curious role as marital counsellor between husband and wife, advising Sara what news to include – and what to omit – when she wrote to Coleridge. Both Poole and the Wedgwoods were suspicious of Wordsworth's influence, but it is difficult to discount the simple impression that Coleridge was glad to be free of his domestic existence for a while. The sentimentality with which he idealised it at a distance, particularly his feelings for his children, only confirms this. He seemed guiltily aware of this predicament, and would soon write anxiously to Poole that he did not want Sara "imagining that I do not feel my own & her absence as I ought to feel it".[72]

12

One person Coleridge did not see in London that September was Charles Lamb. In the dispute with Charles Lloyd over *Edmund Oliver*, Lamb found himself drawn into an anti-Coleridge faction with Southey, and much hurtful gossip was exchanged. Some time in the summer he sent Coleridge a wholly uncharacteristic letter, mocking the friend he had once revered, with a series of satirical "Theological" enquiries, which show the unconscious marks of his betrayed – and perhaps adolescent – hero-worship. They included such questions as "Whether God loves a lying Angel better than a true Man?", and "Whether the higher order of Seraphim Illuminati ever sneer?"[73]

That Lamb had ever thought of Coleridge as an angel or a seraph, speaks for itself. But the reproach that Coleridge was a divinity fallen from grace (exaggerated respect followed by exaggerated condemnation) was to be a pattern of disillusion repeated in many subsequent friendships. Lamb, however, never really lost the warmth of his feelings for Coleridge. They were soon recovered after his return from Germany, by which time Lloyd's mental imbalance (which led eventually to the asylum) had become evident even to Southey. Indeed Lamb's profound respect for Coleridge could even here be traced beneath the ironies, when he concluded: "I now submit to your enquiries the above Theological Propositions, to be by you defended, or oppugned, or both, in the Schools of Germany, whither I am told you are departing, to the utter dissatisfaction of your native Devonshire, & regret universal of England . . ."[74] This was already something like an olive-branch, in the Lamb manner. Southey was far less magnanimous, and vented his spleen in public, through the medium of a review.

Notices of the *Lyrical Ballads* only began to appear in October, after Coleridge's departure for Germany, and for the most part they were puzzled but impressed. The *Analytical*, the *Monthly* and the *British Critic*, while expressing reservations, quoted at length, and picked out "The Nightingale", "Tintern Abbey", and "The Thorn" for particular praise. Most remarkably of all, remembering its political posture, the *Anti-Jacobin* described the whole collection as having "genius, taste, elegance, wit, and imagery of the most beautiful kind", though this review did not appear until April 1800.

But the fullest of the early articles appeared in the *Critical Review* of October 1798, and was an unsigned demolition job by Southey, which heaped scorn on "The Idiot Boy" and "The Thorn", and then savaged the *Mariner.* "Many of the stanzas are laboriously beautiful; but in connection they are absurd or unintelligible . . . We do not sufficiently understand the story to analyse it. It is a Dutch attempt at German sublimity. Genius has here been employed in producing a poem of little merit."[75]

Both Coleridge and Wordsworth were understandably offended by this hostility from a man who should at least have proved a literary ally, whatever his personal feelings. More damaging still, it was probably this piece that first convinced Wordsworth that the *Mariner* was the weak link in the collection, because the most novel and ambitious. The "Dutch" jibe implied a drunken second-rate imitation of Bürger.

Unknown to either of them, it was Lamb himself who took up the cudgels on their behalf in a private letter to Southey of November. It is a remarkable demonstration both of Lamb's disinterestedness, and of his acute literary perception. It also represented what the younger generation would soon come to feel almost universally about Coleridge's ballad.

> I am sorry you are so sparing of praise to the "Ancient Mariner;" – so far from calling it, as you do, with some wit, but more severity, "A Dutch Attempt" etc, I call it a right English attempt, and a successful one, to dethrone German sublimity. You have selected a passage fertile in unmeaning miracles, but have passed by some fifty passages as miraculous as the miracles they celebrate. I never so deeply felt the pathetic as in that part,
>
> A spring of love gush'd from my heart,
> And I bless'd them unaware –
>
> It stung me into high pleasure through suffering. Lloyd does not like it; his head is too metaphysical, and your taste too correct . . .[76]

13

Coleridge left one other hostage to literary fortune in London. This was his twenty-three-page quarto containing "Fears in Solitude", "France: an Ode", and "Frost at Midnight", which was unexpectedly taken on by Joseph Johnson, in exchange for a useful £30 credit to be drawn in Hamburg.[77] The edition appears to have been circulated very quietly: a copy was sent to George Coleridge in Ottery, Southey bought another, and Sara Coleridge (in one of her rare literary comments) described the first poem, with something like surprise in December (as if she had not seen it before) as "very beautiful".[78]

It received four short, but very favourable reviews, though there was some adverse notice of Coleridge's political outspokenness, from both the radical and the conservative press. This indicated the narrow path he was attempting to tread between two increasingly polarised factions. The *Critical* thought he had become a patriot "alarmist"; while the *British Critic* still lamented his "preposterous prejudices against his country".[79] In fact, in its delicate and ambitious balancing of private and public voices – actually combined in "Fears in Solitude" – it is the most accomplished of his early collections.

The running order of the three poems, carefully chosen by Coleridge, takes the reader from the private world of the Conversation Poems into the public stance of the "Ode", and back again. Its three-part structure is itself an ideological statement, which courageously links together the pattern of Coleridge's life from the days of Pantisocracy to the "retirement" in the Quantocks. It is both political and confessional, a provocative combination of literary styles and subject-matter, which attempts to record the representative experience of a "Friend of Liberty" in those confused and passionate years of the 1790s. It was for this reason that Joseph Johnson, perhaps the greatest radical publisher of his day – the friend of Godwin, Blake, and Mary Wollstonecraft – was evidently so keen to issue the quarto, much to Coleridge's own surprise. "I had introduced myself to Johnson, the Bookseller, who received me civilly the first time, cordially the second, affectionately the third – & finally took leave of me with tears in his eyes."[80]

The opening poem, "Fears in Solitude", begins in "a green and silent spot . . . a small and silent dell" in the Quantocks, where Coleridge is once more alone with his "dreams of better worlds" amid the wild flowers and the skylarks. He then launches into a long and intricate political meditation, touching upon his hopes for political change, his fears of France, his sense of guilt at being considered an "enemy" of his own country. He accuses the conservative English of warmongering, and the radicals of corruption. He speaks "most bitter truth, but without bitterness". Yet his own position is full of contradictions, and he falls back on a beautiful but anxious hymn of loyalty:

> O native Britain! O my Mother Isle!
> How shouldst thou prove aught else but dear and holy
> To me, who from thy lakes and mountain-hills
> Thy clouds, thy quiet dales, thy rocks and seas,
> Have drunk in all my intellectual life . . .[81]

The poem ends with a return to "beloved Stowey", his cottage and his family, evoked with the magic, pastoral power of a Samuel Palmer picture.

The central poem, "France: an Ode", is a public statement of his changing attitude to the revolution, from the fall of the Bastille (stanza two), the coming of the Terror and the declaration of war (stanza three), to the invasion of neutral Switzerland (stanza four). It is probably his most successful exercise in the Miltonic mode, using a refined and chastened version of the language of "Religious Musings", but still carrying a powerful body of epic imagery which sustains the historical importance of his subject. His picture of France awakening in 1789, part terrible giant, and part fretful child, is often quoted by political essayists, and has the force of one of Goya's paintings:

> When France in wrath her giant-limbs upreared,
> And with that oath, which smote air, earth and sea,
> Stamped her strong foot and said she would be free,
> Bear witness for me, how I hoped and feared! . . .[82]

Coleridge goes on to describe the troubled state of English radicals during the period of the Terror, and the onset of the European war. He shows how they tried to remain loyal to the principles of liberty enshrined in the revolution, while increasingly horrified by the violence and excesses of the French themselves:

> "And what," I said, "though Blasphemy's loud scream
> With that sweet music of deliverance strove!
> Though all the fierce and drunken passions wove

A dance more wild than e'er was maniac's dream!
Ye storms, that round the dawning East assembled,
The Sun was rising, though ye hid his light![83]

This emphasis on the fanaticism and atheism which Coleridge feared, while yet hoping in the broad sunrise of liberty, seems a faithful reflection of his *Watchman* period, with all its stormy struggles. He still hoped that "conquering by her happiness alone", and bringing peace and justice to the "low huts of them that toil and groan", France would eventually "compel the nations to be free".

But then, in the spring of 1798, came the terrible disillusion of the French invasion of Switzerland, with all its attendant bloodshed, and the overwhelming realisation that France was now acting again like a brutal imperial power. The imagery here takes on poignant echoes of the Quantock days:

Forgive me, Freedom! O forgive those dreams!
I hear thy voice, I hear thy loud lament,
From bleak Helvetia's icy caverns sent –
I hear thy groans upon her blood-stained streams![84]

It was these passages that Daniel Stuart described in his editorial as containing "some of the most vigorous lines we have ever read".

In the final stanza, Coleridge continues to defend the idea of liberty, by withdrawing it from the immediate political conflict, and passionately identifying it with the indestructible force and beauty of nature. (Shelley was to adopt a similar position, though with very different revolutionary implications, in his "Ode to the West Wind" of 1819.) Here the public Ode moves back into the private, visionary world of the two Conversation Poems, which are placed on each side of it in the quarto. Liberty is glimpsed in the "homeless winds" over the Quantock heaths, and the ocean waves beyond Porlock and Lynton:

And there I felt thee! – on that sea-cliff's verge,
Whose pines, scarce travelled by the breeze above,
Had made one murmur with the distant surge!
Yes, while I stood and gazed, my temples bare,
And shot my being through earth, sea, and air,
Possessing all things with intensest love,
O Liberty! my spirit felt thee there.[85]

The quarto then closes with "Frost at Midnight", in which his child Hartley seems to become the symbol of all he hoped for in the future, a new generation promising a life blessed equally by liberty and nature. The tryptich of poems thus formed was in many ways Coleridge's testament to the first decade of his adult life as a writer, moving from his own childhood to that of his son. In Germany he would celebrate his twenty-sixth birthday.

14

There were various last-minute preparations: £30 in cash was set aside for Sara, the Wedgwoods arranged for Coleridge to draw German currency from a commercial agent of theirs in Hamburg, Von Axen; and an enormous travelling coat was purchased for twenty-eight shillings, as heavy as a rug, with huge pockets for books and a spectacular collar big enough to fold entirely over Coleridge's head like a night-cap.[86]

Coleridge and his overcoat, in company with John Chester and the Wordsworths, left London on the mail for Yarmouth on 14 September. Besides the travel-letters to Stowey, he had agreed to send articles and translations to Stuart at the *Morning Post*. From Yarmouth on the 15th he sent an emotional farewell to Poole: "I am on the point of leaving my native country for the first time – a country, which, God Almighty knows, is dear to me above all things for the love I bear to you. – Of many friends, whom I love and esteem, my head & heart have ever chosen you as the Friend – as the one being, in whom is involved the full & whole meaning of that sacred Title." He commended Sara into Poole's keeping.[87]

On 16 September 1798 the packet sailed out of Yarmouth at eleven in the morning on a brisk south-westerly, and the author of the *Ancient Mariner* found himself for the first time in open seas. As England dropped away below the horizon, his thoughts were not for his poems, but for his children. "When we lost sight of land, the moment that we quite lost sight of it, & the heavens all round me rested upon the waters, my dear Babies came upon me like a flash of lightning – I saw their faces so distinctly!"[88] Then, unexpectedly, both the Wordsworths began to be violently seasick. Coleridge paced the deck, observing the mounting grey waves of the North Sea with interest, "neither sick or giddy, but gay as a lark".[89]

NINE

Der Wanderer

1

Coleridge's visit to Germany was planned as a three-month tour, but lasted for ten. During this time he reverted in many ways to the life of a bachelor student – learning the language, studying science and metaphysics, working on Schiller and Lessing as "special subjects", and touring much of the north German countryside between Lübeck and the Hartz Mountains. His Notebooks and letters show the liveliest interest in German manners and folk customs, and voracious reading (and translating) of German poetry and newspapers. He worked very hard, despite some serious drinking and several bouts of opium-taking at times of acute homesickness.

The winter of 1798–9 was to prove the hardest of the century, and for many weeks he was cut off from all communications with home, mail being blocked by frozen rivers and snow-bound roads. But his intense sociability, quite different from the Wordsworths, carried him through as he moved with increasing ease in German society, visiting and dining out, and making a wide circle of new friends. The experience subtly changed many of his attitudes, both literary and political, and gave him a strong new sense of his loyalty to his "Mother Isle".

The two-day crossing from Yarmouth to Cuxhaven set the tone for much of the tour. While William and Dorothy remained closeted below decks, Coleridge rapidly got on terms with all the other passengers, drinking with a Dane, buffooning with an old Prussian, and discussing politics with a Swedish nobleman. "I partook of the Hanoverian's & Dane's wines, & Pine apples – told them some hundred Jokes, and passed as many of my own. Danced all together a sort of wild dance on the Deck – Wordsworth and Sister bad as ever."[1]

The Dane, rapidly succumbing to his own brandy and Coleridge's charm, was soon announcing that they had "Un Philosophe" in their midst: "Vat imagination! vat language! vat fast science! vat eyes – vat

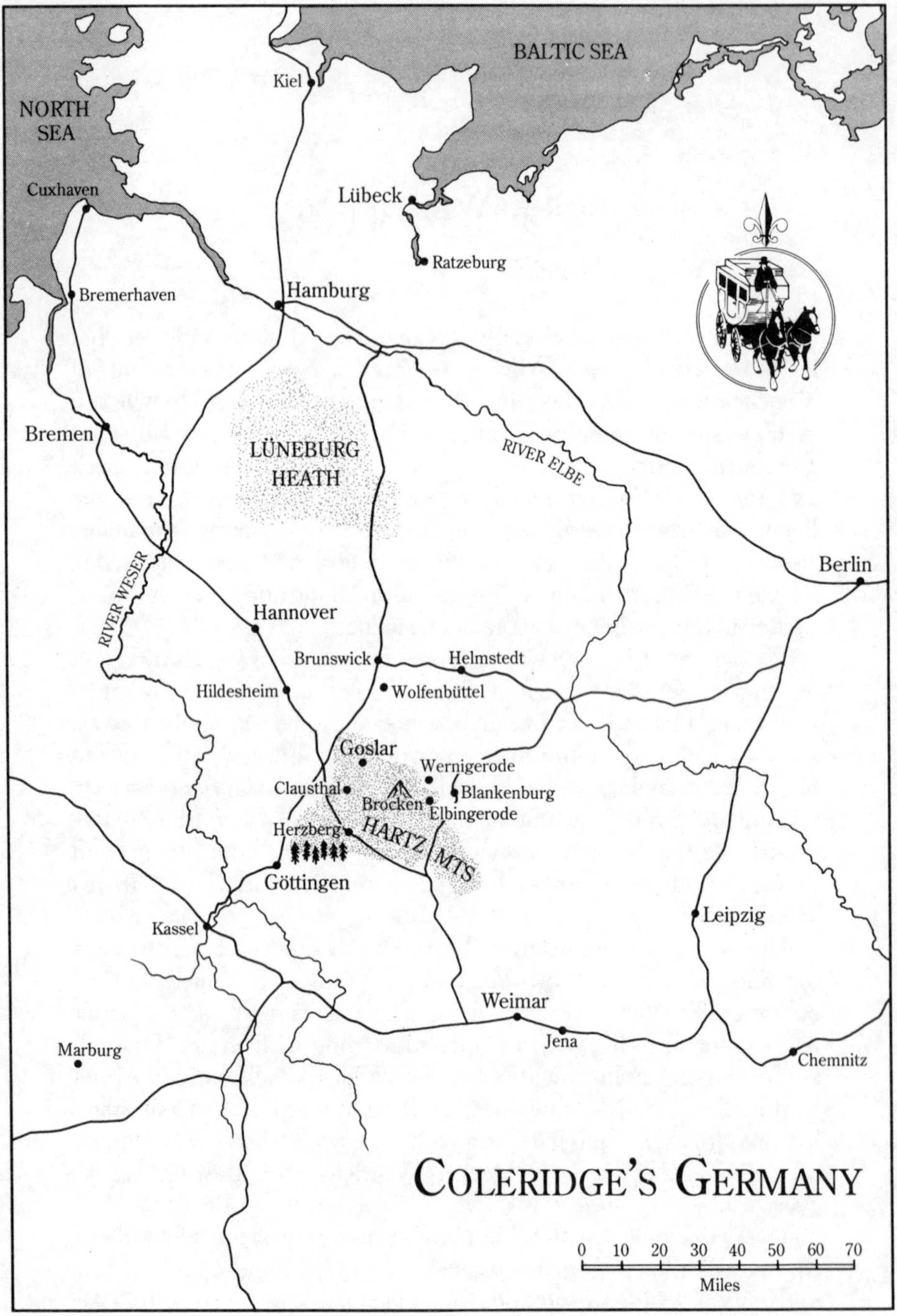
BALTIC SEA
NORTH SEA
Kiel
Lübeck
Cuxhaven
Ratzeburg
Bremerhaven
Hamburg
Bremen
LÜNEBURG HEATH
RIVER ELBE
RIVER WESER
Berlin
Hannover
Brunswick
Helmstedt
Hildesheim
Wolfenbüttel
Goslar
Wernigerode
Clausthal
Blankenburg
Brocken
Elbingerode
Herzberg
HARTZ MTS
Göttingen
Leipzig
Kassel
Weimar
Jena
Marburg
Chemnitz
0 10 20 30 40 50 60 70
Miles

COLERIDGE'S GERMANY

a milk vite forehead! – O my Heafen! You are a God!" All of which Coleridge recorded with Kubla-like complacency.

But at night he wrapped himself in his greatcoat and dozed quietly on the deck, watching the shifting movements of the stars, and the glitter of the sea.

> The Ocean is a noble Thing by night; a beautiful white cloud of foam at momently intervals roars & rushes by the side of the Vessel, and Stars of Flame dance & sparkle & go out in it – & every now and then light Detachments of Foam dart away from the Vessel's side with their galaxies of stars, & scour out of sight, like a Tartar Troop over a Wilderness! – What these stars are, I cannot say – the sailors say, that they are the Fish Spawn which is phosphorescent.[2]

At four o'clock in the morning, still out of sight of land, he noticed a wild duck swimming alone on the sea. "A single solitary wild duck – You cannot conceive how interesting a thing it looked in that round objectless desert of waters."[3]

2

Once safely anchored in the mouth of the Cuxhaven estuary the following evening, Coleridge immediately began a letter to Sara: "Over what place does the Moon hang to your eye, my dearest Sara? To me it hangs over the left bank of the Elbe; and a long trembling road of moonlight reaches from thence up to the stern of our Vessel, & there it ends . . . Goodnight, my dear, dear Sara! – 'every night when I go to bed & every morning when I rise' I will think of you with a yearning love, & of my blessed Babies!"[4] They docked at Hamburg on 19 September 1798, and disembarked into "an ugly City that stinks in every corner", where the hotel rooms were filthy, but the claret excellent and cheap.

They remained in Hamburg for a fortnight, tramping out to Altona and all over the city, using their letters of introduction to Von Axen, Johnson's friend Remnant, and various other booksellers and merchants, including the younger brother of the poet Klopstock, proprietor of a Hamburg newspaper. This produced an introduction to the poet himself, on the 21st, whom Coleridge regarded as "the venerable father of German poetry".

He described their interview at length, with the curious spectacle of Wordsworth discussing Milton in French, while Coleridge himself discussed the "elder German Poets" in Latin. He noted how Klopstock's enormous swollen legs and solemn powdered periwig contrasted strangely with his cheerful manner and quick gestures, "lively in his motions as a boy", which still showed the author of the "Odes". However he was indignant when Klopstock talked "great nonsense about the superior power which the German language possessed, of *concentering meaning*".

The talk moved into smoother waters with general satisfaction over Nelson's great victory over the French at the Battle of the Nile, just announced; and closely shared feelings about the revolution. "At the beginning of the French Revolution Klopstock wrote some fiery Odes in praise of France – he received high & honorary Presents from the French Republic, &, like our Priestley, was invited to the French Legislature, which he declined. But when French Liberty metamorphosed herself into a Fury, he sent back the Presents with an Ode, expressing his Recantation."[5]

Coleridge was moved to tears by this meeting, and promised to translate some of the Odes into English. But he could not quite forgive the periwig: "it is an honor to Poets & Great Men that you think of them as parts of Nature; and any thing of Trick & Fashion wounds you in them as much as when you see Yews clipped into miserable peacocks. – The author of the Messiah should have worn his own Grey Hair."[6]

Coleridge's extensive Hamburg letters to Poole and Sara were packed with such lively observations. He ranged over everything that met his eye, nose, ear or mouth: recipes for German soups ("I have tasted 20 kinds"); the universal use of brass doorbells ("an incessant Kling, kling, klang . . . Bürger alludes to this in the 'Lenore'"); the styles of tobacco pipes ("cane, clay, porcelain, wood, tin, silver, and ivory"); the construction of the hackney-coaches of Hamburg; the fantastic signboards above the shops; the prostitutes of Altona; or the largest organ he had ever seen in the Church of St Nicholas.

He was particularly struck by the popularity of English fashions among the German youth, and the general warmth towards England. ". . . to be an Englishman is in Germany to be an Angel – they almost worship you . . . It is absolutely false that the literary Men are Democrats in Germany – Many *were*; but like me, have *published* Abjurations of the French – among which number are Klopstock, Goethe (the author of the 'Sorrows of Werter') Wieland, Schiller & Kotzebu."[7] This did not however prevent innkeepers and hoteliers charging them exorbitant prices, which especially irritated Wordsworth.

The difference between Coleridge's and Wordsworth's financial resources quickly became apparent during this fortnight. When they were initially looking for rooms, Coleridge was invited by the Swedish nobleman to stay in plush apartments as the "great superb Hotel de Hamburgh"; but Wordsworth meanwhile had been to immense trouble to find them cheap rooms at Der Wilder Man on the market-place, and himself slept at the Sea Man's Hostel.[8]

At Der Wilder Man Coleridge was awoken by the screaming of "distressful" poultry beneath his window. By the 22nd they were all "in a state of Oscillation between Weimar & some village near Hamburg – Frightened at the expenses of Travelling . . ."[9] The following day Coleridge and John Chester rode thirty-five miles out to prospect the quiet but fashionable resort of Ratzeburg, set amidst the lakes south of Lübeck.

Here they found an elegant little country town, approached across a bridge over the lake, surrounded by beautiful woodlands – "exquisite walks, for Autumn & for Winter; the tints on the trees & lakes – the icicles & the snow."[10] A small military garrison attracted a mixed society of moneyed burghers and retired nobles, all very pro-English. "Rule Britannia" was struck up when they went to a local concert, and at the table d'hôte they were given a feast "in honor of Nelson's victory". From the houses on the island hill-top, there was a view up-lake of the seven spires of Lübeck.[11] Coleridge got an introduction to the Protestant pastor, whose Rectory was positioned close to the church on the very shores of the lake, and discussed terms for three months' board and lodging, at thirty-six marks a week.

But back in Hamburg on the 27th, Wordsworth found these terms exorbitant. After anxious discussions, it was decided rather surprisingly that the party should divide up. It is clear that Wordsworth, who was about to enter upon one of his most intensive and brilliant periods of composition, was really looking for complete rustic seclusion, while Coleridge wanted a much more social existence, where he could practise the German language and study its culture. Coleridge noted regretfully: "Wordsworth & Sister determined to go on, & seek, lower down, obscurer & cheaper Lodgings without boarding."[12]

Less explicit, perhaps, was Wordsworth's desire to be completely alone with Dorothy, who ever since the Tintern Abbey expedition had become something like her brother's Muse, magically holding open the gateway back into the Cumberland childhood. The growing intensity of this relationship seems well understood by Coleridge, who came to regard it, as his German letters show, as something sacred to Wordsworth and intimately associated with his poetry. Though he often expressed his longing to be with them in Germany, and they with him, an exquisite tact held them apart, pouring all their mutual feelings into innumerable letters exchanged throughout this winter and the following spring, though very few have survived.

The two men went on a last evening walk together, out to Altona, seeing a child riding on the ramparts on a goat, and a melancholy sunset filling the dark woods with a "brassy mist".

They stayed in Hamburg for the Feast of St Michael on 29 September, which cheered them all, and then Coleridge and Chester removed to Ratzeburg for the winter, while Wordsworth and Dorothy slipped deep into Lower Saxony, finally discovering cheap lodgings in the old medieval town of Goslar, 200 miles south in the remotest part of the Hartz Mountains. The only strange thing was that Wordsworth did not write for nearly six weeks, a silence which Coleridge regarded as "ominous" though he did not say why.[13]

Coleridge reported all this to Poole, with his great relief at finally obtaining their Goslar address from Dorothy. Apparently Wordsworth was working hard, but not much at German; as for himself, "I work at nothing else, from morning to night."[14]

3

The avuncular concern with which Poole oversaw and tried to direct Coleridge's German labours from far off in England is remarkable. He wrote with the lengthy, well-intentioned fussiness of some elderly moral tutor, who has to deal with a brilliant, wayward, but favourite pupil. He was brisk about the separation: "The Wordsworths have left you – so there is an end of our fears about amalgamation, etc. I think you both did perfectly right . . . You will, of course, hear frequently from Wordsworth."

He was stern about the work to be done. "You are now, dear Col, fixed in Germany, and what you have to do is to attend *wholly* to those things that are better attained in Germany than elsewhere . . . I should spend no time to send anything to Stuart . . . *Begin* no poetry – no original composition – unless translation from German may be so called . . . Beware of being too much with Chester . . . Live with Germans. Read in German. Think in German." He was severely encouraging about the regime to be held to. "Make a strict arrangement of your time and chain yourself down to it ... It would counteract a *disease* of your mind – which is an active subtlety of imagination ... This many of your friends falsely call irresolution. No one has more resolution and decision than you."[15]

There is a distinct echo here of the earnest, anxious, George Coleridge, writing to his undergraduate brother at Cambridge, five years before. That Coleridge continued to depend on such paternal counselling in adulthood, from the "beloved" friend far less intellectually gifted than himself, revealed the childlike aspect in his nature which showed no signs yet of maturing. But of course Coleridge, with his chameleon gifts, may deliberately have cultivated this aspect for Poole's benefit. When no further letters reached Ratzeburg after 8 October (they were held up in the frozen Elbe) until the beginning of December, he wrote to both Poole and Sara with increasing desperation.[16]

Yet life at Ratzeburg was evidently very pleasant. He was immediately befriended by the pastor, and slipped into a comfortable regime of morning studies, afternoon walks, and evening entertainments. By mid-November, he wrote: "we have a deep snow and a hard frost, and I am learning to skate – There are Balls and Concerts every week – & I am pressed by all the Ladies to dance."[17]

He became a favourite among the pastor's children, and skilfully turned household existence into a non-stop language lesson, as he fondly recalled.

> It was a regular part of my morning studies for the first six weeks of my residence at Ratzeburg, to accompany the good and kind old pastor, with whom I lived, from the cellar to the roof, through gardens, farmyard, etc, and to call every, the minutest, thing by its German name. Advertisements, farces, jest books, and the conversation of children while I was at play with them, contributed their share to a more home-like acquaintance with the language, than I could have acquired from works of polite literature, or even from polite society.[18]

He went on several winter expeditions, one of them by boat up the lake – before it too froze over – to the "old fantastic Town" of Lübeck on the Baltic, with its medieval ramparts, spired gateways, and ancient churches staffed by pastors all in huge white ruffs, "exactly like the pictures of Queen Elizabeth". He delighted in all curious customs. "In the evening I wish myself a painter, just to draw a German Party at Cards – One man's long Pipe rested on the Table, smoking half a yard from his mouth by the fish-dish; another who was shuffling, and of course had both hands employed, held his pipe in his Teeth, and it hung down between his Thighs, even to his ancles – & the distortions which the attitude & effort occasioned made him a most ludicrous Phiz."[19] He felt he could have loitered a week in the churches: "every picture, every legend cut out in gilded wood-work, was a history of the manners & feelings of the ages."[20]

When the lake froze over completely in December, he took part enthusiastically in the skating. His descriptions of this are fascinating, for he sent them to Wordsworth as well as Sara, and so inspired the famous passage of Cumberland skating in *The Prelude* which Wordsworth wrote that winter in Goslar. The verbal resemblances are in places exact. Coleridge wrote:

> In skating there are three pleasing circumstances – the infinitely subtle particles of Ice, which the Skate cuts up, & which creep & run before the Skater like a low mist, & in sun rise or sun set become coloured; 2nd the Shadow of the Skater in the water seen thro' the Transparent Ice, & 3rd the melancholy undulating sound from the Skate not without variety; & when very many are skating together, the sounds and the noises give an impulse to the icy Trees, & the wood all round the lake *tinkle!*[21]

Wordsworth, in the long childhood sequence, "Fair seed-time had my soul . . ." which later became Book 1 of *The Prelude*, turned to his memories of skating in "the frosty season" in the Lake District. He recalled the cottage windows blazing in the twilight, the village clock tolling six, and the sound of voices and skate-blades echoing out into the gathering darkness:

> . . . The precipices rang aloud;
> The leafless trees, and every ice crag
> Tinkled like iron, while the distant hills
> Into the tumult sent an alien sound
> Of melancholy, not unnoticed, while the stars,
> Eastwards were sparkling clear . . .[22]

Dorothy wrote back teasingly to Coleridge: "You speak in rapture of the pleasures of skating . . . in the North of England amongst the mountains whither we wish to decoy you, you might enjoy it with every possible advantage. A race with William upon his native lakes would leave to the heart and imagination something more Dear and valuable than the gay sight of Ladies and countesses whirling along the Lake of Ratzeburg."[23] In this exchange, there is again a hint of the sharp differences in their social approach to Germany; a little jealousy from Dorothy; and for the first time clear evidence of the Wordsworths' desire to draw Coleridge away from Stowey the following year.

Coleridge felt his friends' absence in Goslar very much, and towards Christmas sent them a light, but deeply affectionate set of "English hexameters" which he had composed one night while lying in bed, "ill and wakeful". Had they all been together, this might have been yet another blank verse Conversation Poem, but instead he cajoled his feelings into a bouncing metre, to be read "with a nod of the head in a humoring recitativo". Nonetheless it contained depths of emotion:

> William, my head and my heart! dear Poet that feelest and thinkest!
> Dorothy, eager of soul, my most affectionate sister!
> Many a mile, O! many a wearisome mile are ye distant,
> Long, long comfortless roads, with no one eye that doth know us.[24]

There was, he said, "a great deal more, which I have forgotten, as I did not write it down." But in another passage, describing the pains in his eyes (he had caught an eye infection, perhaps while skating, and had styes), he unearthed a further hidden memory of his own home at Stowey. "What a life is the eye!" he exclaims, and then imagines a man who is in some way symbolically blind to domestic affections:

> Him that is utterly blind, nor glimpses the fire that warms him;
> Him that never beheld the swelling breast of his mother;
> Him that ne'er smiled at the bosom as babe that smiles in its slumber;
> Even to him it exists, it stirs and moves in its prison;
> Lives with a separate life, and "Is it the spirit?" he murmurs:
> Sure, it has thoughts of its own, and to see is only its language.[25]

This mysterious theme of blindness was to appear in much of his later poetry. It must have struck the Wordsworths as strange, in one who could evidently see and feel for them with such immediacy.

When Wordsworth sent a passage of his own poetry, the section which now begins, "There was a Boy, ye knew him well, ye

Cliffs / And Islands of Winander!" Coleridge responded with all that perception and delight which had become indispensable to their friendship. At first, he admitted that in the "general bustle of pleasure" with which he read the whole letter, the lines had "only puzzled" him. But now on rereading he saw that "they are very beautiful, and leave an affecting impression. That 'Uncertain heaven received / Into the bosom of the steady lake,' I should have recognised any where; and had I met these lines running wild in the deserts of Arabia, I should have instantly screamed out 'Wordsworth!' . . ."[26]

4

Though Coleridge continued to receive "long and affectionate" letters from the Wordsworths throughout the winter, he was cut off from all news from England until early January.[27] Only a letter of 1 November from Sara arrived a month later, informing him that little Berkeley had been seriously ill after a smallpox inoculation.

Coleridge wept passionately as he imagined this, delivering himself of "the stress and tumult of my animal sensibility". Sara had moved to Bristol to nurse the children: "O my babies! – Absence makes it painful to be a Father! – My Wife, believe and know that I pant to be home & with you."[28]

Despite this outburst of paternal emotions (which Poole feared would distract his German studies), Coleridge did not yet set his return date to England, though Sara must still have hoped that the original three months would not last much beyond January 1799. Instead he turned his attentions to family Christmas in Ratzeburg.

His descriptions of the festive season contain one of the earliest known records, in English, of the customs of the Christmas tree and Father Christmas (which were much later popularised in Britain by Queen Victoria's German husband, Prince Albert).

> On the Evening before Christmas Day one of the parlours is lighted up by the Children, into which the parents must not go; a great yew-bough is fastened on the Table at a little distance from the wall, a multitude of little Tapers are fastened in the bough, but not so as to burn it until they are nearly burnt out – & coloured paper etc hangs and flutters from the twigs. – Under this bough the Children lay out in great neatness the presents they mean for their parents.[29]

Coleridge participated enthusiastically in this ceremony at the pastor's house, where eight or nine children ran about, tenderly hugging their parents, who both dissolved into tears. He identified with the father, who "clasped all his children so tight to his breast, as if he did it to stifle the Sob that was rising within him. – I was very much affected. And the Shadow of the Bough on the wall, on the wall & arching over on the Ceiling, made a pretty picture – & then the raptures of the very little ones, when at last the Twigs & thread leaves began to catch fire, & *snap* – O that was a delight for them!"[30] He does not mention how the incipient conflagration was avoided.

While the children's presents were given under the tree on Christmas Eve, those from the parents were brought on Christmas Day by a mysterious forerunner of the modern Father Christmas. This was one of those "multitude of strange wild superstitions" which fascinated Coleridge among the folk customs.

> Formerly, & still in all the little Towns & villages through the whole of North Germany, these Presents were sent by all the parents of the village to some one Fellow who in high Buskins, a white Robe, a Mask, & an enormous Flax Wig personates Knecht Rupert – i.e. the Servant Rupert. On Christmas night he goes round to every house, & says that Jesus Christ, his Master, sent him there – the Parents & older children receive him with great pomp of reverence, while the little ones are most terribly frightened.

One of the things that most struck him about this ritual was the way that the children, having been "let into the secret" of Knecht Rupert's real identity at the age of seven or eight, instinctively continued the charade for their smaller brothers and sisters: "it is curious, how faithfully they all keep it!"[31] He saw this as an example of the co-existence of rationalism and religion, with the collusions of folk-superstition, which seemed almost universal in Germany, whether in the Protestant north or Catholic south.

Another example occurred in the ancient insignia against witchcraft, which appeared everywhere on country buildings: "both on Inns, Stables, & Farms there are ALWAYS nailed up at both Gables two pieces of wood . . . the crosses often shaped into horns & horses heads. This, they believe universally, keeps off the Evil Spirit who in a ball of fire would come into their chimnies. – Here *all* the higher classes, except the Clergy *perhaps*, are Infidels – all the *People* grossly superstitious."[32]

5

On 4 January 1799, Coleridge at last received a long letter from Poole, and immediately sat down to answer it with a detailed description of his German studies and future plans. "I am quite well: calm & industrious. I now read German as English . . . On very trivial, and on metaphysical Subjects I can talk *tolerably* – so so! – but in that conversation, which is between both, I bungle ridiculously."

He now unveiled his revised plan to travel south and enrol himself in the University of Göttingen until the end of the academic year in May. Here he would embark on two extensive pieces of literary work. The first would be a series of letters, later perhaps to form a book, addressed to his patron Josiah Wedgwood on the history and folk-customs of the "Bauers, or Peasants" in Germany. The second was to be a life of Lessing, "interweaved with it a true state of German Literature, in it's rise & present state".[33]

The former would eventually appear – in fragmentary but brilliant form – in *The Friend*, while the latter, though never completed, would lay the basis for his extensive use of German literary and critical theory in his lectures after 1808. An original idea for a German travel book, though already partly assembled in his letter-journals, was later dismissed as too ephemeral.

Coleridge seems to have been unaware of the heartache that this sudden extension of his plans, from a three-month to an eight-month sojourn abroad, would inevitably cause Sara. This insensitivity eventually aroused great resentment in his wife. Yet he was genuinely determined to make the most valuable possible use of his time, and he answered Poole's disciplinarian strictures with energy.

> . . . I have imperiously excluded all waverings about other works – ! That is the disease of my mind – it is comprehensive in it's conceptions & wastes itself in the contemplations of the many things which it might do! – I am aware of the disease, & for the next three months, if I cannot cure it I will at least suspend it's operation . . . The Journey to Germany has certainly *done me good* – my habits are less irregular; & my *mind* more in my *own power*! But I have much still to do![34]

Coleridge also reassured Poole about the Wordsworths' plans. They had not rejoined him, but were now touring through the Hartz Mountains to visit Nordhausen. "Wordsworth is divided in his mind, unquietly divided, between the neighbourhood of Stowey & the N. of England. He cannot think of settling at a distance from *me*, & I have told him that I *cannot* leave the vicinity of Stowey. His chief objection to Stowey is the want of Books –"[35]

He thought that Dorothy's presence had prevented Wordsworth from getting full advantage from German society, or working up new literary materials instead of his own poetry: "he might as well have been in England as at Goslar, in the situation which he chose, & with his *unseeking* manners . . . His taking his Sister with him was a wrong Step – it is next to impossible for any but married women . . . to be introduced to any company in Germany. Sister is considered as only a name for Mistress."[36]

This unexpectedly sharp criticism perhaps disguised a touch of jealousy at Wordsworth's singleness of mind in pursuing his own poetic path, and sharing it so intimately with Dorothy. Coleridge alone knew the value of what his friend was writing, and himself longed to return to the life of "dear *independent* Poetry", when his German labours were complete. Yet far more than Wordsworth, he felt the pressures – both moral and financial – to justify his intellectual endeavours abroad; and he responded to the professional expectations of his friends – Poole, the Wedgwoods, Stuart – that he become a specialist in German affairs.

A long letter to Wedgwood in February, which contained the first part of his "History of the Bauers", written as an academic essay on the emancipation of the German peasantry (and singularly dull compared with his travel-letters) showed this dutiful effort to avoid "waverings" into poetry. His Notebooks are similarly packed with long lists of German vocabulary, formal studies of German metrical forms, and extensive biographical notes on Lessing.[37]

Only occasionally do these entries take on his distinctive touch of critical originality, such as his concept of power in poetry arising from a combination of clarity and obscurity.

> The elder Languages fitter for Poetry because they expressed only prominent ideas with clearness, others but darkly . . . i.e. Feelings created by obscure ideas associate themselves with the one *clear* idea. When no criticism is pretended to, & the Mind in its simplicity gives itself up to a Poem as to a work of nature, Poetry gives most pleasure when only generally & not perfectly understood. It was so by me with Gray's *Bard*, & Collins' odes – *The Bard* once intoxicated me, & now I read it without pleasure.

Coleridge was here reaching towards a complex idea of poetry that was more than mere youthful "intoxication"; it had to be both intelligible *and* mysterious, the proper subject of a critical, adult mind playing over it in detail. "From this cause it is that what *I* call metaphysical Poetry gives me so much delight."[38]

Ironically the middle part of this passage has often been taken out of context, to suggest a purely "magical" reading of poetry, best when "not perfectly understood", as if obscurantism was the consequence of his German metaphysical interests. In fact the study of German language immensely increased his critical attention to English, and his subtle theories of the imagination arose in part from this early intensive period of translating between the two languages,* and his growing attention to what was intellectually "visible" and defined by words, and what remained "invisible" and evocative. Years later he would describe this in his Shakespeare lectures, in a wonderful phrase, as the activity of the imagination "hovering between images" of fixed meaning.[39] It was a "hovering" that he first learned in his German studies.

6

Coleridge and Chester finally departed for Göttingen on 6 February 1799, embarking on a freezing, six-day journey southwards to the Hartz Mountains. They travelled the 200 miles in a series of antiquated German stagecoaches, during the coldest week of the century, breaking their journey at Hannover where they were entertained "with Spartan Frugality & payed with Persian Pomp".[40] Icy winds blew through the split panelling of the coach – "a Temple

*Coleridge organised a personal dictionary of German words under ten generic categories, which indicate an unusual approach to his new "language world". These were: (1) Names of Spirits, Men, Birds, Beast, Fishes and Reptiles; (2) Sensation, Passion, Touch, Taste, and Smell; (3) Sight and Motion; (4) Sound and Motion; (5) Inanimate Things on the Land, the Productions of Nature; (6) Inanimate Things in Air, Heaven, Fire & Water .. including all subterranean things; (7) The Works and Inventions of Man, Clothes, Houses, Machinery, Ceremonies, Festivals; (8) Science and the Operations of Intellect; (9) Time & Space & their Relations; (10) Composite Terms, in which Art illustrated by Nature, or Nature by Art. (*Notebooks*, I, 354) These categories suggest the way he approached language poetically, less a taxonomy of objects, but rather as a creative power in itself, "re-inventing" the world in terms of human perceptions, rather like the Epic Poem which he was continually urging upon Wordsworth. These lists are punctuated with detailed records of the price of food, wine, spirits, lodgings, and travel; together with the occasional brilliant notations as from his walks round the lake of Ratzeburg. "Severity of the Winter – the Kingfisher, its slow short flight permitting you to observe all its colours, almost as if it had been a flower." (*Notebooks*, I, 381) of all the Winds of Heaven!!" – and at night the postillion frequently stopped the journey because the roads were obliterated by snow.

Well fortified with brandy, Coleridge continued to observe everything around him, the lamps in the passing cottage windows, the delicious twists of sweet white bread at a village fair, the touching sight of a family of twelve itinerant Jews sharing a miserable bed of straw at an inn, with their dogs sleeping at their feet. "There was one very beautiful Boy among them, fast asleep, with the softest conceivable opening of the Mouth, with the white Beard of his Grandfather upon his right cheek . . . The Jews are horribly, unnaturally oppressed & persecuted all throughout Germany."[41]

Gradually the bleak, snow-bound heaths of Prussia gave way to the soft, rounded hills of the Hartz, and shortly before Göttingen they saw a party of thirty horse-sledges, driven by wild-looking students with elegantly befurred ladies, skimming in cortège through the snow, with cracking whips and jangling sleigh-bells.

They finally reached the small university city, nestling among the hills, on the evening of 12 February, and took lodgings "in a damn'd dirty hole in the Burg Strasse".[42] Later they transferred to better rooms, owned by one of the professors, in what is now Winder Strasse, the long main street running from the cathedral to the market-place, next to the beautiful medieval *gasthaus* known as Schroder's (now marked by a plaque). It was the centre of the student quarter, surrounded by beer-cellars, and close to the magnificent university library, "two *immense* large Rooms, ornamented with busts & Statues".[43]

Coleridge had earlier been given a "melancholy" picture of Göttingen, "of its dullness – of the impossibility of being introduced into mixed societies etc etc" – but soon found its extraordinary university life to be quite otherwise. He applied for his matriculation, and took letters of introduction to Professor Heyne, "a little, hopping, over-civil, sort of a Thing who talks very fast & with fragments of coughing between every ten words", who proved to be extremely courteous and arranged for him to have special borrowing privileges at the library, "which properly only the Professors have".[44] He inscribed himself for lectures in theology, physiology, anatomy and natural history,[45] and was delighted to find a mass of materials for his study of Lessing and early German literature.

Even more pleasing, he was called on by a group of English students at the university, many of whom had Cambridge connections. Among these were Charles and Frederick Parry, brothers of the celebrated Arctic explorer, Sir William Parry; and Anthony Hamilton of St John's College. Two other men, Clement Carlyon and George Greenough, also became close friends, and later published amusing reminiscences of their adventures together, which suggest that Coleridge's social life at Göttingen could hardly have been less dull.

Anthony Hamilton was the first to dispel any lingering notions of Teutonic melancholy by taking Coleridge on his first weekend to a session of something called the Saturday Club. Coleridge was astonished by the experience. "Such an Evening I never passed before – roaring, kissing, embracing, fighting, smashing bottles & glasses against the wall, singing – in short, such a scene of uproar I never witnessed before, no, not even at Cambridge. – I drank nothing – but all, except two of the Englishmen, were drunk – & the party broke up a little after one o'clock in the morning."[46]

He was particularly amazed, in what we are to believe was his unaccustomed state of sobriety, by a drinking game with a sword, which involved each man skewering his hat on the blade in turn, "Hat over Hat, still singing", until everyone collapsed in a frenzied mass-embrace. Coleridge found this besotted, puppy-like student kissing "a most loathsome Business", but it gave him much food for reflection.

Describing the scene later to Sara, with appropriate strictures, he ruminated gravely on the sense it gave him of his own altered attitudes to life. "I thought of what I had been at Cambridge, & of what I was – of the wild & bacchanalian Sympathy with which I had *formerly* joined similar Parties, & of my total inability now to do aught *but meditate* – and the feeling of deep alteration in my moral Being gave the scene a melancholy interest to me!"[47]

For the first three months at Göttingen, Coleridge plunged into his academic studies, regularly attending lectures – especially those of J. F. Blumenbach on natural history and anthropology – and painstakingly transcribing his Lessing materials at the library. He met both Blumenbach and the theologian J. G. Eichhorn for informal seminars. He said he now worked harder "than I trust in God Almighty, I shall ever have occasion to work again". He found the work of transcription "body-and-soul wearying Purgatory", but he greatly enjoyed his general reading, especially in "the works of all those German poets before the time of Lessing, which I *could not*, or could not *afford* to buy". He did in fact invest in some £30 worth of books, chiefly metaphysics – nearly a quarter of his annual allowance, as he told Wedgwood – "with a view to the one work, to which I hope to dedicate in silence the prime of my life."[48] This is an oblique reference to the world of Kantian metaphysics, which he had first seen beckoning him in his Notebooks of 1796.

He was excited, as he had never been at Cambridge, by all the academic luminaries attracted by the university, and solemnly listed the roll-call of distinguished professors at Göttingen to Sara: "among which the names of Mosheim, Gesner, Haller, Michaelis, Pütter, Kästner, Heyne, Letz or Less, Blumenbach, Lichtenburg, Plank, Eichhorn, Meiners, and Jacobi are as well known to the Literati throughout Europe, as to their own Countrymen."[49] Perhaps he felt, as Stuart once shrewdly observed, that he himself would only really have been happy in occupying a university post.

This intensive period at Göttingen also gave him a sense of sharing in the intellectual life of Europe, of being part of a broad community of world-renowned scholars, which shaped much of his subsequent writing, and distinguished him sharply from the purely provincial aspect of English thought. His whole notion of "criticism" – of the application of philosophic principles to imaginative literature – was to be European rather than English; and the fundamental importance which he gave to religious and metaphysical ideas, in later controversies over both literature and politics, profoundly reflects the atmosphere of Romantic reaction and mysticism which was then spreading throughout the universities of Germany – at Göttingen, at Jena, at Leipzig. Coleridge found something Teutonic in his own soul, so the bright spirit of the Quantock Hills rose up to meet the misty enchantments of the Hartz Mountains.*

*Coleridge's interest in Lessing reflects his personal identification with the life of the European intellectual. Gotthold Ephraim Lessing (1729–1781) was intended by his pastor father for a career in the Church, but fell in love with dramatic literature, became one of Germany's first freelance writers and earliest champions of Shakespeare. He wrote plays and dramatic criticism, becoming resident critic at the national theatre in Hamburg, and a close friend of Kleist's. His restless life, travelling all over Germany, fascinated Coleridge, and features prominently in his biographical notes. (*Notebooks*, I, 377) He was one of the first European critics to interpret the new Romantic spirit in terms of Shakespearean, rather than French neo-classical, drama and he greatly influenced A. W. Schlegel who wrote a brilliant essay on him in 1804, describing his "boldly combining mind" in which "new chemical connections and *interpenetrations* take place". (See Bibliography, Walter Jackson Bate, p. 94) Coleridge was first attracted to Lessing by a portrait of him he saw in young Klopstock's house in Hamburg in September 1798. His enthusiastic comments make the element of self-identification very evident: "His eyes were uncommonly like mine – if anything, rather larger & more prominent . . . The whole Face seemed to say, that Lessing was a man – of quick & voluptuous Feelings; of an active but light Fancy; acute; yet acute not in the observation of actual Life, but in the arrangements & management of the Ideal World – (i.e.) in taste, and in metaphysics." (*Letters*, I, p. 437)

7

Meanwhile, throughout February and March, there was a complete absence of letters from England, since the Elbe remained frozen and very little domestic mail reached Hamburg.[50] Coleridge was increasingly anxious about Sara and the children, and wrote tender letters in March to Stowey, even though he knew they would remain at Cuxhaven until the spring thaw.

> Why need I say, how anxious this long Interval of Silence has made me? I have thought & thought of you, and pictured you & the little ones so often & so often, that my Imagination is tired, down, flat and powerless; and I languish after Home for hours together, in vacancy; my *feelings* almost wholly unqualified by *Thoughts* . . . I am deeply convinced that if I were to remain a few years among objects for whom I had no affection, I should wholly lose the powers of Intellect – Love is the vital air of my Genius, & I have not seen one human Being in Germany, whom I can conceive it *possible* for me to *love* – no, not one.[51]

Yet even these letters have a curious abstraction and lack of tact about them. Sara would hardly have been reassured by the thought of his remaining abroad for "a few years", or his failure to find some other lovable Being in Germany. They mention no definite return date, and show a strange inability to enter into her own feelings of abandonment. Moreover, the lively accounts of student life which accompany them ironically contradict his tales of "vacancy" and homesickness, to a degree that Coleridge seems to have been quite unaware.

In fact Sara's situation was far worse than he knew. Her letters to Poole show how terribly she had suffered during little Berkeley's illness. The baby had been badly disfigured by smallpox and never really recovered its strength. Poole persuaded her to keep all these details secret from her husband. She had grown thin, and lost much of her luxurious hair, so that she wore a wig for the rest of her life.[52] Then, on 11 February (just before Coleridge's arrival at Göttingen), little Berkeley Coleridge suddenly died in a fit of convulsions at Bristol. Sara almost entirely broke down, and was taken in by Robert Southey and Edith at their house in Westbury. Again, Poole persuaded her to keep this news from Coleridge, because of the "violent effect" he imagined it would have on him, and the disruption it would cause in his German studies.

In these repeated interventions of Poole, and Sara's repeated compliance with them, there was an extraordinary over-protectiveness towards Coleridge. It was as if his genius was too unstable and too childlike to bear the full emotional responsibilities of parenthood. By treating him like this, they both perhaps conspired to make it true. For Sara, it became a nightmare ordeal which she had to bear alone; she was forced into the suffering, adult role in their relationship, powerless to express her real feelings, and condemned to wait passively for the consolations of a man who appeared increasingly distant, irresponsible and wayward.

Over a month after Berkeley's death, Poole finally decided to inform Coleridge of the bare facts, in a brisk, manly, uplifting letter posted on 15 March, which eventually reached Göttingen on 4 April.

> It was long contrary to my opinion to let you know of the child's death before your arrival in England. And I thought, and still think myself justified in that notion, by the OVER-anxiety you expressed in your former letters concerning the children . . . The truth is, my dear Col, it is idle to reason about a thing of this nature . . . Don't conjure up any scenes of distress which never happened. Mrs Coleridge felt as a mother . . . and in an exemplary manner, did all a mother could do. *But she never forgot herself.* She is now perfectly well, and does not make herself miserable by recalling the engaging, though, remember, mere instinctive attractions of an infant a few months old.[53]

Poole was not an unfeeling man, and the brusqueness of this letter, and the dismissive references to Sara's sufferings, can only be read as a direct reflection of his worries about Coleridge. Ten days later, Sara too was finally allowed to write. Her letter was agonising, and now openly expressed her misery at his absence.

> O my dear Samuel! it is a suffering beyond your conception! You will feel, and lament the death of your child, but you will only recollect him as a baby of fourteen weeks, but I am his Mother, and have carried him in my arms . . . I cannot express how ardently I long for your return, or how much I shall be disappointed if I do not see you in May . . . Our dear little Hartley you will discover is grown a little. He has a most agreeable little tongue; he talks of his Father every day . . . – I am much pleased to see you wrote that you "languish to be at home". O God! I hope you never more will quit it![54]

8

When Coleridge first heard of his child's death, he went for a long walk in the open fields around Göttingen, and threw stones into the river as he had done as a boy at Ottery.[55]

He found he could not weep: he felt stunned and morally "perplexed" by the meaningless of death, that "giddies one with insecurity, & so unsubstantiates the living Things one has grasped and handled!" His letters show that it took several weeks for him to admit all his complex feelings of grief and guilt to himself.

His first reaction to Poole was to quote Pascal and insist on a kind of abstract optimism: "My Baby has not lived in vain . . . *nothing* is hopeless. – What if the vital force which I sent from my arm into the stone, as I flung it in the air & skimm'd it upon the water – what if even that did not perish! – It was *life*! – it was a particle of *Being* – !it was *Power*! – & *how could* it perish – ?"[56] He soothed himself with such speculations.

He copied out for Poole one of Wordsworth's "Lucy" poems, "A Slumber did my spirit steal", describing it as a sublime epitaph: "whether it had any reality, I cannot say. – Most probably, in some gloomier moment he had fancied the moment in which his Sister might die."[57] To Coleridge the death of his child seemed almost equally imaginary. Then he announced firmly that he would not be ready to return for six or eight weeks, he had such a "vast quantity of materials" to collect in the library. "I am very busy, very busy indeed! – I attend several Professors, & am getting many kinds of knowledge; but I stick to my Lessing – The Subject more & more interests me . . ."[58]

His first letter to Sara, two days later, was similarly abstracted. Berkeley's death, he said, made him "discontented" with Priestley's doctrine on "the future existence of Infants". He sent an epitaph of his own, but admitted it had been written a few weeks before, for another child of an English friend of his whose infant "had died before its Christening". He felt this had been a kind of premonition. He now hoped to be home "at the end of 10 or 11 weeks".[59]

He felt that the child's death might bring them closer together, and for the first time he openly referred to their marital quarrels, though blaming himself not Sara. "When in Moments of fretfulness and Imbecillity I am disposed to anger or reproach, it will, I trust, be always a restoring thought – 'We have wept over the same little one – & with whom am I angry? – with her who so patiently and unweariedly sustained my poor and sickly Infant through his long Pains.'"[60]

Coleridge's strange and dreamlike reaction to his child's death can easily be misinterpreted as callousness. Yet in reality it seems more a form of self-defence, or displaced guilt. He insisted on continuing his German studies, yet his grief and anxiety gathered momentum as April went by.

Clement Carlyon observed his fondness for walking on the old medieval ramparts of Göttingen, listening to the nightingales that filled the long colonnades of oak trees.[61] Mentioning these in his next letter to Poole, Coleridge was suddenly able to express the reality of his feelings more fully.

> ... What a gloomy Spring! But a few days ago all the new buds were covered with Snow ... There are a multitude of Nightingales here – poor things! they sang in the Snow. – I thought of my own verses on the Nightingale, only because I thought of Hartley, my *only* child! – Dear Lamb! I hope, *he* won't be dead, before I get home. – There are moments in which I have such a power of Life within me, such a conceit of it, I mean – that I lay the Blame of my Child's Death to my absence – *not intellectually*; but I have a strange sort of sensation, as if while I was present, none could die whom I intensely loved.[62]

He ended this letter even more nakedly. "My dear Poole! don't let little Hartley die before I come home. – That's silly – true – & I burst into tears as I wrote it." Yet perhaps such things should still better have been written to his wife.

Despite all these protestations of grief and homesickness, Coleridge showed great firmness of purpose in remaining at Göttingen. He clearly felt that completion of his studies was, in the end, more important than any domestic consolation he could bring to Sara. There were several times when he considered a precipitate return in April, but resisted. He was shaken by Sara's letter – which reached him a fortnight after Poole's. There is some suggestion that he briefly fell back on opium to insulate himself.

In mid-April, Wordsworth and Dorothy suddenly appeared in Göttingen, after a long tour through the Hartz, and urged him to go back with them at once to England. Even this appeal he withstood. On 23 April he again wrote to his wife, this time with something like abruptness:

> Surely it is unnecessary for me to say, how infinitely I languish to be in my native Country & with how many struggles I have remained even so long in Germany! – I received your affecting letter, dated Easter Sunday; and had I followed my impulses, I should have packed up & gone with Wordsworth & his Sister, who passed thro', & only passed thro', this place, two or three days ago . . . But it is in the strictest sense of the word impossible that I can collect what I have to collect, in less than six weeks from this day; yet I read and transcribe from 8 to 10 hours every day . . . This day in June I hope, & trust, that I shall be in England![63]

He then tried to soothe her with the beautiful description of the children's Christmas celebrations in Germany, adding an account of country life round Göttingen – the peasants' children, the shepherds, the healing superstitions connected with the gallows. He ended with a touching little poem, "three stanzas which, I dare say, you will think very silly" but which expressed "a yearning, yearning, yearning *Inside*":

> If I had but two little wings
> And were a little feath'ry Bird,
> To *you* I'd fly, my Dear!
> But Thoughts, like these, are idle Things –
> And I stay here.[64]

Understandably, perhaps, none of this quite mollified Sara. When she next wrote, there was a new bitterness in her tone, and she pointedly remarked on the unfavourable reception which the *Lyrical Ballads* was receiving. Moreover, Coleridge's return date continued its steady process of slippage, moving back irresistibly from May to June, and then to July. Once again he had contrived to be absent at a crucial moment in their married life, and the fissures and misunderstanding deepened and spread.

Poole was equally anxious about the effect of Wordsworth's departure from Germany, but here again Coleridge made a determined show of his independence, and emphasised his loyalty to Stowey. In May he recounted in further detail how he had refused to fall in with their plans, having spent the day walking with them in the countryside. "They were melancholy & hypp'd – W. was affected to tears at the thought of not being near me, wished me, of course to live in the North of England . . ."

He assured Poole that he would never do this, as it would be unsuitable for Sara ("a place where she would have no acquaintance"), and besides there were no proper libraries for his work. "Finally, I told him plainly, that *you* had been the man in whom I *first* and in whom alone, I had felt an *anchor*! . . . W. was affected to tears, very much affected . . . But my Resolve is fixed, *not to leave you till you leave me!*"[65] He then proceeded with a discussion of possible new houses for the summer in the Quantocks.

But Poole, like Sara, may have had his doubts. The repeated mention of Wordsworth's tears may rather have expressed Coleridge's own emotions, and certainly the magnet of Wordsworth in the north was soon to draw him like a compass needle. Indeed, throughout this long spring at Göttingen, one is aware of Coleridge falling into a kind of double life, repeatedly telling Sara and Poole of one set of loyalties, while secretly acting on other impulses which were actually shaping his career and future plans.

Sometimes he even teased Poole deliberately with his waywardness. Among his learned papers, he said, he would bring back a scheme to manufacture parchment from old shoes; a method of grafting apples on to oak saplings; and a speculative process for obtaining "Aqua fortis from Cucumbers". But perhaps this was the opium talking through his anxieties.[66]

9

Despite the domestic tragedy in England, one thing became very clear: Coleridge was beginning to enjoy himself enormously in the university atmosphere of Göttingen. If he worked hard, he also relaxed with the greatest vigour. He revelled in the company both of his learned German professors and of his wild young English fellow students. The erudition of the German scholars – especially Blumenbach's investigations into natural history, and Eichhorn's rationalist and textual criticism of the Bible – fascinated him, and spilled over easily into his social life. "The Professors here are exceedingly kind to all the Englishmen; but to me they pay the most *flattering* attention – Especially, Blumenbach and Eichhorn. – Nothing can be conceived more delightful than Blumenbach's lectures; & in conversation he is indeed a most interesting man."[67]

Many evenings were spent in this witty, scholarly circle, which included the Orientalist Thomas Tyschen, who taught Coleridge Old German and Gothic forms. Coleridge was four or five years older than his fellow students, and as a published author, was treated with particular hospitality. It made English academic life appear narrow and parochial. "My God! a miserable Poet must he be, & a despicable

Metaphysician whose acquirements have not cost more trouble & reflection than all the learning of Tooke, Porson & Parr united. With the advantage of a great Library Learning is nothing, methinks . . ."

In this heady atmosphere he imagined, besides his Life of Lessing, the pleasures of leisurely assembling "some horribly learned book, full of manuscript quotations from Laplandish and Patagonian Authors – possibly, on the striking resemblance between the Sweogothic & Sanscrit Languages, & so on!"[68]

The younger English students formed an admiring group round him, dazzled by his talk, impressed by his poetry, and fascinated by his eccentricities (which by now give the impression of being well-cultivated). They were a lively and intelligent group: Clement Carlyon, then twenty-two, a Fellow of Pembroke College and future doctor; George Greenough, twenty-one, a natural scientist and future President of the Geological Society; and Charles Parry, twenty, another future doctor. Professor Blumenbach's son also joined this set, talking late into the night on every subject under the sun and moon – geology, folk customs, religion, linguistics, witchcraft, agriculture, and always Coleridge's beloved metaphysics.

Carlyon remembered his "natural good-humoured effrontery" in challenging the opinions of those about him, and making them all think in new ways. On one occasion, "Coleridge made the profound, although seemingly trivial, remark that no animal but man appears ever to be struck with wonder. He was fond of amusing himself and us by asking the definition of some particular word, closing the enquiry, after each had exercised his ingenuity, with his own, which we seldom failed, with due submission to him, to consider the best."[69]

Carlyon contrasted his casual clothes and distracted appearance with his intensity of manner and amusing, partly unconscious, arrogance.

> When in company, his vehemence of manner and wonderful flow of words and ideas, drew all eyes towards him, and gave him pre-eminence, despite his costume, which he effected to treat with great indifference. He even boasted the facility with which he was able to overcome the disadvantage of negligent dress; and I have heard him say, fixing his prominent eyes upon himself (as he was wont to do, whenever there was a mirror in the room), with a singularly coxcomical expression of countenance, that his dress was sure to be lost sight of the moment he began to talk; an assertion which, whatever may be thought of its modesty, was not without truth.[70]

Carlyon's shrewd observation of Coleridge's fascination with his own image in the mirror can be seen as almost a psychological facet of his personality: the self-reflective and self-dramatising element.

Charles Parry wrote home to his family in May with a similar assessment of his new, extraordinary friend. He presented him as almost the most singular phenomenon in all Göttingen. "Coleridge is much liked, notwithstanding many peculiarities. He is very liberal towards all doctrines and opinions, and cannot be put out of temper." His peculiarities included his "abstruse" speculations, his "devoted attachment to his country", his wild enthusiasm in conversation on any topic. His friends suffered from "the mysticism of his metaphysics", but felt he had "a good heart, and a large mass of information, with superior talents".

Parry was particularly impressed by the way Coleridge outpointed the German professors in philosophical arguments, overwhelming their "strongholds" with his fervour. "Eichhorn, one of the principal theologists in Germany, and a lecturer here, seems, from all accounts, to be doing his utmost to destroy the evidences on which we ground our belief . . . Coleridge, an able vindicator of these important truths, is well acquainted with Eichhorn, but the latter is a coward, who dreads his argument and his presence."

As a poet, Coleridge "severely criticizes his own productions. His best poems have, perhaps, not yet appeared in print." Parry was struck by how hard Coleridge studied. "He is, at present, engaged on a work, which will be no less interesting in Germany than in England – A History of German Poetry, from the earliest times to the present day, including a particular review of Lessing's Works. It will probably extend to two quarto volumes."[71]

He also loved Coleridge's flamboyant style: whenever he met Pütter, the Professor of History, walking on the ramparts, he always doffed his hat with a low old-fashioned bow. Pütter was the only academic in the faculty – according to Coleridge – who professed "pure Christianity", and therefore deserved true respect in the English fashion.

10

In early May, far from hurrying his Lessing studies to a conclusion, Coleridge announced that he intended a walking tour in the Hartz Mountains, to pay his respects to the Brocken spectre, and observe the springtime celebrations in the countryside. He borrowed a map from Parry, and enquired if anyone wished to join him.[72] Immediately the whole group – Chester, Carlyon, the two Parrys, Greenough, and the young Blumenbach – volunteered, and on 11 May began what Coleridge christened the "Carlyon-Parry-Greenation". (He was "never above a pun", observed Carlyon patiently.)

They were away for a week, climbing the Brocken, and then returning on an exhausting and circuitous course through the little country villages – Rübeland, Blankenburg, Wernigerode, and Wordsworth's erstwhile retreat at Goslar. Coleridge described this journey in two long and brilliantly detailed letters to Sara, and both Carlyon and Greenough recalled it at length many years afterwards.

Carlyon gives the impression that Coleridge – though he suffered dramatically from swollen feet, and agonisingly stubbed toes ("my whole frame seemed going to pieces with fatigue . . . my key-note Pain") – drove them on relentlessly, and never stopped talking. "When we were ascending the Brocken, and ever and anon stopping to take breath, as well as survey the magnificent scene, a long discussion took place on the sublime and beautiful. We had much of Burke, but more of Coleridge . . . Many were the fruitless attempts made to define sublimity satisfactorily, when Coleridge, at length, pronounced it to consist in a suspension of the powers of comparison."[73]

This, incidentally, was an idea that had first struck him on listening at night to the "thunders and howling of the breaking ice" at Ratzeburg, when he had reflected that "there are sounds more sublime than any sight *can* be, more absolutely suspending the power of comparison, and more utterly absorbing the mind's self consciousness, in its total attention to the object working upon it."[74] But he had already used the effect, poetically, in the *Mariner*, in the haunting passage describing the unearthly growling and roaring of the icebergs.[75] It was the sort of "mysticism" that so fascinated his young companions.

In his own letters, Coleridge leaped from one impression to the next: waterfalls, caves, witches on the Brocken (they missed the spectre), May Pole dancing, a pig fair, an iron ore smelting ("white & blue flares"), wild duck, salamanders, a Cranach altar-piece, a Giant's rib, tales of bewitchment and petticoats.

He described the endlessly unrolling panorama of forest valleys. "We travelled on & on, O what a weary way! now up, now down, now with path, now without it; having no other guides than a map, a compass, & the foot-paces of the Pigs."[76] They slept in country inns, on straw; and Coleridge – "a wise but an indulgent Mentor" – insisted they regaled themselves constantly with coffee, bacon, and Schnapps in milk (a mixture he defined as "sheathed" spirits).

He drew interest from every incident: when they met a wild party of students from Halle, dressed bizarrely in leather jackets, sabres, and "great three cornered Hats, with small iron chains dangling from them", he asked young Blumenbach if it was a uniform, and was delighted with the reply: "He said No! – but that it was a Student's *Instinct* to play a character, in some way or other."[77]

At many of the inns, a *stammbuch* or visitors' album was kept, and Coleridge began to compose a memorial poem of their tour, which he finally entered in the album at Elbingerode. Beginning with the panorama from the Brocken, "woods crowding upon woods, hills over hills", the poem charts their descent through the endless fir-trees, the curious "hollow Sound" of bird-song echoing, and the sudden unexpected vision of an "old romantic Goat" sitting in a clearing. It then rises again, with a note of genuine homesickness and yearning, which suggests very well the complexity of his feelings during these last weeks in Germany:

> O "dear dear" England, how my longing Eye
> Turn'd Westward, shaping in the steady Clouds
> Thy sands & high white Cliffs! Sweet Native Isle,
> This Heart was proud, yea, mine Eyes swam with Tears
> To think of Thee; & all the goodly view
> From sov'ran Brocken, woods and woody Hills,
> Floated away, like a departing Dream,
> Feeble and dim.[78]

It had the makings of another Conversation Poem, but Coleridge was conscious that he could not sustain it. He sent it to Sara, but wrote to Poole: "O Poole! I am homesick . . . my poor Muse is quite gone – perhaps, she may return & meet me at Stowey."[79]

Years later, in the *Sibylline Leaves*, he made one of his characteristic and inspired additions, which deepens the whole tone of the poem, giving it a sudden philosophic implication. Looking back, he now felt he had travelled with a new, sad knowledge:

> . . . In low and languid mood: for I had found
> That outward forms, the loftiest, still receive
> Their finer influence from the Life within; –
> Fair cyphers else: fair, but of import vague
> Or unconcerning, where the heart not finds
> History or prophecy of friend, or child . . .[80]

It was not quite true that his Muse had departed. Besides the original poems he sent to Sara and the Wordsworths from Germany, which turn largely on the theme of absence and homesickness, he also completed a number of short but very polished verse-translations. These were evidently offshoots of his study of German poetry. They included a number of lyric pieces by Friedrich Leopold Stolberg: "On a Cataract", "William Tell's Birth-Place", "The British Stripling's War-Song," and "Hymn to the Earth" in dashing hexameters, a metre that particularly attracted him because of its qualities of rapid, "improvised" speech and description:

> Travelling the vale with mine eyes – green meadows and lake
> with green island,
> Dark in its basin of rock, and the bare stream flowing in brightness . . .[81]

Other translations, or imitations, were drawn from Goethe, Lessing, popular German folksongs, and the playwright Schiller.

Schiller was then probably the most fashionable German author for English readers, the gothic romanticism and nationalism of his plays striking an immediate chord, and when Coleridge returned home he would find the London publishers far more interested in Schiller than the recherché Lessing.

Some of these poems are direct, almost academic, translations; others are peculiarly Coleridgean forms of imitation, in which a few lines from the original would inspire what was virtually a new poem. This manner of jumping-off from a foreign original would prove wonderfully, and sometimes dangerously, congenial to Coleridge. When he later published them in newspapers, he was frequently tempted to disguise his sources, thus beginning the long and tortured history of his "plagiarisms" from German materials. Initially the disguise was unnecessary, for his transformations of the originals were complete and characteristic of his own voice.*

---

*Coleridge first published two, partially plagiarised poems from the German of Salomon Gessner and Friederike Brun – both, incidentally, Swiss poets – in 1802 (see Chapter 13). But ten years later he began the wholesale, unacknowledged use of A. W. Schlegel in his lectures, and the silent incorporation of large extracts from Schelling and Kant in the philosophical sections of the *Biographia*, and various occasional essays on aesthetics. The significance of these, and many other plagiarisms will be considered in volume two, but textually the whole subject has been exhaustively examined. (See Bibliography, Thomas MacFarland and Norman Fruman; and Thomas MacFarland's earlier study *Coleridge and the Pantheist Tradition*, Oxford, 1969.) Here it is worth noticing that for Coleridge, plagiarism begins in translation – and specifically the attempt to carry over and interpret German literature and philosophy into an insular, English culture. If psychologically it was a form of kleptomania, then intellectually it was a form of smuggling valuables across a closed border.

Even something as deeply Teutonic and sentimental as Goethe's "Mignon's Song" from *Wilhelm Meister*, drawing on the old German tradition of *lieder*, takes on the magical quality of Coleridge's dream-landscapes:

> Know'st thou the land where the pale citrons grow,
> The golden fruits in darker foliage glow? . . .[82]

The Hartz tour, made in such lively and amusing company, reawakened all Coleridge's happiest memories of the open-air life of the Quantocks. He was at the centre of a young and admiring circle once more, he revelled in the exchange of libraries for landscapes, he felt deeply the "dance of Hills" which excited a corresponding "motion" in his own imagination.[83] Several times, both to Sara and Poole, he remarked on the visions it brought him of home: "sometimes I thought myself in the *Coombes* about Stowey, sometimes about Porlock, sometimes between Porlock and Linton – only the Stream was somewhat larger."[84] He was back again in the land of "Kubla Khan".

It also brought him (as Parry remarked), a growing sense of his love of England, an unsophisticated patriotism, which began to seem far stronger than all the doubts and hesitations he had expressed in "Fears in Solitude" – a poem which he had read to Carlyon. This was to mark a steady shift in his political views, which soon became evident in the journalism he would write for Stuart on his return. His position was still radical and anti-ministerial, but he had an increasing sense of England's isolated position in the continuing war with revolutionary France.

Carlyon noted this in one discussion that took place over glasses of Médoc at the table d'hôte in Clausthal on 17 May, just before their return to Göttingen.

> The Pittites of our party, from having Coleridge opposed to them, got decidedly worst off, and we were content to leave him thenceforth in undisputed possession of the field of politics . . . And although, upon the above occasion, consistently with his early associations, he stoutly defended Fox against Pitt, there is abundant evidence, in much of his subsequent writings, to show that no one was better able than himself to depict the difficulties of the appalling crisis with which that great minister had to contend . . .[85]

On their last night of the tour Coleridge cheerfully described to Poole the mood of jovial chauvinism that had united the party. "We returned and spent the evening with a round of old English Songs, of which God Save the King & Rule Britannia were, as you may suppose repeated no small number of Times – for being abroad makes every man a Patriot & a Loyalist – almost a Pittite!"[86] There was little irony in this, and nothing could be further from the subversive mood of the Welsh tour five years earlier with Hucks. The implied change in himself, and in the international situation, would eventually provide Coleridge (as Wordsworth, too) with one of the great intellectual and moral challenges of his life.

Returning to Göttingen, on 19 May, Coleridge still stubbornly delayed setting a definite date for his departure home. There was further work to be done on Lessing, and he wanted to visit the library at Wolfenbüttel where Lessing had held a post between 1770 and his death in 1781. But his prevarication obviously had deeper motives now – his guilt over the death of Berkeley had become, at some level, reluctance to return to domestic life with Sara, despite all his protestations; and the sublime irresponsibility of his student life charmed him from anxieties like opium itself.

11

Towards the end of May, he wrote a long letter to his patron Josiah Wedgwood, trying to summarise his academic activities in the most organised manner.

> What have I done in Germany? – I have learnt the language, both high & low German; I can read both, & speak the former so fluently, that it must be *torture* for a German to be in my company . . . my pronunciation is hideous. 2ndly, I can read the oldest German, the Frankish & the Swabian. 3dly – I have attended the lectures of Physiology, Anatomy, & Natural History with regularity, & have endeavoured to understand these subjects. – 4th – I have read & made collections for an history of the Belles Lettres in Germany before the time of Lessing – & 5thly – very large collections for a Life of Lessing.[87]

He added that he had "six huge letters" prepared for Wedgwood on the history of the German peasantry, one of which had already been sent. Finally, he intended to use statistics and materials gathered in German to examine the arguments of Thomas Malthus' essay on *Population*, and open up some broad questions concerning "Godwin's & Condorcet's Extravagancies" of philosophy: "Is the march of the Human Race progressive, or in Cycles? – But more of this when we meet."[88]

His expenses, particularly on books, had been great, and he hoped to "*anticipate* for 40 or fifty pounds" his annuity for 1800. All this would be justified by the one great work of metaphysics he was planning to write, when he was resettled in England, and had repaid his debts "before Christmas" with preliminary publications of his German work.[89]

Virtually all these plans would eventually alter, or go astray. The life of Lessing would be replaced by his translations of Schiller; the letters on the Bauers would be promised in November 1800, but never appear; the studies of German poetry and folklore would only emerge gradually in later lectures, *The Friend* of 1809, and glancingly in the *Biographia* of 1817; the dispute with Godwin would be diverted into long hours of personal discussion in London. The highly ordered picture he outlined to Wedgwood was something of a chimera, and was wholly characteristic of Coleridge's genius for projecting a mass of brilliant works which would never actually leave his desk.

Yet there can be little doubt that he had worked as hard, and read as widely, in Germany as he claimed. The whole expedition profoundly affected his views on literature, politics, religion, and metaphysics. What was to prove most difficult for him, was to shape these materials into a working career: as Poole had warned, it was the ranging, adventurous and undisciplined quality of his imagination which was the danger and the "disease". Yet it was precisely this quality which gave such life to his travel accounts. The impromptu "journey of enquiry" was in many ways his natural literary form, whether in prose or poetry or the lecture. The regular, systematic study was the furthest from his instinctive intellectual gait.

One thing that Coleridge did faithfully send to the Wedgwoods as requested, by his friend Anthony Hamilton, was a specially commissioned pastel portrait by a local Göttingen artist. He appears to have had two executed, for the other eventually became the property of Thomas Ward, probably inherited from Poole, and has survived. It was perhaps the most Romantic of all the pictures ever done of him: the long, dark locks falling over his collar in wild confusion; the huge eyes turned reflectively upon the viewer; the full mouth in voluptuous repose. The artist had made him, unconsciously, a brooding, tender, continental figure from the world of *Young Werther*: Coleridge as a member of the *sturm und drang* generation, wholly absorbed in his inner world of thoughts and feeling. Looking at it made him shiver, he said, with his own mortality: "I should not like to die by land or water before I see my wife & the little one that I hope yet remains to me!" This, he admitted, was self-dramatisation – "an idle sort of feeling" – though he knew it would have its subtle effect on Wedgwood.[90]

12

Nearly a month later, on 24 June, Coleridge finally packed up his books which were sent ahead in a chest to Cuxhaven, and departed from Göttingen. On the eve of his leave-taking, there was a tremendous party for him, given by Professor Blumenbach, at which he dazzled all the professors and their wives with his brilliant talk and execrable pronunciation. Carlyon recalled "something inexpressibly comic in the manner in which he dashed on, with fluent diction, but the very worst German accent imaginable, through the thick and thin of his subject". It was probably on this occasion that he held forth on Immanuel Kant, and was much amused "by a young lady's expressing her surprise that he, not being a German, could possibly understand Kant's philosophical writings, which were not even intelligible *to her*!"[91]

Coleridge's homeward journey was, not unexpectedly, circuitous. First he and Chester made another ascent of the Brocken, taking a coach to Clausthal, accompanied by Carlyon and Greenough, who seemed incapable of abandoning him. They reached the summit at sunset on the 24th, but again the "spectre-hunters" were disappointed; after a night on straw at the inn, they returned to the peak at dawn, but again without any sightings. Instead they were "amply repayed by the sight of a Wild Boar with an immense Cluster of Glow-worms round his Tail & Rump".[92]

Then they walked slowly to Brunswick, where further delaying reinforcements arrived in the shape of the Parry brothers.

It emerged that Coleridge had proposed in all seriousness an expedition to Scandinavia, evidently in the footsteps of Mary Wollstonecraft – "a pedestrian tour together through parts of Denmark, Sweden, and Norway". The Parrys had been waiting to receive permission from their father, which they had just obtained. For a moment it looked as if Coleridge would whirl them all off across the

Baltic, but he finally pleaded homesickness. Perhaps nothing so vividly illustrates his powers of enchantment over his young circle as this fantastic expedition, and the disappointment with which its postponement was received.

It was, however, to be *merely* a postponement. "He promised, however to return and make the projected northern tour with us the ensuing spring. This afforded some consolation to the Parrys, who, after hastening, immediately on receipt of their father's answer, from Göttingen to overtake us, were naturally not a little disappointed at the thought of returning thither . . . their object unaccomplished." Coleridge's vision retained its powers over them, nonetheless, for the following summer Greenough, Carlyon and Charles Parry actually made this journey.[93]

Coleridge spent a few unsatisfactory days trying to obtain Lessing materials at the Wolfenbüttel library. He and Chester then walked at a cracking pace the twenty-three miles from Brunswick to Helmstedt, where they "rummaged old Manuscripts", examined priceless sketches by Holbein, Raphael, and Correggio, and were hospitably received by the local academics.

By now the travellers had the appearance of wandering scholars, not to say tramps, with stinking clothes and various sores and swellings from the summer heat. Chester had St Antony's Fire in his leg, "& his Arse is sore"; but Coleridge was in ecstatic state of dereliction. He had no travelling chest or portmanteau, and only one clean shirt. "Heaven! I stink like an old Poultice," he cheerfully informed Greenough in a farewell letter. "I should mislead any Pack of Foxhounds in Great Britain/ Put a Trail of Rusty Bacon at a Furlong Distance & me at a mile, and they would follow *me* . . . if I caught only the Echo of a Tally Ho! I should climb into a Tree!" He made his last greeting in the style they had come to expect of him: "Soul of Lessing! hover over my Boxes! Ye Minnesänger! fly after them! – Dear Greenough! Dear Parry! Carlyon, Fred – I go –"[94]

In his Notebooks he scrawled a list of presents to send back from England: William Cowper's poems for Professor Blumenbach; Wordsworth's poems for Professor Wiedemann (professor of anatomy, chemistry, and mineralogy); and for Greenough – "mem. to send the whole of the works of that interesting writer, Mr. S. T. Coleridge . . . as I have a superficial acquaintance at the least with that celebrated gentleman."[95]

TEN

JOURNEYMAN

1

While giving the impression of tremendous speed, Coleridge successfully loitered all the way back to England. Having left Göttingen on 24 June, he arrived breathlessly at Stowey more than a month later at the end of July 1799, his chest of metaphysical volumes now trailing behind him at Cuxhaven. In a letter to Sara, he had imagined landing directly in the West Country at Shurton Bars, and then making the "lonely walk" of four miles across the fields into her arms. "It lessens the delight of the thought of my Return that I must get at you thro' a tribe of *acquaintances*, *damping* the freshness of one's Joy!"[1] In fact he almost certainly stopped off in London to see Daniel Stuart, for the first of his Stolberg translations appeared in the *Morning Post* in August; and he also borrowed some much needed clean laundry from Wordsworth's lawyer brother Richard at Holborn.[2]

There is no record of his reception at Stowey, but it cannot have been unmixed delight: within a fortnight Sara had gone to visit the Southeys who were on holiday at Minehead. Poole was of course overjoyed at his return, but for Sara there were recriminations and anxieties: her husband's long absence, the death of Berkeley, uncertainty about their future home, the heavy overdrawing on the Wedgwood annuity. She also insisted on a reconciliation with Robert Southey, after all his kindness.

Coleridge undertook this in an awkward letter of 29 July, which reflects something of the strained domestic circumstances he had returned to. "I have been absent, Southey! ten months, & little Hartley prattles about you; and if *you* knew, that domestic affliction was hard upon me, and that my own health was declining . . . I am perplexed what to write, or how to state the object of my writing."[3] The change of tone from the ebullient Göttingen letters, and the first mention of ill-health for many months, tells its own story.

In Coleridge's absence, Southey had been acting *in loco parentis*, and Sara had been drawn towards her sister's much more stable household – a reassertion of the old Fricker family loyalties which was to emerge ever more strongly in future years. Southey, moreover, had undermined Sara's confidence in her husband's genius and ability to sustain his own family financially. He had attacked the *Lyrical Ballads* in the press, and privately criticised "France: an Ode" – which had been reprinted in the *Spirit of the Public Journals* – as a surrender of his political principles.[4] He disapproved of the Wedgwood annuity, and had been drawn into Charles Lloyd's machinations against Coleridge which had also temporarily alienated Lamb. Sara had written to Poole when staying at Westbury: "It is very unpleasant for me to be often asked if Coleridge has changed his political sentiments, for I know not properly how to reply. Pray furnish me."[5]

Ironically, it was during this summer that the celebrated cartoon reappeared in the *Anti-Jacobin* anthology, showing Coleridge as the long-eared ass, in the supposedly dangerous radical company of Lloyd and Lamb, with all the other English Jacobins. One begins to understand why Coleridge had prevaricated so long in the peaceful and friendly academia of Germany.

Yet Coleridge's innate generosity of spirit was revealed in such adverse personal circumstances. Having agreed to a reconciliation, largely for Sara's benefit, he pressed home towards common ground with Southey, and concluded his letter:

> Southey, we have similar Talents, Sentiments nearly similar, & kindred pursuits – we have likewise in more than one instance common objects of our esteem and love – I pray and intreat you, if we should meet at any time, let us not withhold from each other the outward Expressions of daily Kindliness; and if it not be any longer in your power to soften your opinions, make your feelings at least more tolerant towards me.[6]

A further letter was despatched on 8 August, while Sara was still at Minehead, dealing with Lloyd's mischief-making and assuring Southey that he had always spoken of his brother-in-law with "respect & affection" to Poole and Wordsworth. Poole also wrote diplomatically, urging the reconciliation, and insisting that Lloyd's behaviour was the consequence of "a diseased mind". As a result, the Southeys and Sara came back together to Stowey in mid-August, and the two men formally embraced each other in the middle of Lime Street – a rather unusual gesture, which Coleridge had perhaps brought back from the Continent.[7]

The two families spent much of the next six weeks in each other's company: house-hunting in Somerset, visiting George Coleridge's family at Ottery; and on a walking expedition through Devon by Dartmouth and Totnes, whose leafy tidal estuary he considered very "tame" by comparison with the wild, beloved coastal path through Porlock, Culbone and Lynton.[8] Coleridge should have been working up his German materials, but the delight of returning to "Kubla Khan" country – indeed perhaps working on that poem – easily side-tracked him, and he had some idea of taking a house with Sara by the sea, between Watchet and Kilve.

Moreover the Muse had returned in original form: besides the translations he sent to Stuart, he began an epic in hexameters with Southey, to be entitled "Mahomet"; and wrote the "Lines Composed in a Concert Room", with their echoes of childhood and the singing of the Abyssinian Maid. He also collaborated with Southey on a satirical ballad, "The Devil's Thoughts", which was published with spectacular success in the *Morning Post* on 6 September.[9]

The first three stanzas of this inspired piece of political cartooning were composed by Southey as he hummed in front of the shaving-mirror one morning at Stowey; the remaining fourteen were dashed off by Coleridge over breakfast.[10] It was a last return to the provocative, radical humour of their Bristol days. Drawing on the popular tradition of the broadsheet ballad, the poem tells how His Satanic Majesty makes a little excursion from his "brimstone bed" to visit his "snug little farm the Earth", and see how his "stock" is appreciating in the capable hands of rich lawyers, doctors, merchants, booksellers, and those who own cottages "with a double coach-house".

Much fun is made with imagery drawn from the Bible and Milton (who is referred to in a footnote as "that most interesting of the Devil's biographers"). Pitt – not mentioned by name – is compared to "Noah and his creeping things" going up into the Ark; and there are sharp asides on the slave trade and appalling conditions in the Cold Baths prisons. Yet the satire is very broad and good-natured – with none of the factional fury of the earlier "War Eclogue" aimed against the Prime Minister. Stuart obviously regarded it as wholly suitable for the newspaper, which was trying to establish a new position of moral opposition to the ministry, independent of both the old Foxite Whigs and the discredited pro-French radicals. The Devil is less of a Jacobin than a representative of moral and political hypocrisy, who takes from the poor to give to the rich, and supports all those who trade on the weak and vulnerable and sick.

Aerial view of Quantock Hills, Somerset, showing villages and paths frequented by Coleridge and Wordsworth, 1797–8, down to the Bristol Channel at East Quantoxhead and Kilve (bottom left). Village of Holford, with its two wooded coombes, nestles in hills at centre left; Dowsborough Hill shows top left with Stowey (hidden behind trees). The flint track of Longstone Hill curves across central ridge, from Alfoxden (isolated house in trees, left) to West Quantoxhead (village, extreme right). This now can be compared with map, Coleridge's West Country. (*Aerofilms Ltd*)

Ash Farm above Culbone Combe, near Porlock. The probable site of Coleridge's opium dream that produced "Kubla Khan". (*Photograph by author*)

Culbone Church in the Combe, between Ash Farm and the sea. (*Photograph by author*)

Interior of Shrewsbury Unitarian Chapel, dominated by the panelled pulpit where Coleridge preached in January 1798.

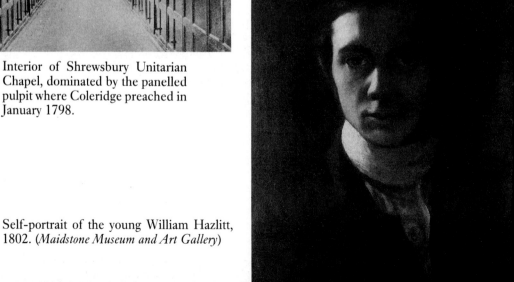

Self-portrait of the young William Hazlitt, 1802. (*Maidstone Museum and Art Gallery*)

Coleridge's Cottage: Nether Stowey

Alfoxden Park

The Holford Coombs

Foreground shows the lane from Nether Stowey down into Holford, with Alfoxden obscured by trees on right: the walk during which the *Ancient Mariner* was begun runs through the pines on the top horizon over Longstone Hill.

The Glen

Streams from the Quantock Hills converging in Holford Glen, where Coleridge, Wordsworth and Dorothy often met to plan poetry ("The Brook"), and listen to nightingales.

Line drawings of Quantock area made by Edmund New, 1914.

Engraving of Göttingen, showing the foothills of the Hartz mountains. Dated 1836.

Friedrich Klopstock. (*Mary Evans Picture Library*)

G. E. Lessing. (*Mary Evans Picture Library*)

Friedrich Schiller. (*Mary Evans Picture Library*)

Immanuel Kant. (*Mary Evans Picture Library*)

Weather effects on the fells above Derwent Water. (*Landscape Only*)

Greta Hall and Keswick Bridge with Latrigg fell behind. Engraving. (*The British Museum*)

Perdita Robinson. Portrait by Thomas Gainsborough, 1781–2. (*Waddesdon Manor*)

William Godwin, 1802, by James Northcote. (*National Portrait Gallery, London*)

Humphry Davy, 1803, by Henry Howard. (*National Portrait Gallery, London*)

THE POET AND JOURNALIST

The wanderer above the sea of mist by Caspar David Friedrich, 1818. (*Kunsthalle, Hamburg*)

The Maid of Buttermere, "Sketch'd from Life" by James Gillray, 1802. (*Carlisle Library*)

Coleridge, 21st March 1804. Pencil drawing by George Dance. (*The Wordsworth Trust*)

Coleridge, 1804. After a portrait by James Northcote, made just before departure for Malta. (*The Wordsworth Trust*)

Occasionally Coleridge's stanzas reach a visionary intensity, which were recalled by a later generation of Romantic poets:*

> He saw an Apothecary on a white horse
> Ride by on his vocations,
> And the Devil thought of his old Friend
> Death in the Revelations.[11]

Stuart published the poem anonymously, and later said it sold out the edition of the paper and marked an upswing in the circulation which increased tenfold over the next three years. It certainly convinced him that every attempt must be made to hire Coleridge as a staff-writer now that he was returned from Germany.

Southey was also impressed by the fluent way Coleridge had developed his original doggerel into balladic form. He had undertaken to edit the new volume of the *Annual Anthology*, a highly popular year-book of literary work, and he now began to press Coleridge to return to "Christabel" and complete it in time for publication as the opening item in the 1799 edition. He argued that this would be the best showcase for Coleridge's new work. Poole was perhaps also behind this idea, for both men were keen to prevent Coleridge giving any more of his valuable work anonymously to Wordsworth's *Lyrical Ballads* should an expanded second edition appear.[12] Coleridge initially agreed, though increasingly anxious about finances, he felt that some "money-book" from his German materials must be the first priority.

The genial humour of "The Devil's Thoughts" reflects something of the patriotic feelings with which Coleridge had returned to England. At Ottery with his brothers, while feasting on "Roast

---

*Both Shelley and Byron published versions of Coleridge's poem, freely adapting it without acknowledgment: respectively, "The Devil's Walk" (1812) and "The Devil's Drive" (1813). In Shelley's case it later provided the seed for his great propaganda poem of 1819, "The Mask of Anarchy", which contains this stanza:

> Last came Anarchy: he rode
> On a white horse, splashed with blood;
> He was pale even to the lips,
> Like Death in the Apocalypse.

(See Richard Holmes, *Shelley: the Pursuit*, 1974, p. 106–7.) Coleridge's poem again reappeared in various pirated pamphlets during the Reform Bill agitation of 1830–32, with illustrations by Cruikshank and Thomas Landseer. By this time its authorship was credited to Richard Porson, Coleridge's old Professor of Greek, a proper Attic irony.

Fowls, mealy potatoes, Pies, & Clouted Cream", he had refused all the old political arguments and joined in rousing toasts to Church and King. He acknowledged the irony of the situation, but wrote cheerfully to Poole: "Who such a friend as I am to the system of Fraternity could refuse such a Toast at the Table of a Clergyman and a Colonel – his Brothers? So, my dear Poole! I live in Peace."[13]

2

Yet he did not have domestic peace, and was increasingly restless in his separation from the Wordsworths. Throughout September he was trying to obtain Alfoxden again, to lure them south;[14] and he wrote a series of long letters on the future of their poetry. Much thought was given to the fragments of the future *Prelude* he had seen in Germany. (These are referred to, confusingly, sometimes as the "Poem to Coleridge", sometimes as "The Recluse", and are now known to scholars as the "1799 Prelude".) About 10 September he wrote a significant proposal for what he saw as the major literary task facing Wordsworth. It is striking how clearly he could see his friend's *magnum opus*, as opposed to the vague, shimmering outline of his own future work glimpsed through the contradictory demands of journalism, poetry, metaphysics, and German study, which pulled him momently in different directions.

For Wordsworth, there was one, overwhelming and epoch-making task which the age itself imperiously demanded.

> My dear friend . . . I wish you would write a poem, in blank verse, addressed to those, who, in consequence of the complete failure of the French Revolution, have thrown up all hopes of the amelioration of mankind, and are sinking into an almost epicurean selfishness, disguising the same under the soft titles of domestic attachment and contempt for visionary *philosophes*. It would do great good, and might form a part of "The Recluse", for in my present mood I am wholly against the publication of any small poems.[15]

This proposal Wordsworth would interpret after his own fashion, in the form of autobiographical witness to his own struggles between revolutionary Utopia and nature. But he came to regard Coleridge as the only man who could see him through – indeed oversee him – during the next five years that this task would take. In a sense,

Coleridge had here abandoned his own Epic pretensions (so wonderfully described in 1797) into his friend's keeping, a gesture of renunciation both heroic and curiously tragic.

Yet the proposal also marks a forthright recognition of his own position. To see the French Revolution as a "complete failure" might seem an abrupt apostasy of his old hopes, even though such doubts had been implicit since the earliest days of Pantisocracy. Yet the statement marks a new realism, an affirmation that "the amelioration of mankind" was still the grand object in view; that "domestic" retirement – as celebrated for instance by Thelwall – was no real solution; and that the work of "visionary *philosophes*" (so much his own work) was more than ever vital to the literary cause. In its own way, it was a declaration of his own intent to go out again into the public sphere, chastened and determined.

3

As autumn advanced, Coleridge still avoided any clear plan of action, or literary commitments. Professionally he was being drawn in three different directions at once: Poole and Southey wished him to stay in the West Country, working on his German books, writing poetry, and perhaps taking a few private pupils; Stuart wanted him in London, writing topical verse and political articles for the *Morning Post*; Wordsworth wanted him in the north to continue the experimental work begun in the *Lyrical Ballads.* Coleridge's personal compass would oscillate round these three cardinal points – the West Country, London and the Lakes – for many months to come; and in some ways his uncertainty about his true direction would dominate his life for the next four years.

With his fatal genius for being all things to all men, for trying to please everyone at once, and for trying to fulfil expectations on every hand, he fell into a pattern of prevarication and fragmentation in much of his work. He dreamed more than he planned, he planned more than he could execute, leaping from one brilliant conception to the next, never still or concentrated for more than a few weeks at a time.

At the heart of this restless whirling and sparking lay the problem of his domestic life with Sara, profoundly disrupted by his ten months in Germany. They could not find a new house together in Somerset or Devon, and on the return to Stowey at the end of September they were soon engulfed in practical difficulties, which gave him no peace to work. Little Hartley's health registered the disruptions: first he seriously injured a bone falling downstairs at Southey's lodgings in Exeter; then he caught scabies so the whole cottage at Stowey had to be fumigated, while he was painted with brimstone ointment and his parents wore foul-smelling mercurial belts; and finally Sara shut his arm in a door, bruising it severely.[16]

Then the cottage flooded in the autumn rains, and Coleridge caught pneumonia on his walks. He wrote in growing exasperation: "Our little Hovel is afloat – poor Sara tired off her legs with servanting – the young one fretful & noisy from confinement exerts his activities on all forbidden Things – the house stinks of Sulphur – I however, sunk in Spinoza, remain as undisturbed as a Toad in a Rock; that is to say, when my rheumatic pains are asleep."[17]

But the disturbance was deep in the rock: walks in the rain, doses of opium, no German work, and more long reading of travel books – always a sure sign of restlessness – this time J. G. Stedman's *Narrative of a Five Year Expedition in Guiana, on the Wild Coast of South America.* He wrote Southey an account of the vultures there, and defended them as valuable scavengers who prevented plague by feeding on carrion, while the "noble Eagle" was by comparison "not only useless but a murderer".[18]

In early October, Coleridge fled to the Wedgwoods' house at Upton in Wiltshire, to discuss Lessing; while Sara laundered all the linen in the cottage and burned Hartley's infected clothes. Coleridge had heard from Wordsworth, who promised that the great blank verse poem, now intended as a "tailpiece" to "The Recluse", would be dedicated to him. This touched Coleridge deeply, and made him secretly determined to find some excuse for going north. "To be addressed, as a beloved man, by a thinker, at the close of such a poem as 'The Recluse', a poem *non unius populi*, is the only event, I believe, capable of inciting in me an hour's vanity," he wrote back to Wordsworth. He added that it would be a kind of creative vanity at one remove: "self-elevation produced *ab extra*"; yet what he needed was that same impulse *ab intra*, from within himself.[19]

Even at Upton he was too unwell and unsettled "to be comfortable"; and moved back briefly to Stowey where "young Brimstonello" was improving. More reading in old folios by the fire, when the family had gone to bed, set him dreaming again of travel and poetry. "If I begin a poem of Spinoza," he confided to his Notebooks, "thus it should begin: I would make a pilgrimage to the burning sands of Arabia, or etc etc to find the Man who could explain to me there can be *oneness*, there be infinite Perceptions – yet there must be a *one*ness, not an intense Union but an Absolute Unity . . ."[20]

Meanwhile he assured Southey he would set about completing "Christabel" "with all speed".[21] He ordered a great quiver of newly cut pens from Thomas Ward, with ghastly puns about writing "till *Pen*tecost, filling whole *Pen*tateuchs", and signing his thanks with heavy irony "from Apollo's Temple in the odoriferous Lime-Grove . . ."[22]

4

Speed, when it came, took the form of movement rather than composition. Coleridge began to whirl around his compass points. He suddenly informed Sara that he must go to Bristol to chase up his book-box, and if necessary from thence to London. He timed his departure almost telepathically, for the missing box arrived in Stowey forty-eight hours later. She sent messages to retrieve him, but in vain: she had no news of him for nearly six weeks, and they did not meet again until early December. Without telling her, he had gone to see the Wordsworths. Curiously her letters to Poole during the interim are philosophical: she took a holiday with Hartley at Kilve, and awaited developments. By now she must have understood that there was little immediate chance of Coleridge "subsiding" into domesticity: what she hoped for was some prospect of financial security, and this indeed he would do his best to manage in the coming months.

At Bristol, Coleridge burst in upon Cottle with a thousand schemes, and was introduced to laughing-gas by Dr Beddoes' new assistant at the Pneumatic Institute, the young Cornish chemist Humphry Davy. Davy was as fascinated by poetry as by intoxication (with Coleridge they sometimes became the same thing), and soon joined the ranks of Coleridge's youthful admirers. He would become Coleridge's most important contact in the scientific world, and in later years would introduce him to the Royal Institution as a lecturer.*

---

*Humphry Davy (1778–1829) still represents the old eighteenth-century unity between scientific and literary cultures, like Erasmus Darwin, Jefferson, and Priestley before him. (See "Coleridge's Circle") Originally attracted equally by poetry and chemistry, Davy's published works would include much verse, and a treatise on fly-fishing. Coleridge was always fascinated by his lectures, many of which he later attended in London, and drew from his papers on chemical and electrical experiments numerous analogies with the workings of poetry and criticism. Later Coleridge's own scientific interests drew him towards the German *Naturphilo-*

footnote continued overleaf

This first meeting was curtailed by news from Durham that Wordsworth was depressed and ill. No further excuse was wanting, and on 22 October Coleridge and Cottle were rattling northwards in the publisher's stylish postchaise. Immediately Coleridge's Notebooks leaped into life once more, as they had in the Hartz, noting the appearance of streams, thatched cottages, and the autumnal foliage, "a lovely light yellow . . . red, or rather *poppy* color'd".[23]

They reached Sockburn-on-Tees four days later, where they found Wordsworth in rude good health, comfortably established in the large manor farmhouse belonging to his old friends the Hutchinsons. There was a blissful reunion, and high-spirited introductions to the Hutchinson family: Tom, the Yorkshire farmer, and his three animated sisters, Mary, Sara, and Joanna. Coleridge immediately set out to charm the entire family, melting northern reserve with all his wit, self-mockery and flights of wildest fantasy about his adventures in the Hartz. He noted cheerfully: "Few moments in life so interesting as those of an affectionate reception from those who have heard of you yet are strangers to your person."[24] Dorothy was particularly pleased to show off Coleridge to her greatest childhood friend, Mary Hutchinson (for whom she had written the sketch at Racedown), while the middle sister, Sara, then twenty-four, looked on with sunny, sceptical amusement. Coleridge, capable of adapting himself with equal ease to a professorial soirée in Germany as to a Yorkshire farmhouse kitchen, did not disappoint.

But Wordsworth was impatient, after the long separation, to hurry his friend off alone on a conducted tour of the kingdom of his childhood, so long envisioned in his poetry in Germany. Within twenty-four hours they were striding westwards towards the Lake District, with a bemused Cottle trying to keep up with them on a small pony. He, or the animal, gave up at Greta Bridge. The two continued across the Pennines, eating "gobbets of Bread & Cheese" on the march, and coming down through Troutbeck to the sudden, silvery expanse of Lake Windermere with all the dark hills of Cumberland rising beyond.

---

footnote continued.

sophie, and concepts of a universal Life Force, though he decisively rejected Evolution on religious grounds. (See Kathleen Coburn, "Coleridge: A Bridge between Science and Poetry", in *Coleridge's Variety*, edited by John Beer, Macmillan, 1974.) As Coleridge's Notebooks show, he did not share Wordsworth's doubts about empirical and analytic methods ("we murder to dissect"), and he can be strikingly scientific in his observations of plants, animals, geology, and – above all – human psychology. Davy had enormous respect for his intellectual capacity (see Chapter 14), and in 1807–1808 would make great efforts to establish him as a public lecturer.

They had been joined at Temple Sowerby by Wordsworth's sailor brother, John, another important introduction for Coleridge into the Wordsworth clan: a tall, silent, kindly man of deep and inarticulate feeling, passionately devoted to his elder brother and sister. John had joined the merchant navy, and was on shore-leave between two East India voyages. The three men took the ferry across the lake, and entered into the heartland at Hawkshead, where Wordsworth had been to school, slowly working their way back through Rydal to Grasmere. From here they began an extensive exploration of the whole district, which lasted for the first fortnight of November, reaching out to Ullswater, Borrowdale, Ennerdale, Wasdale Head, and Buttermere. (See map.)

For Coleridge, all his previous wanderings in the Quantocks and the Hartz were brought to fruition in this dazzling discovery of the Lakes, with its high fells, its rocky waterfalls, its spreading waters, and its miraculously sudden shifts of light and cloud. From the moment he saw the River Greta, his Notebooks began to flood with fresh observations and visionary reflections: "River Greta near its fall into the Tees – Shootings of water threads down the slope of the huge green stone – The white Eddy-rose that blossom'd up against the stream in the scollop, by fits & starts, obstinate in resurrection – It *is the life* that we live. Black round spots from 5 to 18 in the decaying leaf of the Sycamore."[25]

He was overwhelmed by the great crags all round the horizon: "Ghost of a mountain – the forms seizing my Body as I passed & became realities – I, a Ghost, till I had reconquered my Substance."[26] The sunny mists that rose and descended seemed like "the luminous gloom of Plato".[27] The expanse of Ullswater transfixed his eyes, perusing and enquiring, as he tested his perceptions: "a large Slice of calm silver – above this a bright ruffledness, or atomic sportiveness – motes in the sun? – Vortices of flies? – how shall I express the Banks waters all fused Silver, that House too its slates rainwet silver in the sun, & its shadows running down in the water like a column."[28]

The words seemed to bubble up and fuse in new forms as he wrote. The variety of the light filled him with a new sense of wonder: "over the forke of the Cliff behind, in shape so like a cloud, the Sun sent cutting it his thousand silky Hairs of amber & green Light – I step two paces, and have lost the Glory, but the edge has exactly the soft richness of the silver edge of a cloud behind which the Sun is travelling! – The fog has now closed over the Lake, & we wander in darkness . . ."[29] He saw "violet Crags"; a hill "like a Dolphin so beautiful in the Lines of Snow"; archipelagos of little islands in the lakes like "Pleiads" of stars.

He climbed the waterfalls of Scale Force between Crummock and Buttermere, and lived out its beauty and violence: "the chasm thro' which it flows is stupendous – so wildly wooded that the mosses & wet weeds & perilous Tree increase the Horror of the rocks which *ledge* only enough to interrupt not stop your fall – & the Tree – O God! to think of a poor Wretch hanging with one arm from it."[30] As he wrote to Dorothy from Keswick on 10 November: "You can feel what I cannot express for myself – how deeply I have been impressed by a world of scenery absolutely new to me . . . It was to me a vision of a fair Country. Why were you not with us Dorothy? Why were not you Mary with us?"[31]

As Wordsworth had no doubt intended, the idea of settling in the Lakes now rose vividly before them. He in turn wrote to Dorothy, in the same letter: "C. was much struck with Grasmere & its neighbourhood & I have much to say to you, you will think my plan a mad one, but I have thought of building a house there by the Lake side. John would give me £40 to buy the ground . . . we shall talk of this . . ."[32] This scheme was to bring the Wordsworths back to Grasmere in December, and Coleridge in the summer to Keswick, though not without many difficulties and much discussion.

John Wordsworth had to depart early for his next voyage, and they climbed Helvellyn together as a kind of pledge for the future. Coleridge wrote a moving account of this ceremonial – one of his earliest experiences of serious fell-walking – in which their ideal of friendship consecrated in the beauty of the natural world emerges with extraordinary power. This short section of his letter to Dorothy is indeed close to the form of a Conversation Poem, with all its visionary intimations, yet held back in a prose medium which was increasingly Coleridge's most intense and instinctive response to life. Even in its steady, unfolding rhythms, it is markedly shaped and poetic. Landscape and emotion are fused with complex undertones of valediction.

> We accompanied John over the fork of Helvellyn on a day when light & darkness coexisted in contiguous masses, & the earth & sky were but *one*! Nature lived for us in all her grandest accidents – we quitted him by a wild Tarn just as we caught a view of the gloomy Ulswater. Your Br. John is one of you; a man who hath

solitary usings of his own Intellect, deep in feeling, with a subtle Tact, a swift instinct of Truth & Beauty. He interests me much.[33]

There was, too, an implied sadness that Coleridge himself still stood outside this magic circle: how he longed to be "one of them" himself. For already he was also being called away again, to the southern compass point, by news from London.

A letter from Stuart, probably forwarded by Cottle from Bristol, now reached him at Keswick proposing a contract as a staff-writer on the *Morning Post*. Professionally he was attracted by the offer, and financially his debt on the Wedgwood account made it difficult to refuse. (Wordsworth was also in debt to Josiah for £100, drawn in Germany, which he did not manage to return until July 1800.)[34] London offered him resources and libraries for his German work, so long delayed, and also a kind of staging post between Poole and Wordsworth.

He wrote crisply to Southey (but not to Sara), that he would accept the post, "which, if it turn out well, will enable me & Sara to reside in London for the next four or five months – a thing I wish extremely on many . . . accounts."[35] He did not explain how he came to be in "such a distant corner of the Kingdom", except to say he had been alarmed by Wordsworth's health (which had been perfectly satisfactory); and he was utterly silent about the Lakes. Then he delayed his departure for a further week of fell-walking, and a visit to Thomas Clarkson, the campaigner against the slave trade, at Eusemere.* It was difficult to tear himself away: "Monday Morning – sitting on a Tree Stump at the brink of the Lake by Mr Clarkson's – perfect serenity; that round fat backside of a Hill with its image in the water . . ."[36]

---

*Another influential dissenter, Thomas Clarkson (1760–1846), reformer and Vice-President of the Anti-Slavery Society, later befriended Coleridge in the darkest days of his opium addiction. Besides his *History of the Abolition of the Slave Trade* (1808), he wrote studies of Quakerism and William Penn. His wife Catherine became an intimate of Dorothy's, and we learn much from their letters of the shifting Wordsworth-Coleridge alliance. During this first Eusemere visit, Coleridge was still clearly in the ascendant: "C. was in high spirits and talk'd a great deal. W. was more reserved . . . He seems very fond of C. laughing at all his jokes and taking all opportunities of showing him off." Coleridge's ecstatic reaction to the Lakes did not prevent him making fun of well-heeled Lake tourists – "Gold-headed Cane on a pikteresk Toor" – and cursing Sir Michael Le Fleming for his "damned white-washing" of Rydal Hall, where they had trespassed – as he put it – with their feet, in return for Sir Michael's "Trespass on the Eye". (*Notebooks*, I, 508, 514)

5

Even when Coleridge finally separated from Wordsworth on 18 November, he could not bring himself to go directly south. Instead he leaped into a coach and shot back across the Pennines to Sockburn to see Dorothy and the Hutchinsons. He remained for two or three days, an oasis of happiness, flirting with everyone, and working suddenly on a new ballad, to be called "Love". It was now that he entered in his Notebooks a single, and perhaps tragic phrase: "The long Entrancement of a True-love's Kiss".[37]

Coleridge later described this second visit to Sockburn as one of those "spots of enchantment" where his poetry was renewed, and he fell in love with Sara Hutchinson. Certainly the phrase from his Notebook was incorporated in the first of the "Asra" poems – poems secretly dedicated to Sara Hutchinson – which he wrote the following year, "The Keepsake". It recalls an early morning walk with "Emmeline", an embroidered handkerchief given as a token, and something of Sara's particular mixture of humour and quick sympathy:

> I yet might ne'er forget her smile, her look,
> Her voice, (that even in her mirthful mood
> Has made me wish to steal away and weep,)
> Nor yet the entrancement of that maiden kiss . . .[38]

Three years later, when he was certainly deeply in love, he added a retrospective entry for 24 November 1799, which traces his fall to one vividly remembered incident which has all the accidental quality of truth. "Nov 24th – the Sunday – Conundrums & Puns & Stories & Laughter – with Jack Hutchinson – Stood round the Fire, et Sarae manum a tergo longum in tempus prensabam . . ."[39] The Latin part of this entry reads in full: "and I held Sara's hand for a long time behind my back, and then for the first time, Love pierced me with its dart, envenomed, and alas! incurable."

Yet the contemporary evidence tends to suggest that Coleridge, in his own fashion, had fallen indiscriminately in love with the whole Hutchinson family, rather as he had done eight years before with the Evanses. Their friendship with the Wordsworths, the world of northern hospitality, the poetic magic of their landscape, had all cast their spell over him. The emotional warmth he had clearly lost in his relations with his wife was here promised renewal. There is a strong suggestion that initially, at least, he was attracted equally by Mary

Hutchinson, and he would later emphasise that he "did not then know Mary's & William's attachment".[40] This denial seems to imply that he recognised how closely his feelings for the Hutchinson sisters were in fact bound up with his feelings for Wordsworth. He fell in love with the women surrounding his closest male friend, just as he had done when he met the Fricker sisters with Southey. It is not perhaps coincidental that "Emmeline" was the name Wordsworth also used in his early poems about Mary, whom he was eventually to marry in 1802.

These enchanted days at Sockburn were inextricably associated with the rapid composition of the ninety-six lines of his ballad "Love", which transposed all his emotions immediately to the plane of medieval legend: a love-lorn minstrel wooing his Lady Genevieve, his "bright and Beauteous bride". Poetry, playful flirtation, and a little posing as the moon-struck bard, were perhaps not really separated at this stage:

All thoughts, all passions, all delights,
Whatever stirs this mortal frame,
All are but ministers of Love,
 And feed his sacred flame.

Oft in my waking dreams do I
Live o'er again that happy hour,
When midway on the mount I lay,
 Beside the ruined tower.

The moonshine, stealing o'er the scene
Had blended with the lights of eve;
And she was there, my hope, my joy,
 My own dear Genevieve!

She leant against the armèd man,
The statue of the armèd knight;
She stood and listened to my lay,
 Amid the lingering light.[41]

Coleridge had been much impressed on his walks by the effigy of a medieval knight in chain-mail, carved on the family tomb belonging to the Conyers, in Sockburn church. It must have reminded him of the old family tombs at Ottery. But unlike most crusader memorials, the "armèd knight" at Sockburn rested his feet on a monstrous "wyverne" or dragon-serpent, and local legend associated the heroic killing of this monster with an ancient standing stone or "greystone" in the nearby fields.[42]

Coleridge's love of folklore, and the way it came to possess even the natural elements in a landscape, was aroused. "In the North every Brook, every Crag, almost every Field has a name – a proof of greater Independence & a society more approaching in their Laws & Habits to Nature."[43] He included the "greystone" in an early draft of his ballad, later changing it to the symbolic "mount" where the minstrel lies "midway" in contemplation; while the "wyverne" is altered, lamia-like, into a beautiful but fiendish woman who lures the knight to his destruction.

The poem becomes a tale within a tale, with psychological implications about the fatality of love: the minstrel can only win his lady by recounting the destruction of the knight, who is "crazed" by his experience, and dies in the arms of his beloved:

> And that she nursed him in a cave;
> And how his madness went away,
> When on the yellow forest-leaves
> A dying man he lay . . .[44]

Moved by this story, Genevieve embraces the bard, and the ballad appears to end in a moment of voluptuous happiness for the poet. But Coleridge achieves a brilliant touch of uncertainty, in the final line, but using the same words, "bright and beauteous", to describe Genevieve as had been used previously to describe the knight's fiendish vision of the *femme fatale*, "an angel beautiful and bright". The implication, striking like a sudden unresolved chord, is that both loves are a kind of malediction; and at some level this seems to reflect his situation with Sara Hutchinson.

Coleridge originally considered this poem as part of a longer ballad, closely associated with the world of "Christabel", which was to be called "The Tale of the Dark Ladie". But he was so excited with its form, and its proof of his recovered powers, that he immediately submitted it to the *Morning Post* on his return to London.

It appeared on 21 December with a characteristic editorial note distinguishing between his role as poet and political commentator:

> . . . as it is professedly a tale of antient times, I trust, that "the affectionate lovers of venerable antiquity" (as Cambden says) will grant me their pardon . . . it is possible that now, even a simple story, wholly unspiced with politics or personality, may find some

> attention amid the hubbub of Revolutions, as to those who have remained a long time by the falls of Niagara, the lowest whispering becomes distinctly audible.[45]

It eventually became one of his best-known poems, after the *Mariner*, and directly inspired John Keats to write "La Belle Dame Sans Merci" in 1820, which has many echoes of its music, theme, and setting.

Coleridge remained at Sockburn for a week, almost as if he were in hiding, writing neither to his wife nor Poole, and immersed in the company of Dorothy, Mary and Sara. The vivacity and tenderness of these women evidently gave him something he had not found in Germany, nor on his return to Stowey. The contrast between the two Hutchinson sisters must have fascinated him: Mary rather tall and tranquil, with that deep sense of inner calm that so attracted Wordsworth; Sara altogether more quick and outgoing, a small energetic figure with a mass of auburn hair, responding to his jokes, neat and rapid in the house, eager on country walks. Later observers – De Quincey, Keats, Coleridge's own daughter – would describe her as homely in appearance, with a pronounced underjaw, expressive of her determination and good humour. (But Keats would also add, as late as 1817, "enchanting".)

Perhaps one of the keys to Sara's distinction, and her love of poetry – which would make her Coleridge's most faithful amanuensis – was the early period of her childhood in Cumberland. She was brought up in the house of a strange, kindly, autodidact relative known as James Patrick of Kendal, "the Intellectual Pedlar", whom Wordsworth would use as a model for the figure of the Wanderer in *The Excursion*. She had an independence and originality of mind, all her own; and would prove one of the most steadfast and practical of all the women who attached themselves to the Lake District circle. She was no "beauteous Bride" or angelic fiend or temptress; but she was a strong, attractive woman who offered that quality most seductive to Coleridge – emotional security and endless good nature: a promise of home.

On 26 November he finally caught the all-night coach for London, and his new career. The following day, awaking at dawn, he pulled out his Notebook and made a strange, symbolic entry, describing a flock of starlings glimpsed from his carriage window over the low, wintry landscape.

"Starlings in vast flights drove along like smoke, mist, or any thing misty without volition – now a circular area inclined in an Arc – now a

Globe – now from complete Orb into an Elipse & Oblong – now a balloon with the car suspended, now a concaved Semicircle – & still it expands & condenses, some moments glimmering & shivering, dim & shadowy, now thickening, deepening, blackening!"[46]

This image haunted him for years after: he recalled it while climbing alone over Scafell Pike in 1802, and rephrased it twice in his Notebooks in 1803.[47] It is an image of shifting energy and imagination; a protean form or a force-field, lacking fixed structure or outline; a powerful personality without a solid identity, or unified will – "without volition". Clearly, this was some sort of self-image for Coleridge, both stimulating in its sense of freedom, of "vast flights"; and menacing in its sense of threatening chaos or implosion, "thickening, deepening, blackening".*

6

Back in London he immediately took lodgings at 21 Buckingham Street, between the Thames and the Strand near the *Morning Post* offices, summoned Sara and Hartley to join him, and set to work with ferocious energy to establish himself as a journalist. During the next five months he would write seventy-six articles or "leading paragraphs" for Stuart, largely on foreign affairs and constitution matters. His first piece, a brilliant and detailed analysis of the new French constitution proclaimed by Bonaparte, appeared promptly the following Saturday 7 December.

There was one last regretful memory of the Lakes, as he gazed out of his lodging windows at the dark shapes of the city: "harsh contrast compared with the universal motion, the harmonious System of Motions, in the country & every where in Nature. – In this dim Light London appeared to me as a huge place of Sepulchres thro' which Hosts of Spirits were gliding."[48] Then he set to work.

His initial plan was to do freelance literary work in the mornings at Buckingham Street, and to oversee "the literary and political department" of the newspaper, both as editor and leader-writer, during the afternoons.[49] Besides general political commentaries, he wrote

*In 1802 he would specifically apply it to his irrational state of mind in sleep, dream, opium or sexual passion. Like many of his later self-images, it drew on the symbolism of birds and flight, always closely associated for him with his powers of imagination and creativity. Virginia Woolf would unconsciously use this passage to describe Coleridge in one of her essays: "he seems not a man, but a swarm, a cloud, a buzz of words, darting this way and that, clustering, quivering, and hanging suspended." (See Bibliography.) She too saw in the starlings something of what he might become in history.

directly about many of the leading public figures of the day: Pitt, Bonaparte, Benjamin Constant, Washington, Fox, Sheridan and Lord Grenville (the Foreign Minister). In trying to redefine the new moderate, anti-ministerial position of the *Morning Post* based on "certain fixed and announced principles", Coleridge quickly hit upon a central theme of his mature political writing, one very different from the "flame-coloured" enthusiasms of his Bristol lectures and the *Watchman*. This theme was an attack on the fanaticism which now increasingly polarised British war-time politics into Jacobin and anti-Jacobin wings: a fanaticism which he would analyse with growing subtlety, as both a political and a psychological phenomenon. His argument was that extremism on the left only encouraged extremism on the right, leading to oppressive and hard-line attitudes and measures.

Coleridge called for a new realism among the friends of liberty, and the creation of a moderate, centralised body of liberal opinion, opposed to Pitt but equally opposed to "zeal both anti-jacobin and anti-gallican".[50]

An early leader of 12 December, "Advice to the Friends of Freedom", defined this position by calling the radicals to order.

> Passion makes men blind; and these men, by the alarms which their intemperate zeal, unfixed principles, and Gallican phraseology excite, form around the Minister a more effective phalanx of defence, than all his body-guard of Loan-jobbers, Contractors, Placemen and Pensioners, in and out of Parliament. But these are times in which those who love freedom should use all imaginable caution to love it wisely . . . Good men should now close ranks. Too much of extravagant hope, too much of rash intolerance, have disgraced all parties: and facts, well adapted to discipline us all, have burst forth even to superfluity.[51]

This new note of sobriety accurately reflected his own political development, clearly signalled in "France: an Ode", his letters from Germany, and his private reflections to Wordsworth on the poet's task *après le déluge*. It became something of the house-style of Stuart's paper.

He wrote cheerfully about his labours to Southey on Christmas Eve. "I am employed from I-rise to I-set – i.e. from 9 in the morning to 12 at night – a pure Scribbler. My Mornings to Booksellers' Compilations – after dinner to Stewart, who pays *all* my expences here . . . For Stewart I write often his leading Paragraphs, on Secession,

Peace, Essay on the new French Constitution, Advice to Friends of Freedom . . ." He was also contributing topical poems, such as a "Christmas Carol", and a satire on a politician's rubicund nose.[52] He reckoned to pay off the £150 overdrawn on the Wedgwood annuity by April 1800, when he could "return" to the Lessing biography.

His articles were not always delivered on time, but he worked well under deadline pressures – a significant discovery – and in February he three times volunteered to report on all-night sittings at the House of Commons, working from eight in the evening to three in the morning in the "hideously crowded" reporters' gallery, taking down speeches by Pitt and Fox and writing them up (verbatim reporting was still illegal) for the next day's paper. He was fascinated by this glimpse of the parliamentary power struggle at first hand. "The elegance, & high-finish of Pitt's Periods even in the most sudden replies, is *curious*: but that is all. He *argues* but so so; & does not *reason* at all . . . Fox possesses all the full & overflowing Eloquence of a man of clear head, clean heart, & impetuous feelings. He is to my mind a great orator. All the rest that spoke were mere creatures."[53]

Coleridge found the whole journalistic process both exhausting and stimulating, and it gave him a taste for the national debate of public issues that he never subsequently lost. He was deeply interested in the formation of public opinion in the metropolis, and this sense of the importance of London life for a man of letters was to distinguish him sharply from Wordsworth's commitment to solitary writing in the Lake District.

He confided ironically to Josiah Wedgwood after the first two months:

> We Newspaper scribes are true Galley-Slaves . . . Yet it is not unflattering to a man's Vanity to reflect that what he writes at 12 at night will before 12 hours is over have perhaps 5 or 6000 Readers! To trace a happy phrase, good image, or new argument running thro' the Town, & sliding into all the papers! Few Wine merchants can boast of creating more sensation . . . But seriously . . . they are important in themselves, & excellent Vehicles for general Truths. I am not ashamed of what I have written.[54]

His own reputation was altering as a result of his position on the *Morning Post*. When he had arrived in London from Germany, he was still known as some wild West Country firebrand poet, the author of "The Devil's Thoughts". The *Anti-Jacobin* had republished the Gillray cartoon of "The New Morality" with a libellous caption. "He has left his native country, commenced citizen of the world, left his poor children fatherless and his wife destitute. *Ex his disce* his friends Lamb and Southey!" Though advised by attorneys to prosecute, he sensibly let it go.[55]

Daniel Stuart gave a very different assessment of the strengths and weaknesses which he now revealed in Fleet Street.

> To write the leading paragraph of a newspaper I would prefer him to Mackintosh, Burke, or any man I ever heard of. His observations not only were confirmed by good sense, but displayed extensive knowledge, deep thought and well-grounded foresight: they were so brilliantly ornamented, so classically delightful. They were the writings of a Scholar, a Gentleman and a Statesman, without personal sarcasm or illiberality of any kind. But when Coleridge wrote in his study without being pressed, he wandered and lost himself.[56]

Coleridge began to enjoy his new life in the metropolis. He was soon reconciled with Charles Lamb (who, unlike Southey, was incapable of bearing a grudge), and was dining out regularly with him, Godwin, Stuart, Humphry Davy (visiting from Bristol), the publisher Longman, and various literary ladies who admired his poetry – Mary Hays, Charlotte Smith, Mrs Barbauld, and his favourite, Perdita Robinson,* who celebrated the author of "Kubla

*Mary "Perdita" Robinson, fashionable beauty and Shakespearian actress, had once been mistress to the Prince Regent, before turning her charms upon poetry and the gothick novel. (See "Coleridge's Circle".) Among the rather severe and starchy blue-stockings, Coleridge loved her raffish glamour and enthusiastic approach to life. "She is a woman of undoubted Genius . . . She overloads every thing; but I never knew a human Being with so *full* a mind – bad, good, & indifferent, I grant you, but full, & overflowing." (*Letters*, *I*, p. 562) Perdita's "Ode to S. T. Coleridge", composed between December 1799 and her death in December 1800 contains the following passage:

> Now by the source, which lab'ring heaves
> The mystic fountain, bubbling, panting,
> While gossamer its net-work weaves,
> Adown the blue lawn, slanting!
> I'll mark thy 'sunny dome', and view
> Thy 'caves of ice,' thy fields of dew!
> Thy ever-blooming mead, whose flow'r
> Waves to the cold breathe of the moon-light hour!

Coleridge urged Southey to include her work in the *Annual Anthology*, and when she was dying exchanged affectionate letters with her from the Lakes. In "A Stranger Minstrel", a poem set on Skiddaw, he has the voice of the mountain itself praise her "song and witching melody" (see Chapter II). He was always grateful for her appreciation of "Kubla Khan", and in volume two I will consider how far Perdita's own experience of opium may have influenced Coleridge's preface to the poem of 1816, and even the arrival of the Person from Porlock.

Khan" in her own verses.[57] He attended plays, and critically followed a course of lectures by Mackintosh.

Rather surprisingly, Sara and Hartley also flourished at Buckingham Street, and a new domestic harmony – of a rather noisy kind – was established. Coleridge's regular departures for the newspaper office, as well as his regular income of four or five guineas a week, may have helped to soothe Sara, and she was pregnant again in January 1800. As before, Hartley was the barometer of this improved atmosphere, and the three-year-old was certainly rumbustious. "Hartley is quite well, & my talkativeness is his, without diminution on my side ... Tomorrow Sara & I dine at Mister Gobwin's as Hartley calls him – who gave the philosopher such a Rap on the shins with a ninepin that Gobwin in huge pain *lectured* Sara on his boisterousness. I was not at home."[58]

By comparison Coleridge found the good behaviour and "cadaverous Silence" of Godwin's children "quite catacombish." He put this down to the tragic death of Mary Wollstonecraft, though he felt her influence had greatly improved Godwin "in heart & manner" since they last met.[59]

Coleridge now began a real intimacy with Godwin, arguing long into the night about politics and theology, until the erstwhile atheist slowly changed his opinions. Godwin subsequently described Coleridge as one of the "four principal oral instructors" of his life, leading him to a new appreciation of the divinity in all things. "My theism, if such I may be permitted to call it, consists in a reverent and soothing contemplation of all that is beautiful, grand, or mysterious in the system of the universe ... into this train of thinking I was first led by the conversations of S. T. Coleridge."[60]

So struck was Godwin by Coleridge's warmth and magnetic personality that he began to keep a series of personal notes with the vague idea of writing a biographical essay about him, at some future date, though these always remained in manuscript. After recording the curious details of his early life, Godwin noted that Coleridge still planned to write an Epic poem, beginning at thirty-five (1807), "meditated" for three years, composed in two, and to comprise "all his accumulations". Coleridge "always longed to know some man whom he might look up to, by that means to increase his sentiment of the importance of our common nature: every man knows himself to be little."[61] Psychologically, all this fascinated Godwin.

Coleridge in turn teased him relentlessly on the "pedantry of atheism", particularly tickled by Godwin's frequent expression,

"'God bless him, to use a vulgar Phrase'".[62] He modestly admitted the value of their discussions, but gravely put down any improvement in Godwin's "poetic & physiopathic feeling" to the influence of his daughter – the future Mary Shelley, then aged one.[63] Hartley also announced that he would marry Mary.

7

Indeed Coleridge was now attempting to redirect the efforts of all his friends. He became a positive firework box of schemes and projects. During these months in London we find him advising Lamb to start contributing to the newspapers; Southey to give up editing, write a history of the Levellers and concentrate on finishing his Epic poem, "Madoc"; and Humphry Davy to write "a compact compressed History of the Human Mind for the last Century" (a Coleridgean project if ever there was one). He did not always expect to be taken entirely seriously, as he told the latter. "Take my nonsense like a pinch of snuff – sneeze it off, it clears the head."[64]Even wilder fluctuations appeared in his own life-schemes.

Like the flock of starlings, each scheme appeared to expand or contract, according to Coleridge's correspondent, faithfully reflecting what each one wished to hear. Southey wished to return to the Continent, and accordingly in December Coleridge was considering "a pleasant little Colony for a few years in Italy or the South of France".[65] But this of course depended on peace with Bonaparte. By January this scheme had expanded to include Humphry Davy and Wordsworth, "precious Stuff for Dreams".[66] At the same time he was pressing Poole to find a larger house in the Quantocks, at Stowey or Aisholt, which might suit Sara.[67] Her pregnancy meant at any rate that they must be settled definitely by August at latest, and she clearly favoured the West Country. In February Coleridge also considered sharing Alfoxden with Southey;[68] and in March with Wordsworth. By May, when Southey had left for Portugal, the idea for the colony had moved back to the Lakes, and now included both Davy and Godwin.[69] Coleridge had no doubt forgotten, by this stage, that he had also promised to tour Scandinavia in the summer with his Göttingen friends.

Yet these mercurial shifts had their own underlying logic. In the first place Coleridge needed a place big enough to work undisturbed: "a House with a Garden, & large enough for me to have a Study out of the noise of Women & children – this is absolutely necessary for me."[70] In the second place, the old Pantisocratic ideal of a group of like-minded friends living in close proximity in the country, whether in England or abroad, still inspired him. His domestic life with Sara was not enough, and his rapid shifts of plan can be seen as a constant attempt to orchestrate his friends into some viable combination of talents and personalities. Moreover his choice of friends to be "colonised" was extraordinarily perceptive of what Hazlitt would later call "the spirit of the age": Wordsworth, Southey, Godwin, and Davy represented a real intellectual elite of the time.

In the third place, Coleridge was struggling to reconcile two fundamental loyalties in his life, now at opposed points on his compass: Tom Poole and William Wordsworth. By mid-March 1800 it was clear that they could never be reunited, as in the old Quantock days. He wrote candidly to Poole, hoping for some measure of understanding.

> I would to God, I could get Wordsworth to re-take Alfoxden – the Society of so great a Being is of priceless Value – but he will never quit the North of England – his habits are more assimilated with the Inhabitants there – there he & his Sister are exceedingly beloved, enthusiastically . . . Certainly, no one, neither you, or the Wedgwoods, altho' you far more than any one else, ever entered into the feeling due to a man like Wordsworth – of whom I do not hesitate in saying, that since Milton no man has *manifested* himself equal to him.[71]

Poole had been impressed by Coleridge's impact on the *Morning Post*, and looked forward eagerly to the fruits of his German work. He saw that London was stimulating for his friend, and told him: "I am happy you begin to feel your power." The Lakes represented a threat in his eyes, and he now frankly charged Coleridge "with prostration in regard to Wordsworth". There is evidence that both Lamb and the Wedgwoods felt the same.[72] Coleridge, under increasing pressure with his work, denied the charge – "Have I affirmed anything miraculous of W.?" – and insisted that his newspaper work only showed the power of gaining "a few more paltry guineas" than he had supposed. "On the contrary, my faculties appear to myself dwindling, and I do believe if I were to live in London another half year, I should be dried up wholly . . ."[73]

Indeed by March 1800, Coleridge's commitments in London had become very heavy. He had undertaken a verse translation of the three parts of Schiller's *Wallenstein* for Longman; and as a result of a brilliant newspaper profile of Pitt, Stuart was pressing him for a series on Bonaparte and other leading statesmen, to be called "The Men and the Times". Stuart also wanted him to take "half-shares" in the *Morning Post* and his evening paper, the *Courier*, which would give him a full-time editorial post worth £2,000 per annum.[74] He had also contracted for some form of German travel book with Longman.

He tried to explain to Poole that none of these schemes, though they represented great professional success, really fulfilled his long-term plans. He had told Stuart that he "would not give up the Country, & the lazy reading of Old Folios for two Thousand Times two thousand pound – in short that beyond £250 a year, I considered money as a real Evil – at which he stared." He added that a writing career should be carefully divided between limited journeyman work, for pay and self-publicity; and absolute literary work done in leisure and independence. There should be no middle road, or wasteful compromising of talent. "I think there are but 2 good ways of writing – one for immediate, & wide impression, tho' transitory – the other for permanence – Newspapers the first – the best one can do is the second – that middle class of translating Books etc is neither the one or the other." He would only consider newspaper writing as a financial supplement, for a few months each year; and as for the Schiller work – "O this Translation is indeed a *Bore – never, never, never* will I be so taken in again."[75]

The strain of newspaper work had also affected his relations with Sara. On 2 March, she and Hartley left to stay with friends, and Coleridge moved in with the Lambs at 36 Chapel Street, in Islington. He wrote confidentially in Latin to Southey about their difficulties, saying that she was a wonderful mother, but had no appreciation of his "studies, temperament, and – alas – infirmities". "Non possumus omni ex parte felices esse" – "we can never be happy in all respects."[76] It was the first clear admission of the marital incompatibility that had long been evident in his way of life.

8

Coleridge arrived at Lamb's with "three ponderous German dictionaries"; a set of seventeenth-century political dialogues; a huge box of letters, poems, and sermons; a pair of razors and a soap box; and a voluminous five-penny floral dressing-gown decorated with hieroglyphics, in which he used to sit translating *Wallenstein* looking suspiciously "like a conjuror", according to Lamb.[77]

Reverting to bachelor status, he worked hard, drank hard, and talked unstoppably: the model of a Bohemian freelance journalist. Lamb described his company as "a continuous feast".[78] In one twenty-four-hour period he drafted his 3,000-word profile of Pitt, and completed 50 blank verse lines of his German translation.[79] This did not prevent many wild evenings with Lamb and Godwin, which sometimes ended in drunken but good-natured arguments on their perennial theological and political topics.

After one of these sessions Coleridge wrote an expressive note of apology, which perfectly captures the intoxicating effect of his company.

> Dear Godwin, The Punch after the Wine made me tipsy last night – this I mention, not that my head aches, or that I felt after I quitted you, any unpleasantness, or titubancy – ; but because tipsiness has, and has always, one unpleasant effect – that of making me talk *very* extravagantly; & as when sober, I talk extravagantly enough for any *common* Tipsiness, it becomes a matter of nicety in discrimination to know when I am or am not affected. – An idea starts up in my head – away I follow it thro' thick & thin, Wood & Marsh, Brake and Briar – with all the apparent Interest of a man who was defending one of his old and long-established Principles – Exactly of this kind was the Conversation with which I quitted you . . . We shall talk wiselier with the Ladies on Tuesday.

The letter then closed with a characteristic last jab. "The Agnus Dei & the Virgin Mary desire their kind respects to *you*, you sad Atheist."[80]

The profile of Pitt, which appeared on 19 March 1800, was the finest example of Coleridge's early journalism in a national newspaper. It was completely original in its style and conception: a psychological analysis of the Prime Minister's political shortcomings, seen in terms of his moral education and empty rhetorical powers. Coleridge had been making many such innovations during these months in the style of public debate, finding novel angles of attack and analysis.

On 22 January he had published a detailed verbal study of one of Lord Grenville's papers on the necessity of prosecuting the war with France, showing how minute errors in grammar, the false figures of speech, served to disguise illogical political and strategic thinking. (This was a type of political criticism popularised over a century later by George Orwell in his concept of "non-speak".) He showed, for example, how the misplacing of one verbal connective – "also" – in a single sentence cast doubt on Grenville's entire analysis of the French military campaigns in Europe.[81]

Lamb, always one of his most sensitive readers, was ecstatic about this "very novel and exquisite manner in which you combined political with grammatical science", and commented with blissful hyperbole: "It must have been the death-blow to that ministry. I expect Pitt and Grenville to resign. More especially the delicate and Contrellian grace with which you officiated, with a ferula for a white wand, as gentleman usher to the word 'also', which it seems did not know its place."[82]

Other novelties included an obituary of General George Washington, cast in terms of a psychological concept of "commanding genius" as opposed to mere "talented" leadership;[83] and an "Analysis or Skelton" of a parliamentary debate, in which the arguments of the ministry and the opposition were laid out in parallel columns of newsprint, like a biblical commentary, so that the closed, mirror-thinking of both sides was effectively demonstrated.[84]

But the profile of Pitt was his masterpiece. Coleridge's aim was to show that Pitt's prosecution of the war against revolutionary France, and his suppression of dissenting opinion at home, arose out of a fundamental inability to grasp human and moral realities. As a statesman, he had become a "denatured" personality, cut off from the feelings, aspirations, and sufferings of ordinary people. He lacked the human imagination of a great political leader (like, for example, Washington). He lived in a world of verbal abstractions, moral clichés, and deadened emotions, which had no living connections. Coleridge began this subtle and formidable indictment with an incisive critique of Pitt's elitist political upbringing.

> William Pitt was the younger son of Lord Chatham; a fact of no ordinary importance in the solution of his character, of no mean significance in the heraldry of morals and intellect. His father's rank, fame, political connections, and parental ambition were his mould:- he was cast, rather than grew . . . From his early childhood it was his father's custom to make him stand up on a chair, and declaim before a large company; by which exercise, practised so frequently, and continued for so many years, he acquired a premature and un-natural dexterity in the combination of words, which must of necessity have diverted his attention from present

objects, obscured his impressions, and deadened his genuine feeling.[85]

Coleridge was here using a developed form of David Hartley's "associative" psychology – that moral feelings attach themselves to our early experience of external objects – to suggest a crucial gap between intellect and feeling in Pitt's political education. And in that striking epigram, that Pitt's character was "cast" like a piece of iron in an industrial mould, rather than steadily "growing" like a plant according to natural laws, he was extending a Burkian notion of slow, steady, harmonious development out of tradition and rooted human experience, towards his own concept of organic form.

The critique continues, with autobiographic echoes, in his description of Pitt's student life. "At college he was a severe student; his mind was founded and elemented in words and generalities, and these too formed all the superstructure. That revelry and that debauchery, which are so often fatal to the powers of intellect, would probably have been serviceable to him; they would have given him a closer communion with realities . . ."[86] (Here Coleridge was perhaps making an oblique reference to his own colourful career at Cambridge, certainly packed with "realities".)

When Pitt became Prime Minister at the perilously early age of twenty-four, he was entirely unprepared to respond to the moral and intellectual challenge of the French revolutionary movement. He suppressed reform, he instituted a network of spies and informers, he prosecuted a vengeful European war, he taxed the poor, and he gave way to the "panic of property" and commercial interests.

His entire ideological position, continued Coleridge, was based on received ideas, entrenched abstractions, and linguistic generalities: "Atheism and Jacobinism – phrases, which he learnt from Mr Burke, but without learning the philosophical definitions and involved consequences, with which that great man accompanied those words . . . Press him to specify an *individual* fact of advantage to be derived from a war – and he answers, SECURITY! Call upon him to particularise a crime, and he exclaims – JACOBINISM!"[87] Pitt was, therefore, necessarily blind, rigid, narrow, callous in feeling, callow in doctrine: "a young man, whose feet had never wandered; whose very eye had never turned to the right or to the left; whose whole track had been as curveless as the motion of a fascinated reptile!" (Certainly, as Hazlitt had observed, most unlike his accusor.)

Coleridge summarised this sweeping and frontal attack in a major rhetorical passage, whose imagery was drawn deep from his own poetic experience, and whose terms brilliantly anticipate the concept of the "natural man", the man of sensibility formed as a child of nature, which Wordsworth would explore in the *Prelude*. Here Pitt is condemned as an aberration, *contra-natura*, a withered, mechanical production of the previous Lockian age, profoundly at odds with the Romantic spirit of striving intellect and generous emotion. It was a passage that seized upon the astonished readers of the *Morning Post*:

> A plant sown and reared in a hothouse, for whom the very air, that surrounded him, had been regulated by the thermometer of previous purpose; to whom the light of nature had penetrated only through glasses and covers; who had had the sun without the breeze; whom no storm had shaken;* on whom no rain had pattered; on whom the dews of Heaven had not fallen! – a being, who had had no feelings connected with man or nature, no spontaneous impulses, no unbiassed and desultory studies, no genuine science, nothing that constitutes individuality in intellect, nothing that teaches brotherhood in affection! Such was the man – such, and so denaturalised the spirit, on whose wisdom and philanthropy the lives and living enjoyments of so many millions of human beings were made unavoidably dependent.[88]

It is clear from this tremendous jeremiad that Pitt, as in the previous "War Eclogue" of 1798, has become a largely symbolic figure, representative of the cruelty, illiberalism and worst features of

---

* Wordsworth was deeply impressed by this passage, and unconsciously used its images later in Book IX of *The Prelude*, to describe his own naïve and insular state of mind (the innocent Englishman abroad) when he first arrived in revolutionary Paris in 1791, reacting like a tourist to the ruins of the Bastille, and not yet aware of the tremendous historical forces now unleashed throughout France:

> . . . Amused and satisfied, I scarcely felt
> The shock of these concussions, unconcerned,
> Tranquil almost, and careless as a flower
> Glassed in a green-house, or a parlour shrub
> When every bush and tree, the country through,
> Is shaking to the roots . . .
>
> *The Prelude*, 1805, Book IX, lines 85–90

Indeed I suspect that much of Coleridge's journalism, together with his poetry and talk, profoundly affected the way Wordsworth finally interpreted his own experiences in France (See *The Prelude*, 1805, especially Book X, lines 690–1006). The pattern of Coleridge's journalistic development has been admirably assessed by John Colmer in *Coleridge: Critic of Society*, Oxford 1959.

the English political reaction; just as Castlereagh would become for Shelley.[89] Moreover, through the negative features of this attack, there begins to rise a positive portrait of the statesmanlike qualities which Coleridge admired: qualities of intellect and feeling combined, the opposite of a "denaturalised spirit". Coleridge would also assign these to the poet. In both he required "mind and heart" in harmony with nature. The attack was compared to the letters of Junius, and even Hazlitt would later call it "masterly and unanswerable".[90]

It was as a result of this essay that Stuart began to press Coleridge to take up a permanent post. In the space of four months, Coleridge, with his formidable skills of literary assimilation, had adapted himself to the newspaper idiom of the day, abandoning the radical pyrotechnics and sermonising manner of the *Watchman* to address a national audience. He had then proceeded to transform it along Romantic lines.

Just as he had made the popular ballad into a new literary form, taking up where Bürger had left off, so he had now taken the political leader from the hands of Edmund Burke, and made it into a new language of opposition and philosophical demand. It was perhaps the first major example, in the public sphere, of post-revolutionary rhetoric, in which the language of the Rights of Man had been modified into what may be called the Rights of Nature. Coleridge would spend the next twenty years attempting to expand and explore the implications of this position, and defend it against the charge of apostasy.

9

Throughout this hectic month of March, Coleridge was also continuing his work on Schiller's *Wallenstein*, corresponding alternately with Poole and Wordsworth about his summer plans, and cheerfully burning the candle with Lamb, Godwin, and assorted literary ladies. Lamb wrote contentedly to his friend Manning on 17 March.

> Coleridge has been with me now for nigh three weeks, and the more I see of him in the quotidian undress and relaxation of his mind, the more cause I see to love him and believe him a *very good man* . . . He is engaged in Translations, which I hope will keep him this month to come. – He is uncommonly kind and friendly to me. – He ferrets me day and night to *do something*. He tends me, amidst all

> his own worrying and heart oppressing occupations, as a gardner tends his young *tulip*.[91]

The first part of *Wallenstein* was finished, with a tremendous effort, on 20 April. Coleridge would later say, while engaged on Part Two, that the work of translation "wasted and depressed my spirits, & left a sense of wearisomeness & disgust which unfitted me for anything but sleeping or immediate society".[92] He had hoped to catch the contemporary fashion for Schiller, in large part generated by *The Robbers*, and Longman pressed him unmercifully for completion, while Lamb agreed to correct the proof sheets.[93] In the event, the project was a financial disaster, earning him only £50 in advances, while Longman lost £250 on the combined editions.[94] It probably also served to undermine his confidence in the long-projected Life of Lessing.

Yet the *Wallenstein* fascinated him as a study in Romantic leadership, and taught him a practical grasp of dramatic construction and character-creation. This had considerable influence on his later analysis of Shakespeare's plays. In his notes on the working manuscript, he already summarises some significant contrasts between the two playwrights.

> Wallenstein is a finer psychological than dramatic, and a more dramatic than a tragic character. Shakespeare draws *strength* as in Richard the Third, and even when he blends weakness as in Macbeth – yet it is weakness of a specific kind that leaves the strength in full and fearful energy. – But Schiller has drawn weakness imposing on itself the love of power for the sense of strength (a fine conception in itself, but not tragic . . .[95]

Schiller only completed the *Wallenstein* trilogy in 1799, and Coleridge was working from a manuscript copy. Based on the historical figure who commanded the forces of the Austrian Emperor, and used Kepler as his astrologer, the trilogy is a study in power and betrayal, which marks Schiller's reaction against the French Revolution and is sometimes thought to have been an early reflection on Bonaparte's character. The themes of leadership, freedom, historical necessity, and personal idealism, closely relate to the ideas that Coleridge was beginning to explore in his political journalism.

After the "sturm und drang" of *The Robbers*, the trilogy represents Schiller's attempt, under the influence of Goethe, to remodel German classical drama along Shakespearean lines, with a variety of rapid scenes, contrasted characters, and shifts of dramatic tone using both verse and prose. Coleridge's decision to translate the work for Longman (omitting the first part, *Wallenstein's Camp*, as unsuitable) was made not for mere commercial considerations, but because he recognised immediately its literary significance and topical value in his own development. Despite his disenchanted references to the slog of translation work at the time, he was proud of his work, and long afterwards described it as "a specimen of my happiest attempt, during the prime manhood of my intellect, before I had been buffeted by adversity or crossed by fatality".[96]

He always remained deeply admiring of Schiller, and remarked in 1833:

> He outgrew the composition of such plays as *The Robbers*, and at once took his true and only rightful stand in the grand historical drama – the *Wallenstein* – not the intense drama of passion – he was not master of that – but the diffused drama of history . . . The *Wallenstein* is the greatest of his works; it is not unlike Shakespeare's historical plays – a species by itself. You may take up any scene, and it will please you by itself; just as you may in *Don Quixote*, which you read *through* once or twice only, but which you read *in* repeatedly.[97]

This last distinction, moving from structural to psychological appreciation, is characteristic of Coleridge's Romantic criticism; while taking the whole of European literature for its frame of reference.

Much of the power of the drama, which is set in Germany during the time of the Thirty Years War, arises from the conflict of loyalties surrounding two national leaders, Wallenstein and his Lieutenant-General Octavio Piccolomini. The pressures of loyalty and betrayal are exemplified by Octavio's son, Max Piccolomini, a divided character whose ambiguous position (he is also in love with Wallenstein's daughter, Thekla) strongly appealed to Coleridge. There is also an Astrologer, and a rich body of dramatic imagery drawn from "the science of the stars", fates, and a very Teutonic form of nature-mysticism.

Coleridge translated freely, inevitably with strong echoes from Shakespearean blank verse; but in many of Max Piccolomini's speeches he successfully expands Schiller's original text into a graceful, resonant, English form that seems closely related to the Conversation Poems. Here, for example, in Act II scene 4 of *The*

Piccolomini, Max reflects upon the influence of nature and myth in his childhood, while talking to Thekla. (In modern editions of the play, the passage appears at Act III scene 4, and only runs to nine lines in the German.)

> The intelligible forms of ancient poets,
> The fair humanities of old religion,
> The Power, the Beauty, and the Majesty,
> That had their haunts in dale, or piny mountains,
> Or forest by slow stream, or pebbly spring,
> Or chasms and wat'ry depths; all these have vanished.
> They live no longer in the faith of reason!
> But still the heart doth need a language, still
> Doth the old instinct bring back the old names,
> And to yon starry world they now are gone,
> Spirits or gods, that used to share this earth
> With man as with their friend; and to the lover
> Yonder they move, from yonder visible sky
> Shoot influence down: and even at this day
> 'Tis Jupiter who brings whate'er is great,
> And Venus who brings every thing that's fair![98]

10

Coleridge managed to write two more leaders for the *Morning Post* before his planned four months of journalism was up. Stuart was still pressing for a profile of Bonaparte, to pair in the Plutarchian manner with that of Pitt. Though promised, and several times announced – it was never completed, though a story went about that the French Ambassador in London privately informed the paper that Bonaparte was eagerly expecting a "eulogy" from Mr Coleridge. Coleridge later gave this as his reason for not publishing the piece, which seems somewhat unlikely.[99]

Instead he produced a fiery review of a reactionary pamphlet by the erstwhile reformer Arthur Young, closing it in high style.

> We have, alas! too often mistaken newspaper anecdotes of rogues in Paris for the annals of the French nation since the revolution; and in our rage against a phantom of Jacobinism, have shamefully neglected to calculate the blessings from the destruction of Feudalism. The vine of liberty shall not be blasphemed by us, because the Noahs of the revolutionary deluge, who first planted it, were made drunk by its untried fruits.[100]

With this parting shot from the liberal wing against the ministry, he left Chapel Street on 2 April and bounced north to the Lakes on a visit, as Lamb regretfully put it, "to his God, Wordsworth".[101] As he travelled about for the next three weeks, the final sheets of *Wallenstein* were posted back to Lamb for correction.

Wordsworth, Dorothy, John Wordsworth and Mary Hutchinson were now established in the famous cottage at Town End, just outside Grasmere, with its beautiful views over Grasmere Lake, and its little garden cut back into the hillside behind. (It had been a tiny inn, the Dove & Olive Branch, and was only later named Dove Cottage.) Spring was arriving, and Coleridge remained with his friends until 2 May, walking all over the district looking for possible houses, among which he spotted the elegant shape of Greta Hall, perched on a little hill beneath Skiddaw, just north of Keswick. He collected flower seeds for Lamb, made notes on the epitaphs in Grasmere churchyard, and listening to bells tolling "thro' a mist in Langdale vale" – a melancholy sound that would appear in the second part of "Christabel".[102]

There was also a mysterious reference in his Notebooks to the romantic keepsake which appeared in his first Asra poem: "A little of Sara's Hair in this Pocket".[103] Had Mary brought over this teasing memento from Sockburn? Or had he contrived one of his sudden dashes over the Pennines? But it is not known that he definitely saw Sara Hutchinson again until the following winter, and Tom Hutchinson was busy settling into a new farm, Gallow Hill, near Scarborough.[104]

Coleridge took advantage of the calm of Grasmere to write a strategic letter to Josiah Wedgwood. He had been forced to draw a further £20 advance on his annuity, but despite the difficult finances, he felt the winter had been well used.

> For these last six months I have worked incessantly – and have lived with as much economy as is practicable by any man . . . In this engagement of translating the prolix Plays of Schiller I made too a very, very foolish bargain . . . of their Success I have no hope . . . But with all this I have learnt that I have Industry & Perseverance – and before the end of the year, if God grant me health, I shall have my wings wholly unbirdlim'd.[105]

He modestly made no mention of the successes of his journalism, perhaps because he felt Wedgwood would regard it as ephemeral work. The repeated image of the bird breaking free from lime-covered twigs (a local method of trapping) suggested poetry stirring in him again; and it would come back to haunt him in the difficult months ahead.

To Southey, who was finally departing for Lisbon to recover his health and write a history of Portugal, Coleridge sent godspeed and a last reminder of the colony dream. "If you stay longer, than the year on the Continent, *I and mine will join you* – & if you return at that Time, you must join us. Where we shall be, God knows! but in some interesting Country it will be, in Heaven or Earth."

As he closed this letter, he was swept by sudden memories of the Pantisocratic days, purged of all bitterness, and intensified by the sense of parting, changing, and moving on into adulthood. His postscript overflowed with emotions which must have embarrassed Southey, as much as touched him. "The time returns upon me, Southey! when we dreamt one Dream, & that a glorious one – when we ate together, & thought each other greater & better than all the World beside, and when we were bed fellows. Those days can never be forgotten, and till they are forgotten, we cannot, if we would, cease to love each other."[106] The best Southey could manage in return was to ask Coleridge to be his literary executor in case he should be "summoned on the grand tour of the universe". But he had been impressed by the journalism, and urged Coleridge to publish a new volume of poetry.[107]

At Grasmere, a very different plan was afoot, for Wordsworth had decided to publish a second, enlarged edition of the *Lyrical Ballads*, for which he wanted Coleridge's help both as co-author and as editor. Cottle's first edition had sold out, as the book's reputation spread in London, and Wordsworth had recovered the copyright and offered it through Coleridge to Longman. In June Longman bought it for £80, with republication planned for autumn 1800.[108]

The prospect of returning to collaborative work with Wordsworth during the summer – with a completed "Christabel" as his main contribution to the new edition – exerted a powerful influence on Coleridge's still unsettled plans. Both men were making a deliberate sacrifice of literary independence to pursue this scheme: Wordsworth was giving up work on "The Recluse" to concentrate on miscellaneous "Pastoral Poems" (already pouring from his pen since the move to Grasmere); while Coleridge was abandoning any idea of separate publication of his ballads and Conversation Poems. It would soon emerge for whom this sacrifice was most costly.

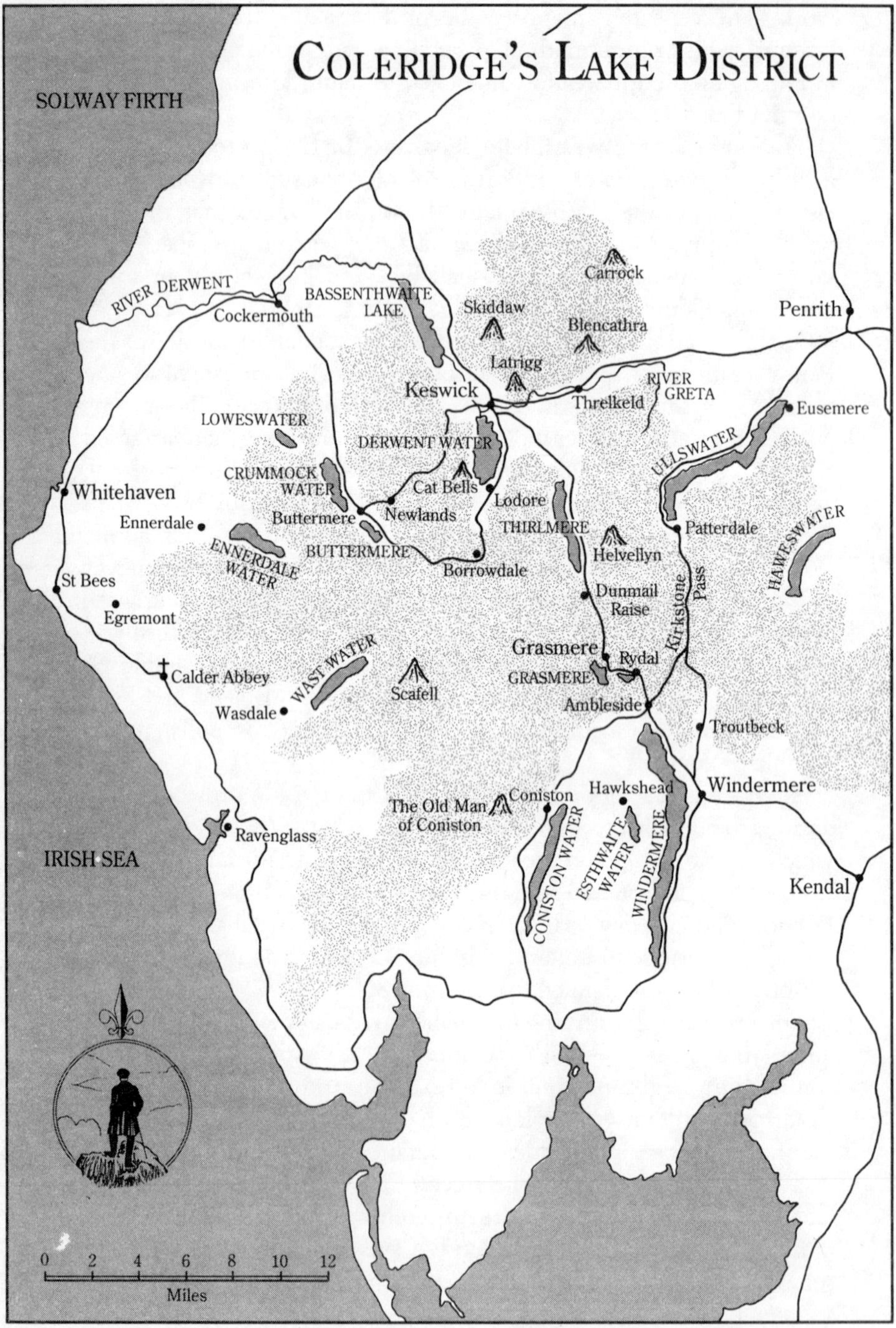
COLERIDGE'S LAKE DISTRICT
SOLWAY FIRTH
RIVER DERWENT
Cockermouth
BASSENTHWAITE LAKE
Skiddaw
Carrock
Blencathra
Penrith
Latrigg
Keswick
Threlkeld
RIVER GRETA
Eusemere
LOWESWATER
DERWENT WATER
ULLSWATER
CRUMMOCK WATER
Cat Bells
Lodore
Whitehaven
Ennerdale
Buttermere
Newlands
THIRLMERE
Patterdale
HAWESWATER
ENNERDALE WATER
BUTTERMERE
Borrowdale
Helvellyn
St Bees
Dunmail Raise
Kirkstone Pass
Egremont
Grasmere
Rydal
GRASMERE
Calder Abbey
WAST WATER
Scafell
Ambleside
Wasdale
Troutbeck
Hawkshead
Windermere
The Old Man of Coniston
Coniston
Ravenglass
IRISH SEA
CONISTON WATER
ESTHWAITE WATER
WINDERMERE
Kendal
0 2 4 6 8 10 12
Miles

ELEVEN

Laker

1

On 4 May 1800 Coleridge hastened back to Bristol, collected Sara and Hartley and, basing himself at Poole's, began a final search for a possible house in the West Country. But it seems clear that his heart was already set upon the Lakes, with various auxiliary schemes to attract both Godwin and Humphry Davy northwards.

To Godwin he wrote in a mood of dreamy optimism on 21 May:

> If I cannot procure a suitable house at Stowey, I return to Cumberland & settle at Keswick – in a house of such prospect, that if, according to you & Hume, impressions & ideas *constitute* our Being, I shall have a tendency to become a God – so sublime & beautiful will be the series of my visual existence. But whether I continue here, or migrate thither, I shall be in a beautiful country – & have house-room and heart-room for you; and you must come & write your next work at my house.[1]

In June he saw much of Davy at the Pneumatic Institute, announcing in passing that he intended to translate Blumenbach's *Natural History* and would require scientific advice.[2] He also arranged with Cottle (and his partner, Biggs) to print the projected second edition of the *Lyrical Ballads* in Bristol for Longman to sell in his splendid London bookshop. Davy was co-opted to correct the proofs when they were ready. Thus Coleridge steadily drew his friends into the orbit of great new literary schemes, with a characteristic mixture of heady dreams and surprising practicalities.

It is not clear what Sara Coleridge made of these developments, attached as she was to the Bristol of her childhood, and the fast friendship that had developed with Tom Poole at Stowey. Since Coleridge's departure for Germany in the autumn of 1798, she had only lived with her restless husband for a few months at a time – the longest at Buckingham Street lasting but ten weeks – and the prospect of steady domestic happiness must have looked somewhat remote. Perhaps she saw in his lyrical descriptions of Greta Hall the best chance of putting down new roots in a house where he would be happy; and the expected child – due in September – held out fair promise of renewed family life together. But, like Poole, she worried increasingly about the influence of Wordsworth, and the constant disruption of her husband's professional career that he seemed to produce.

Professional matters were, indeed, piling up into a series of unfulfilled commitments, only too typical of freelance life. Although Coleridge was able to return the advance of £20 to Wedgwood on 12 June, from newspaper earnings, his financial position with his publishers required the greatest effort if he was ever to be "unbirdlimed" before the end of the year. His major commitments were as follows: completion of Part Two of *Wallenstein* for Longman (advance of £50); completion of a German travel book for Longman (advance of £20); completion of an anthology or "bookseller's compilation" for Phillips (advance of £25). On top of this he had now undertaken the editing of the *Lyrical Ballads* for Wordsworth. The life of Lessing – patiently awaited by the Wedgwoods – was not yet begun, and in reality seemed ever more remote.

Against this, he had established an invaluable connection with the *Morning Post*; and Stuart, though disappointed that he had not joined the staff, was always willing to pay handsomely for whatever articles or poems he submitted henceforth. In fact Coleridge did manage to fulfil two of these engagements in the next six months – the *Wallenstein* was completed in August, and the *Lyrical Ballads* was edited by December. Then the Wedgwood annuity for 1801 came to his rescue (Josiah had waived the German overdraft), and he did not return to regular journalism until the spring of 1802. Nevertheless, lack of funds remained a constant problem, and he frequently borrowed small sums from friends – Wordsworth, Poole and others – which was to cause several awkward confrontations in the future.

All this was hardly unusual for a young writer with a growing family, and it probably worried Sara more than him. His real professional difficulties lay within himself: the problem that Poole had identified in Germany – lack of concentration of his efforts, a thousand brilliant projects without the corresponding energy to execute them. Yet when he did execute, it was still with astonishing speed, power and assurance.

Just as physically he was a lazy, easy-going man, yet capable of tremendous feats of walking and climbing; so mentally, he was a drifter and dreamer, yet capable of sudden, short bursts of extreme imaginative intensity. All his friends – Southey, Poole, Stuart, Wordsworth – came to acknowledge this in their own way, though they never ceased to be puzzled by it; and sometimes, later, to despair of it.

For Coleridge himself, it became a subject of obsessive anxiety and self-analysis, though not untouched by fascination and even pride, which led him to delve increasingly into his own psyche, probing and questioning, until the problem of creativity itself eventually became his central, commanding concern. This inward spiralling of his imagination, as his Notebooks show, began with his new phase of life in the Lake District, where he had hoped – as he told Godwin – that the landscape would transform him into a god.

2

Coleridge "rearrived at Grasmere", as he put it, with Sara, Hartley and his customary comet's train of book-chests, on Sunday 29 June 1800. He had conveniently caught flu on the way, at Liverpool, and immediately retired to Wordsworth's back bedroom with "a brace of swollen eyelids", leaving Sara and Dorothy to sort out the ensuing chaos, which halted Dorothy's meticulous Journal for three weeks. She had already been over to Keswick to make arrangements with Mr William Jackson, the wealthy carrier who owned Greta Hall. Soon, however, they were all blissfully sailing in Wordsworth's boat on Grasmere Lake.

Coleridge started making notes on the beautiful crags and waterfalls round Ambleside. He already felt himself a native of the place, and laughed at the summer tourists with their picturesque guidebooks: "Ladies reading Gilpin's etc while passing by the very places instead of looking at the places."[3] He himself was already *looking* with passionate delight, and carefully shaping what he saw into *plein-air* sketches as in the Quantock days: "Going up the Force notice the Sheepfold the higher – of whose parallelogram is faced with fern, one a plume, the rest bunches of parsley fern – & the fold inclosed a curve of the path of a mountain beck."[4]

He went quickly to work on the manuscript of the *Lyrical Ballads*, now planned as two volumes, sending a long detailed letter to Cottle on the running order of Wordsworth's poems, a clean copy of "Love" which was to be included, and some seventy detailed alterations to the *Mariner*, ranging from entire new stanzas to minute corrections of spelling and punctuation.[5]* He wrote to Stuart – once again promising the Bonaparte article, "on my word & honor" – but more practically, promising "as a friend" to remain at his service for particular articles and poems in the coming months.[6]

To Davy, he sent a long account of nitrous oxide experiments which interested them both, and promised that when he had "dis-embrangled" his affairs he would "attack chemistry, like a Shark". The prospect of Greta Hall filled him with anticipatory delights. "My dear fellow, I would that I could wrap up the view from my House in a pill of opium, & send it to you! I should then be sure of seeing you in the fall of the year. But you *will* come."[7]

Sara seemed reasonably pleased with their northern translation, and Hartley, now nearly four, seemed to embody something of his father's mood of release. "Hartley is a spirit that dances on an aspin leaf – the air, which yonder sallow-faced & yawning Tourist is breathing, is to my Babe a perpetual Nitrous Oxyde. Never was more joyous creature born."[8]

Curiously it was Wordsworth who most worried Coleridge, seeming rather depressed and withdrawn, troubled with pains in his side when he attempted to write, and weighed down by the amount of work to be done on the new edition. Coleridge bustled about him, actually calling him "a lazy fellow", and promising to take all the editorial work off his hands. This promise he faithfully performed over the next three months. He threw himself into the role of wizard, as he had done with Lamb. "I trust . . . I have invoked the sleeping Bard with a spell so potent, that he will awake & deliver up that Sword of Argantyr, which is to rive the Enchanter GAUDY-VERSE from his Crown to his Fork."[9]

---

*In correcting the *Mariner* at Wordsworth's urging, Coleridge removed much gothic spelling ("the Ancyent Marinere") and archaic phrasings ("the eldritch sea" for "the rotting sea"). These were evident improvements. But Wordsworth's distrust of the bizarre also led to the sad omission of some remarkable images, such as Coleridge's original use of the folk-legend of the "Hand of Glory", to present the resurrection of the dead ship's crew on return to harbour, in Part VI. Thus the whole of the following stanza was summarily removed:

> They lifted up their stiff right arms,
> They held them strait and tight;
> And each right-arm burnt like a torch,
> A torch that's borne upright.
> Their stony eye-balls glitter'd on
> In the red and smoky light.
>
> *P.W.*, p. 204n

On the evening before their departure from Grasmere for Keswick, they sailed out to the island on Grasmere Lake for a picnic. They made a fire, hung a kettle over a fir branch, and feasted and danced around the blaze in a happy family circle which became a sort of dedication of the summer, a ritual that must have reminded Coleridge of the ceremonies of the great Kubla.

> I lay & saw the wood, & mountains, & lake all trembling, & as it were *idealized* thro' the subtle smoke which rose up from the clear red embers of the fir-apples which we had collected. Afterwards, we made a glorious Bonfire on the Margin, by some alder bushes, whose twigs heaved & sobbed in the uprushing column of smoke – & the Image of the Bonfire, & of us that danced round it – ruddy laughing faces in the twilight – the Image of this in a Lake smooth as that sea, to whose waves the Son of God had said, PEACE![10]*

On 24 July Coleridge and his family finally left Grasmere, and travelled the fifteen miles northwards to Greta Hall, crossing over the high rolling pass of Dunmail Raise, along the western flank of Helvellyn, and down to Keswick on Derwent Water, beneath the huge guardian shapes of Latrigg Fell and Skiddaw. Coleridge immediately climbed to the roof, and sat writing letters to his friends. One was headed: "From the leads on the housetop of Greta Hall, Keswick, Cumberland, at the present time in the occupancy and usufruct-possession of S.T. Coleridge, Esq., Gentleman-poet and Philosopher in a mist."[11] It described his position very well.

---

*It is one of those strange resonances of Romantic biography that this description of their feast and fire at the water's edge, with its undertones of Pantheistic ceremonial, would be echoed a generation later by Trelawny's beautiful evocation of the ritual burning of Shelley's drowned body on the beach near Spezia, in the presence of Byron and Leigh Hunt. "The lonely and grand scenery that surrounded us so exactly harmonized with Shelley's genius, that I could imagine his spirit soaring over us. The sea, with the islands of Gorgona, Capraja, and Elba, was before us . . . After the fire was well-kindled we repeated the ceremony of the previous day; and more wine was poured over Shelley's dead body than was consumed during his life. This with the oil and salt made the yellow flames glisten and quiver. The heat from the sun and fire was so intense that the atmosphere was tremulous and wavy. The corpse fell open and the heart was laid bare." (*Recollections of the Last Days of Shelley and Byron*, 1858, by E. J. Trelawny, Chapter 12) It is almost as if the moment of Romantic dedication in the Lakes of 1800 was harmonically related across twenty-two years with the moment of Romantic mourning and loss, in Italy in 1822. But conventional literary history has no form of chronology to connect such events.

3

It seems wonderfully appropriate that Greta Hall had originally been built as an astronomical observatory. Positioned on a small but commanding hill, just beyond the stone pack-bridge over the River Greta at the northern end of the town, it offered spectacular views of the surrounding fells and a huge, ever-changing dome of Cumberland sky. To this day, its white façade can be seen shining out of Keswick from almost every peak of the encircling fells – most impressively perhaps from Cat Bells across Derwent Water – a sort of landlocked lighthouse, upon which the lonely fell-walker can always get an accurate compass fix in his wanderings.

Their new landlord, Mr Jackson, had rebuilt it on the scale of a squire's country house, three storeys high, with an echo of the observatory retained in its two unusual drum-shaped wings at the front. It had fine airy rooms, large commanding windows on three sides, marble fireplaces, and a big back-kitchen. Beyond the sloping lawns, the Greta encircled the property in a horse-shoe shape, the river bank at the back being planted with a delightful walk of trees. At the front several acres of vegetable garden ran down to the bridge and the Keswick road. Mr Jackson occupied the snug rooms at the back of the house with his housekeeper, old Mrs Wilson (who became a sort of fairy godmother to Hartley), and let the entire front to Coleridge for £42 per annum, including furniture. He was to prove the kindest and most indulgent of landlords, his first act of generosity being to waive the first six months' rent, and give Coleridge the run of his 500-volume library, "well-stored with Encyclopaedias, Dictionaries, & Histories etc".[12]

Coleridge initially took as his study the magnificent first-floor chamber on the left of the frontage, with spectacular views of the fells – "a whole camp of giants' tents" – Derwent Water and Borrowdale to the south-west, Bassenthwaite to the north-west. "I question if there be a room in England," he crowed to Godwin (with further pressing invitations), "which commands a view of Mountains & Lakes & Woods & Vales superior to that, in which I am now sitting."[13] He could define "six distinct Landscapes" in the panorama of lakes and hills, across which "mists, & Clouds, & Sunshine make endless combinations, as if heaven & Earth were forever talking to each other."[14]

His bedroom with Sara next door, on the right of the frontage, also commanded a magnificent view of southern fells towards Helvellyn, whose shifting morning light and shade hypnotised him. "My Glass, being opposite to the Window, I seldom shave without cutting myself. Some Mountain or Peak is rising out of the Mist, or some slanting Column of misty Sunlight is sailing cross me; so that I offer up soap & blood daily, as an Eye-servant of the Goddess Nature."[15]

The study-room, with its fireplace and rapidly filling bookshelves and visionary windows, was to be endlessly described in his Notebooks and letters over the next three years, at various times of day and night, with all the differing moods of sunset, sunrise, starlight, and storm. It became an emblem of his own imagination working in solitude, a magic cell of human thought in the vastness of nature, the focus both of delight and of despair.

4

Throughout August and September, while Sara awaited the birth of their child, Coleridge explored the surrounding fells and worked on the manuscript of the *Lyrical Ballads*, setting aside the life of Lessing and all his other publishing commitments. In taking on Greta Hall, in going against the advice of Poole and the Wedgwoods, in abandoning his opening on the *Morning Post*, he had made an enormous investment in his partnership with Wordsworth and his own literary future as a poet. He wrote a number of poems this summer inspired by his first experience of fell-walking, notably "The Mad Monk", "A Thought Suggested by a View of Saddleback in Cumberland", and "A Stranger Minstrel", dedicated to Perdita Robinson on a climb of Skiddaw. These show a transition between the blank verse of the Conversation Poems towards the much tighter, traditional lyric form of his later emblematic poems. They are full of strange voices and inexplicable visions, which point towards the tremendous, confessional outburst of the "Dejection" ode:

I heard a voice from Etna's side;
   Where o'er a cavern's mouth
   That fronted to the south
A chesnut spread its umbrage wide:
A hermit or a monk the man might be;
   But him I could not see:
And thus the music flow'd along,
In melody most like to old Sicilian song:

'There was a time when earth, and sea, and skies,
The bright green vale, and forest's dark recess,
With all things, lay before mine eyes
In steady loveliness:
But now I feel, on earth's uneasy scene,
Such sorrows as will never cease;–
I only ask for peace;
If I must live to know that such a time has been!'

This haunting passage from the opening of "The Mad Monk" returns to the question of visionary powers, and the lost Paradise, initiated in "Kubla Khan". (Xanadu has become Sicily, and the Khan has gone into pastoral retirement on a mountain-top.) The poem is unresolved, but Wordsworth would also later take it up, closely using the phrasing and rhythms of the second stanza, to develop the theme of the "Immortality" Ode in 1802.[16]

None of these poems would have been written without the Lake District world which now absorbed Coleridge. A curious symbolic incident took place on his first ascent of Skiddaw in early August, as he told Poole. "I was standing on the very top of Skiddaw, by a little Shed of Slatestones on which I had scribbled with a bit of slate my name among the other names – a lean expressive-faced Man came up the Hill, stood beside me, a little while, then running over the names, exclaimed, *Coleridge!* I lay my life, that is the *Poet Coleridge.*"[17] Coleridge, for once, remained silent, gazing out over the glittering waters of Bassenthwaite far below.

Coleridge's chief effort was concentrated on finishing "Christabel", an attempt to return to the inspiration of the Quantock days, which caused him endless struggles – "every line has been produced by me with labour-pangs". It delayed the completion of the *Lyrical Ballads* copy for Biggs and Cottle, and caused Wordsworth evident irritation. Doggedly Coleridge tramped back and forth over the hills between Keswick and Grasmere, seeking encouragement from the Wordsworths and visions from the mountains.

He filled his Notebooks with beautiful descriptions of these expeditions, which made him tanned and fit, though he drank heavily and worried increasingly. He later told Josiah Wedgwood: "The wind from Skiddaw & Borrowdale was often as loud as wind need be – & many a walk in the clouds on the mountains did I take; but all would not do – till one day I dined out at the house of a neighbouring clergyman, & some how or other drank so much wine, that I found myself on the hither Edge of Sobriety. The next day, my verse making faculties returned to me, and I proceeded successfully . . ."[18] Despite these pressures, there is still no evidence that he resorted to opium until much later in the autumn.

On 29 August Coleridge had a large section of Part Two completed, and with the manuscript in his pocket made a triumphant journey to Grasmere along the entire ridge of the Eastern Fells – crossing Great Dod, White Side, and Helvellyn, and slithering perilously down by Nethermost Pike to Dunmail Raise in the dark. He recorded this first of his epic solo fell-walks in a brilliant series of running *plein-air* sketches, which catch not only the physical sensation of the climber – "as I bounded down, noticed the moving stones under the soft moss, hurting my feet" – but also the spiritual effect of moving alone through such a high, wild, naked landscape. These prose-notations were a new form of Romantic nature-writing, as powerful in their way as his poetry; rapid, spontaneous, miraculously responsive to the changing panorama of hills he moves through, and containing a sort of telegraphic score of his emotional reactions.* This is what he wrote at the climactic point of Helvellyn, as the light was failing; a description which gives one of the first literary records of Striding Edge, which has become perhaps the most famous "airy traverse" in all the Lakeland fells.

> Am now at the Top of Helvellin – a pyramid of stones – Ulswater. Thirlemere. Bassenthwaite. Wyndemere, a Tarn in Patterdale. On my right Two tarns, that near Grasmere a most beautiful one, in a flat meadow. Travelling along the ridge I came to the other side of those precipices and down below me on my left – no – no! no words can convey any idea of this prodigious wilderness. That precipice fine on this side was but its ridge, sharp as a jagged knife, level so long, and then ascending so boldly – what a frightful bulgy

*The originality and power of Coleridge's fell-walking Notebooks and letters has only recently received some attention. His use of emotional notations comparable to a musical score; his breaking of the conventional eighteenth-century picturesque window or frame of description – using panoramic sweeps rather than fixed perspectives; and his subversion of the old guide-book formulas; all deserve further exploration. Excellent preliminary studies have appeared, by Molly Lefebure, "The First of the Fellwalkers", in her *Cumberland Heritage*, London 1970; and by William Ruddick, "Notes on the lakeland fells", in *Coleridge's Imagination*, edited by Richard Gravil, Lucy Newlyn and Nicholas Roe, Cambridge UP, 1985. Robert Gittings and Jo Manton sensitively contrast his descriptive style with that of Dorothy's *Journals* (but in the latter's favour) in *Dorothy Wordsworth*, Oxford 1985. Among many other aspects, Coleridge is the first to introduce the impression of physical effort, travelling bodily through a landscape, and perilous immediacy (with the implied doubt that he will ever return). His greatest inheritor is, perhaps, Alfred Wainwright.

precipice I stand on and to my right how the Crag which corresponds to the other, how it plunges down, like a waterfall, reaches a level steepness, and again plunges! – The Moon is above Fairfield almost at the full! – now descended over a perilous peat-moss then down a Hill of stones all dark, and darkling, I climbed stone after stone down a half dry Torrent and came out at the Raise Gap. And O! my God! how *did* that opposite precipice look – in the moonshine – its name Stile Crags.[19]

Dorothy recorded his arrival that night at Dove Cottage in her Journal. "At 11 o'clock Coleridge came when I was walking in the still clear moonshine. He came over Helvellyn. Wm was gone to bed and John also . . . We sate and chatted till ½-past three, W. in his dressing gown. Coleridge read us a part of Christabel. Talked much about the mountains etc etc." The following day, indefatigable, Coleridge cleared away brambles in the little garden and "discovered a rock seat in the orchard". He noted: "the beards of Thistle & dandelions flying above the lonely mountains like life, & I saw them thro' the Trees skimming the lake like Swallows."[20]

The day after they walked round Stickle Tarn, and went to the summer fair at Grasmere. Dorothy concluded the day on a note of idyllic happiness. "We drank Tea immediately afterwards by candle-light. It was a lovely moonlit night. We talked about a house of Helvellyn. The moonlight shone only upon the village it did not eclipse the village lights and the sound of dancing and merriment came along the still air. I walked with Coleridge and Wm up the Lane by the Church, and then lingered with Coleridge in the garden. John and Wm were both gone to bed, and all the lights out."

The third day, Coleridge returned over Helvellyn to Keswick, accompanied by Wordsworth as far as the ridge, dreaming of the poet's house on the mountain-top. With such expeditions, skimming like his swallows outwards and back to Greta Hall over the forgetful hills, Coleridge's summer slipped rapidly away into autumn.

5

On 14 September, Sara gave birth to a boy at half past ten in the evening. For once, Coleridge was present. His first impulse was to call him Bracy, after the minstrel in "Christabel". The child was very ill for several weeks, and he was finally christened Derwent, perhaps to appease the spirit of the place. Thereafter, as Coleridge noted, followed "an interval, during which I travelled much."[21]

In fact his professional situation had suddenly become critical: Wordsworth had rejected "Christabel" for the *Lyrical Ballads*. All his other commitments and debts came crowding in upon him, and for the first time in his life Coleridge experienced a complete writing-block. On 30 October he would confide in his Notebook: "He knew not what to do – something he felt, must be done – he rose, drew his writing-desk suddenly before him – sate down, took the pen – & found that he knew not what to do."[22] The only thing that appeased him at this moment was that baby Derwent laughed for the first time at six weeks old, and noticed the trees along the Greta bending in the autumn winds.[23]

The rejection of "Christabel" seems to have been a wholly unexpected blow for Coleridge. In early September, Wordsworth had sent the manuscript of Part One to Biggs and Cottle to be set up in type, and the broad contents of the two volumes was defined. On Coleridge's insistence, the collection was now to be published under Wordsworth's name alone; he also agreed to the *Mariner* being removed from the front to the back of volume one.

They had discussed a new, critical preface, and Coleridge's Notebooks suggest he may have initiated Wordsworth's famous line of argument concerning "emotion recollected in tranquillity". His jottings during late August include this superb sequence of natural observation and critical response: "An eminently beautiful object is Fern, on a hill side, scattered thick but growing single – and all shaking themselves in the wind . . . A child scolding a flower in the words in which he had himself been scolded & whipt, is *poetry* / past passion with pleasure . . . so poetry . . . recalling of passion in tranquillity . . ."[24] It is interesting, and wholly characteristic, that this crucial perception should have arisen from Coleridge's observation of little Hartley's behaviour, a child of nature. (Indeed this end-page of the Notebook is stained with rain-drops, and scribbled over with a child's chalk, presumably Hartley's learned annotations.) The 6,000-word preface eventually contained the first full statement of Wordsworth's theory of poetic language.

On 20 September, Wordsworth sent a first draft of the preface to Cottle, including the following paragraph. "For the sake of variety, and from a consciousness of my own weakness, I have again requested the assistance of a friend who contributed largely to the first volume, and who has now furnished me with the long and beautiful poem of CHRISTABEL, without which I should not yet have ventured to present a second volume to the public."[25] Wordsworth subsequently deleted the phrase "long and beautiful"; and on 10 October the entire paragraph.

Between these dates, Coleridge had brought over the completed manuscript of "Christabel" Part Two to Grasmere. He had been working under great pressure, for his finances had forced him to begin further freelance contributions for Daniel Stuart, and Derwent throughout this time continued very ill. His letters show that he was also worried about Wordsworth's health – for it was still his friend's mysterious pains, not his own, which bothered him. He wrote to Stuart on 30 September: "Wordsworth's health declines constantly – in a few days his Poems will be published, with a long poem of mine. Of course, you will procure them. The Preface contains our joint opinions on Poetry."[26]

Dorothy's Journal records the subsequent visit, over four days. On 4 October: "Coleridge came in while we were at dinner very wet. – We talked till 12 o'clock. He had sate up all the night before writing Essays for the newspaper. – His youngest child had been very ill in convulsion fits. Exceedingly delighted with the 2nd part of Christabel." On the 5th: "Coleridge read a second time Christabel – we had increasing pleasure. A delicious morning. Wm and I were employed all the morning in writing an addition to the preface. Wm went to bed very ill after working after dinner." On the 6th: "A rainy day. Coleridge intending to go but did not get off. We walked after dinner to Rydale. After tea read The Pedlar. Determined not to print Christabel with the LB."

There is no further comment. Coleridge left the next day, and Dorothy, "weak and unwell" herself, went to bed early. One can conclude that it had been a stressful visit for all of them. The only substitute scheme that emerged was that "Christabel" should be printed the following year in a luxury edition with "The Pedlar"; but this was never done. Coleridge made no immediate remark in his Notebook, except to record that on 10 October, "the first snow fell on Skiddaw".[27]

There were of course sound literary reasons why the ballad should have been excluded. Coleridge later enumerated these in letters to Davy and to Wedgwood. To begin with, it was too long for an anonymous contribution; and it was unfinished. Curiously, Wordsworth never seems to have raised the latter objection, and would later say that he preferred Part One on its own, with the perceptive observation that it was only Part Two which raised the "expectation" of an end in narrative terms.[28] Then its style of medieval balladry was "discordant in its character" with Wordsworth's poetry of rural life: though this objection applied equally to the *Mariner.*[29]

But finally, said Coleridge, "the poem was in direct opposition to the very purpose for which the Lyrical Ballads were published – viz – an experiment to see how far those passions, which alone give any value to extraordinary Incidents, were capable of interesting, in & for themselves, in the incidents of Common Life."[30] Again, this was true, except that it entirely ignored the original purpose of Coleridge's contributions as conceived in the Quantocks, which was precisely to explore "preternatural" as opposed to rural tales.

What had happened was clear: Wordsworth, from a position of apparent weakness, had ruthlessly come to dominate the terms of the collaboration. Having used Coleridge – even, one might think, having exploited him – as advisor and editor, drawing him up to the Lakes for that very purpose, he had entirely imposed his own vision of the collection on the final text. The extraordinarily dismissive note which he now attached to the *Mariner*, further bears this out.[31]* In literary terms, he was absolutely true to his own genius in this. But in terms of their friendship, their shared vision of a life dedicated to poetry in the Lakes, it was little short of a catastrophe. Coleridge had

---

*Wordsworth's note, which Coleridge did not see before it appeared in print in the second edition, read as follows: ". . . the Author was himself very desirous that [The *Ancient Mariner*] should be suppressed. This wish had arisen from a consciousness of the defects of the Poem, and from a knowledge that many persons had been much displeased with it. The Poem of my Friend has indeed great defects; first, that the principal person has no distinct character, either in his profession of Mariner, or as a human being who having been long under the control of supernatural impressions might be supposed himself to partake of something supernatural: secondly, that he does not act, but is continually acted upon: thirdly, that the events having no necessary connection do not produce each other; and lastly, that the imagery is somewhat too laboriously accumulated. Yet the Poem contains many delicate touches of passion, and indeed the passion is everywhere true to nature; a great number of the stanzas present beautiful images, and are expressed with unusual felicity of language; and the versification, though the metre itself is unfit for long poems, is harmonious and artfully varied . . ." (See Stephen Gill, who gives a very perceptive account of this whole episode, in *William Wordsworth: A Life*, Chapter 7, Oxford, 1989.) Wordsworth's four objections, the faintness of his praise, and the disparaging tone in which he presumes to speak for Coleridge himself, are astonishing when one considers the original terms of the collaboration. Compared to Charles Lamb, one may feel he understands almost nothing of the poem's power. But most disturbing of all, Coleridge later took on these criticisms as comments on the weakness, not of his poem, but of his own personal character (see Chapter 12).

submitted himself to Wordsworth in the most humiliating and damaging way; while Wordsworth had shown extraordinary insensitivity to the effect that this rejection would have on Coleridge's powers and self-confidence.

Coleridge was slow to admit all this to himself: he was brisk in his letters about it to his friends, and he continued faithfully his editorial work, even to the extent of copying out the first 200 lines of Wordsworth's "Michael", the poem that was to substitute for "Christabel", in November. He remained unstinting in his praise of Wordsworth's poems. It was not until December that he admitted something of what had occurred: "as to our literary occupations they are still more distant than our residences – He is a great, a true Poet – I am only a kind of Metaphysician. – He has even now sent off the last sheet of a second Volume of his Lyrical Ballads."[32] The possessive pronoun said it all.

6

As to "Christabel", it may be doubted if it could – or should – have ever been "completed", though Coleridge would dream of it for nearly thirty years after, and give various accounts to Gillman and others of the putative plot-line. Much of it became a sort of illusory construction in his head: though the written text of both Parts was never longer than 677 lines in total, he would claim to Davy on 9 October that it ran "up to 1300 lines", and to Poole two days later that it had "swelled" to 1400 lines.[33] By the following April it was "a Legend in Five Acts", ready to be printed by the Bulmerian Press with illustrations.[34]

Such wild claims began to extend to much of his other writing – he promised to Stuart the Bonaparte essay on no less than three occasions; to Longman the life of Lessing and the German travel book; to Wedgwood the essays on German folk culture. Here one can trace the desperate prevarications of the overburdened freelance, combining with the first sinister wish-fulfilments and seductive mania of opium-addiction. In November he admitted something of this to Wedgwood: "I had gotten myself entangled in the old Sorites of the old Sophist, Procrastination – I had suffered my necessary businesses to accumulate so terribly, that I neglected to write to any one – till the Pain, I suffered from not writing, made me waste as many hours in dreaming about it, as would have sufficed for the Letter-writing of half a Life."[35] He was talking here of his correspondence simply; but it was even more true of his professional writing, and poetry.

Yet there were technical reasons, so to speak, why "Christabel" would always remain a fragment; and it can be argued that these have entire and even beautiful poetic validity. Indeed, had Wordsworth chosen to print Part One alone, together with *Mariner*, Coleridge would have already done enough to establish the dual Romantic archetypes of his "preternatural" world – the outcast sailor and the seduced maiden, the masculine and the feminine principle subjected to the daemonic ordeal, in their corresponding mythological settings, the boat at sea and the castle in the wild wood.

The combined force of these psychic visions, with their tremendous summonings of traditional folklore and Romantic psychopathology, would certainly have unbalanced the rural plain-style to which Wordsworth had committed the *Lyrical Ballads*. But publishing them would also have been sufficient to reveal Coleridge in his unique poetic originality at this crucial moment in his career, instead of muffling his reputation for nearly two decades. He would have felt himself a "true Poet", and much might have been spared him.

The main technical reason for incompletion is evidently structural. "Christabel" is not (like the *Mariner*) based on the traditional form of a ballad tale, with its rapid sequence of unfolding action. From the very opening lines, its form is chant-like, trance-like. Its power derives from a haunting suggestiveness of atmosphere, an incantation of psychological symbols and spells, which defy any normal narrative development. As they stand, the two Parts represent a balance of these evoked forces, rather than a cumulative action.

Part One, set in a legendary version of the Quantocks, with all its rustling shadows and bright winking details, is a form of night-haunting, an obscure but profoundly disturbing seduction scene. (A lesbian reading, a gothic-vampire reading, a daemonic-nature reading are all possible.) Part Two, so skilfully transferred by Coleridge to the landscape of the Lakes and the legendary north, is by contrast a piece of "daylight witchery", more like a scene of hypnosis or possession, full of suspended courtly imagery and allegoric overtones, a waking dream of uneasy talk and gestures.

The two Parts are thus night and day versions of the same, inexplicable trance. They offer minimal dramatic development. In Part One, Christabel's innocence, as a "child of Nature" so fascinating to Coleridge, is presented in terms of her dead mother; in Part

Two, it is explored in relation to her emotionally "dead" father, Sir Leoline. In both, though action is constantly threatened, the only true movement is purely thematic: the awakening of sexual feelings, the arrival of spring, the daemonic forces of the green forest entering the dark, oppressive castle (like an adolescent's poltergeist) seizing upon both child and father in the person of Geraldine. The bard Bracey's intervention, with his allegoric dream, actually delays action – and moves it off-stage – rather than furthering it. We are taken backwards into the memories and unconscious feelings of the suspended participants, a world of broken friendships and frustrated loves.

The sense of passionate emotions and explosive energies, locked and spellbound, frozen, dumb, struggling for release but always contained, becomes the ultimate character of the poem. Hence to develop the "plot" would be to break the "spell", to dissipate the essentially dream-like quality of the involuted, slumbering enigma. At some level, Coleridge must surely have known this:

> Yea, she doth smile, and she doth weep,
> Like a youthful hermitess,
> Beauteous in a wilderness,
> Who, praying always, prays in sleep.
> And, if she move unquietly,
> Perchance, 'tis but the blood so free
> Comes back and tingles in her feet.
> No doubt, she has a vision sweet.[36]

Finally there is the mysterious character of Geraldine. She is perhaps the most extraordinary of all Coleridge's poetic creations, an embodiment of pure sexual energy almost like an unstable chemical element in constant transformation. A damsel in distress, witch, sorceress, lamia-snake, nature goddess, daemonic spirit, (and something of a boudoir vamp) – she depends completely for her power on this protean ambiguity, which cannot be sustained within the moral limitations of dramatic action. To develop her would be to destroy her, and this too Coleridge must have known. Her power, most of all, depended on the fragmentary, open form of the poem.

There is one further consideration. Of all Coleridge's major poems, it is most difficult to see what inspired "Christabel", where it came from in his imagination. Years later he would say that certain lines of Richard Crashaw on St Theresa, and her martyrdom, may have suggested "the first thought of the whole poem".[37]* The idea of innocence is as central to the conception as that of guilt is to the *Mariner*: the paradox being that both bring forms of nightmare suffering, of martyrdom. But the personal resonances are far more problematic: the "child of nature" theme suggests distant echoes of Dorothy Wordsworth, and something of the ambiance and undertones of the early Wordsworth household at Alfoxden. Hartley, too, is a kind of projected presence, appearing most explicitly in the unexpected coda to Part Two, "A little child, a limber elf,/Singing, dancing to itself . . ."[38]

But if "Christabel" draws on any autobiographical sources, they must be much deeper than these, perhaps to the roots of Coleridge's own childhood at Ottery, the early dreams, the lost sister, the disrupted household, the longings for love. Geraldine is Coleridge's most explicit treatment of sexual power, and she is ambiguous, menacing, enchanting, perhaps vengeful. The trance she throws over Christabel's powers of speech, suggests some shadowy confrontation between sexual and creative energies. And she touches on a central problem in Coleridge's own psychological make-up – the

---

*Coleridge became fascinated by the life, work, and psychology of the great Spanish mystic, St Theresa of Avila, and began a study of her in June 1810 (*Notebooks*, III, 3911). He had also been writing about questions of religious visions, hallucinations, and diabolic possession in *The Friend*, a subject I shall return to with relish in volume two. The following passage from Richard Crashaw's "A Hymn to the Name and Honour of the Admirable Saint Teresa" (1652) seems relevant to "Christabel", both in its theme and its hypnotic verse-movement:

> . . . For she breathes All fire.
> Her weake breast heaves with strong desire
> Of what she may with fruitless wishes
> Seek for amongst her Mother's kisses.
> Since 'tis not to be had at home
> She'll travel to a Martyrdom.
> No home for her confesses she
> But where she may a martyr be.

Other bibliographic sources for the ballad have been pursued by A. H. Nethercote in *The Road to Tryermaine* (1939); but a wider field of study seems indicated, which might include the Lamia-Lilith figure in Philostratus and Burton; the folktales of the Sleeping Beauty or the fairy Oberon (see C. M. Wieland); the female monsters of Greenland and Scandinavia collected in "The Destiny of Nations"; and even the Jungian concept of the vengeful Anima. Some of these themes are explored by Jonas Spatz in "Sexual Initiation in Coleridge's Christabel", PMLA, No. 90, January 1975; Susan M. Luther, *Christabel*, Salzburg Studies, 1976; and by implication in Bram Dijkstra's *Idols of Perversity: Fantasies of Feminine Evil*, Oxford, 1986. The immense impact of the poem on Shelley and Byron; on John Keats ("The Eve of St Agnes"); on Tennyson ("The Lady of Shallot"); and the whole Pre-Raphaelite Movement, belongs to volume two; as well as Coleridge's later reflections in the Notebooks (e.g. II, 2207; or III, 3720).

threat of one personality being "possessed" by another, more dominant one. But of all the longer poems, "Christabel" is the least consciously confessional, the most deliberately invented, the most magically contrived.

Just here, perhaps, lay Coleridge's greatest psychological impediment to completion. The whole thrust of his new Lakeland writing in the Notebooks was towards self-consciousness, achieved through observation of the natural world and his responses to it. He was seizing upon the outward landscapes, analysing them, and internalising their effects. His whole instinct was turning towards this form of confessional writing, in his letters, his Notebooks, and his poetry.

Even in Part Two of "Christabel", this new pressure of the confessional becomes evident in several passages, which almost break out of the assumed ballad form, further fragmenting it: the lament for lost friendship, "Alas! they had been friends in youth" – which always delighted Hazlitt – and the coda on Hartley, are notable examples of this, which almost exist as separate poems, and have been frequently anthologised as such. Bracey's dream of the dove and the snake also takes on a malevolent, sexually suggestive internal menace of its own, which raises autobiographical issues of power and submission.[39]

Between 1798 and 1800 Coleridge had, essentially, outgrown the naïve, dream-like ballad form of "Christabel", and could never recover its spontaneity. Prevented by Wordsworth from the satisfaction of immediate publication, he could not easily release himself from its imaginative hold upon his own development. He tried to go back, when he should have been free to leap forward – as he had done so often in his literary work. In consequence, over the next months – and indeed years – he mourned the loss of one kind of creative power when he should have been celebrating the gain of another. Hence the paradox that so often in the letters and poems of the 1801–4 period – and most memorably in "Dejection" – he describes this apparent loss of creativity in the most brilliant and imaginative new ways. He opposed the poet and the metaphysician, when he himself was now both.

7

The long struggle to finish "Christabel" had thrown him fearfully back in his "bread-and-beef occupations", as he told Godwin and Poole, "Dunning Letters etc etc – all the hell of an Author".[40] Through October he tried to make up some ground by showering articles and poems on Stuart, but they were not, significantly, original work. A series of essays on "Monopolists and Farmers" were based on materials supplied by Poole; and one poem, "Inscription for a Seat by the Road Side", was a revision of one of Wordsworth's rejected pieces "On the Naming of Places" for the *Lyrical Ballads*. His own poem on the subject – half-sketched in the Notebooks – was never worked up, an ominous sign. "The Sopha of Sods – whole life – sliding down Lattrig – Snow-tree – planting & sowing – poem hid in a tin box – stooping from sublime Thoughts to reckon how many Lines the poem would make."[41]

His deeper, instinctive reaction was to throw himself out on to the fells, abandoning himself to the wild autumnal weather, walking and climbing till he was exhausted, and fuelling himself on brandy and – now – opium. It was not exactly a search for oblivion, but through physical effort and danger, to submit himself to the great healing forces of nature. His eyelids swelled from exposure to the wind, his hands were cut on the crags, his legs ached with muscular pains that soon became rheumatic.[42]

On 11 October, just after the first snow had fallen, he climbed Carrock Fell – still one of the loneliest of the great Cumberland peaks, beyond Latrigg up the Caldew Valley to the east of Keswick. Here, as he laconically recorded in his Notebook, "almost broke my neck".[43] His account to Davy a week later has all the visionary intensity of a prose poem, the bleak wilderness of the outer landscape faithfully mirroring the wilderness within.

> On this mountain Carrock, at the summit of which are the remains of a vast Druid Circle of Stones, I was wandering –; when a thick cloud came on, and wrapped me in such Darkness that I could not see ten yards before me – and with the cloud a storm of Wind & Hail, the like of which I had never before seen & felt. At the very summit is a cone of Stones, built by the Shepherds, & called the Carrock Man . . . At the bottom of this Carrock Man I seated myself for shelter; but the wind became so fearful & tyrannous that I was apprehensive, some of the stones might topple down upon me. So I groped my way further down, and came to 3 Rocks, placed in this wise [*sketch*] – each supported by the other like a Child's House of Cards, & in the Hollow & Screen which they made I sate for a long while sheltered as if I had been in my own Study, in which I am now writing. – Here I sate, with a total feeling worshipping the power & "eternal Link" of energy.[44]

This passage has an almost allegoric force, like something out of Bunyan. The imaginative connection between his solitary study, and the solitary fell-tops, was to become a vital metaphor in his writing about the Lakes. And such wild "wanderings" were to become a physical resort, almost as powerful as the inner one of opium. This particular expedition ended with a sudden, benevolent break in the clouds, and "as if by enchantment" a great blue panorama opening to the south, with a bright rainbow above. "I descended by the side of a Torrent, & passed or rather crawled (for I was forced to descend on all fours) by many a naked Waterfall, till fatigued & hungry (& with one finger almost broken, & which remains swelled to the size of two Fingers) I reached the narrow vale, & the single House nested in Ashes & Sycamores." Here he took black bread and milk from the farmer's wife, and promised to return with medicine for her rheumatic pains – which for a moment made him forget his own. "I wish much to go off with some bottles of Stuff to the poor Creature – I should walk 10 miles, as ten yards."[45]

This was the last of Coleridge's fell-walking expeditions of the autumn, as the Lake District weather rapidly deteriorated, and the chill damp winds began to penetrate the front rooms of Greta Hall. His eyes became inflamed – "they are so blood-red, that I should make a very good Personification of Murder" – he had boils on his neck, and increasing rheumatic pains in his legs.[46] He began regular purchases of a local opium-based pain-killer, the notorious "Kendal Black Drop"[47] He spent more time alone in his study, struggling with his writing-block, sitting up later into the night, and beginning to gather the first of those haunting sound-images which cluster around the poem "Dejection: an Ode". "October 21 – Morning – 2 o'clock – Wind amid its branches makes every now & then such a deep moan of pain, that I think it my wife asleep in pain – A trembling Oo! Oo! like a wounded man on a field of battle whose wounds smarted with the cold."[48] It is remarkable how such images enter his Notebooks and letters more than a year before the poem itself was conceived: the distillation of two long winters' misery.

Snow fell, covering the whole landscape in November, and even Hartley became ill. As Coleridge's imagination closed in on itself, shuttered off like the hills, and opium took its hold, he began to have a recurrence of those terrible nightmares which had seized on him in childhood. He tried to break out of the besieging circle of illness and introspection, tramping fifteen miles over the snow-bound road to Grasmere at the end of the month to help with the final corrections of the *Lyrical Ballads*. But even here the nightmares pursued him, a mixture of bodily and sexual horrors. Dorothy's Journal sympathetically records his "great boils", his illness, and his retreats to bed.

His own Notebooks are vividly explicit.

> A most frightful Dream of a Woman whose features were blended with darkness catching holding of my right eye & attempting to pull it out – I caught hold of her arm fast – a horrid feel – Wordsworth cried out aloud to me hearing my scream – heard his cry & thought it cruel he did not come: but did not wake till his cry was repeated a third time – the Woman's name Ebon Ebon Thalud – When I awoke, my right eyelid swelled.[49]

The sinister name seems to have come from his memory of *The Arabian Nights*, which has a story about a drug-dealer Ebn Thaher. Such dreams would become a specific and terrible affliction over the next three years, reaching their climax in the winter of 1803 when he actually feared the onset of sleep itself, a characteristic of opium addiction, also described at length by De Quincey. This experience too he would transform into the moving, confessional poetry of "The Pains of Sleep".

But in this Grasmere dream, it was perhaps the half-suppressed feeling of Wordsworth's "cruelty", withholding his power to rescue Coleridge, that was most significant. From now on, the psychological pattern of the friendship was changing rapidly, with Wordsworth moving into the position of strength and self-reliance formerly occupied by Coleridge; and Coleridge himself becoming the weaker, dependent partner, struggling to reassert his sense of professional purpose. This dialogue of strength and weakness powerfully informs much of the new poetry they would both write, reaching its fullest expression in the closely associated major Odes "Intimations of Immortality in Early Childhood" and "Dejection", whose very titles indicate their divergent paths. From now on, too, Coleridge began to question the wisdom of his move to the Lakes, and look with growing desperation for some alternative life scheme abroad.

8

These doubts first surfaced in a letter of 1 November to Josiah Wedgwood, when he wrote to apologise about overdrawing on the 1801 annuity by £40. Coleridge tried to enthuse about all the delights of Greta Hall, but found himself instead sadly recalling the old securities of his friendship with Tom Poole at Stowey. "I used to feel myself more at home in his great windy Parlour, than in my own cottage. We were well suited for each other – my animal Spirits corrected his inclinations to melancholy; and there was some thing both in his understanding & in his affection so healthy & manly, that my mind freshened in his company, and my ideas & habits of thinking acquired day after day more of substance & reality."[50] The unspoken comparison was surely with Wordsworth, still his greatest friend, and yet now striding relentlessly ahead on the path of his great poetry.

To Poole himself he wrote of a scheme to go to London with a dramatic Romance, which he had been sketching in his Notebooks, "The Triumph of Loyalty".[51] Hartley and Derwent, he said, brought him the greatest pleasure, when they were not ill; as for his own body, it was "a very crazy machine", the weather racked him with rheumatism, and he spent more and more time in bed. He was aware of financial obligations, work slipping by, a sense of fatally lost momentum. "Altho' I am certain, that I have been greatly improving both in knowledge & power in these last twelve months, yet still at times it presses upon me with a painful Weight, that I have not evidenced a more tangible utility. I have too much trifled with my reputation."[52] Again, the unspoken reference is to Wordsworth.

To Davy, in December, he spoke of another, more metaphysical scheme, an analytic essay on Pain. "I want to read something by somebody expressly on *Pain*, if only to give an *arrangement* to my own thoughts, though if it were well treated, I have little doubt it would revolutionize them. – For the last month I have been tumbling on through sands and swamps of Evil, & bodily grievance."[53]

To Godwin he spoke with even greater desperation of a huge, 1,400-page work of geography which would follow "the most celebrated Travels into the different climates of the world", a truly Coleridgean dream.[54] He was painfully aware that his original plan of attracting these friends to the Lakes, to form an intellectual colony, had melted away.

The one significant source of relief arrived in the person of Sara Hutchinson – who came to spend the winter at Grasmere. It was she, and not his wife, who now entered into the beleaguered world of his imagination; and it was under these conditions that the good-humoured flirtations of Sockburn changed into something far more intimate and serious. This profound shift of feeling in Coleridge was, from the beginning, closely involved with his sense of lost power, his first prolonged resort to opium, and his emergent feelings of rivalry with Wordsworth. Sara Hutchinson therefore stands in a complex and ambiguous position, both a symbol of possible renewal in Coleridge's emotional life, and also a fantasy-figure – an alternative to domestic duties, an escape from professional pressures, a temptingly unattached woman who offered – quite differently from Dorothy – a further hold on the intimate heart of Wordsworth's household.

The Wordsworths themselves felt this, and wishing to cheer and encourage their friend, undoubtedly fostered the friendship in these early days. Visits were exchanged between Grasmere and Greta Hall, in December and January. Coleridge gave Sara Hutchinson a Christmas present of Anna Seward's *Original Sonnets*, which he inscribed light-heartedly "to Asahara, the Moorish Maid" – an early version of the romantic code-name of his Notebooks and poems, "Asra".

Wordsworth had ordered through Longman a copy of William Withering's *British Plants* (1796), with two botanical microscopes, for himself and Coleridge to pursue their nature studies within doors during the winter; and Asra copied five pages of native plant-names into Coleridge's Notebook, a gesture of confidence on both sides, for he rarely allowed others to make entries – and his wife, never. (In this list they first recorded the local name, "Forget-me-not".)[55] He later fondly recalled a winter afternoon at Grasmere spent reading Bartram's *Travels* with Asra, "when William and Dorothy had gone out to walk".

These small details suggest the nature of their growing intimacy, with Asra falling into the role of amanuensis and practical helper, sharing books, listening to his metaphysics, and encouraging that delight in nature that still sustained him. For Sara Coleridge, wrapped up in the children and domesticities of Greta Hall, Sara Hutchinson's companionship may have appeared at first a welcome distraction for her ailing husband. Certainly his affection for his children remained reassuringly constant.

Shortly before Christmas he took Hartley out to pay his respects to the moon, as in the old days at Stowey. "Hartley was in my arms the other evening looking at the Sky – he saw the moon glide into a large Cloud – Shortly after, at another part of the Cloud several Stars sailed in. Says he – 'Pretty Creatures! they are going in to see after their mother Moon.'"[56] These images, too, would enter into his poetry, slowly absorbed in the coming months, and gathering poignant resonance from his own loneliness and suffering:

Thou first and chief, sole sovereign of the Vale!
O struggling with the darkness all the night,
And visited all night by troops of stars,
Or when they climb the sky or when they sink . . .[57]

He now busied himself with the final editorial work on the *Lyrical Ballads*, writing covering letters for review copies being sent to influential public figures like William Wilberforce, and Charles James Fox. But his own literary affairs came to an absolute standstill.[58] He held off Longman's demands for the Lessing with dramatic accounts of his illness, and still vainly promised at least the German travel-letters for January. He gossiped to Godwin about the London theatre, but admitted to Thelwall that his ideas were drifting into abstruser regions.

> My literary pursuits are, 1. the Northern Languages, the Sclavonic, Gothic & Celtic, in their most ancient forms . . . 2. as a serious object, a metaphysical Investigation of the Laws, by which our Feelings form affinities with each other, with Ideas, & with words. As to Poetry, I have altogether abandoned it, being convinced that I never had the essentials of poetic Genius, & that I mistook a strong desire for original power.[59]

This was a tragic statement of his loss of intellectual self-confidence after the first six months at Greta Hall. Yet perhaps it also contained a first shadowy attempt to distinguish himself from Wordsworth's success, to which he had sacrificed so much and so deliberately. One can glimpse something new stirring in that extraordinarily flexible and resourceful mind: the hope of recreating himself imaginatively out of the sense of failure itself. First he had deserts of opium, illness, and domestic unhappiness to cross; and endless unavailing visions of escape to live through. But he would do it, he would endure, he would write.

TWELVE

Lover

1

In January 1801 Coleridge's health altogether collapsed, and for three months he retreated to the upper rooms of Greta Hall. He shuffled between bed and sofa, reading deeply in metaphysics – Giordano Bruno, Hobbes, Locke, Kant – scribbling in his Notebooks, and gazing out through his panoramic windows at the harsh winter beauty of the fells and lakes, with their ever-changing effects of light and weather.

His physical symptoms were spectacularly varied and unpleasant: rheumatic fevers, swollen leg joints, boils, agonising nephritic pains, and a swollen testicle diagnosed as a hydrocele. The local surgeon-apothecary treated him with a corresponding variety of nostrums: leeches, poultices, vinegar fomentations, sal ammoniac rubs, bark infusions, and brimstone; to which he added Kendal Black Drop as a blessed nightly panacea against pain. He was soon deep in opium, heavily laced with brandy, which combined with his metaphysics to carry him away into clouds of unknowing, from which he would occasionally descend to write long, luridly brilliant letters to his friends – Godwin, Poole, Davy, Thelwall. His medical complaints themselves took on epic proportions, wildly comic or tragic by turns, yielding labyrinthine literary schemes, shadowy metaphysical castles, and superb bright fragments of natural imagery.

2

It is significant, in this first period of really serious opium addiction, that though he thought much about poetry, he did not actually write it. Opium was no fuel for the constructive imagination, but a barrier against pain and anxiety, and a febrile encouragement to his long night-speculations and dreams of literary glory.

In his lucid hours, Coleridge was perfectly aware of this situation. He wrote characteristically to Poole one night in February:

> I have begun to take Bark, and I hope, that shortly I shall look back on my long & painful illness only as a Storehouse of wild Dreams for Poems, or intellectual Facts for metaphysical Speculation. Davy in the kindness of his heart calls me the Poet-philosopher – I hope, Philosophy & Poetry will not neutralize each other, & leave me an inert mass. But I talk idly – I feel, that I have power within me: and I humbly pray to the Great Being, the God & Father who has bidden me "rise & walk" that he will grant me a steady mind to employ the health of my youth and manhood in the manifestation of that power . . . O my dear dear Friend! that you were with me by the fireside of my Study here, that I might talk it over with you to the Tune of the Night Wind that pipes its thin doleful climbing sinking Notes like a child that has lost its way and is crying aloud, half in grief and half in hope to be heard by its Mother.[1]

These hopes, these images – the lost child going back even to his traumatic night on the banks of the Otter – were all to reappear in his great confessional poem "Dejection".[2] Moreover, the growing religious orthodoxy – the need for a merciful, fatherly divinity to bless and release his powers – seemed to arise directly in response to the growing guilt he felt about his opium-taking, his prostration and procrastination. He would later, in May, speak directly to Poole of "the Disgust, the Loathing, that followed these Fits & no doubt in part too the use of the Brandy & Laudanum which they rendered necessary."[3]

In his study he still took immense pleasure in the natural world viewed from his windows, in his books, in regular visitations by his children, in the friendly attentions of a household cat. His Notebooks and letters are particularly full of the sayings and doings of little Hartley, now five years old, ebullient and precocious like a projection of his own youthful spirit. "From morning to night he whirls about and about, whisks, whirls, and eddies, like a blossom in a May-breeze."[4]

Many of his observations of Hartley connected with his own theories of language and poetry, developing from the primitive workings of the imagination. He watched the boy building a model fireplace, from stone blocks, in which the fire itself was also represented by a stone: "four stones, fireplace – two stones, fire – arbitrary symbols in Imagination".[5] Father and son would hold long, elaborate conversations as they gazed together out on the fells, describing what they saw and felt, just as little Sam had once talked to the Reverend John at Ottery long ago.

On 17 March, Coleridge made this detailed entry which touches upon his advancing concepts of the relations between mental representation and language.

> Tuesday – Hartley looking out of my study window fixed his eyes steadily & for some time on the opposite prospect, & then said – Will yon Mountains *always* be? – I shewed him the whole magnificent Prospect in a Looking Glass, and held it up, so that the whole was like a Canopy or Ceiling over his head, & he struggled to express himself concerning the Difference between the Thing & the Image almost with convulsive Effort. – I never before saw such an Abstract of *Thinking* as a pure act & energy, of *Thinking* as distinguished from *Thoughts*.[6]

One wonders, however, what effect these strange, intense cross-questionings must have had on the child; and what Sara Coleridge must have felt with her husband shut away upstairs in the house, a sort of metaphysical lighthouse keeper, lost amidst his books and laudanum tinctures. When Wordsworth came on a visit towards the end of March, Coleridge lay "abed – nervous", dreamily watching the prismatic colours turning in his tumbler of medicine. "Wordsworth came – I talked with him – he left me alone – I shut my eyes – beauteous spectra of two colours, orange and violet . . . abstract Ideas – & unconscious Links!!"[7]

Yet when Asra came on the same visit – she was preparing to return to Yorkshire via Penrith – he sat up happily reading with her from Bartram's *Travels*. They discovered a passage of topographical description which he suddenly applied, "by a fantastic analogue & similitude", to the structure of Wordsworth's poetic imagination. Wordsworth's mind in all its power seemed to him like the harsh but fruitful geography evoked by Bartram, germinating trees like poems. "The soil is a deep, rich, dark Mould on a deep Stratum of tenacious Clay, and that on a foundation of Rocks, which often break through both Strata, lifting their back above the Surface. The Trees, which chiefly grow here, are the gigantic Black Oak, Magnolia, Fraxinus excelsior, Platane, & a few stately Tulip Trees."[8] It was an analogy that years later he would use in Chapter 22 of the *Biographia*.[9]

Coleridge made no further remark about Asra's departure, only his imagination whirled on after her, and he plunged for relief further into his metaphysics. The result was four enormously long philosophic letters to Josiah Wedgwood, in which he attacked the empirical doctrines of Descartes and Locke, and laid the basis for his own idiosyncratic form of idealism.[10] Although these letters do not mention Kant, his Notebooks show that he was now reading the German philosopher, and enthusiastically considering the concepts of time and space as subjective "categories" of mental perception, rather than as objective facts of empirical data.[11] Wedgwood later admitted that he put these epistles aside, unreadable and unread. But the pottery-king observed stoutly to Poole: "from the cursory view I took of them he seems to have plucked the principal feather from out of Locke's wings."[12]

Coleridge himself wrote wildly to Poole that metaphysical excitements and "intensity of thought" had left him feverish and sleepless, and Wordsworth had fervently entreated him to desist. Indeed his philosophical claims, and references to "minute experiments with Light & Figure", have the grandiose tones of opium.

> If I do not greatly delude myself, I have not only completely extricated the notions of Time, and Space; but have overthrown the doctrines of Association, as taught by Hartley, and with it all the irreligious metaphysics of modern Infidels – especially, the doctrine of Necessity. – This I have *done*; but I trust, that I am about to do more – namely, that I shall be able to evolve all the five senses, that is, to deduce them from *one sense* & to state their growth, & the causes of their difference – & in this evolvement to solve the process of Life & Consciousness.[13]

A mighty claim indeed, but one which was to haunt him for the rest of his life with the possibilities of a grand metaphysical opus reconciling idealism with Christian doctrines of revelation and salvation.

Yet this long withdrawal into illness and opium, isolated in the remote firelit world of his study, a sort of hermit's retreat, served Coleridge in its own way. Imaginatively speaking, it was a question of taking stock of his powers, *reculer pour mieux sauter.* Digging back into his own mind and beliefs, he found the beginnings of a new literary identity, the poet-philosopher in a mist, whose very bafflement and intellectual frustrations gave him a new form of Romantic subject-matter. While Wordsworth gained the authority of poetic success, Coleridge found the authority of his poetic failure. Failure, prostration, imaginative crisis, itself became something upon which he, as a writer, could exercise brilliant lines of poetic enquiry and self-dramatisation. At times, he could even see himself as his own Mariner – "Mind shipwrecked by storms of doubt, now mastless, rudderless, shattered, – pulling in the dead swell of a dark & windless Sea."[14]

The painful uncertainties of his inner visionary world now themselves supplied him with the richest imaginative materials, which – like the *Mariner* and "Christabel" – were beyond the range of Wordsworth's appreciation. The medium of this new vision was increasingly prose – in his letters and Notebooks – though prose of extraordinary imaginative life and subtlety. And out of this prose, which began in confession and self-analysis, was gradually formed a wholly new instrument of literary and philosophical criticism.

On 25 March he wrote an astonishingly vivid letter to William Godwin, which demonstrates this process of self-transformation. Its apparent subject – like the later "Dejection" ode – is his own failure to produce poetry. But its metaphoric life, humour, and self-mocking energy, become paradoxically an evocation of those very imaginative powers he had claimed to have lost. He argued that the original poet in him was dead; but he proved – with a kind of exultation – that a new poet-philosopher was being born in the study at Greta Hall, surrounded by the images of the fells he had climbed.

> In my long Illness I had compelled into hours of Delight many a sleepless, painful hour of Darkness by chasing down metaphysical Game – and since then I have continued the Hunt, till I found myself unaware at the Root of Pure Mathematics – and up that tall smooth Tree, whose few poor branches are all at its very summit, am I climbing by pure adhesive strength of arms and thighs – still slipping down, still renewing my ascent. – You would not know me – ! all sounds of similitude keep at such a distance from each other in my mind, that I have *forgotten* how to make a rhyme – I look at the Mountains (that visible God Almighty that looks in at all my windows) I look at the Mountains only for the Curves of their outlines; the Stars, as I behold them, form themselves into Triangles – and my hands are scarred with scratches from a Cat, whose back I was rubbing in the Dark in order to see whether the sparks were refrangible by a Prism. The Poet is dead in me – my imagination (or rather the Somewhat that had been imaginative) lies, like a Cold Snuff on the circular Rim of a Brass Candle-stick, without even a stink of Tallow to remind you that it was once

> cloathed and mitred with Flame. That is past by! – I was once a Volume of Gold Leaf, rising & riding on every breath of Fancy – but I have beaten myself back into weight and density, & now I sink in quicksilver, yea, remain squat & square on the earth amid the hurricane, that makes Oaks and Straws join in one Dance, fifty yards high in the Element.[15]

What one senses in such a passage is not restriction, but release; not depression, but delight. The talk of loss and failure is consistently contradicted by the excitement and spontaneity of the leaping rhythms and metaphors. Coleridge finds his salvation in the irrepressible life of language itself. This would be the pattern for the future, even in the blackest moments of despair in his Notebooks. The controlling images seem to pour out inexhaustibly to Godwin like a torrent of enchantments. (The effect is curiously like the experience of the Sorcerer's Apprentice.) Yet they all rise so naturally from the objects round his study room: the branches at the window, the cat in his lap, the candlestick at his desk, the goldleaf on his books, the wind whirling about the hills outside. All are symbols of the imagination actively at work. Moreover, like his fell-walking studies, they still celebrate his perception of the powers of nature, the "link of energy", which surge about him even in the stillness of the sickroom.

Out of these long winter nights of self-analysis, and the cloud of metaphysics, the first tentative outlines of his theory of the creative imagination were beginning to emerge in philosophical form. To Poole he wrote:

> My opinion is this – that deep Thinking is attainable only by a man of deep Feeling, and that all Truth is a species of Revelation. The more I understand of Sir Isaac Newton's works, the more boldly I dare utter to my own mind & therefore to *you*, that I believe the Souls of 500 Sir Isaac Newtons would go to the making up of a Shakespeare or a Milton . . . Newton was a mere materialist – *Mind* in his system is always passive – a Lazy Looker-on on an external World. If the mind be not *passive*, if it be indeed made in God's Image, & that too in the sublimest sense – the Image of the *Creator* – there is ground for suspicion, that any system built on the passiveness of the mind must be false, as a system.[16]

Here already lies the seed of the active, shaping imagination, "the esemplastic power", which he would define in the *Biographia*.

3

At last, with the arrival of spring weather over the fells in April, Coleridge slowly began to recover. "With the fine weather I revive, like a Parlour Fly; but every change in this changeful Climate throws me on my back again, with inflamed eyes, rheumatic fever, & latterly a sort of irregular *Gout*."[17] His financial situation had again temporarily resolved itself, with the publisher Phillips' advance of £25 paid off after a solicitor's letter ("which amused me infinitely – I felt like a man of this World"); and Longman's £30 advance on Lessing finally liquidated by Wordsworth with money from the *Lyrical Ballads* contract – a gesture of justice as well as kindness towards his collaborator.

Domestic harmony was less easily attained, and Dorothy's account of the visit to Greta Hall in April suggests strong marital tensions. She now told Mary Hutchinson (perhaps with Asra in mind) that she considered Coleridge and his wife fundamentally "ill-matched". She tried to be fair to Sara Coleridge, but her sympathies are evident: "She is indeed a bad nurse for C., but has several great merits . . . She would have made a very good wife to many another man, but for Coleridge!! Her radical fault is want of sensibility, and what can such a woman be to Coleridge? She is an excellent nurse to her sucking children . . ." Yet Coleridge, in his moods, his abstractions, his hypochondriac delights, and his opium flights, may have been more of a child for Sara than Dorothy ever appreciated. Dorothy's solution was to imagine him basking in some exotic climate, until restored to his magicianhood: "at Lisbon, in the South of France, or at one of the Western Isles".[18]

Coleridge consolidated his recovery with startling rapidity in May. At first he went about on a crutch, spinning wild schemes for the summer.[19] To Davy, just appointed director of the Royal Institution in London, he announced a plan to set up a chemistry laboratory in Keswick, and wanted to know about Herschel's work on the "Thermometric *Spectrum*".[20] To Southey, returned after his year at Lisbon, he suggested sharing the household at Greta Hall.[21] To Tom Poole, he revived the Pantisocratic scheme, with a plan to "settle near Priestley, in America" accompanied by Wordsworth and two or three stout Cumberland farmers.[22]

To Wordsworth himself, he talked longingly of emigration to the Azores, at St Miguel; or at Nevis on the Pinney estate in the West Indies. Wordsworth took this so seriously that in July he actually wrote privately to Poole, asking for a loan of £50 to defray Coleridge's travelling expenses.[23] (When Poole refused, Coleridge – who still owed him £37 – was unreasonably offended, and broke off correspondence for several weeks, no doubt sensing his old friend's strong disapproval of such visionary escapes from his professional duties. But they were soon reconciled.[24])

Coleridge's real mood, as he climbed up that "rock of Convalescence" is well caught in a further summons to Southey.

> Yes, Sir! we will go to Constantinople; but as it rains there, which my Gout loves as the Devil does Holy Water, the Grand Turk shall show the exceeding attachment, he will no doubt form towards us, by appointing us his Vice-roys in Egypt – I will be Supreme Bey of that showerless District, & you shall be my Supervisor. – But for God's sake, make haste & come to me, and let us talk of the Sands of Arabia while we are floating in our lazy Boat on Keswick Lake, with our eyes on massy Skiddaw, so green & high.[25]

Meanwhile, tranquilly enough, he decided to appease Sara by beginning Hartley's formal education with lessons in natural history. Father and son crawled together about the vegetable gardens of Greta Hall, examining ant-heaps. "Ants having dim notions of the architecture of the whole System of the world, & imitating it, according to their notion in their ant-heaps . . . Hartley's intense wish to have Ant-heaps near our house: his *Brahman* love & awe of Life."[26]

By June he was back out on the fells, climbing over Easedale and seeing below the glimmering lake and church tower, "places wherein To wander & wander for ever & ever."[27] He found a long, narrow hollow formed in one of the rocks, exactly "like a Coffin", and there tried burying himself symbolically, with a sycamore bush shading his face, and a single tall foxglove set heraldically at his feet. "Exactly my own Length – there I lay & slept – It was quite soft. June 18, 1801. Thursday."[28]

4

But real health had not returned – he relapsed continually with swollen leg joints, and agonising attacks of "irregular gout", and the opium dosing continued. No serious work was being done, apart from reading. In late June he concentrated sufficiently to correct the draft of a tragedy that Godwin had sent him from London, and enjoyed a visit from the poet Sam Rogers (who carried away with him memories of a recitation of "Christabel", phrases of which would eventually find their way to Walter Scott). He urged Godwin, like Southey, to join him at Greta Hall – requests which emphasise his sense of intellectual isolation – and continued his dreams of escape. "I shall go in the first Vessels that leave Liverpool for the Azores, (St Michael's to wit) & these sail at the latter end of July. – Unless I can escape one English Winter & Spring, I have not any rational prospect of Recovery."[29] It is notable that he did not include his wife and children in these plans.

In early July, an unsolicited advance of £50 suddenly arrived from Josiah Wedgwood, with which he was able to pay off his "Keswick Bills, rent, etc", and the household finances were set fair again until Christmas.[30] Almost immediately Coleridge packed his bag, departing not for the Azores but for Asra.

His explanation to Sara was in every sense academic: he needed to study the works of Duns Scotus and other medieval philosophers at the great cathedral library of Durham. In the event it transpired that the library held only one work by Scotus, and the learned librarian, when asked for Leibnitz, grandly referred Coleridge to a microscope-maker in the city who had permanent displays of zoological specimens. ("Heaven & Earth! – he understood the word '*live Nits*'.")[31]

Durham was only eight miles from George Hutchinson's new farm at Bishop Middleham, where Asra was staying. Coleridge arrived at Middleham on 16 July, and after desultory visits to Durham, concocted a plan to go and stay with her other brother Tom, at his farm at Gallow Hill, near Scarborough on the Yorkshire coast, where he could officially undertake a recuperative regime of sea-bathing. He and Asra rode the sixty miles together on horseback, arriving on 31 July and remaining for ten days.[32]

Coleridge, whose left knee was conveniently swollen ("pregnant with agony") submitted to a local doctor's prescription of "horse-exercises & warm Sea-bathing" every day. He was advised to use the enclosed salt-water baths, but characteristically plunged into the open sea the moment he reached the beach, having "Faith in the Ocean". "I bathed regularly, frolicked in the Billows, and it did me a proper deal of good."[33]

But more good was found in the soothing female company of Asra, and Mary, who nursed him and cooked fine meals at the farmhouse, and indulged him in long, flirtatious evenings in the big, firelit kitchen. In his role as convalescent, he was installed with leg up on the sofa, innocently caressed and cuddled by both Asra and Mary. Secretly he now tasted moments of erotic paradise which he never forgot.

Coleridge's freedom, or irresponsibility, of behaviour during this largely clandestine visit (he gave Southey a humorously bowdlerised account) is remarkable. It shows his almost desperate longing for physical tenderness, for almost puppy-like petting and comforting, which he had long since ceased to find at Greta Hall. He is quite explicit about this in his Notebooks this summer, analysing his wife's remoteness of feeling with resigned detachment, and clearly implying sexual frigidity.

> Sara's ... coldness perhaps & paralysis in all *tangible* ideas & sensations – all that forms *real Self*... Nothing affects her with pain or pleasure as it is but only as other people *say it is* – nay by an habitual absence of *reality* in her affections I have had a hundred instances that the being beloved, or the not being beloved, is a thing indifferent; but the *notion* of not being beloved – that wounds her pride deeply. I have dressed perhaps washed with her, & no one with us – all as cold & calm as a deep Frost ... (She) is uncommonly *cold* in her feelings of animal Love.[34]

But what this note avoids, is why and how his own feelings – once so richly amorous and domestic in the Clevedon and Stowey days – had also grown cold, irritable and impatient with Sara. Ever since Germany he had been moving away from his wife; restless in his travels, unsettled in his work, fatally attracted by the apparent freedom of the Wordsworth household. Now with his creative struggles, his illness, the isolating effects of opium, he was seeking emotional escape: fantasies of exotic climates, revived dreams of a Pantisocratic colony, flirtations with the Hutchinson sisters. Yet he was also seeking, in his own instinctive way, a genuine convalescence: a revival of his powers, a revival of love, a renewal of his sense of worth as a man.

Something of this was caught in a curiously formal little poem he now wrote, and despatched to the *Morning Post*, entitled "On Revisiting the Sea-Shore, After Long Absence". The last time he had seen the sea was at Porlock.

> God be with thee, gladsome Ocean!
>   How gladly greet I thee once more!
> Ships and waves, and ceaseless motion,

And men rejoicing on thy shore . . .
Dreams (the Soul herself forsaking),
Tearful raptures, boyish mirth;
Silent adorations, making
A blessed shadow of this Earth![35]

The poem was formal (like a lyric by Samuel Rogers) because it was public. For Coleridge now found himself having to disguise the reality of his private feelings, a further inhibition to his poetry. It was only in the Asra poems, not intended for publication, that he was able to record directly the secret paradise of Gallow Hill.

In these he described a number of rapturous incidents: lying with Asra under a willow tree, both their heads cradled on Mary's lap; carving their names on a tree trunk; lying on the sofa in the kitchen in the firelight, with Asra's body pressing a "brooding warmth" against his breast; and one unforgettable moment of tenderness when all three curled on the sofa while Mary stroked his brow and Asra tickled his cheek with her eyelash.

All these appear in "A Day-Dream", which was not published until 1828. The extraordinary intimacy and innocence of these moments are strikingly childlike, as if Coleridge had regained his lost boyhood, and was feeding off a sudden flood of maternal caresses that had always been withheld from him at home. Evidently they took place in an atmosphere of teasing and laughter, with Asra and Mary probably unaware of the profoundly erotic chords they were touching in Coleridge. He was indeed behaving like a "sucking child", and his awareness of such feelings of specific desire, to be maternally fed and caressed, become almost explicit in another version of the incident and the poem, carefully disguised as "The Day-Dream: From an Emigrant to his Absent Wife":

. . .I guess
It would have made the loving mother dream
That she was softly bending down to kiss
Her babe, that something more than babe did seem,
A floating presence of its darling father . . .[36]

Innocent as they were, these sensations came back to haunt Coleridge with obsessive sexual force, especially in later moments of depression and opium. A few weeks later he brokenly recalled Asra's physical warmth in his Notebooks: "Prest to my bosom & felt there – it was quite dark. I looked intensely toward her face – & sometimes I *saw it* – so vivid was the spectrum . . . sopha / Lazy Bed – Green [? marine] – the fits of Light & Dark from the Candle going out in the Socket – Power of association – that last Image how lovely to me now."[37]

He recollected the "different parts of her Dress". He remembered his pleasure in "Endeavoring to make the infinitely beloved Darling understand all my knowledge", and how she had made him "learn the art of making the abstrusest Truth intelligible & interesting".[38] Even nine years after, he would still be amazed how the powers of association led his thoughts of her back to the Gallow Hill kitchen, the firelight, and the domestic tenderness of that summer. He was then, in March 1810, trying to analyse the problem philosophically, in the midst of a desperate opium crisis, but the old images vividly asserted themselves, fresh with amorous suggestions:

> I began strictly and as a matter of fact to examine that subtle Vulcanian Spider-web Net of Steel . . . in which my soul flutters inclosed with the Idea of your's – to pass rapidly as in a catalogue thro' the Images only, exclusive of the thousand Thoughts that possess the same force, which never fail instantly to awake into vivider flame the for ever and ever Feeling of you: – The fire, Mary, you, & I at Gallow-Hill; or if flamy, reflected in children's round faces – ah whose children? – a dog – that dog whose restless eyes oft catching the light of the fire used to watch your face, as you leaned with your head on your hand and arm, & your feet on the *fender* – the fender thence – Fowls at Table – the last dinner at Gallow Hill, when you drest the two fowls in that delicious white Sauce . . . ten thousand links, and if it please me, the very spasm & drawing-back of a pleasure which is half-pain, you not being there.[39]

It is here that the Notebooks have a greater confessional authority than the Asra poems: they are more precise, more revealing, more vulnerable. The intricate patterns of imagery and sexual suggestion are both subtle and daring: the obsessional sequence of entwined objects – spider's web, firelight flame, eyes, children, doting dog, legs on the fender, fowls on the table, white sauce on the fowls, the "spasm of pleasure" – enact the agonising dance of memory and desire with terrible and beautiful conviction.

To convert such experiences into the language of the Conversation Poems, with their pastoral decorum, was increasingly difficult for Coleridge. He needed a new language, intimate and rapid as thought, profoundly confessional, closer to his own wonderful talk: and this he found in his exhilarated, image-packed, prose. But all through the autumn and winter following the Gallow Hill visit, he was struggling to translate the experience into a poetic form, halfway between the public lyric and the fully confessional declaration. It emerged first as the private verse "Letter to Sara Hutchinson", and then as the Ode "Dejection" which he austerely edited for publication in the *Morning Post*.

In its first form, later censored from the Ode, Coleridge would at last succeed in describing the sofa incident at Gallow Hill with some degree of explicitness, and a new simplicity of emotional statement. But he knew, only too well, that unlike Wordsworth's advances in the lyric form, this could never be used for professional purposes. It was too close to his own life and sufferings; it was too close to home. And in the last two lines of this stanza, the language itself flinches away into propriety, even as he speaks to Asra.

> It was as calm as this, that happy night
> When Mary, thou, & I together were,
> The low decaying Fire our only Light,
> And listen'd to the Stillness of the Air!
> O that affectionate & blameless Maid,
> Dear Mary! on her Lap my head she lay'd –
>   Her Hand was on my Brow,
>   Even as my own is now;
> And on my Cheek I felt thy eye-lash play.
> Such Joy I had, that I may truly say,
> My spirit was awe-stricken with the Excess
> And trance-like Depth of its brief Happiness.[40]

5

Coleridge reluctantly quitted Gallow Hill on 9 August, and after a week of penitential sulphur bathes at Dinsdale, returned to Keswick, carefully timing his arrival to coincide with the long-promised visit from Southey and his family. The presence of Edith Southey at Greta Hall evidently soothed Mrs Coleridge, and in the holiday atmosphere of boating and walking the worst of the domestic confrontation between Coleridge and his wife was at least postponed. Coleridge sent shamelessly flirtatious doggerel to Mary and Joanna at Gallow Hill ("Nota bene. I'm married, / and Coals to Newcastle must never be carried"), but his thoughts circled round Asra.

The Wordsworths were away in Scotland, but he continued to dream of their happy household. Climbing over the fells with Southey, talking of Sicily and the Azores, he came across a pulsing pool of spring-water in the grass, and immediately saw it as an emblem of the Wordsworth-Hutchinson circle, so sure of each other's loyalties and affection. "The spring with the little tiny cone of loose sand ever rising & sinking at the bottom, but its surface without a wrinkle. – W.W. M.H. D.W. S.H."[41] He did not add his own initials, as he had done on the "Rock of Names" which they had earlier carved on Dunmail Raise. But the image slipped into another Asra poem, the blank verse "Inscription for a Fountain on a Heath", with its consoling promise to the traveller of coolness and refreshment.

> Quietly as a sleeping infant's breath,
> Send up cold waters to the traveller
> With soft and even pulse! Nor ever cease
> Yon tiny cone of sand its soundless dance . . .
> Here Twilight is and Coolness: here is moss,
> A soft seat, and a deep and ample shade.
> Thou may'st toil far and find no second tree.[42]

With the onset of autumn, it became clear to Coleridge that neither Wordsworth nor Southey would ever accompany him into winter exile abroad. In reality, he now had only two practical alternatives: London or Stowey. He reopened correspondence with Poole and Daniel Stuart, assuring the former that there had been no "falling off" of his affection, and suggesting to the latter that he might rejoin the *Morning Post*. "I will assuredly make the attempt to write some good prose for you; but I must first give *the Poetics* a complete *Jog*."[43] In September he sent Stuart a series of verse epigrams for publication, and also discreetly asked for a complimentary subscription to be sent to Asra. "Wordsworth & myself have one very dear Friend to whom the pleasure of seeing a paper during the time I wrote in it would be greater, than you can easily imagine."[44]

To Godwin on 22 September he gave a clear hint of his unsettled position at Greta Hall.

> If I am absolutely unable to go abroad – (and I am now making the last effort by an application to Mr John Pinny respecting his House at St Nevis, & the means of living there) I may perhaps come up to London, & maintain myself, as before, by writing for the Morning Post. – If I come, I come *alone*. – *Here* it will be imprudent for me to

stay, from the wet & the cold – even if every thing within doors were . . . well suited to my head & heart . . .[45]

In October, Southey left for Dublin to take up a post as Secretary to the Irish Chancellor, with a salary of £200 per annum, a characteristically efficient career move which was certainly not lost on Sara Coleridge. But Coleridge waved it aside to Poole: "of course the *opening* is great. – Men of Talents are at present in great request by the Ministry – had I a spark of ambition, I have opportunities enough – but I will be either far greater than all this can end in, even if it should end in my being Minister of state myself, or I will be nothing."[46] Sara probably found it difficult to imagine Coleridge as a Minister of State, and gloomily dwelt on the alternative.

On 21 October, his twenty-ninth birthday – "who on earth can say that without a sigh!" – the first snow fell, and Coleridge wrote to Southey of his own imminent departure. "Yesterday the snow fell – and today – O that you were here – Lodore full – the mountains snow-crested – & the dazzling silver of the Lake – this cloudy, sunny, misty, howling Weather! . . . I move southward in the hope that warm Rooms & deep tranquillity may build me up anew."[47] An "Ode to Tranquillity" was accordingly despatched to the *Morning Post*, a further warrant to Stuart of his professional intentions.[48]

But he lingered long enough at Greta Hall to superintend a little ceremony for Hartley. This was the traditional rite for boys of leaving off baby's petticoats for trousers, which was performed at the beginning of November. It touched his father deeply, and reminded him of all he had lost in domestic happiness.

Hartley . . . ran to & fro in a sort of dance to the Jingle of the Load of Money, that had been put in his breeches pockets; but he did not roll & tumble over and over in his old joyous way – No! it was an *eager* & solemn gladness, as if he felt it to be an awful aera in his life. – O bless him! bless him! bless him! If my wife loved me, and I my wife, half as well as we both love our children, I should be the happiest man alive – but this is not – will not be.[49]

The Wordsworths called on him at Keswick just before his departure and Dorothy noted in her Journal for 10 November: "Every sight and sound reminded me of him – dear, dear fellow, of his many walks to us by day and by night. I was melancholy, and could not talk, but at last eased my heart by weeping – nervous blubbering, says William."

6

By 16 November 1801, Coleridge was back in London, occupying bachelor lodgings found for him by Stuart, at 10 King Street, between Covent Garden and Fleet Street. Flinging himself into the oblivion of newspaper work, he immediately dashed off three long and brilliant articles on the newly formed Cabinet of Addington's administration. He plunged back gratefully into metropolitan society, seeing Godwin, Davy, Lamb and many others. "I saw so many People on Monday and walked to & fro so much, that I have been ever since like a Fish in air, who, as you perhaps know, lies panting & dying from excess of Oxygen."

Looking back at his isolation in the Lakes, he described his friendship with Wordsworth and Dorothy in a phrase too often quoted out of its humorous context to be properly understood. It was a piece of impiety conjured up for Godwin: "A great change from the society of W. & his sister – for tho' we were three persons, it was but one God – whereas here I have the amazed feeling of a new Polytheist, meeting Lords many, & Gods many."[50]

There was much talk in London of the peace treaty to be signed with Bonaparte, and in his sense of liberation, Coleridge half-planned a flit over to France with Davy to observe the new regime at first hand, and write about it for the *Morning Post*.[51] But instead his flit took him westwards to Stowey – despite Stuart's protests – departing on Boxing Day, and remaining for the first three weeks of January 1802 in the company of Poole and the Wedgwoods, planning metaphysical works on "Time and Space". He then returned to London on 21 January to attend Davy's scientific lectures at the Royal Institution ("to renew my stock of metaphors"). He took extensive chemical notes, and resumed work for the newspaper until the end of February.[52]

Throughout this time he sent a stream of letters to Grasmere, Keswick, and Gallow Hill, attempting to sort out his future. He now knew of Wordsworth's decision to marry Mary Hutchinson, and this produced a whirlpool of contradictory emotions. The genuine pleasure of seeing his friends settling their lives so securely in the Lakes was shadowed by terrible feelings of jealousy and despondency. More than ever he felt threatened with exclusion from the magic circle, and longed for reassurance through Asra. An expressive fragment of his correspondence with her (much of it later destroyed) survives from this period: "If I have not heard from you very recently, and if the last letter had not happened to be full of explicit love and feeling, then I conjure up shadows into substances – and am miserable."[53]

At the same time, his wife was astonished to receive a series of wild proposals about emigration, which indicate his equally strong desire to break away from the Lakes and establish their family life anew. "What do you say to a two years' Residence at Montpellier – under blue skies & in rainless air? In that case, we would go . . . from Liverpool to Bordeaux by Sea – . But I must first work. Southey would go that way to Lisbon – & spend some months with us."[54] He also teased her with his social success in London, a subject which he knew would appeal to her: "I assure you, I am quite a man of *fashion* – so many titled acquaintances – & handsome Carriages stopping at my door – & fine *Cards*." He said that if he remained for three months in the capital "passing criticisms on furniture & chandeliers", and receiving compliments from elegant women ("the *sweet* (N.B. musky) Lady Charlotte" – a distinct jab there) he would be a "Thing in Vogue – the very *tonish* Poet & Jemmy Jessamy fine Talker in Town".[55]

Yet inwardly he was full of doubts, and struggling to face up to his accumulated problems: procrastination and uncertainty about his writing; continual ill-health and use of opium (he had already discussed this earnestly with Poole); and an emotional life increasingly divided between his wife and Asra. His Notebooks, which are full of his metaphysical reading at the "old Libraries" – Paracelcus on witches, Baxter on preternatural spirits, a "Collection of Revelations & Visions" – also attempt to deal with his personal situation. He tried presenting the issues to himself in objective terms as if they belonged to another man. "A lively picture of a man, disappointed in marriage, & endeavoring to make a compensation to himself by virtuous & tender & brotherly friendship with an amiable Woman – the obstacles – the jealousies – the impossibility of it. – Best advice that he should as much as possible withdraw himself from pursuits of morals etc – & devote himself to abstract sciences."[56]

Sometimes he saw his lack of purpose as a metaphysical problem: "Something inherently mean in action. Even the Creation . . . disturbs my Idea of the Almighty's greatness – would do so, but that I conceive that Thought with him Creates."[57] At other times, he expressed his indecision as a single, highly suggestive, poetic image: "The soul a Mummy embalmed by Hope in the Catacomb."[58]

He saw that his personal crisis could be used for a whole "series of

Love Poems", which would explore the imagery of Love "in all the moods of the mind", whether philosophic, fantastic, mystical, religious, or those of "simple Feeling". They would comprise "all the practice, & all the philosophy of Love".[59] Here he was consciously beginning to shape the series of Asra poems, which in the following autumn he would group around "Dejection", for publication where possible. These entries also show that his personal crisis, far from overwhelming him, was becoming his real literary subject and leading him out of the cul-de-sac of "Christabel".

He turned to his friends as well, and not only to Poole, Southey and the Wordsworths. After an argument with Godwin, who had recently remarried, and felt himself neglected, Coleridge used the process of peace-making – one in which he was always adept and tender – to write an astonishingly intimate letter about his own failings as a man and husband. This shows a critical self-awareness of agonising acuteness. He told Godwin quite openly of his "domestic Discord", and the "heart-withering conviction" that though he could never be happy without his children, he could only be miserable with their mother. He admitted that he could be unreliable as a friend, lacking "steadiness & self-command", and often appearing "boisterous & talkative in general company" to the point of vanity. Yet he added that, as an author, he had neither vanity nor ambition – "I think meanly of all, that I have done". This itself produced unnatural "Langour, & Despondency" in his professional life.

To these faults, he added a vivid analysis of his own character and temperament, using Godwin's own language of associative psychology, together with one of his own unforgettable bird-images. It is balanced marvellously between solemnity and self-mockery.

> You appear to me not to have understood the nature of my body & mind. Partly from ill-health, & partly from an unhealthy & reverie-like vividness of *Thoughts*, & (pardon the pedantry of the phrase) a diminished Impressibility from *Things*, my ideas, wishes, & feelings are to a diseased degree disconnected from *motion & action*. In plain and natural English, I am a dreaming & therefore an indolent man. I am a Starling self-incaged, & always in the Moult, & my whole Note is, Tomorrow, & tomorrow, & tomorrow.

He saw how throughout his life he had lacked the "self-directing Principle", and how weak he was in resisting external pressures and impulses. "If I might so say, I am, as an *acting* man, a creature of mere Impact."[60]

Godwin noted privately: "I could write a character of Coleridge – the solemn – the superemphatical – the mass of immeasurable complacence in his own rare & unfinished conceptions, yet conceptions brought forth with throes indescribable. Look to his writings – the deeper he dives, the more absolutely beyond all comprehension."[61]

Coleridge's formidable self-indictment does not entirely escape the paradox of self-celebration; once again, the precision and energy of the language make their own plea for forgiveness. It would be endlessly repeated in Coleridge's private Notebooks over the next decade. It is also revealing to see how closely it corresponds to Wordsworth's criticisms of the Ancient Mariner as a dramatic character. For Coleridge was self-dramatising and establishing a literary persona as well.

To the normal human response, which Godwin himself must have made – what do you intend to do about these weaknesses? – Coleridge's implicit answer was, not to change them, but to explore and exploit them.

He would not – could not – break out of his cage; but he would make it a place to sing, his "whole Note". From his wife, from Asra, from the Wordsworths, from Lamb, from all his friends – he simply asked for love and understanding in return. To Coleridge, entranced by the vision of himself, that did not seem so very much. And sometimes his friends thought the same.

7

For all his deprecation of "motion and action", Coleridge was once again in whirling activity at the end of February 1802. He had just written a fourth article for Stuart on the Cabinet changes, and was negotiating with a bookseller for the trip to Paris to cover the imminent signing of the Peace of Amiens, including a tour through France and Switzerland.[62] Then news reached him from Grasmere that Asra had fallen ill, in consequence of the extremely awkward position in which his love-letters had placed her. This becomes plain from the "Letter to Sara Hutchinson", in which Coleridge speaks of the "complaining Scroll" he wrote to Asra, "which even to bodily sickness bruis'd thy Soul".[63] The Wordsworths had heard rumours of an open break between Coleridge and his wife. Abandoning all his professional commitments in London, he left King Street on 29 February and hurried north to Gallow Hill, arriving on 2 March, where he remained for ten days, helping Mary and Tom to nurse her.[64]

Very little is known about this crucial visit, in which Coleridge, also facing up to the reality of Mary's forthcoming marriage to Wordsworth, attempted to resolve the nature of his "virtuous & tender & brotherly friendship" with Asra. If they were ever to have become lovers, it would surely have been now, after the four months' absence from Greta Hall, the long soul-searching, and the passionate correspondence. It is impossible to know what intimacies took place, though the "Letter" is full of physical tenderness and what can only be described as Asra's generous bedded warmth and maternal body-heat:

> Sister & Friend of my devoutest Choice!
> Thou being innocent & full of love,
> And nested with the Darlings of thy Love,
> And feeling in thy Soul, Heart, Lips, & Arms
> Even what the conjugal & mother Dove
> That borrows genial Warmth from those, she warms,
> Feels in her thrill'd wings, blessedly outspread . . .[65]

This is one of the most sensuous of all passages in Coleridge's poetry, the erotic confusion between lover and nurse held in the hot, palpitating image of the receptive, tender mother dove. (It would be censored from "Dejection".) Yet it seems finally to insist on sexual innocence. Certainly what Coleridge agreed with Asra during those days at Gallow Hill was a form of renunciation, though the rightness of this would haunt him for the rest of his life.* The importance of his

*A number of scholars have worried at the nature of this renunciation, its reality or otherwise; and the world of sexual fantasy it opened up for Coleridge, especially after 1804. (See works cited in my preface, Note I.) Some have suggested sado-masochistic implications; others have speculated on masturbatory obsessions; Norman Fruman has written of the "final, frozen recoil from the warm and vivid world of Nature and the natural man" (see "Coleridge's Rejection of Nature", in *Coleridge's Variety*, 1985, op. cit.); and William Empson has remarked tartly: "one could not invent a more decisive moral object-lesson in favour of adultery" (see *Coleridge's Verse: A Selection*, 1972, op. cit.). A characteristic early fantasy appears in the Notebooks for December, 1803: "When in a state of pleasurable & balmy Quietness I feel my Cheek and Temple on the nicely made up Pillow in Caelibe Toro meo [on my celibate couch], the children in making this decision is also made clear in the draft poem. The terms on which they would now all live simultaneously together and apart is viewed by Coleridge with grief and self-pity:

> My own peculiar Lot, my house-hold Life,
> It is, & will remain, Indifference or Strife.
> While *ye* are *well & happy*, 'twould but wrong you
> If I should fondly yearn to be among you –
> Wherefore, O wherefore! should I wish to be
> A wither'd branch upon a blossoming Tree?[66]

Coleridge's Notebook is silent upon this visit, except to record that he "wept aloud" when he finally left on the mail on 13 March, in "a violent storm of snow & Wind".[67] On 15 March he was back at Keswick.

He remained at Greta Hall for just four days, and then walked over the windswept Dunmail Raise to spend the weekend at Grasmere. He arrived at dusk on Friday 19 March, as Dorothy anxiously recorded, "his eyes were a little swollen with the wind. I was much affected with the sight of him, he seemed half stupified." They stayed up late talking, and Dorothy's spirits were "much agitated". A letter also arrived from Asra at Gallow Hill.

During the weekend they talked of Wordsworth's marriage, and the plan to settle his affairs by a visit to Annette Vallon in France beforehand. Then Coleridge returned to Greta Hall, where the Wordsworths promised to join him the following week. When they came on 28 March, Wordsworth brought over the first four stanzas of

---

fire-gleam on my dear Books, that fill up one whole side from ceiling to floor of my Tall Study – & winds, perhaps are driving the rain, or whistling in frost, at my blessed Window . . . O then what visions have I had, what dreams – the Bark, the Sea, all the shapes & sounds & adventures made up of the Stuff of Sleep & Dreams, & yet my Reason at the Rudder: O what visions, (μαστοι) as if my Cheek & Temple were lying on me gale o' mast on – Seele meines Lebens ! [soul of my Life !] – & I sink down the waters, thro Seas & Seas – yet warm, yet a Spirit –." (*Notebooks*, I, 1718). Coleridge himself explains, "Pillow – mast high"; that is, a transliteration of the Greek, *mast-oi*, breasts; and Kathleen Coburn further glosses the coded fantasy: "me gale o' mast on: Greek, μεγαλόμαστοὖ large breasted." For further, perhaps Freudian, light on the punning, transliterated connection between swaying ships, high masts, and large breasts, reconsider Illustration I by Gustave Doré. But for the time being I modestly leave the reader to reflect on the possibilities of all these themes within my narrative, with two *caveats*: that Coleridge always had profound religious objections to divorce; and that there is little in the psychoanalytic line about relationships (with the exception, perhaps of his mother) that Coleridge does not explore with the greatest enthusiasm – in his letters and *Notebooks* – for himself.

the "Immortality" Ode which he had begun the previous day, picking up phrase for phrase the great theme of despondency and hope which Coleridge had already set out in "The Mad Monk". In reply, Coleridge secretly began to write the first version of "Dejection" in the form of the verse "Letter" to Asra, which is set in his study at Greta Hall on the stormy Sunday night of 4 April. The previous day, he and Wordsworth had climbed Skiddaw together.

8

A series of fragmentary Notebook entries record the poem's inception through the last days of March and the beginning of April. "A Poem on the endeavor to emancipate the soul from day-dreams & note the different attempts & the vain ones . . . Poem on this night on Helvellin; William & Dorothy & Mary – Sara & I . . . Poem on the length of our acquaintance; all the hours I have been thinking of her etc. Waterfall – tiny – & Leaf – still attracted still repelled . . . Great Mars making a circle under the Moon, on a white cloud."[68] But many other images also coalesced: from his Lake District walks, the kitchen at Gallow Hill, and those long nights in his study, going as far back as his lonely letter about the melancholy night-wind to Poole in the first winter of 1800.

The original manuscript draft is written on the pages of a vertically ruled accounts ledger, which Coleridge had intended for his wife's household bills.[69] As Coleridge put it in his Notebook: "No one can leap over his Shadow; Poets leap over Death."[70]

The difference between the first version ("Letter to Sara Hutchinson") and the final published version ("Dejection: an Ode") of the autumn are very great. They reveal the split between Coleridge's inner world of tempestuous emotions, and the outer persona of the public philosopher-poet who wrote for the *Morning Post.* The first version is a passionate declaration of love and renunciation, of almost hysterical intensity; the final version is a cool, beautifully shaped, philosophical Ode on the loss of hope and creative power, "the shaping spirit of Imagination". Coleridge moved from one to the other by a process of supreme artistic discipline, cutting, editing and self-censoring. Both versions carry their central themes with absolute conviction; but the split between the two suggests an agonising division of spiritual life, almost a kind of schizophrenia.

The first version is almost twice as long as the final one: 340 against 139 lines. It is unashamedly confessional throughout, mentioning Sara, William, Dorothy and Mary by name; and describing the failure of his marriage in painful detail: "two unequal Minds . . . two discordant Wills". Autobiographical passages subsequently censored from "Dejection", include his deprived boyhood at Christ's Hospital (". . . for cloistered in a city School / The Sky was all, I knew, of Beautiful"); the tender fireside scenes at Gallow Hill; the bitter contrast between the households at Grasmere and Keswick; the sense of his beloved children as hostages to fortune ("how they bind / and pluck out the Wing-feathers of my Mind, / Turning my Error to Necessity"); and the overwhelming image of Asra as the warm unattainable "conjugal & mother Dove".

The movement of the verse in the first version is swift and spontaneous, a true letter, and the tone is simultaneously exalted and self-pitying; while in "Dejection" the verse is cunningly shaped into eight irregular stanzas, and the outpouring of grief is carefully controlled and led into a climax of joy and blessing. The first version overwhelms the reader with its intimacy, its torrent of lament and letting-go, which is both shocking and compulsive. The final version holds the reader in an act of high, rhetorical attention, around the proposition that external nature cannot heal the poet (as Wordsworth believed it could) whose own powers are failing:

> I may not hope from outward forms to win
> The passion and the life, whose fountains are within.[71]

Yet however much "Dejection" is to be preferred as a finished work of art, the "Letter" draws more directly on Coleridge's true imaginative life. It is richer in, and closer to, those irrepressible sources of imagery which fill his Notebooks and private correspondence: the wind and sunlight over the fells, the moon and stars, the seasonal energy of plants and birds, the life of his children, the longing for love, friendship and a happy home. When he writes in the central passage (used in both versions) of his loss of confidence in a living, active, benevolent universe:

> O Sara! we receive but what we give,
> And in *our* Life alone does Nature live.
> Our's is her Wedding Garment, our's her Shroud –[72]

those contrasted images of the bridal dress and the winding sheet have more power and conviction in a poem that has evoked, in such confessional detail, the failings of an actual marriage and the frustrations of an unattainable love. Autobiography, in other words, gives the real authority to the vision of the poem; and to censor and deny it was for Coleridge an act of terrible self-discipline and self-deprivation.

Such differences between the public and private versions suggest the difficulty of Coleridge's situation as a poet, increasingly evident through the summer, in which he built up a whole body of Asra poems which he was unable to publish freely, without obvious betrayal. Yet it is still arguable that "Dejection", in its reduced and disciplined form, is the more universal work. It is a poem of Romantic crisis, in which Coleridge celebrated that paradox already apparent in his letters – that the subject of failure, of lost imaginative power, could itself produce great poetry, vividly imagined and metaphysically argued. "Dejection" takes its place in a dialogue with Wordsworth's "Immortality Ode" (not finished for a further two years) about the nature of human hope and creativity. They eventually formed part of a continuing Romantic tradition of spiritual self-examination and crisis, further explored in Shelley's "Ode to the West Wind" and Keats' "Melancholy". It was thus, by a further paradox, one of the most fruitful poems Coleridge ever wrote.*

---

*This literary grouping of Romantic "crisis-odes" and lyrics has been brilliantly explored by Lionel Trilling and Harold Bloom, "Romanticism", in *The Oxford Anthology of English Literature*, vol. II, 1973. While the central theme common to all the poets is the questioning of creative and visionary powers, and the assertion of various forms of hope and spiritual endurance, the underlying implications are perhaps theological. Beyond the problem of personal "authenticity" seems to lie the question whether life – or literature – can have real meaning without some form of Divine continuity or assurance within the structure of reality. These difficult issues have been most recently raised by George Steiner in *Real Presences*, Faber 1989, who considers the question, familiar to Coleridge, of whether language itself ultimately depends on the notion of Divine articulation within the universe. (See "Religious Musings", *P.W.*, p. 132, "For all that meets the bodily sense I deem,/Symbolical, one mighty alphabet"; and "Frost at Midnight", *P.W.*, p. 242.) The immense impact of "Dejection" itself, radiating far beyond the Lake District circle, will later emerge for example in the poem Shelley wrote in Italy in 1818, "Stanzas written in Dejection, near Naples".

THIRTEEN

Metaphysical Mountaineer

1

For Coleridge, the writing of "Dejection" was itself an act of release. During the summer of 1802 he sent carefully edited versions to Southey, to Tom Wedgwood and to a new friend William Sotheby. He was proud of the work, as he put it, "for the Truth & not for the Poetry".[1]

But at Grasmere the poem was initially greeted with dismay. On 21 April, Dorothy saw only the personal implications of his grief. "Coleridge came to us, and repeated the verses he wrote to Sara. I was affected with them, and was on the whole, not being well, in miserable spirits. The sunshine, the green fields, and the fair sky made me sadder; even the little happy, sporting lambs seemed but sorrowful to me." For Wordsworth it was a challenge that could only be answered in poetry.

At Greta Hall, as Coleridge later told Southey, there was a confrontation with his wife, in which he first openly threatened separation. This seems to have occurred in May, and after bitter home-truths shouted on both sides, to Coleridge's amazement the atmosphere in the household was transformed. His explanation to Southey is long and revealing on both sides:

> Mrs Coleridge was made *serious* – and for the first time since our marriage she felt and acted, as beseemed a Wife & a Mother to a Husband, & the Father of her children – She promised to set about an alteration in her external manners & looks & language, & to fight against her inveterate habits of Thwarting & unintermitting Dyspathy – this immediately – and to do her best endeavors to cherish other *feelings*. I on my part promised to be more attentive to all her feelings of Pride, etc etc and to try to correct my habits of impetuous & bitter censure. We have both kept our Promises . . . I have the most confident Hopes, that this happy Revolution in our domestic affairs will be permanent . . .[2]

One result of this entente was that Mrs Coleridge was soon "breeding again". Coleridge gives the impression of an armed truce, a sort of domestic Peace of Amiens, rather than a true recovery of love. But throughout the spring and summer he speaks no more of dejection, and refers to "Love & Concord" in his house in July.

Even Dorothy noticed the difference, and was amazed to report that Mrs Coleridge sent some clean clothes over to Grasmere for Coleridge when he was staying there in June ("the first time she ever did such a thing in her life"). But she still thought that even in this renovated state, Mrs Coleridge was the "lightest weakest silliest woman!"[3]

Coleridge himself was getting fit again, and did not seem exactly "a wither'd branch" at Grasmere. One evening he came over Grisedale Hause carrying an enormous bag of books for Wordsworth, having beaten through a "furious wind", and survived the attack of a "vicious cow, luckily without horns". Dorothy noted: "he looked and *was* well – strong he must have been for he brought a load over those Fells that I would not have carried to Ambleside for five shillings." Dorothy also referred to him as "our physician Coleridge" when writing to Asra.[4]

Indeed Wordsworth gives a remarkable buoyant picture of Coleridge in his "Stanzas in Thomson's Castle of Indolence", written in May 1802. Describing himself as a "weary Wight" driven by the "tempest strong" of verse-writing, he gives a very different impression of his companion from Keswick:

> With him there often walked in friendly guise,
> Or lay upon the moss by brook or tree,
> A noticeable Man with large grey eyes . . .
> Heavy his low-hung lip did oft appear,
> Deprest by weight of musing Phantasy;
> Profound his forehead was, though not severe . . .
> Noisy he was, and gamesome as a boy;
> His limbs would toss about him with delight,
> Like branches when strong winds the trees annoy . . .
> He would have taught you how you might employ
> Yourself; and many did to him repair, –
> And certes not in vain; he had inventions rare . . .
> Long blades of grass, plucked round him as he lay,
> Made, to his ear attentively applied,
> A pipe on which the wind would deftly play;
> Glasses he had, that little things display,

The beetle panoplied in gems and gold . . .
He would entice that other Man to hear
His music, and to view his imagery;
And, sooth, these two were each to the other dear . . .[5]

Coleridge's rapid recovery from the "Dejection" crisis is characteristic; both physically and mentally he was still astonishingly resilient, and his wife's capacity to adapt to the Asra situation – within limits – evidently helped. Indeed had they each demanded less of their marriage, and consciously settled for something more humdrum, it might have been a more enduring relationship.

But Coleridge's renunciation of Asra did not banish her from his mind. Though he did not see her again during the summer, he corresponded with her regularly – "my darling Sara" – and continued to work on other Asra poems, bringing some of them over to Grasmere on 4 May. The Wordsworths connived at this poetical worship, setting up a curious series of monuments to her over the fells: the rock of names, Sara's Seat (a bank of moss, planted round with flowers), and Sara's Gate.

Coleridge had set himself a long German poem by Saloman Gessner to translate as a poetic exercise, and the result was "The Picture, or, the Lover's Resolution", in which he adapted a romantic scene from Gessner to form the basis of a blank verse account of his lovelorn fell-wanderings. Though full of fine descriptive passages, which evoke the Lakes as he had previously evoked the Quantocks, the poem substitutes the gothic gloom of a Teutonic lover for more personal feelings. But at least these he could publish.

Here Wisdom might resort, and here Remorse;
Here too the love-lorn man, who, sick in soul
And of this busy human heart aweary,
Worships the spirit of unconscious life
In tree or wild-flower. – Gentle lunatic![6]

The "lunatic's" actual letters to Asra are thoroughly domestic, full of accounts of the children, which are expressive in a quite different way. Once again, Hartley is often the unconscious medium through which his father reveals himself. Coleridge wrote to Asra in June:

> Hartley told his Mother, that he was thinking all day – all the morning, all the day, all the evening – "what it would be, if there

were *Nothing*! if all the men, & women, & Trees, & grass, and birds & beasts, & the Sky, & the Ground, were all gone: *Darkness & Coldness* – & nothing to be dark & cold," . . . Hartley's *attachments* are excessively strong – so strong, even to places, that he does not like to go into town – or on a visit. The field, garden, & river bank – his Kitchen & darling Friend – they are enough; and Play fellows are burthensome to him – excepting *me* – because I can understand & sympathize with his wild Fancies – & suggest others of my own . . . My best Love –[7]

Coleridge also wrote to his brother George, in one of his increasingly infrequent efforts to maintain contact with Ottery, giving a contented enough account of life at Greta Hall. "Mrs S. Coleridge is but poorly; however her Disorder menaces me with no other Event, I suspect, than that of *a New Life*." The letter skirts professional difficulties but suggests that Coleridge was casting around for subjects to write on. "As to my Studies, they lie chiefly, I think, in Greek & German. (Hartley made me laugh the other day by saying, that Greek Letters were English Letters *dried up*.)"[8]

2

But the real subjects – poetry, metaphysics, fell-walking (now inextricably linked) – soon appeared in July and August.* On 12 July

* Coleridge's passion for climbing hills and scaling mountain peaks – evident during the Welsh tour, in the Quantocks, in the Hartz, in the Lake District, and later in Sicily – seems to have some deep imaginative correspondance with his metaphysical enquiries. Peaks and hill-tops are frequently given mystical significance in his poetry – for example in the climbing poem to Charles Lloyd, "To a Young Friend"; in "This Lime-Tree Bower"; in "The Mad Monk"; and in "A Stranger Minstrel". The panoramic view from a peak – as we shall see on Scafell – often brings moments of intense vision. Moreover the urge to climb out of civilisation, to get *above and beyond*, may suggest a sort of intellectual claustrophobia, a longing to free himself not merely from the restraints of domesticity, but from a narrow English culture. He climbed, as it were, to see across the whole of Europe. It is also true that the cult of mountain-tops, of spiritual communing with nature in her remotest places, becomes a characteristic of Romanticism as a whole. Beginning perhaps with Gray and Walpole's Swiss tour in search of the sublime in 1740, it is expressed equally in Wordsworth's visions from Snowdon and the Alps (both curiously baffled) in *The Prelude*; or the haunting paintings of Caspard David Friedrich's wanderers, gazing out from mountain spurs, hill-top escarpments, or perilous sea-cliffs. (See Gert Schiff, "An Epoch of Longing" in *German Masters of the Nineteenth Century*, Metropolitan Museum of Art, New York, 1981.) This Romantic mountain tradition infiltrates deep into nineteenth-century English feeling, producing consequences as diverse as the foundation of the British

the Wordsworths left Grasmere on a long expedition to Gallow Hill, and then France to see Annette Vallon. They remained away until after William and Mary's marriage in Yorkshire, and did not return to Grasmere until October. Their absence seems to have had a curiously liberating effect on Coleridge.

A new visitor appeared at Greta Hall, the poet and dramatist William Sotheby, whose sonnets Coleridge had once included in the collection made at Bristol. A warm friendship quickly sprang up: Sotheby, a sensitive and amusing man in his mid-forties – "you, my dear Sir! looked at a Brother Poet with a Brother's Eyes" – drew Coleridge out in long conversations ("unpardonably loquacious") and after his departure, encouraged Coleridge to begin a literary correspondence.[9] This was exactly the kind of audience that Coleridge needed at that moment: spontaneous, relaxed, highly intelligent, and above all, perhaps, outside the Wordsworthian sphere of influence.

Between July and September, Coleridge wrote six long and brilliant letters to Sotheby, which mark his emergence as a Romantic critic. They initiate many of the subjects he would later treat at length in the *Biographia*: the role of the poet, the functioning of the imagination, the nature of poetic language, and for the first time his awareness of a "*radical* Difference" between himself and Wordsworth.[10]

The prose of these letters is even finer than in those written to Godwin, and among the best that Coleridge ever wrote. His description of the poet at work is unforgettable, moving around the philosophical problem he had defined in "Dejection", and taking it forward in a vivid series of active images. He now argues that the poet is a metaphysician who actively engages with nature, who goes out of himself, who *hunts down* the otherness of being. Coleridge's revived belief in these powers shines out:

Alpine Club (1857), and – particularly relevant to Coleridge – Gerard Manley Hopkins' poem, "No worst, there is none", (1885) which ends:

> O the mind, mind has mountains; cliffs of fall
> Frightful, sheer, no-man-fathomed. Hold them cheap
> May who ne'er hung there. Nor does long our small
> Durance deal with steep or deep. Here! creep,
> Wretch, under a comfort serves in a whirlwind: all
> Life death does end and each day dies with sleep.

(See *Tourists, Travellers and Pilgrims*, by Geoffrey Hindley, Hutchinson 1983.)

> It is easy to cloathe Imaginary Beings with our own Thoughts & Feelings; but to send ourselves out of ourselves, to *think* ourselves in to the Thoughts and Feelings of Beings in circumstances wholly & strangely different from our own: hoc labor, hoc opus: and who has achieved it? Perhaps only Shakespeare. Metaphysics is a word, that you, my dear Sir! are no great Friend to. But yet you will agree, that a great Poet must be, implicitè if not explicitè, a profound Metaphysician. He may not have it in logical coherence, in his Brain & Tongue; but he must have it by *Tact*: for all sounds, & forms of human nature he must have the *ear* of a wild Arab listening in the silent Desert – the *eye* of a North American Indian tracing the footsteps of an Enemy upon the Leaves that strew the Forest; the *Touch* of a Blind Man feeling the face of a darling Child.[11]

Each of these three startling comparisons to the poetic process had been earned by Coleridge, after much thought. The Arab in the desert appears in two of his later poems, and the Notebooks at Greta Hall. "Mother listening for the *sound* of a still-born child – blind Arab list'ning in the wilderness."[12] The blind man feeling the face of his child arose from Coleridge's sensations of caressing Derwent in the dark, and also watching Sara cuddle her child.

Even the Red Indian is really Coleridge out on the fells. Once below Scafell that summer, he identified a party that had walked before him – consisting of a boy, a girl, a donkey and a dog – purely by their footprints. His annotations, measured against his walking-stick, suggest he would have survived well with a Susquehanna hunting party. "Brock Crag . . . came to the four-foot Stone, on which there are the clear marks of 4 feet, the first a beast's foot, so wide, the next a boy's shoe in the mire, the 3rd notch in my stick . . . the third a dog's Foot of the natural size, the fourth a child's Shoe, marked with the first notch . . . (The Shepherd Girl measuring her foot, to see if she wax'd, in the mark of the Boy's shoe)."[13]

Besides much else of critical interest, these letters contain his first version of the celebrated distinction between fancy and imagination, which was to become so important in the *Biographia*: "Fancy, or the aggregating Faculty of the mind – not *Imagination*, or the *modifying*, and *co-adunating* Faculty".[14] They also proclaim, in the very teeth of "Dejection", his continuing faith in some fundamental unity between the mind of man and the activities of nature. "Nature has her proper interest; & he will know what it is, who believes & feels, that every

Thing has a Life of its own, & that we are all *one Life*. A Poet's *Heart & Intellect* should be *combined, intimately* combined & *unified*, with the great appearances in Nature – & not merely held in solution & loose mixture with them, in the shape of formal Similies."[15]

These six letters, by themselves, could have formed a short critical treatise on Romantic poetry, had Coleridge considered this kind of publication. They begin to formulate a reply to Wordsworth's preface to the *Lyrical Ballads* (though this had been originally based on his own conversation), by challenging Wordsworth's notions of the lyric plain-style as too limited for an entire theory of poetic language. But Coleridge confided to Sotheby, in one of his comic-heroic bird images, that metaphysical criticism too often overwhelmed his own poetic impulse: "for I believe that by nature I have more of the Poet in me." When he began a poem in his study, too often he "beat up game" of a very different intellectual kind. ". . . Instead of a Covey of poetic Partridges with whirring wings of music, or wild Ducks *shaping* their rapid flight in forms always regular (a still better image of Verse) up came a metaphysical Bustard, urging its slow, heavy, laborious, earth-skimming Flight, over dreary & level Wastes."[16]

Yet it is the familar paradox that nothing could be less laborious or dreary than these letters. Coleridge's own delight in this correspondence with Sotheby was later revealed in September, by the sudden supremely impractical suggestion that Sotheby return to the Lakes from London and take five rooms for his family at Greta Hall.[17]

3

Coleridge's health and spirits continued good throughout July and August, except for occasional bowel attacks: "they are a seditious Crew". He copied out for Asra, with mock horror, an extract from Richard Warner's recent *Tour Through the Northern Counties*, describing the tourists' sights of Cumberland, which included "the gigantic Intellect & sublime Genius of COLERIDGE" at Keswick. Warner does not seem to have found the poet moping. "The animated, enthusiastic, & accomplished COLERIDGE, whose residence at Keswick gives additional charm to its impressive Scenery, inspired us with Terror [*A lying Scoundrel!*] while he described the universal Uproar [*O Lord! what a lie!*] that was awakened thro' the mountains by a sudden Burst of involuntary Laughter in the Heart of their Precipices . . ."[18]

He had his own idea for presenting the Lakes to the tourists. "I have often thought of writing a set of *Play-bills* for the vale of Keswick – for every day in the Year – announcing each Day the Performances, by his Supreme Majesty's Servants, Clouds, Waters, Sun, Moon, Stars, etc."[19] In this ebullient mood, even Hartley sometimes found his father too much: "Don't ask me so many questions, Papa! I can't bear it."[20]

At the beginning of August, Coleridge decided to relieve Greta Hall by taking himself off into the heart of the precipices, on a solitary expedition. He planned a strenuous nine-day walking and climbing tour across the central fells, going out as far as the sea at St Bees, and coming back over Scafell, the highest and wildest of the Lake District peaks. This he recounted in a superb letter-journal to Asra, written en route between 1 and 9 August, which forms the first literary description of the peculiarly English sport of fell-walking. Coleridge was in effect inventing a new kind of Romantic tourism, abandoning the coach and the high-road for the hill, the flask and the knapsack.

He drew himself a sketch-map of his intended route,[21] and set off on Sunday morning 1 August, with a converted besom-stick or broom-handle for his staff, and a climber's knapsack made from a large square of "natty green oilskin" folded into a string bag. The preparing of the staff, which "left the Besom scattered on the kitchen floor", particularly annoyed Mrs Coleridge.

In the knapsack he carried a spare shirt, stockings, cravat, and night-cap (which seems to have been Coleridge's equivalent of a sleeping-bag), together with paper twists of tea and sugar, his Notebook, and half a dozen quills with a portable inkwell.[22] His route ran south-westwards, on the first leg, up Newlands and over the passes into Buttermere and Ennerdale, in brisk windy sunlit weather.

At Buttermere, he drank tea outside the little inn, "and read the greater part of the Revelations", tuning his mood to the wild heights ahead. He must also have noticed in passing the handsome innkeeper's daughter, Mary Robinson, who was "celebrated by tourists under the name of *The Beauty of Buttermere*", as he would later write about a famous scandal associated with her "gap-toothed" charms, for the *Morning Post*.[23]

Moving on in increasingly exultant mood, he observed the waterfall of Scale Force, "which glimmered thro' the Trees, that hang before it like bushy Hair over a madman's Eyes", then climbed over the uncharted fells towards Ennerdale, watching the sunset from a remote sheepfold, "for of all things a ruined Sheepfold in a desolate place is the dearest to me, and fills me most with Dreams & Visions & tender thoughts of those I love best." He lodged the night with an old shepherd, a friend to Mr Jackson's, at the foot of the lake.[24]

The next day he passed along the mountains north of Wasdale, recording a wonderful evocation of those formidable presences, which always seem to brood with mysterious menace over the solitary traveller: "the Monsters of the Country, bare bleak Heads, evermore doing deeds of Darkness, weather-plots, & storm-conspiracies in the Clouds". Reaching the coast at St Bees, he spent two days pacing the hard sand, visiting Egremont and Calder Abbey, and sleeping fully clothed at "a miserable pot-house, dining on gin and water".

On 4 August, he turned inland again, pushing eastwards round Wastwater, "whole new world of Images in the water!", crossing the screes with their red streaks running in broad stripes through the stone, and into the wilderness at Kirk Fell, below Scafell Pike, where he stayed with a farmer known to Wordsworth. "I was welcomed kindly, had a good Bed, and left it after Breakfast."[25]

On 5 August he made his ascent of Scafell, clambering up the side of a torrent, and bringing his letter-journal up to date on the very summit, with "huge perpendicular Precipices" at his feet.

> O my God! what enormous Mountains these are close to me . . . the Clouds are hast'ning hither from the Sea – and the whole air seaward has a lurid Look – and we shall certainly have Thunder – yet here (but that I am hunger'd & provisionless) *here* I could lie warm, and wait methinks for tomorrow's Sun; and on a nice Stone Table am I now at this moment writing to you – between 2 and 3 o'clock as I guess, surely the first Letter ever written from the Top of Sca' Fell! . . .

Beyond the terrible abysses, the "frightfullest" cliff drops ("one sheep upon its only Ledge"), the huge sheer plunging pillars of bare lead-coloured stone all round him, his gaze lifted northwards to the distant paradise of Borrowdale, the Castle Crag, and Derwent Water, "and but for the haziness of the Air I could see my own House – I see clear enough where it stands." He sealed his letter with wafers kept in his portable inkhorn: "you shall call this Letter when it passes before you the Sca' Fell Letter; I must now drop down, how I may into Eskdale."[26]

He had seen, clearly enough, a vision of his own life from that majestic and terrible vantage point: beleaguered by precipices, menaced by thunder, haunted by visions of home, but all the time the quill pen moving companionably over the paper, talking, talking, talking, even in that wilderness.

The descent from Scafell Pike, made by sliding down a stepped series of sheer rock ledges, chafing the skin of his chest with friction burns, and making his muscles tremble with exhaustion and vertigo, produced an effect of almost religious intensity. He had thrown his faithful broomstick before him, only to find that with two ledges left to drop, he could neither continue down, nor climb back up. For a moment he was panic-stricken, lodged like the sheep on the face of that huge mountain-side, utterly alone.

His reaction to this situation (a climber's nightmare) and his description of it, shows Coleridge at his finest pitch: a comic hero beset by tragic visions, spiritual, intelligent, and supremely self-aware of his own psychological drama:

> My Limbs were all in a tremble – I lay upon my Back to rest myself, & was beginning according to my Custom to laugh at myself for a Madman, when the sight of the Crags above me on each side, & the impetuous Clouds just over them, posting so luridly & so rapidly northward, overawed me. I lay in a state of almost prophetic Trance & Delight – & blessed God aloud, for the powers of Reason & the Will, which remaining no Danger can overpower us! O God, I exclaimed aloud – how calm, how blessed am I now: I know not how to proceed, how to return; but I am calm & fearless & confident; if this Reality were a Dream, if I were asleep, what agonies had I suffered! what screams! – When the Reason & the Will are away, what remains to us but Darkness & Dimness & a bewildering Shame, and the Pain that is utterly Lord over us, or fantastic Pleasure, that draws the Soul along swimming through the air in many shapes, even as a Flight of Starlings in a Wind.[27]

He had no need to tell Asra that this was the dilemma of his whole life now: between reality and dream, courage and submission, writing and opium. Would his imaginative genius sustain him as a rational mind, a soul; or condemn him to be a screaming flock of bird-like impulses shifting in every wind?

Coleridge finally escaped from Scafell by clever use of a vertical gulley, or chimney, in the rock, slipping down "between two walls, without any danger or difficulty", his knapsack on his hip. Below, he sat out the overtaking thunderstorm in another sheepfold, and afterwards shouted out all their names – Asra, the Wordsworths, his children – across the valley, when "Echo came upon Echo".[28] He wished he could remain there for ever, by the mountains and lonely tarns, like some mad, gentle shepherd, "a wanderer seeking his Sheep forever, in storm & snow especially."[29]

But he returned, by Coniston, Bratha and Grasmere, on 9 August, "quite sweet and ablute", his boot-soles ripped and his trouser-knees in tatters.[30] He told his wife tactfully that the whole expedition had cost him just thirteen shillings, of which four shillings had been given away "to Bairns, & foot-sore Wayfarers". Sara replied that this did not include the price of clothes repairs.

4

Almost immediately after his return, Charles and Mary Lamb arrived unannounced on the doorstep of Greta Hall, finally come to see the wizard in his northern kingdom. Despite dark looks from Sara, Coleridge received them "with all the hospitality in the world" and they remained for three weeks, touring the Lakes until early September, in his company. This opportunely put off all further questions of work.

Lamb was delighted with Coleridge's study, observing that it very properly contained a blazing fire even in midsummer: it was "a large antique ill-shaped room, with an old-fashioned organ, never played upon, big enough for a church, Shelves of scattered Folios, an Eolian Harp, & an old sofa". He pretended to be nervous of the vast panorama of surrounding fells, "great floundering bears & monsters they seemed"; but Coleridge immediately hurried him up Skiddaw and Helvellyn, and took him into Borrowdale to pay his respects to the waterfall of Lodore.

Lamb afterwards told Coleridge, "I shall remember your mountains to the last day I live. They haunt me perpetually."[31] He was now convinced that there was such a thing "as that which tourists call *romantic*"; though he added to his friend Manning that they made rather "a spluttering about it, and toss their splendid epithets around them".[32]

He made no comment on Coleridge's marital situation. But he clearly felt that his friend was too cut off from London, and remarked that for himself he would "mope & pine away" without Fleet Street and the Strand. "Still, Skiddaw is a fine Creature."[33] But there was something about this visit that determined Lamb to be "sober".

5

At the end of August, Coleridge wrote Asra a study of the Lake District waterfalls, several of which he had visited with Lamb. He described Lodore in Borrowdale as "the Precipitation of the fallen Angels from Heaven, Flight & Confusion, & Distraction, but all harmonized into one majestic Thing."[34] He had crawled up Moss Force, near Buttermere, on hands and knees, slipping on the spongy vegetation, and cutting his hands where the rock was bare. He found the "stretched & anxious state of mind" while climbing, made his impressions more vivid.

He was fascinated by the dynamics of the flowing water, and tried to convey the complex appearance of life and deliberate movement. "The mad water rushes thro' its *sinuous* Bed, or rather prison of Rock, with such rapid Curves, as if it turned the Corners not from the mechanic force, but with foreknowledge, like a fierce & skilful Driver; great Masses of Water, one after the other, that in twilight one might have feelingly compared them to a vast crowd of huge white Bears, rushing, one over the other, against the wind – their long white hair shattering abroad in the wind."[35] He compared the different structures of Moss Force, Scale Force and Lodore, and considered the latter unequalled by anything he had seen in prints and sketches of the Scottish and Swiss cataracts.

Water as usual made him metaphysically aware of the underlying energies of nature, and transcendental implications, as if a waterfall was a kind of perpetual Brahman prayer-wheel, worshipping its maker.

"What a sight it is to look down on such a Cataract! – the wheels, that circumvolve in it – the leaping up & plunging forward of that infinity of Pearls & Glass Bulbs – the continual *change* of the *Matter*, the perpetual *Sameness* of the *Form* – it is an awful Image & Shadow of God & the World."[36]

6

After Lamb's departure, Coleridge at last returned to his writing-desk and began to submit material to the *Morning Post.* He started with a series of four long articles, which ran throughout September, making a Plutarchian comparison between the French Republic under Bonaparte and the Roman Republic under the Caesars. He also submitted a substantial body of poetry which included "Dejection", and several of the other disguised Asra poems of the summer, together with twenty brief epigrams.

To Tom Wedgwood he was deliberately dismissive of his efforts: "The Poetry, which I have sent, has been merely the emptying out of my Desk. The Epigrams are wretched indeed; but they answered Stuart's purpose better than better things. – I ought not to have given any signature to them whatsoever."[37] But the truth seems to be that, within the restrictions implied by the Asra materials, Coleridge was now attempting to establish his poetic identity separate from Wordsworth. Certainly he had never previously published such a continuous series of poems in the newspaper, as this autumn.

The series ran as follows:

6 September: "The Picture, or, the Lover's Resolution", the account of his lovelorn hill-wanderings adapting the German poetry of Gessner, which runs to 186 lines.

11 September: "Hymn before Sun-rise, in the Vale of Chamouni", a psalm-like praise of the mountains and waterfalls, 85 lines long, which is also – as will be seen in a moment – partly an adaption.

17 September: "The Keepsake", the earliest of his Asra poems, sufficiently illusive to be published unaltered.

24 September: "Inscription for a Fountain on a Heath", which uses the emblem of the dancing sand in the spring as a symbol of love.

4 October: "Dejection: an Ode", which was selected to appear on the day of Wordsworth's and Mary's marriage, and which Coleridge must have considered as a kind of epithalamium in its specially edited version.

7 October: "An Ode to the Rain", a piece of fluent light verse, humorously looking forward to the departure of unwelcome guests from Greta Hall. (Not, one assumes, Charles and Mary Lamb.)

11 October: the main body of the epigrams, including one which ironically uses Annette's name, in a teasing reference to Wordsworth's wild oats in France.

16 October: "Answer to a Child's Question", a lyric poem for Hartley on the language of birds.

19 October: "The Day-Dream: From an Emigrant to his Absent

Wife", a carefully domesticated adaption of the erotic Asra poem describing their dalliance at Gallow Hill, "A Day Dream".

Particular light is thrown on Coleridge's attempt to re-invent his poetic persona this autumn, for the readers of the *Morning Post*, by the true history of the "Chamouni" poem, which contains an even more elaborate mystification than the Asra poems. Here Coleridge became involved in a self-disguising strategy that entailed both deception and downright plagiarism. Psychologically the case is fascinating, for it shows him trying to play the role of the inspired bard of popular conceptions, while actually suppressing his own poetic vision.

Coleridge originally set out to use material from his mountain-climbing and waterfall letters and journals as the basis for a poem evoking the transcendent energies he had continually glimpsed upon the fells. His vision upon Scafell and Carrock, and his perilous studies of Moss Force and Lodore, certainly provided him with marvellous perceptions already gathered. But Coleridge was unable to transfer these into poetry – indeed the whole conception of "transferring" what already existed so intensely in his prose was questionable. Instead, he fell back on the device of translating and adapting a short German poem, by Friederike Brun, about the mountains and glaciers at Chamonix, to provide the structure for a conventional and overtly religiose poem full of booming Teutonic piety.

Even in the best passages, closest to his own observations, this foreign rhetoric weakens the borrowed verse by comparison with his own prose:

> And you, ye five wild torrents fiercely glad!
> Who called you forth from night and utter death,
> From dark and icy caverns called you forth,
> Down those precipitous, black, jagged rocks,
> For ever shattered and the same for ever?
> Who gave you your invulnerable life,
> Your strength, your speed, your fury, and your joy,
> Unceasing thunder and eternal foam?[38]

The rhythms are powerful, but one looks in vain for the manic white bears, the prayer-wheels, or the falling angels. All have been suppressed. Lamb, for one, immediately noticed the difference, and pronounced himself "offended" by the Swiss mountains Germanically shouting "God" to each other, when he had only ever heard the "Cumbrian mountains" echoing with Coleridge's own shouts, syllables "assuredly of no Godlike Sound".[39]

Coleridge published the poem without acknowledgment to Brun (the usual newspaper convention of the day was to state, "from the German"). Instead he added a very beautiful introductory note developing the poetic fiction that he had written the poem among the frozen icefields of Chamonix; though of course he had never been to Switzerland in his life. "The beautiful *Gentiana major*, or greater gentian, with blossoms of the brightest blue, grows in large companies a few steps from the never-melted ice of the glaciers. I thought it an affecting emblem of the boldness of human hope, venturing near, and, as it were, leaning over the brink of the grave."[40] As it happened, this too was based upon Friederike Brun's footnotes.

These were not perhaps very serious falsifications (Brun's poem was only twenty lines as against Coleridge's eighty-five). But they are significant in the light both of Coleridge's later, and graver, plagiarisms; and of his self-doubts about his own poetic authority. He was now inventing a bardic role, for public admiration, and cutting himself off from his own true sources in nature which, by tragic irony, were ever more richly present in his private writing, to Asra, to Sotheby, and in his own Notebooks.

On the day before publication, 10 September, he tried to explain something of the situation to Sotheby. While on Scafell, he told his sympathetic friend:

> I involuntarily poured forth a Hymn in the manner of the *Psalms*, tho' afterwards I thought the Ideas etc disproportionate to our humble mountains – & accidentally lighting on a short Note in some swiss Poems, concerning the Vale of Chamouny, & its Mountain, I transferred myself thither, in the Spirit, & adapted my former feelings to these grander external objects. You will soon see it in the Morning Post – & I should be glad to know whether & how far it pleased you.[41]

But even here he could not bring himself to mention Brun's poem by name; and it was not in fact noted until after his death, in an article by Thomas De Quincey in 1834.[42] Worst of all, what he had actually "poured forth" on Scafell, was completely suppressed.

7

As autumn returned, so did dejection. Alone in his study, he found himself sometimes bursting into tears. There was a recurrence of domestic rows with Sara: "ill-tempered Speeches sent after me when I went out of the House, ill-tempered Speeches on my return, my friends received with freezing looks, the least opposition or contradiction occasioning screams of passion."[43] So he told Tom Wedgwood.

In October, his bad dreams began again – a sure sign of renewed opium-taking: school nightmares, a distorted vision of Dorothy as a fat, bloated, red-haired harpy; and a grim vision of being "followed up & down by a frightful pale woman who, I thought, wanted to kiss me, & had the property of giving a shameful Disease by breathing in the face."[44] All kinds of sexual guilt were thinly disguised here. He sympathised intensely with Hartley's new-found fear of the dark, when the child begged for a candle at night to keep at bay the appearance of ugly faces, which *seemed* to fill the bedroom: "the Candle cures the SEEMS."[45]

In long letters he tried to entice Southey to winter with him at Greta Hall (having failed with Sotheby), and then resorted to his old habit of dreaming up wildly ambitious literary projects: a two-volume history of English prose ("these will be finished by January"); a monograph on the subject of poetry; an Epic on the Fall of Jerusalem; and finally an entire encyclopaedia. Southey wrote back crisply: "As to your essays etc etc, you spawn plans like a herring: I cnly wish as many of the seed were to vivify in proportion . . ."[46]

In the privacy of his Notebook, Coleridge reverted to one of his faithful consoling bird-images: "I lay too many Eggs (in the hot Sands of this Wilderness, the World!) with Ostrich Carelessness & Ostrich Oblivion. The greater part, I trust, are trod underfoot, & smashed; but yet no small number crawl forth into Life, some to furnish Feathers for the Caps of others, & still more to plume the Shafts in the Quivers of my Enemies, of them that lie in wait against my Soul."[47] It was a curious mixture of truth and paranoia.

By the end of October 1802 the old winter pattern was reasserting itself strongly: escape from Greta Hall, emigration plans, newspaper work for Daniel Stuart. A new element appeared in an invitation from Tom Wedgwood to join him in the West Country, where they could mature a plan to recuperate together in the south of France. Tom was in fact mortally ill, dosing himself with drugs, and desperate for a travelling companion. His physical state fluctuated even more than Coleridge's, and his moods were as uncertain. But Coleridge grasped eagerly at the idea, despite his boasted incompetence in anything more than dictionary French: "as to Pronunciation, all my Organs of Speech, from the bottom of the Larynx to the Edge on my Lips, are utterly and naturally Anti-gallican". The idea of helping someone evidently more desperate than himself promised a sort of release: "If only I shall have been any Comfort, any Alleviation, to you – I shall feel myself at ease."[48]

His wife, who was expecting the new baby in January, received this news with barely suppressed fury. Coleridge left Greta Hall on 4 November 1802, taking the chance of a missed coach-connection to spend the day with Asra, who was staying with relatives at Penrith. This precipitated a long and angry exchange of letters between Coleridge and Sara, which continued through November and December. But these gradually became more conciliatory in tone, until he was again calling her "my dear Love" and the old teasing "Sally Pally".

During this correspondence, Coleridge analysed both their characters at length, to Sara's disadvantage, adding the considered opinion that "in sex, acquirements, and in the quantity and quality of natural endowments whether of Feeling, or of Intellect, you are the Inferior."[49] He also expressed the wish that Asra might attend Sara on her lying-in, "because you will hardly have another opportunity of having her by yourself & to yourself, & of learning to know her, such as she really is." His lack of marital tact had become quite formidable. Yet there was a sort of unworldly earnestness in some of what he said, which must still have touched his wife: "how much of our common Love & Happiness depends on your loving those whom I love, why should I repeat?"[50]

He was also open with her on the subject of opium, which he was now consciously hiding from most of his friends: "once in the 24 hours (but not always at the same hour) I take half a grain of purified opium, equal to 12 drops of Laudanum – which is not more than an 8th part of what I took at Keswick, exclusively of Beer, Brandy, & Tea, which last is undoubtedly a pernicious Stimulant."[51] The idea that tea was the most dangerous in his battery of drugs may have been a joke; or just a further provocation.

8

As so often, at the very moment when he appeared most unfixed and purposeless, Coleridge produced another brilliant burst of journalism for Stuart, written almost on the wing. During October and November he published a series of open letters to Charles James Fox, challenging his view of Bonaparte as a peacemaker in Europe. These were profoundly influential in London and shifted the *Morning Post* towards an increasingly patriotic stance. He also wrote an incisive analysis of the phenomenon of Jacobinism in England, simultaneously attacking its philosophy, and defending those who had been misled by it. This article, of which he was justly proud, appeared on 21 October 1802, and marks an historic point in the crisis of English radicalism.

Under the ironic title, "Once a Jacobin Always a Jacobin", Coleridge asked why government circles should be so relentless in their persecution of erstwhile radicals, arguing his old case for political unity in a world of fanaticism. Why should the whole English nation be "clapped under hatches"? Why should one-time radicals be so vindictively pursued? "Is it because the creed which we have stated, is dazzling at first sight to the young, the innocent, the disinterested, and to those who, judging of men in general, from their own uncorrupted hearts, judge erroneously, and expect unwisely?"

Here he was undoubtedly speaking for a whole generation of those who had once been excited by the first hopes of the French Revolution, and he courageously implicated himself in the argument. Yet he strenuously denied that he had ever been a convert "to the system of French Politics", or the abolition of property; and in this last denial he was of course covering up his old Pantisocratic ideals.[52]

He ended the article on the offensive, stating that he was contemptuous of those "who would turn an error in speculative politics into a sort of sin against the Holy Ghost, which in some miraculous and inexplicable manner shuts out not only mercy but even repentance". The parallel between political and religious fanaticism would later be developed in *The Friend.* Lamb read these political essays "daily", and said he was "particularly pleased" with the Jacobin broadside: "it was plausible *ad populum.*"[53]

But most memorable among this crop of newspaper work, and most characteristic of his extraordinary versatility, was a parallel series of five sensational articles on the celebrated Lake District scandal of the Beauty of Buttermere, which appeared in the *Morning Post* between 11 October and 31 December. Here Coleridge convincingly transformed himself into a popular journalist producing a scoop story. He gave it a colourful "human angle"; yet also found literary undertones and psychological subtleties worthy of one of the Border Ballads.

The "Beauty" was Mary Robinson, the innkeeper's daughter he had glimpsed on his tour. She had been seduced into a Scottish elopement by a handsome, unscrupulous, confidence-trickster, John Hatfield, travelling under the assumed name of the Honourable Colonel Alex Augustus Hope MP.[54]

Coleridge did some rapid investigative reporting, conducted interviews, collected local press pieces, embroidered on rumours, until his dramatic instalments of the unfolding story became the talk of London. They ran initially under the title of "The Romantic Marriage" and then, as the plot thickened, "The Keswick Imposter". He packed them with all the necessary, novelettish details of love-letters ("put into my hand"); of dashes "at dusk" over the Glaramara Pass; and of a "handsome dressing box" – containing pistols, silver trinkets etc – left behind by the absconding villain.[55]

Coleridge carefully built up Mary as a Romantic child of nature from the Lakes, beautiful and betrayed; while Hatfield became a city-seductor, an Iago-like villain of mysterious – and no less Romantic – evil. Sexual passion was the undoing on Mary's side. But Hatfield's motives remained dark and psychopathic – beneath greed and power, the instincts of a forger, the urges of an adventurer, remained some hidden impulse: perhaps the instinct to corrupt innocence itself.

The story continued to fascinate Coleridge, and eight months later, in August 1803, when Hatfield had been arrested and unmasked, Coleridge attended his trial at the Carlisle Assize. He even interviewed Hatfield in the condemned cell (impersonation of an MP was a capital offence), in a last attempt to explain the engima, but concluded: "*vain*, a hypocrite; it is not by mere Thought, I can understand this man."[56]

One can readily see why the story fascinated him: Mary Robinson was a real-life figure not unrelated to Christabel, while Hatfield had the "motiveless malignity" of a Shakespearean villain. There may also have been something about Hatfield as a "forged" personality, which touched Coleridge more closely, closer than "mere thought".

Wordsworth, Lamb, and De Quincey all left detailed reflections on the Beauty of Buttermere, and several novelists have since taken up the case (most recently Melvyn Bragg). Coleridge himself considered treating the subject fictionally.[57]

Coleridge took his role as yellow journalist with a pinch of salt. His articles – as Special Correspondent from Keswick – have a deliberate degree of purple gothic heightening. "From this time our adventurer played a double game. It seems to have been a maxim with him to leave as few white interspaces as possible in the crowded map of his villainy . . ."[58] He also rather spoiled the solemnity of the proceedings at Carlisle Assize, alarming "the whole Court, Judges, Counsellors, Tipstaves, Jurymen" by "hallooing to Wordsworth" on the other side of the Hall – "*Dinner!*"[59] Hatfield was executed in August 1803; Mary remarried in 1807 and lived happily at Caldbeck in the northern fells.

9

Coleridge's articles were datelined from Keswick, from London, from Bristol, and from Wales: an indication of manic need for motion that had once again overcome him this winter. Stuart had no hope of holding his contributor to a regular contract, though no one else among his staff-writers could produce such a range of poetry, political analysis, foreign policy polemics, and good old-fashioned scoop-writing. Though he visited Greta Hall at Christmas, Coleridge did not settle there again until April 1803, a gap of five months; so Sara Coleridge must also have considered him as something of a freelance husband.

The thread upon which he flew like some brightly coloured bead, was Tom Wedgwood. Having left Greta Hall on 4 November, he was at Cote House the following week, and by 16 November travelling with Tom through the valley of the Usk to visit cousins in Pembrokeshire. They passed by St Clears and Laugharne, where Coleridge interviewed two "fine Parrots screaming away" in a window, and collected epitaphs in the churchyard. "While I took the copy, the Groundsel showered its white Beard on me."[60]

On 21 November they were at Cresselly with the cousins, where they remained until mid-December; Coleridge flirted with "Jessica, Emma, & Frances", gorged himself on clotted cream, dosed himself with ginger tea and laudanum, and wrote his journalism. It was a regime that rather suited him, with the background of Sally

Wedgwood playing on the pianoforte "divinely", as he provokingly informed Sara. "Warm Rooms, warm Bedrooms, Music, pleasant Talking . . . no *difficulties* in my Dreams, no Pains, no Desires."[61]

Travel plans became more and more visionary. "T Wedgwood's hopes & schemes are again all afloat . . . Cornwall perhaps, – Ireland perhaps – perhaps Cumberland – possibly, Naples, or Madeira, or Teneriffe. I don't see any likelihood of our going to the Moon, or to either of the Planets, or fixed Stars – & that is all I can say. Write immediately, my dear Love! & direct to me – where? That's the Puzzle."[62] Coleridge had learned something about Sara's wifely worries, however: winging through this cosmological haze came one solid object: a draft for £50 advance on the Wedgwood annuity, which would pay all the Greta Hall rent and bills, except possibly the butcher's.[63]

News of Sara's premature labour-pains finally spun him north again. Coleridge and Wedgwood arrived at Greta Hall on Christmas Eve, just in time to miss the birth of a daughter – now his third surviving child – another Sara. "I had never thought of a Girl as a possible event," he told Southey, "however I bore the sex with great Fortitude."[64]

Despite special blankets and pots of best butter, Tom was not comfortable at Greta Hall, and soon decamped to his friend Luff's house at Glenridding, over the eastern fells of the Helvellyn range on Ullswater. Coleridge spent most of January 1803 pounding back and forth over the dividing range between Derwent Water and Ullswater: he could not remain in his own house, and he was soon ill again with rheumatics, groin-strain, and swollen hands.[65] Where, in heaven or earth, could he go now?

FOURTEEN

Exile

1

By January 1803, Coleridge's restlessness had become as unappeasable as his opium addiction. Indeed the two seemed closely entwined, driving him through his dreams as through his days. His travel schemes with Tom Wedgwood now projected a comparatively modest expedition "to Paris, thro' Switzerland, to Rome, Naples, & perhaps Sicily" (where the Mad Monk had his cavern).[1] He still thought of some kind of community with the Wordsworths, "in some part of Italy or Sicily" among country people.[2]

He saw Asra at Grasmere, and rode with her "on a double horse" to Keswick, discussing the impossibilities of their friendship. There was now a chance – that Dorothy seems to have foreseen – that she might marry Wordsworth's brother John.[3] Coleridge claimed to greet the prospect tenderly. In 1808 he would write to Stuart, "Had Capn Wordsworth lived, I had hopes of seeing her blessedly married, as well as prosperously."[4]

His walking on the fells this winter was wild and almost obsessive. He had brought back special walking boots from Wales, which he described lovingly in his Notebooks like a true fell-addict, a fine leather upper with an oil-silk cuff six inches above the ankle, and a back-strap for pulling them on. He also noted his special leather-treatment, a compound of "Mutton suet, Hog's Lard, and Venice Turpentine" mixed and melted, and "always put on warm, Shoe or boot being held to the fire, while it is being rubbed in".[5]

On one walk, from Glenridding to Grasmere over Kirkstone Pass in a hailstorm, he almost collapsed from exposure. "I am no novice in mountain-mischiefs; but such a storm as this was I never witnessed, combining the intensity of the Cold with the violence of the wind & rain. The rain-drops were pelted, or rather *slung*, against my face, by the Gusts, just like splinters of Flint . . . My hands were all shrivelled up . . . I was obliged to carry my stick under my arm. O it was a wild business!"[6] The purpose of this expedition was simply to order a trout for Tom's dinner.

2

On 14 January he wrote a magnificent evocation of his fell-walking for Tom, which turned it into a personal Romantic credo. It deserves its place, far more one might think than his "Hymn before Sunrise", in any anthology for Lake District lovers:

> I never find myself at one within the embracement of rocks & hills, a traveller up an alpine road, but my spirit courses, drives, and eddies, like a Leaf in Autumn: a wild activity, of thoughts, imaginations, feelings, and impulses of motion, rises up from within me – a sort of *bottom-wind*, that blows to no point of the compass, & comes from I know not whence, but agitates the whole of me; my whole Being is filled with waves, as it were, that roll & stumble, one this way, & one that way, like things that have no common master. I think, that my soul must have pre-existed in the body of a Chamois-chaser . . . The farther I ascend from animated Nature, from men, and cattle, & the common birds of the woods, & fields, the greater becomes in me the Intensity of the feeling of Life . . . In these moments it has been my creed, that Death exists only because Ideas exist: that Life is limitless Sensation; that Death is a child of the organic senses, chiefly of the Sight; that Feelings die by flowing into the mould of the Intellect . . . I do not think it possible, that any bodily pains could eat out the love & joy, that is so substantially part of me, towards hills, & rocks, & steep waters! And I have had some Trial.[7]

This is more than mere hill-walking, it is an evocation of the state of creativity itself. The process of inspiration, the outpouring of inner being, the artist's confidence in immortality, were all enacted for Coleridge in these wild, solitary journeyings.

But Coleridge could not disappear permanently into the fells, occasionally coming down to Keswick or Grasmere or Glenridding, like some mad shepherd or entranced scholar-gypsy. Though sometimes it seemed his only plan. By the end of January he was off again with Tom, fleeing back to the West Country, where he shuttled throughout February between Cote House, Southey's lodgings at Bristol, and Poole at Stowey.

He told his Bristol friend, Samuel Purkis: "for the last five months of my Life I seem to have annihilated the present Tense with regard to place – you can never say, where *is* he? – but only – where *was* he? where *will* he be?" He was still theoretically following Tom Wedgwood, "a Comet tied to a Comet's Tail", but their combined path "must needs be damnably eccentric, & a defying Puzzle to all Astronomers from La Lande & Herschell to YZ".[8]

He was profoundly upset by Tom's continuing illness, now diagnosed as "a thickening of the Gut" – probably cancer of the stomach – and felt that they would never get away to the Mediterranean. (Tom in fact did go briefly to France in the spring, but soon returned.) Coleridge's final solution was to try an inner trip, a concentrated drug-session with his friend in February. He applied to Sir Joseph Banks, and also to John Wordsworth, for a large supply of Indian Hemp or "Bang". On 17 February he wrote from Stowey to Cote House that the precious package had arrived in the post, from Banks via an intermediary, Samuel Purkis. "Sir Joseph adds in a postscript – 'It seems almost beyond a doubt, that the Nepenthe was a preparation of the Bang known to the Ancients.'" There were no instructions as to the size of the dose.[9] Coleridge enthused as best he could: "We will have a fair trial of *Bang* – Do bring down some of the Hyoscyamine Pills & I will give a fair Trial of opium, Hensbane, & Nepenthe. Bye the bye, I always considered Homer's account of the *Nepenthe* as a *Banging* lie."[10] The experiment took place at Josiah's house at Gunville in Dorset. It was not a success, and by early March Tom had returned to Cote, "hopeless, heartless, planless".[11]

Coleridge's stock as a miracle-worker had rather fallen among the Wedgwoods. Kitty Wedgwood, at Cote, had observed that with Coleridge "an excessive goodness and sensibility is put too forward, which gives an appearance, at least of conceit, and excites suspicion that it is acting."[12] Coleridge left for London a week later, himself much depressed.

3

From Stowey he had written to Southey a long and perceptive letter, analysing their respective marriages and professional situations. He knew that he himself was "talked of, as the man of Talents, the splendid Talker, & as a Poet too"; but he considered Southey the true poet, and that the forthcoming publication of his long poem

Madoc would make his name.[13] Like Wordsworth, Southey had successfully established his private life too.

> You are happy in your marriage Life; & greatly to the honor of your moral self-government, Qualities & manners are pleasant to, & sufficient for, you, to which my Nature is utterly unsuited: for I am so weak, that warmth of manner in a female House mate is necessary to me . . . I am happy & contented in solitude, or only with the common Inhabitants of a Batchelor House: an old woman, and a sharp Child.[14]

He considered it an "evil day" for himself when he married Sara, but he was determined that "it shall not be an evil day for her", in as far as he could be her "Protector & Friend". The trouble was his own weaknesses of temperament: "O dear Southey! I am no Elm! – I am a crumbling wall, undermined at the foundation!" He had two practical solutions: first, that Southey should come to live at Keswick, "& do nothing but great works" – as a kind of substitute for his own failures. Second, that he himself should insure his life for a large sum, and go abroad.[15]

In London he put one part of this scheme into immediate operation, by applying to the Equitable Assurance Society for a Life Policy in favour of Mrs Coleridge, which would bring her £1,000 in the event of his death. Hanging, drowning and suicide were not covered.[16] The premium was high, £27 per annum, and he had some doubts if his "phiz" would past muster, so he determined to "*rouge* a little" if necessary.[17] The Policy, No. T.20743 was dated 7 April 1803 and granted. He never allowed this premium to lapse for the rest of his life.

Southey had doubts about Keswick, which were not resolved until the autumn; and even graver ones about his brother-in-law. He told a friend, William Taylor, in the spring, that while most men were "mere children" compared to Coleridge in intellect, "Yet all is palsied by a total want of moral strength. He will leave nothing behind him to justify the opinion of his friends to the world; yet many of his scattered poems are such, that a man of feeling will see that the author was capable of executing the greatest works." The past tense was ominous.

But Southey added on a kinder note: "It provokes me when I hear a set of puppies yelping at him, upon whom he a great good-natured mastiff, if he came up to them, would just lift up his leg and pass on."[18] Perhaps the real truth was that Coleridge always provoked everything that Southey valued: moral fibre, punctuality, prudence, husbandly virtues. There was something in Coleridge that always escaped him: his self-knowledge perhaps.

Coleridge remained in London for a fortnight, seeing Lamb, Sotheby and Davy. Mary Lamb had one of her recurring fits, and Coleridge took her to the madhouse in a carriage, trying desperately to soothe Charles, who was "cut to the Heart".[19] He felt how all their lives seemed fragile, under threat. He sought relief in larger, smarter gatherings, where he met, among others, Sir George Beaumont, a wealthy art-patron who thought him initially rather *louche.* Davy, himself launched on his dazzling public career, occasionally glimpsed him at these performances.

> I saw him seldomer than usual; when I did see him, it was generally in the midst of large companies, where he is the image of power and activity. His eloquence is unimpaired; perhaps it is softer and stronger. His will is probably less than ever commensurate with his ability. Brilliant images of greatness float upon his mind . . . He talked in the course of one hour of beginning three works, and he recited Christabel unfinished, and as I had before heard it. What talent does he not waste in forming visions, sublime, but unconnected with the real world. I have looked to his efforts, as to the efforts of a creating being; but as yet, he has not even laid the foundations for the new world of intellectual form.[20]

At this time Coleridge was entering in his Notebooks a long, detailed, botanical account of the life-cycle of the caterpillar, from maggot to butterfly, which would later appear in his poems.

> The Caterpillars generally *shift* skins, once a week – they are about 7 weeks in the Caterpillar state – at the end of which time they find out a safe hiding place, where they lie 2 or 3 days, *during which time they shrink & grow shorter*, losing the use of their feet entirely, and appear as in great agony . . . yet when the Shell has completely hardened, it lies motionless unless disturbed by some accident, till the expiration of a certain time, & at length breaks forth into the winged state . . .[21]

Breaking forth into the winged state, in some manner, evidently haunted Coleridge's mind, and such natural emblems were to become increasingly important in his later writing. Yet he remained careless of all immediate practicalities in establishing himself. When a group of Sotheby's rich friends offered to produce a magnificent private edition of "Christabel", on fine paper with decorative illustrations, he waved the offer aside, saying that he would prefer his "lovely Lady" on cheap, Cumberland ballad-paper, when she was ready.[22]

When Longman announced that they would print a third edition of his *Poems* of 1797, he refused to add any of his more recent work – none of the Quantocks poems, none of the Asra poems, not even "Dejection" – and left all the business of proof corrections to Lamb, who wrote sadly in May: "I classed them as nearly as I could, according to dates . . . Can you send me any *wishes* about the book?"[23] Lamb, unlike Southey, felt increasingly affectionate towards his old, unreliable, brilliant friend: "Bless you, old *Sophist*, who next to Human Nature taught me all the corruption I was capable of knowing . . . When shall we two smoke again?"[24]

The renewed threat of war with France finally sent Coleridge back to Keswick, with all possibilities of Continental travel apparently closed. He arrived on 8 April, immediately retreating to his bedroom with influenza for a month. "The Disorder seized in my head in such a way," he told Poole, "that the very idea of writing became terrible to me." He lay gazing out of the wonderful windows, as the spring came over the fells, reading and dozing, and awakening from short sleep clammy with "honey-dew sweats". He thought much of death, and vaguely considered "arranging my MSS, to be published in case I should be taken off".[25] To Poole, it sounded like opium again.

4

The summer of 1803 at Greta Hall – Coleridge's fourth and last before his long-dreamed emigration to the Mediterranean – was richly unproductive. He took longer to get out on the fells than before, and through June and July he was content to bombard Godwin and Southey with his usual spate of magnificent and unrealisable publishing schemes.

To Godwin he announced a vast metaphysical work, "an Instrument of Practical Reasoning", to be prefixed by a twelve-part introduction to the history of logic, from Plato and Aristotle to Descartes, Condillac and Hartley. This would be followed by his own "Organum", which would provide the reader with a detailed analysis of "all *possible* modes of true, probable, & false reasoning, arranged philosophically".[26] This would form a 500-page printed octavo, this first half of which – here Godwin's eyebrow must have stirred – could be ready "for the Printer, at a fortnight's notice".

To Southey, it was a "six or eight" volume "Bibliotheca Britannica, or an History of British literature". This would not only include extracts from the British poets and prose-writers, "everywhere interspersed with biography", but a running history of "metaphysics, theology, medicine, alchemy . . . medicine, surgery, chemistry, etc etc, navigation, travellers, voyagers etc etc."[27] Walter Scott might write on Scottish poets, and various experts on other technical topics. In fact Southey was intrigued by this idea, and Longman was still considering it in 1808. In a way it was an encyclopaedic updating of Coleridge's old idea of the Epic poem.

What Coleridge did do, however, was to produce "certain Explosions in the Morning Post" for Stuart, on the subject of the war with France, which had been renewed in May on the pretext of the disputed sovereignty of Malta. Two articles appeared in July and August, again promising the series entitled "The Men and the Times". Coleridge ranged himself clearly on the side of the government against Fox, arguing with considerable force that England should not be frightened of standing alone against the whole Continental Alliance, in what was now a just conflict against Bonaparte's imperial ambitions. "Englishmen must think of themselves, and act for themselves . . . Let France bribe, or puzzle all Europe into a confederacy against us, I will not fear for my Country . . . the words of Isaiah will be truly prophetic . . . 'They trod the wine-press alone, and of the nations there was none with them.'"[28] Coleridge's eyes were now turned for many reasons, both political and personal, on the Mediterranean. Stuart begged him to continue the series (ever-recalling the profile of Pitt), and develop a philosophical analysis of the leading personalities in the political struggle, both at home and abroad. Coleridge longed to do this, as many Notebook entries show, but he was no longer capable of concentrating his efforts at Greta Hall.

Instead he wrote many beautiful, but fragmentary, entries on little scenes at Keswick: gnats "swarming in the brightness & the Breeze"; an old man resting with his staff in the shade of a rock; clouds and skies viewed through his coloured glasses with their red and yellow lenses; a butterfly madly and purposefully running "up the Stairs of Air"; and as always, his games with his children.[29] Many of these took him far back into his own childhood, like the hot night in July when he heard Derwent in his sleep groaning, and instantly recalled the calf bellowing all those years ago on the night he slept out at Ottery. He brooded on his marriage: "a man who marries for Love – a Frog who leaps into a well – he has plenty of water, but he cannot get out again."[30] It soothed him to think there was some continuity in his life, even if it was only represented by the lulling sounds of the Rivers Greta and Otter.

While he persisted in his attempts to bring Southey to Keswick, other visitors beguiled the time. Among these were William Hazlitt, Samuel Rogers, and Sir George and Lady Beaumont.

Hazlitt was now twenty-five, no longer the innocent of the Quantocks days, argumentative and aggressive, still awkward in company, and now with a roving eye for the girls. He was training as a painter, and had spent the previous summer in Paris studying at the Louvre, and starting what was to become a lifelong cult of Napoleon-worship. He was a convinced republican, and now regarded Coleridge's liberal politics in the *Morning Post* with youthful disdain. Nevertheless he was still profoundly in awe of the Coleridge-Wordsworth circle, and during July, executed "masterly" portraits of both poets, "very much in the manner of Titian's".[31] (Unfortunately, they have not survived.) He also wished to paint Lamb and Southey, and was evidently looking for a patron. Coleridge walked and argued with him, and made tactful introductions to Sir George Beaumont and Tom Wedgwood, which he hoped would further his career. He recorded some fierce arguments over politics and religion.[32]

Hazlitt remained in the district from July till October, during which time Coleridge painted his own wonderfully acute portrait-in-words of his protégé, for Wedgwood. Remarkably, Coleridge seemed to foresee the sensitive essayist and future critic, already appearing through the rather forbidding exterior of the opinionated art student.

> William Hazlitt is a thinking, observant, original man, of great power as a Painter of Character Portraits . . . His manners are to 99 in 100 singularly repulsive – : brow-hanging, shoe-contemplative, *strange* . . . he is, I verily believe, kindly-natured – is very fond of, attentive to, & patient with, children; but he is jealous, gloomy, & of an irritable Pride – & addicted to women, as objects of sexual Indulgence. With all this, there is much good in him – he is disinterested, an enthusiastic Lover of the great men, who have been before us – he says things that are his own in a way of his own – & tho' from habitual Shyness & the Outside & bearskin at least

> of misanthropy, he is strangely confused & dark in his conversation, & delivers himself of almost all his conceptions with a Forceps, yet he says more than any man, I ever knew . . . He sends well-headed & well-feathered Thoughts straight forwards to the mark with a Twang of the Bow-string.[33]

The last phrase, with its characteristic hunting image, is a perfect premonition of Hazlitt's epigrammatic style as a profile-writer and critic in *The Spirit of The Age* (1824).

Coleridge was also right about Hazlitt's sexual nature, which made him restless and unhappy all his life, and finally humiliated him in middle age in an affair with a coquettish teenage maidservant, recounted in his *Liber Amoris*. At Keswick even, Hazlitt rapidly earned a reputation for French-style philandering among the country girls, and some time in October (after Coleridge's letter was written) "narrowly escaped being ducked by the populace, and probably sent to prison for some gross attacks on women".[34] The exact details of this amatory adventure are not known, but Coleridge helped him escape over the hills to Grasmere, lending him shoes and money, and later arranging for his clothes, painting box, and canvasses to be sent discreetly after him to London.[35] Altogether, Coleridge's whole description of Hazlitt is extraordinarily prophetic, showing how quickly he could still be roused by anything that interested and challenged him.

5

The relationship with Sir George and Lady Beaumont – the former an amateur artist himself, the latter a woman of kindly but rather gushing disposition – developed along a different, but familiar pattern. They arrived at Keswick "half-mad" to see Wordsworth, and very cool towards Coleridge, whom they thought vain and worldly. Coleridge immediately turned all his seductive conversational powers upon the rich and aristocratic couple. He told Wordsworth of Lady B, "you may wind her up with *any* Music! – but *music* it must be, of some sort or other." By the autumn they were his passionate admirers.[36]

They offered to build Wordsworth an entire new house on ground near Greta Hall, so he could be closer to his friend (an offer which Wordsworth signally refused); and in the coming years they helped both men generously with money.[37] In August, Coleridge sent them handwritten copies of Wordsworth's "Resolution and Independence" and his own "Dejection" (in a form now addressed to "William" rather than "Sara"), paired together to show the nature of the poetic dialogue between them.[38] In September he sent the "Hymn before Sunrise", and an excerpt from the "Ode to Tranquillity".

In October, he wrote Sir George an immensely long and emotional letter about his political beliefs, confessing his early Jacobin sympathies at Bristol with that curious mixture of guilt and relish which he used to adopt for George Coleridge's benefit. This letter is often given as an example of Coleridge's shameful apostasy from his original radicalism; but that is to ignore the moderate liberal position he had been steadily working towards in his public journalism ever since 1799. Some of the defensive emotion may also have emerged as a result of his arguments with Hazlitt.

The picture he draws of himself in those heady days of lecturing at Bristol is vividly accurate: "Tho' I detested Revolutions in my calmer moments . . . yet with an ebullient Fancy, a flowing Utterance, a light & dancing Heart, & a disposition to catch fire by the very rapidity of my own motion . . . I aided the Jacobins, by witty sarcasms & subtle reasonings & declamations full of genuine feeling against all Rulers & against all established Forms!"[39]

Nevertheless, this letter was clearly designed to enlist Sir George's personal sympathies, emphasising the "bigotry" of Coleridge's family background, and comparing himself – rather wildly – with the young Irish radical Robert Emmett who had just been executed in Dublin for sedition. "Like him, I was very young, very enthusiastic, distinguished by Talents & acquirements & a sort of turbid Eloquence."

What really characterises the letter is not so much apostasy, as self-dramatisation of his youthful career, his "10 months" of sedition, which might have put him in jail "50 times". As he put it, "the very clank of the Chains . . . would not at that time have deterred me from a strong Phrase or striking Metaphor."[40]

The letter was also a subtle piece of flattery towards the rich aristocratic couple ("persons of *your* rank in Society"), whom Coleridge clearly – and correctly – divined as generous future patrons. As he had done previously with the Wedgwoods, he cast himself in the role of the suffering bard, vulnerable and striving for self-knowledge, and very ready to be helped. "I have written, my Heart at a full gallop a down Hill." Given his situation at Greta Hall, it is hard to blame him.

6

As the summer slipped away, without further journalism or poetry, and ever-severer symptoms of opium addiction, Coleridge's emigration schemes rose up again like familiar ghosts. By August he was considering a new and much more independent scheme: a journey to Madeira or Malta, where the British Fleets had established war-time naval bases, and he might secure an administrative post.[41] This had a certain practicality, for his reputation as a commentator on foreign affairs and the government's conduct of anti-French policy would give him value as a civil servant, and he was acquainted with John Stoddart who had just been appointed Judge Advocate in Malta. Moreover the climate of the southern Mediterranean promised balm for all his pains.

Meanwhile Wordsworth, sensing his friend's renewed restlessness, proposed an extensive tour of Scotland, to be undertaken in an Irish "jaunting-car" pulled by an aged horse. This curious vehicle had hanging seats, facing out over the wheels, so that the passengers travelled back-to-back, a symbolic position for the two friends, perhaps. The tour was intended as a concession to Coleridge's ill-health, now described as "atonic Gout", producing a swollen ankle and asthmatic symptoms. Sara Coleridge, who was genuinely anxious about her husband's ill-health, philosophically concurred. "W. is to drive all the way, for poor Samuel is too weak to undertake the fatigue of driving . . . My husband is a good man – his prejudices – and his prepossessions sometimes give me pain, but we have all a somewhat to encounter in this life – I should be a very, very happy Woman if it were not for a few things – and my husband's ill-health stands at the head of these evils!"[42]

They departed with Dorothy on 15 August 1803, on what should have been a blissful return to the simple life of the Quantock days. But Coleridge wrote to Southey: "I never yet commenced a Journey with such inauspicious Heaviness of Heart before."[43] He took with him a travel-notebook, in which he kept one of the fullest topographical accounts of all his trips. An early entry read: "O Asra, wherever I am, & am impressed, my heart aches for you, & I know a deal of the heart of man, that I otherwise should not know."[44]

They proceeded northwards in increasing rain and gloom, through Carlisle (with Hatfield's trial to provide some light relief), Gretna Green, Dumfries, the Falls of Clyde, Glasgow, and the bonny banks of Loch Lomond, which they first glimpsed on 24 August.[45] Both men were rather silent and unwell, without the usual stimulation of actual walking, and Dorothy had to work hard, over-enthusing about the lowering Scottish landscape and reciting her brother's poems to improve the atmosphere. Coleridge noted mournfully that he had "no dear Heart" to recite his *own* verses; "I never hear them in snatches from a beloved Voice, fitted to some sweet occasion, of natural Prospect, in Winds at Night."[46]

Wordsworth said afterwards that his friend seemed "in bad spirits, and somewhat too much in love with his own dejection".[47] While Coleridge told Poole: "I soon found I was a burthen on them; & Wordsworth, himself a brooder over his painful hypochondriacal Sensations, was not my fittest companion."[48]

As before in Germany, they decided to split up, after crossing Loch Lomond on the ferry to East Tarbet. Before they parted at Arrochar on 30 August, Coleridge recorded a Scottish scene that may well have inspired one of Wordsworth's loveliest lyrics, "The Solitary Reaper", not written until 1805. "Never, never let me forget that small Herd boy, in his Tartan Plaid, dim-seen on the hilly field, & long heard ere seen, a melancholy *Voice*, calling to his Cattle! – nor the beautiful Harmony of the Heath, the dancing Fern, & the ever-moving Birches."[49]

The plan was that Coleridge should send his bag back, and return south on foot to Edinburgh. The Wordsworths would proceed west in the jaunting-car, returning in a leisurely fashion by way of Melrose to visit Walter Scott. (They heard him recite "The Lay of the Last Minstrel", which struck them as strangely reminiscent of "Christabel".) They divided their cash, Coleridge generously taking only six guineas from their float of thirty-five. As he slipped away, Dorothy "shivered at the thought of his being sickly and alone, travelling from place to place".[50]

In fact he was much happier, immediately deciding to strike north again along the line of the Scottish forts to Inverness, despite his lack of money and clothes, and a pair of light shoes that split when he dried them in front of a cottage fire. (He had evidently forgotten his fell-boots.) He now tried to exorcise his opium demons in a mad, non-stop, walking bout of eight days, during which he covered 263 miles, reaching Perth on 11 September. On this journey he pushed himself to the extremes of physical and mental exhaustion. He soon took on the appearance of a wild tramp, shoeless but unstoppable, scribbling in his Notebook, subsisting on tea, porridge, ale, and oatcakes. One luxury breakfast consisted of three raw eggs beaten up in two tumblers of whisky and sugar.[51]

At Fort Augustus he was arrested as a spy, but talked his way out and finished up dining with the Governor of the fort. At Fort William, he burst into the inn and collapsed in "an hysterical Fit with long & loud weeping", and was then overcome by diarrhoea, a sure indication of opium withdrawal. With a sort of disassociation he observed the "unutterable consternation" of the landlord and servants, who gabbled in Gaelic and whisked him off to bed, to his own "great metaphysical amusement".[52]

Each night he had terrible dreams, that woke him screaming: "with Sleep my Horrors commence . . . Dreams are no shadows with me; but the real, substantial miseries of Life."[53] But the more outlandish his behaviour became, the kinder the Highlanders seemed to treat him. Finally he attained a disembodied state, and felt he was acting out a sort of Ode to Solitude: "the Nature unmanacled & solitary, the Liberty natural and solitary – I feel here as if I were here to wander on the winds, a blessed Ghost, till my Beloved came to me – go back with her & seek my children."[54]

One clear and highly significant literary conception came to him, that all his future writing would be in some sense autobiographical. "Seem to have made up my mind to write my metaphysical works, as *my Life*, & *in* my Life – intermixed with all the other events / or history of the mind & fortunes of S. T. Coleridge."[55]

At Perth he was called back to reality by perhaps the only kind of news that could have engaged him in this state. Southey had just lost his only daughter Margaret, and in utter grief was coming to Greta Hall for consolation. He wrote within half an hour of arrival: "O dear friend! it is idle to talk of what I feel – I am stunned at present – & this beginning to write makes a beginning of living feeling within me. Whatever Comfort I can be to you, I will . . . my children shall be your's till it please God to send you another."[56] Southey did not perhaps realise how literally Coleridge intended this. He described his own wanderings as a "wild Journey": "I have walked 263 miles in eight Days – so I must have strength somewhere: but my spirits are dreadful, owing entirely to the Horrors of every night – I truly dread to sleep . . . I have abandoned all opiates except Ether be one; & that only in *fits*."

In this letter he also enclosed the terrible verses of "The Pains of Sleep", which he described as "doggerels" but "a true portrait of my nights". They do not present opium visions, as is often thought, but the night-horrors which accompanied withdrawal symptoms from the drug: a ghastly outpouring of suppressed guilts and fears, the black stirred-up sediment of the unconscious mind erupting in the thin hours before dawn.

It was exactly that state of passion and lost reason which he had conjured up on Scafell, as the dream-like condition most to be feared. The verse is spare and rapid, with a breathless muttering somnambular quality, which commands conviction. Not even the Asra poems have this directness. Most terrible of all, it is a faithful self-portrait of Coleridge as he knew himself to be in his worst and weakest moments:

But yesternight I pray'd aloud
In Anguish and in Agony,
Awaking from the Fiendish Crowd
Of Shapes & Thoughts that tortur'd me!
Desire with Loathing strangely mixt,
On wild or hateful Objects fixt:
Pangs of Revenge, the powerless Will,
Still baffled, & consuming still,
Sense of intolerable Wrong,
And men whom I despis'd made strong
Vain-glorious Threats, unmanly Vaunting,
Bad men my boasts & fury taunting
Rage, sensual Passion, mad'ning Brawl,
And Shame, and Terror over all![57]

To admit all this to Southey was also, perhaps, Coleridge's way of sharing his friend's grief, a sort of sacrificial gift. But the difference in their situations was eloquent: Southey had lost a child, Coleridge had lost himself.

By 15 September Coleridge was back at Greta Hall, but not before he had clambered up the crags beneath Arthur's Seat above Edinburgh at sunset, and carefully observed the ships below in the firth, counted 54 peaks on the surrounding mountains, and meditated quite calmly on the smoking chimneys of 10,000 houses, "each smoke from some one family – it was an affecting sight to me!"[58]

7

With Southey and Edith established at Greta Hall (temporarily as they supposed) Coleridge's path of escape was suddenly clear. But he lingered through the last three months of autumn, consoling Southey with many walks over the fells and through Borrowdale. He also entered a period of even more intense introspection and moral stock-taking, now writing long entries almost nightly in his Notebooks. Dreams, self-accusations, stern resolutions, analyses of his friendships, and the most beautiful descriptions of night-sky and landscapes, fill their pages. Sometimes these entries are distorted by opium – he regularly woke the household with his nightmare screaming – at other times they are limpid and touchingly simple.[59]

> I went to the window, to empty my Urine-pot, & wondered at the simple grandeur of the View. 1. darkness & only not utter black indistinguishableness – 2. The grey-blue steely Glimmer of the Greta, & the Lake – 3. The black, yet form preserving Mountains – 4. the Sky, moon-whitened there, cloud-blackened here – & yet with all its gloominess & sullenness forming a contrast with the simplicity of the Landscape beneath.[60]

Sometimes he returned to his love for Asra, the failure of which seemed to take on a new symbolism, representing all he had failed to do in the Lakes. Although apparently despairing, such entries still have a poetic life and force, gathering powerful clusters of imagery, which suggest more than ever that – as in "Dejection" – he was essentially a poet of Romantic crisis.

His birthday entry in October is characteristic of this continuing, steady, unshaken power of vision.

> Slanting Pillars of Light, like Ladders up to Heaven, their base always a field of vivid green Sunshine. – This is Oct. 19. 1803. Wed. Morn. tomorrow my Birth Day, 31 years of age! – O me! my very heart dies! – This *year* has been one painful Dream – I have done nothing! – O for God's sake, let me whip & spur, so that Christmas may not pass without some thing having been done – at all events to finish The Men & the Times, & to collect them and all my Newspaper Essays into one Volume – to collect all my poems, finishing the Vision of the Maid of Orleans, & the Dark Ladie, & make a second Volume, & to finish Christabel . . . The Lake has been a mirror so very clear, that the water became almost invisible – & now it rolls in white Breakers, like a Sea; & the wind snatches up the water, & drifts it like Snow. – And now the Rain Storm pelts against my Study Window! – O Asra Asra why am I not happy!

> why have I not an unencumbered Heart! these beloved Books still before me, this noble Room, the very centre to which a whole world of beauty converges, the deep reservoir into which all these streams & currents of lovely Forms flow – my own mind so populous, so active, so full of noble schemes, so capable of realizing them; this heart so loving, so filled with noble affections – O Asra! wherefore am I not happy! why for years have I not enjoyed one pure & sincere pleasure! – one full Joy! – one genuine Delight, that rings sharp to the Beat of the Finger! – all cracked, & dull with base Alloy![61]

Other entries continued to pour out in November and December: on Hartley, on the moon, on the question of evil, on sunrise over Helvellyn, on bad dreams, on waterfalls, on Plotinus, on candles, on poetry, on his marriage. But no one read them, they were all shut away in his Notebook and his heart.

8

His sense of imminent departure led him to urge Wordsworth to continue the great philosophic poem which he had begun in *The Prelude.* He saw it now in terms of his own forthcoming journey: "a Great Work, in which he will sail; on an open Ocean, & a steady wind; unfretted by short tacks, reefing, & hawling & disentangling the ropes – great work necessarily comprehending his attention & Feelings within the circle of great objects & elevated Conceptions – this is his natural Element."[62]

But he also told Poole, as he prepared to abandon his own household at Keswick, that he feared for the effect of the Grasmere household on Wordsworth's poetic genius. Here jealousy and perception were finely balanced. "I saw him more & more benetted in hypochondriacal Fancies, living wholly among *Devotees* – having every the minutest Thing, almost his very Eating & Drinking, done for him by his Sister, or Wife – & I trembled, lest a Film should rise, and thicken on his moral Eye."[63]

Wordsworth, for his part, arranged a loan of £105 through Sotheby to help pay for Coleridge's journey,[64] and made hasty preparations to have a manuscript book of all his latest poems and parts of *The Prelude* copied out by Dorothy and Asra, for Coleridge to take to the Mediterranean. He also urged, with something like desperation, that Coleridge should map out the structure of the philosophic poem – still imagined as "The Recluse" – to be written in his absence abroad. The unspoken assumption behind this request was that Coleridge would never return alive.

Coleridge finally left Greta Hall on 20 December to spend Christmas at Grasmere. There is no record of his parting from his wife and children. He fell ill at Dove Cottage, and remained there until 14 January 1804, while Dorothy patiently nursed him with hot broth and recorded his nightmare screaming with horror. On a crag above Grasmere, Wordsworth read him "the second Part of his divine Self-biography".[65]

Coleridge entered in his Notebook the possibilities contained in his own biography: "Of a great metaphysician: he looked into his own Soul with a Telescope: what seemed all irregular, he saw & showed to be beautiful Constellations & he added to the Consciousness hidden worlds within worlds."[66]

Revived, as he said, "by a sudden Frost", he then rose up and walked the nineteen miles over the fells to Kendal in four hours thirty-five minutes, and was not tired. "My state of Health is a Riddle," he told Poole.[67]

9

Poole was already in London, temporarily working for the Census, as usual a model of industry and practicality. Faithful to the last, he found Coleridge lodgings at 16 Abingdon Street, in Westminster. From here, Coleridge dashed off six pieces of journalism for Stuart's new evening paper, the *Courier.* He agreed that once abroad, he would supply Stuart with articles on British policy in the Mediterranean. From Abingdon Street he wrote to Sir George Beaumont, now returned to his country estate at Dunmow, on 30 January: "I have reached London, with the resolution of going either to Madeira, or to Catania in Sicily, if I can by any proper way arrange the means of so doing without injury or distress to Mrs Coleridge: and of this I have now little doubt."[68] The following day, having heard from Davy a superb account of Etna, he resolved to go to Sicily via Malta.

It took a further two months to procure passage on a ship, owing to the difficulties of the war-time convoy system, but Coleridge used the time to make surprisingly efficient financial arrangements. The Wedgwood annuity was entirely made over to Mrs Coleridge, all tradesmen's bills paid off, the Life Insurance secured, and Stuart co-opted as his banker in London.[69] The sudden decisiveness of these arrangements, and the series of highly emotional farewell letters he wrote to many friends – Southey, Wordsworth, the Beaumonts, Sotheby, Tom Wedgwood – suggest that he expected to die abroad.[70]

To Asra, who had written a valedictory letter in February that "put despair" into his heart, he sent a copy of Sir Thomas Browne's *Religio Medici* and *Hydrotaphia*, a meditation, as he described it, on Burial Urns – "how *earthy*, how redolent of graves & Sepulchres is every Line!"[71] But perhaps it was not death he hoped for, but a symbolic death of the old self. He concluded with a blessing from "Dejection":

> And all the Stars hang bright above your Dwelling,
> Silent as tho' they watch'd the sleeping Earth![71]

To Wordsworth he wrote:

> O dearest & most revered William! I seem to grow weaker & weaker in my moral feelings – and every thing, that forcibly awakes me to Person & Contingency, strikes fear into me, sinkings and misgivings, alienation from the Spirit of Hope, obscure withdrawings out of Life . . . a wish to retire into stoniness and to stir not, or to be diffused upon the winds & have no individual Existence. But all will become better when once I can sit down, & work: when my Time is my own, I shall be myself again . . .[72]

He had his portrait painted, this time by James Northcote: the last portrait of his youth.[73] The Beaumonts insisted that he spend his final weeks in the splendid comfort of the town house in Grosvenor Square: Sir George pressed an envelope containing £100 into his hand, and Lady Beaumont sent him a specially made travelling-desk, with hidden drawers full of comforts.

There were some revealing last incidents. At Lamb's, Coleridge got drunk and had a blazing row with Godwin, "did thunder & lighten at him" for an hour; and then wrote a most touching letter of apology. (Godwin noted that Coleridge believed in "the trinity, incarnation, fall of man, etc", and thought the war against Bonaparte might last "forty years". He said that Southey "does not desert me in my degradation, though he feels a repulsion against me.")[74]

Coleridge met his old Pantisocratic colleague, George Burnett, in a very low state; and solemnly diagnosed his illness as opium addiction – "such opium-stupidly-wild eyes – O it made the place, one calls the

Heart, feel as if it was going to break." He made great efforts to secure him work with Poole's friend, John Rickman, then secretary to the Speaker of the House of Commons.[75] He also advised Wordsworth to send the manuscript of his poems under parliamentary free-post via Rickman, and when this stratagem was discovered, innocently denied all knowledge of the affair.[76] Meanwhile he prudently gathered letters of recommendation from Rickman, Sotheby, and others, to present to the Governor of Malta.

Shortly before his departure, he received a magnificent letter of valediction from Humphry Davy, now the moving scientific spirit at the Royal Institution.

> In whatever part of the World you are, you will often live with me, not as a fleeting idea but as a *recollection* possessed of creative energy, as an *Imagination* winged with fire inspiriting and rejoicing. You must not live much longer without giving to *all men* the *proof of power*, which those who know you feel in admiration. Perhaps at a distance from the applauding and censuring murmurs of the world, you will be best able to execute those great works which are justly expected from you; you are to be the historian of the Philosophy of feeling. – Do not in any way dissipate your noble nature. Do not give up your birth-right.[77]

Coleridge's reaction was a characteristic mixture of pride, dissembling, and real humility. He gave the letter to Lady Beaumont, then denied that he had intended her to read Davy's praise, then added that both Wordsworth and Davy had always "grossly overrated" him.[78]

10

Coleridge was in Portsmouth by the end of March, waiting to embark on his armed merchant-ship, the *Speedwell.* He had bought new boots, a sunhat, and a pair of green solar spectacles (price one guinea). From here he sent Hartley and Derwent a game of "Spillikins" to remember him by: a new German game which involved scattering a handful of wooden spills on the floor, and trying to pick them up in sequence, without causing the intricate pile to collapse.

He wrote a warm note to his wife. ". . . What we have been to each other, our understandings will not permit our Hearts to forget! – God knows, I weep Tears of Blood, that so it is."[79]

To Southey, he projected one more unwritten epic. "O Southey! from Oxford to Greta Hall – a spiritual map with our tracks, as of two Ships that left Port in Company – It is not for either of us to do it; but a Poet might make a divine Allegory of it."[80]

Almost his last action on land was to try to secure a position for Sara's ne'er-do-well brother, George Fricker. He boarded the ship on 6 April 1804, and scribbled off farewell notes to Wordsworth, Stuart, and Sir George Beaumont, to be taken back by the ship's tender. "Positively, this Night, that Star so very bright over the mast of a noble Vessel – & the sound of the water breaking against the Ship Side – it seems quite a *Home* to me . . . Death *itself* will be only a Voyage – a Voyage not *from*, but to our native Country."[81] Before it got quite dark, he went up to the *Speedwell*'s quarter-deck, and established his observation-post for the long journey ahead. He found that the flat mahogany rudder-case would serve as his writing desk, and the duck-coops around it could be stacked into a sort of armchair for him to sit on. He took up his position, gazing up at the stars, while the caged ducks "quacked at" his legs companionably.[82]

Postscript

So we leave Coleridge, that April night under the stars: a figure suddenly frozen in historical silhouette, like an engraved illustration to his own *Ancient Mariner*, set in a labyrinth of rigging against a phosphorescent, immobile sea. The Poet sailing South into Exile.

*

To publish part one of his Life, this "unfinished" biography, could be considered as an act of appropriate homage (or of folly) to the great master of the suggestive fragment. But it does allow the reader to consider the position *dramatically*, as it were. Suppose Coleridge had indeed died, as he and his friends clearly expected he would, aged thirty-one, somewhere in the Mediterranean in 1804? Suppose his grave now lay, not in the leafy confines of Highgate cemetery, but in the remote volcanic foothills of Mount Etna? Suppose his life had never actually had a part two? How would his reputation now stand?

*

To begin with, the whole "mythos" of his career would surely wear a quite different aspect. He would be seen as part of that meteoric, Romantic tradition of young writers, like Keats, Shelley, or Byron (or even Arthur Rimbaud), who lived and died in a premature blaze of talents. He would be one of the Promethean figures, still moving upwards on the parabola of genius: the fire-bringers, the liberators of spirit, the eternal exiles and idealists. This imagery is already vividly present in Humphry Davy's valediction of 1804.

His literary achievement would have a sharp, bright clarity. It is difficult to think that the shadows of failure, plagiarism, apostacy, or even opium addiction, would mark his reputation in any significant way. On the contrary, his work would be seen as astonishingly ranging, confident, and assured: frustrated only by the marital anxieties and ill-health of his last months in the Lake District.

Coleridge would be recalled as a master of blank verse autobiography in the Conversation Poems, and the "only begetter" of Wordsworth's *Prelude* (which would certainly have remained dedicated to him, as Tennyson dedicated *In Memoriam* to Arthur Hallam). He would be recognised as the spectacular innovator of Romantic ballad forms, and the magician of the haunting, daemonic lyric. (Perhaps "Kubla Khan" would exist purely as an oral memory, uncommitted to manuscript, a true piece of Romantic folklore.)

He would be honoured as an inspired political journalist, the young religious radical and Pantisocrat, who faithfully recorded the fluctuating liberal reaction to the French Revolution and the menacing rise of Bonaparte, between the fall of Robespierre in 1794 and the collapse of the Peace of Amiens in 1803. He would have been acknowledged too as one of the first to recognise the significance of German Romanticism, a brilliant translator, and philosophical interpreter of the drama, folk culture, and idealist metaphysics of the *sturm und drang* period. In all this he would be seen as the great "European" of the early English Romantic Movement.

His more intimate and confessional writing would seem no less impressive. The way his Notebooks developed, especially in the Lake District between 1800 and 1804, make him one of the great English diarists. (See his commanding position in *The English Year*, edited by Geoffery Grigson, Oxford, 1967, 1986.) Not only does he stand within that tradition of exquisite, direct, natural observation that runs in a line from Gilbert White and Dorothy Wordsworth, to Francis Kilvert and Gerard Manley Hopkins; but he also seems to anticipate much of the anxious, modernist, spiritual investigations of W. N. P. Barbellion, or Franz Kafka, or Anaïs Nin.

More than this, he was a pioneer of "outdoor" literature, with his wonderful accounts of fell-walking, hill-climbing, and the experience of mountain-tops, and the constant drama of sky and water. He was perhaps the first writer to recognise "weather" as a subject in itself (both in the day and at night), and this links him particularly with contemporary painters – Constable, Friedrich, and later Turner. While his general letters, ranging from humorous self-portraiture, through travel-writing, literary criticism, to politics and metaphysics, define our sense of the possibilities of the Romantic personality no less surely than those of Keats or Lord Byron.

Indeed, had Coleridge died young; had he always remained as that youthful, archetypal figure on the ship sailing south, we might be tempted to think of him, paradoxically, as already greater than the man he eventually became. If we could stop biography, as we can stop fiction, at the critical chosen moment, we could – it seems – change history.

*

And yet biography cannot stop, because it must conform to the complication, strength, and strangeness of life. (That is its power over fiction, the authority of truth.) Coleridge's future lies richly, tragically, comically, before him. Indeed in human terms the next thirty-two years are more fascinating than anything that has gone before. Not only does he emerge as a controversial public figure – the legendary poet, the lecturer, the critic, the enigmatic metaphysician – but the inner man, the spiritual voyager, enters far wilder and deeper seas. As a true Romantic figure, Coleridge has scarcely yet set sail.

Coleridge's Circle

ALLEN, ROBERT (1772–1805) Close friend of Coleridge's at Christ's Hospital, renowned for good looks and charm. University College, Oxford, and subsequently military surgeon, 2nd Royal Dragoons. Married a merry widow, died of apoplexy in Sudbury.

BANKS, SIR JOSEPH (1743–1820) Explorer, naturalist, accompanied Captain Cook on his first voyage. Founded botanical collection at Kew Gardens, and supplied Coleridge with Indian hemp. President of Royal Society.

BARNES, THOMAS (1785–1841) Editor of *The Times*, cricketer. Christ's Hospital, and Pembroke College, Cambridge. Successively drama critic, parliamentary reporter, and editor (1817). Printed Hazlitt's work but not Coleridge's.

BEAUMONT, SIR GEORGE (1753–1827) Aristocratic patron of the arts, collector, and dilettante landscape painter (pupil of Cozens). A founder of the National Gallery. Houses in London, Leicestershire and Lake District. Generous supporter of Girtin, Constable, Wordsworth, and Coleridge.

BEDDOES, DR THOMAS (1780–1808) Bristol physician and democrat. Contributed to Coleridge's *Watchman*, and later advised him on health matters. Founded Pulmonary Institution at Clifton (1798) where Davy first worked. Father of the poet Thomas Lovell Beddoes.

BOEHME (or BÖHME), JAKOB (1575–1624) German mystical writer, lived in Görlitz working as shoemaker. His transcendental doctrines of dialectical energies (light versus dark etc.) used vivid poetic symbols (rays of the sun etc.) which influenced writers such as William Law, and later Coleridge. See John Beer, op. cit.

BOWLES, REV. WILLIAM LISLE (1762–1850) Poet, and parson in Wiltshire and Gloucestershire. *Sonnets*, first edition 1789, influenced Wordsworth and Coleridge. (See chapter 2.) Wrote a controversial life of Alexander Pope, 1806, which irritated Byron.

BURKE, EDMUND (1729–97) Philosopher, orator, politician. Educated Trinity College, Dublin. Wrote *A Philosophical Enquiry into the Sublime and Beautiful* (1756), a key Romantic text, aged twenty-seven. Member of Parliament for Bristol 1774, associated with Whig reforms. Friend of Fox, opponent of Pitt, until *Reflections on the Revolution in France* (1790), which marked conservative political reaction in England.

BURNETT, GEORGE (1776–1811) A curious version of Coleridge's life as real failure. Born Huntspill, Somerset; educated Balliol College, Oxford, with Southey; Pantisocrat. Then successively rejected by Martha Fricker; failed as Unitarian minister; discharged as army surgeon; hack writer for Richard Phillips; published *Specimens of English Prose Writers of 17th Century* (1807); died prematurely of opium addiction in great poverty.

CHATTERTON, THOMAS (1752–1770) Bristol poet and Romantic prodigy figure, with whom Coleridge sometimes identified, and imagined as a Pantisocrat. Educated Colston's Bluecoat School; found medieval manuscripts in muniment room of St Mary Redcliffe, from which he invented "Thomas Rowley"; died from arsenic and opium overdose in Holborn; works edited by Southey. Coleridge particularly admired his "Excellent Balade of Charitie", "Song from Aella", and "African Eclogues".

CHRIST'S HOSPITAL, SCHOOLBOYS see Bob Allen, Thomas Barnes, George Dyer, Tom Evans, Robert Favell, Frederick Franklin, Charles Valentine, Le Grice, John Gutch, Leigh Hunt, Charles Lamb, Thomas Middleton, John Morgan.

CLARKSON, THOMAS (1760–1846) Reformer, campaigner, Vice-President of the Anti-Slave Trade Society. Lived at Eusemere, Lake District, and Bury St Edmunds. *A Portraiture of Quakerism* (1806), *History of the Abolition of the Slave Trade* (1808); *A Life of William Penn* (1813). With his wife Catherine, later helped Coleridge to battle against opium addiction.

COTTLE, JOSEPH (1770–1835) Bristol publisher, Unitarian. Brother of Amos Cottle, antiquarian. Published works of Coleridge, Wordsworth, Southey, Lovell and Chatterton. Ambitions as epic poet unfortunately produced *Alfred* (1801), *Messiah* (1819), *Fall of Cambria* (1820). Lively and unreliable memoirs of Coleridge, *Early Recollections*, op. cit.

DARWIN, ERASMUS (1731–1802) Doctor, botanist, poet, atheist. Born in Nottingham, settled in Lichfield, member of the Lunar Society. His life's work on botany and evolution published as verse, *The Botanic Garden* (1795); and prose, *Zoonomia, or the Laws of Organic Life* (1796). Grandfather of Charles Darwin.

DAVY, SIR HUMPHRY (1778–1829) Experimental chemist, scientific lecturer, poet; knighted 1812, aged thirty-four. Admirer of Coleridge and Wordsworth. Son of Penzance carpenter, apprenticed to surgeon, taken up by Tom Wedgwood, employed by Dr Beddoes at Clifton; corrected proofs of *Lyrical Ballads*, second edition. Appointed Director of Chemical Laboratory, Royal Institution, London, 1799. Worked on metals, volcanic action, miner's safety lamp, electro-magnetism, all of which fascinated Coleridge. President of Royal Society, 1820.

DYER, GEORGE (1755–1841) Poet, scholar, democrat, Unitarian, hack writer, comic figure in *Elia* essays. Christ's Hospital, tutoring posts, editor of Valpy's classics, bachelor rooms in Clifford's Inn. Mentions Pantisocracy in his poems. He fell drunk into New River, 1823; but married sober, 1824.

EVANS, FAMILY Befriended Coleridge at Christ's Hospital and Cambridge. Of the children – Ann, Elisabeth, Mary and Tom – it is known that Tom joined the East India House as clerk, remained a close friend of Lamb's, and published a paper, the *Pamphleteer*. Mary, Coleridge's first love, married Fryer Todd in October 1795, and lived unhappily ever after; Coleridge met her again in 1808.

FAVELL, ROBERT (1775–1812) Christ's Hospital; Pembroke College, Cambridge; Pantisocrat. Commissioned in 61st Foot, and died courageously at the battle of Salamanca, in Peninsula War.

FOX, CHARLES JAMES (1749–1806) Whig Statesman, son of first Lord Holland, unofficial head of parliamentary Opposition to Pitt. Great friend of Burke until political quarrel 1790. Romantically associated with liberal causes; latterly known for hard drinking and large girth. Died six months after he finally became Prime Minister.

FRANKLIN, REV. FREDERICK WILLIAM (1771–1836) Shared copy of Homer with Coleridge at Christ's Hospital. Later returned as schoolmaster, and then retired as parson to Shropshire: "the fine, frank-hearted Fr –" (*Elia*).

FREND, REV. WILLIAM (1757–1841) Mathematician, tutor at Jesus College, Cambridge; Unitarian and radical. Tried for blasphemy, 1794, and dismissed from University. Friend of Coleridge, Lamb, and Dyer; tutor to Thomas Malthus. *The Principles of Algebra* (1799); *The Beauties of the Heavens Displayed* (astronomical papers, 1804–18). See Frieda Knight, *University Rebel*, 1971.

FRICKER, FAMILY Sara (1770–1845), married Coleridge 1795, lived as part of Southey's household at Greta Hall from 1804. Mary (born 1771), married Robert Lovell 1794, lived with Southeys after his death. Edith (1774–1837) married Robert Southey 1795, lived at Greta Hall from 1803, died insane. Martha (born 1777) rejected George Burnett; Eliza (born 1778), had affair with absconding sea-captain. George (born 1785), joined merchant navy, shipwrecked, press-ganged etc.

FRIEDRICH, CASPAR DAVID (1774–1840) German landscape painter, with powerful pantheistic and mystical overtones. Educated at Copenhagen Academy, settled in Dresden (Schlegel group), with regular painting visits to Baltic coast. Awarded prize by Goethe at Weimar, 1805. Transcendental quality to his work expressed in his titles: "The Cross in the Mountains", "The Monk by the Sea", "The Arctic Shipwreck", "The Wanderer above the Sea of Mist". He celebrated the defeat of Napoleon in 1814 by painting a French dragoon wandering lost in a forest of German evergreens. See William Vaughan, *Romantic Art*, 1978.

GODWIN, WILLIAM (1756–1836) Political philosopher, novelist, biographer, children's publisher. Educated Hoxton Academy, then became atheist. *Political Justice* (1793), *Caleb Williams* (1794), *Memoirs of the Author of the Rights of Woman* (1798), *Lives of the Necromancers* (1834). Married Mary Wollstonecraft, fathered the future Mary Shelley, and published Lamb's *Tales from Shakespeare.* He was fascinated by Coleridge, whom he regarded as one of his "principal oral instructors"; see William St Clair, *The Godwins and the Shelleys*, 1989.

GUTCH, JOHN MATHEW (1776–1861) Journalist, bookseller, banker. Educated Christ's Hospital; in 1803 moved to Bristol, where he edited *Felix Farley's Bristol Journal*; later published Coleridge's essays; printed the first part of the *Biographia*; preserved Coleridge's first known Notebook.

HARTLEY, DAVID (1705–57) Doctor, philosopher, and psychologist. Educated at Cambridge. His theories of behavioural "Necessity", mental "associationism", and medullary "vibrations", widely influenced such writers as Coleridge, Wordsworth, and Godwin. *Observations on Man*, 1749. His works were edited with an important preface by Priestley.

HAZLITT, WILLIAM (1778–1830) Essayist, critic, republican journalist, painter, aggressive fives player. Educated at Unitarian College, Hackney; art student under Northcote; studied in Paris, 1802. Transformed by meeting with Coleridge, 1798. Parliamentary reporter, dramatic critic, radical journalist for the *Examiner*. Lectures 1817–19; *Liber Amoris* (1823); *The Spirit of the Age* (1825); *Life of Napoleon*, 4 vols (1828–30). Became one of Coleridge's most savage and brilliant critics.

HUTCHINSON, FAMILY From Yorkshire. The elder brothers Tom and George became farmers in various parts of the North Country and Wales. Mary (1770–1859) went to school at Penrith, and became an intimate friend of Dorothy's; married Wordsworth in 1802. Sara (1775–1835), became Coleridge's muse "Asra", and lived more or less permanently with the Wordsworths from 1807; Joanna (1780–1841) lived with her brothers.

JOHNSON, JOSEPH (1738–1809) Born in Liverpool, became radical publisher at St Paul's Churchyard, London, where his shop functioned like a literary club. He published work by Blake, Cowper, Wordsworth, Wollstonecraft, Coleridge, Cooper, Paine, and many others.

KANT, IMMANUEL (1724–1804) Major German philosopher (of partly Scottish descent). Born at Königsberg, where he became lecturer, then Professor of Logic and Metaphysics (1770). *Critique of Pure Reason* (1781); *Critique of Practical Reason* (1788); *Critique of Judgement* (1790). He attacked eighteenth century empirical philosophy and Enlightenment atheism, with an immensely subtle system of knowledge and perception, applying concepts of time and space inherent in consciousness, and his famous twelve "categories" of thought (quantity, quality, causation etc.). Coleridge began to grapple with his work in 1796, and used it in essays after 1809. For a brief coherent account, see Roger Scruton, *Kant*, Oxford Pastmasters, 1982.

KLOPSTOCK, FRIEDRICH GOTTLIEB (1724–1803) German poet known for his patriotic *Odes*, and religious epic *Messias* (1748–73) partly inspired by Milton. He introduced the world of Shakespeare, Ossian, Old Nordic and Celtic poetry into the German revival; Coleridge regarded him as the father of German poetry when he met him in Hamburg.

LAMB, CHARLES (1775–1834) Essayist, poet, eccentric, creator of *Elia*. With his sister Mary (1764–1847), one of Coleridge's most intimate and enduring friends, from earliest days at Christ's Hospital. He eventually described Coleridge as "an archangel slightly damaged", and dedicated volume one of his *Works* (1818) to him.

LE GRICE, CHARLES VALENTINE (1773–1858) With Bob Allen, intimate of Coleridge's at Christ's Hospital; Trinity College, Cambridge; wit and clergyman; he married a rich Cornish widow and settled into comfortable obscurity in Penzance. Published "College Reminiscences" of Coleridge and Lamb in *Gentleman Magazine*, 1833 and 1834. His younger brother Samuel (1775–1802), also Christ's Hospital and Trinity, something of a rake, joined the 60th Foot, and died in Jamaica.

LESSING, GOTTHOLD EPHRAIM (1729–1839) German dramatist and critic. *Minna von Barnhelm* (1767); *Emilia Galotti* (1772), *Miss Sara Sampson* (1755). Much admired by Coleridge, who planned to write his biography. See chapter 8.

LLOYD, CHARLES (1775–1839) Elder son of Birmingham banker and philanthropist; poet and epileptic. After *Edmund Oliver* (1798), he married and settled in the Lake District, at Old Brathay, continuing to make minor mischief. *Desultory Thoughts in London*, 1821. Later went to France and died insane.

LOVELL, ROBERT (1770–96) From Bristol Quaker family; Balliol College, Oxford; Pantisocrat. Published *Poems* with Southey, 1794; in same year married Mary Fricker, by whom he had one child. Contributed to Coleridge's *Watchman*. His tragic early death from fever cut short a possibly brilliant career; Southey promised to edit his works, but never did so.

MACKINTOSH, SIR JAMES (1765–1832) Scottish lawyer, publicist, philosopher. Educated in medicine and law at Edinburgh. First married Daniel Stuart's sister, then Josiah Wedgwood's sister-in-law. After defending the French Revolution against Burke, in his celebrated *Vindiciae Gallicae* (1791), he publically repudiated his arguments. Like Coleridge, he went abroad: Recorder of Bombay (1803–12), then returned as Professor of Law. Coleridge grew to dislike his primness.

MIDDLETON, THOMAS FANSHAW (1769–1822) Clergyman, poet, editor. After encouraging Coleridge at Christ's Hospital and Cambridge, he edited the *Country Spectator*, and the *British Critic*. In 1814 appointed first Protestant Bishop of Calcutta; returned to become a Governor of his old school. A Coleridge Memorial Prize, consisting of a statuette of Coleridge, Lamb and Middleton, is still awarded there.

MORGAN, JOHN (?1775–1820) From Unitarian Bristol family; attended Christ's Hospital, and went into business. Reestablished contact with Coleridge in 1807. Supported him through opium struggles, and writing of *Biographia*.

PAINE, THOMAS (1737–1809) Democrat, revolutionary and agitator. *Common Sense* (1776); *The Rights of Man* (1791–92); *The Age of Reason* (1797). Narrowly escaped Robespierre's guillotine; died in poverty, New Rochelle. Campaigner of genius, distrusted by Coleridge.

PANTISOCRATS, AND POTENTIAL RECRUITS Robert Allen, George Burnett,

George Caldwell, Robert Favell, the Frickers, Robert Lovell, Tom Poole, Robert and Thomas Southey, Southey's dog Rover, and Thomas Chatterton (posthumously).

PITT, WILLIAM THE YOUNGER (1759–1806) Statesman, son of the Earl of Chatham, became Prime Minister aged twenty-four in 1783. Initially associated with liberal causes (parliamentary Reform, anti-Slave Trade). After 1792 he prosecuted a bitter war against Revolutionary France, and a policy of repression at home, restricting freedoms of press and assembly, mounting treason trials, and developing a notorious spy-system. See Coleridge's analysis, chapter 9.

POOLE, THOMAS (1765–1837) See chapter 3. In later life Poole kept up an extensive correspondence with Sara Coleridge, and a fatherly interest in Hartley Coleridge.

PRIESTLEY, JOSEPH (1733–1804) Radical, scientist, philosopher, and leading Unitarian. Coleridge's "Patriot, and Saint, and Sage" (1796). He wrote on chemistry, theology, grammar, education, government, and psychology. After a mob burnt down his house and laboratory, he emigrated to America, settling on the Susquehanna. See chapter 4.

PRICE, DR RICHARD (1723–91) Reformer, preacher, Unitarian minister at Newington Green, London. Friend of Priestley, Franklin, Mary Wollstonecraft. He delivered the famous sermon to the Revolution Society at the Old Jewry, November 1789, which sparked off the controversy between Burke and Paine on the future of the French Revolution, to which Coleridge later added his voice in the *Watchman*.

ROBINSON, MARY "PERDITA" (1758–1800) Actress, novelist and poet; famous for her wit, her beauty, and her hats. Painted by Romney, Gainsborough, Reynolds, and Zoffany. She was crippled by arthritis in later life. See chapter 9. In the developing history and cultural climate of Romanticism, it is instructive to consider the titles of some of her *Poems* (1791) – e.g. "Ode to Melancholy", "Ode to the Nightingale", "Monody to the memory of Chatterton", and "Sonnet: the Mariner".

SCHILLER, FRIEDRICH VON (1759–1805) German dramatist and lyric poet, Professor of History at Jena University, 1789. Central figure in the *sturm und drang* period, translated by Coleridge. *The Robbers* (1781); *Wallenstein* (trilogy, 1799); *Maria Stuart* (1800). Collaborated with Goethe on a collection of ballads, 1797–8, like Coleridge and Wordsworth. Later wrote aesthetic essays, drawing on Kant, and influencing Schlegel brothers and Coleridge.

SHERIDAN, R. B. (1751–1816) Playwright, political orator, theatre manager of Drury Lane for thirty years. Greatly admired by Coleridge until he turned down his play *Osorio*.

SOUTHEY, ROBERT (1774–1843) See chapter 3. Poet Laureate, 1813. Besides poetry and criticism, his crisp and penetrating letters suggest the future biographer: *Life of Nelson* (1813), *Life of Wesley* (1820); *Life of Cowper* (1837).

SOTHEBY, WILLIAM (1757–1833) Translator and minor playwright. Educated at Harrow, served in 10th Dragoons, retired to dedicate himself to the classics. Translated Wieland's *Oberon* (1798, which may have influenced Coleridge's "Christabel"), Virgil's *Georgics* (1800); Homer's *Iliad* (1831) and *Odyssey* (1834).

STUART, DANIEL (1766–1846) Newspaper editor and proprietor. Originally apprenticed to the King's Printer, and secretary to the Whig Society of the Friends of the People. Ran *Morning Post* 1796–1803, taking work from Coleridge, Wordsworth, Lamb and Southey; greatly increased its circulation and influence as the leading national daily, critical of government policy. Later used the evening *Courier* to move towards political centre. Ended career owning Wykham Park, Banbury, and as High Sheriff of Oxfordshire.

THELWALL, "CITIZEN" JOHN (1764–1834) Political lecturer, revolutionary, poet. Studied law and divinity, neither of which suited his incendiary temperament. Tried for High Treason with Tom Hardy, Horne Tooke, and Thomas Holcroft in 1794 (all acquitted after some weeks in the Tower of London). After his retreat to Wales (see chapter 7) he settled as a lecturer in elocution – specialising in stammering – at Brixton.

WEDGWOOD, FAMILY Josiah, senior (1730–95), the Staffordshire pottery master, employed Flaxman for his designs. His sons Josiah (1700–1800) and Tom (1771–1805) were patrons to Coleridge, Wordsworth, Davy, and many others. See chapter 7.

WOLLSTONECRAFT, MARY (1759–97) Feminist writer, educationalist, traveller. With Wordsworth, she was one of the few English people who actually witnessed the revolution in Paris. According to Hazlitt, Coleridge met her at Godwin's after her return to London. He had read her *Rights of Woman* (1792), but particularly admired her Scandinavian travel-book, *A Short Residence in Sweden* (1796). Listening to her argue with her philosopher husband Godwin, Coleridge said she was an example of the ascendancy of imagination over intellect.

WORDSWORTH, FAMILY William (1770–1850), poet laureate; Dorothy (1771–1855), diary writer; John (1772–1805), sea-captain; Christopher (1774–1846), Master of Trinity College, Cambridge; Richard (1768–1816), London lawyer.

Bibliography and References

Sources for this Life of Coleridge will be found in the Reference Notes that follow, with major materials first listed separately under "Abbreviations". The reader will also find suggestions for further study and exploration contained *passim* in the footnotes, and "Coleridge's Circle". A fuller bibliography will appear in my second volume, but for the research student I can recommend *Samuel Taylor Coleridge: An Annotated Bibliography of Criticism and Scholarship*, edited by G. K. Hall, Boston, 1983.

I first give below a list of carefully selected provocations and *stimulants*. These are a variety of finely written and usually short texts, which approach Coleridge – or the drama of his work – in a number of different ways that I have found genuinely inspiring in the course of my own research. They include criticism, fiction, and poetry. The list is deliberately brief, and to some degree eccentric: a challenge to the reader to think again.

Bibliography

1 William Wordsworth, *The Prelude*, Book VI, 1805

2 William Hazlitt, "My First Acquaintance with Poets", 1823; and "Mr Coleridge", in *The Spirit of the Age*, 1825; available in *William Hazlitt: Selected Writings*, edited by Ronald Blythe, Penguin Classics, 1987

3 Charles Baudelaire, "L'Albatros", in *Les Fleurs du Mal*, 1859

4 A. C. Swinburne, "Coleridge", in *Essays and Studies*, 1875

5 Walter Pater, "Coleridge", in *Appreciations*, 1889

6 Henry James, *The Coxon Fund*, 1894 (A short story based on J. D. Campbell's biography; see my preface.)

7 Virginia Woolf, "The Man at the Gate", 1940; in *Collected Essays*, vol. 3, Hogarth Press, 1967

8 Herbert Read, "The Notion of Organic Form", "A Complex Delight", and "Coleridge as Critic", all in *The True Voice of Feeling*, 1947; Faber, 1968

9 Humphry House, *Coleridge: The Clarke Lectures*, Rupert Hart Davis, 1953

10 Stevie Smith, "Thoughts on the Person from Porlock", 1957; in *Collected Poems*, Faber, 1975

11 John Beer, *Coleridge the Visionary*, Chatto, 1959
12 Malcolm Lowry, "Through the Panama", a short story in *Hear Us O Lord from Heaven Thy Dwelling Place*, 1961
13 E. P. Thompson, "Disenchantment or Default: a Lay Sermon", in *Power and Consciousness*, edited by Conor Cruise O'Brien, 1969
14 Walter Jackson Bate, *Coleridge*, 1968; Harvard University Press, 1987
15 A. S. Byatt, *Wordsworth and Coleridge in their Time*, London, 1970
16 Thomas McFarland, "Coleridge's Anxiety", in *Coleridge's Variety: Bicentenary Studies*, edited by John Beer, Macmillan, 1974
17 Kathleen Coburn, *In Pursuit of Coleridge*, (an autobiography of her lifetime's research), Bodley Head, 1977
18 Kelvin Everest, *Coleridge's Secret Ministry*, Harvester Press, 1979
19 Marilyn Butler, "The Rise of the Man of Letters", in *Romantics, Rebels and Reactionaries*, Oxford, 1981
20 Claude Prance, *Companion to Charles Lamb: A Guide to People and Places, 1760–1847*, Mansell Publishing, 1983 (This historical dictionary, based on a private collection of 700 volumes of Lambiana, can be read through like a novel of Romantic manners.)
21 Molly Lefebure, *The Bondage of Love: A Life of Mrs Samuel Taylor Coleridge*, Gollancz, 1986
22 Rupert Christiansen, *Romantic Affinities: Portraits from an Age, 1780–1830*, Bodley Head, 1988
23 Sue Limb, *The Wordsmiths at Gorsemere: An Everyday Story of Towering Genius*, Bantam, 1987

References

ABBREVIATIONS USED IN REFERENCE NOTES

(1) Works by Coleridge

Letters – *Collected Letters of Samuel Taylor Coleridge*, 6 vols, edited by E. L. Griggs, Oxford, 1956–71

Notebooks – *The Notebooks of Samuel Taylor Coleridge*, 3 double vols, edited by Kathleen Coburn, Bollingen Series and Routledge, 1957–73

P. W. – *Coleridge: Poetical Works*, edited by E. H. Coleridge, Oxford, 1912, 1980

Complete Poetical Works – *The Complete Poetical Works of Samuel Taylor Coleridge*, edited by E. H. Coleridge, 2 vols, Oxford, 1912, 1975

Biographia – *Biographia Literaria*, edited by J. Shawcross, 2 vols, Oxford, 1907, 1979

Lectures – *Lectures 1795: On Politics and Religion*, edited by Lewis Patton and Peter Mann, Bollingen Series, 1971

Essays – *Essays on his Times*, 3 vols, edited by D. V. Erdman, Bollingen Series, 1978

Watchman – *The Watchman*, edited by Lewis Patton, Bollingen Series, 1970

Friend – *The Friend*, 2 vols, edited by Barbara E. Rooke, Bollingen Series, 1969

Table Talk – *The Table Talk and Omniana*, edited by Coventry Patmore, 1917

(2) Manuscript sources

Dove Cottage – Manuscripts relating to the Wordsworth circle, held by the Wordsworth Trust, Dove Cottage, Grasmere, Cumbria

Bodleian – Manuscripts held at the Bodleian Library, Oxford; notably in the Abinger Collection relating to the Shelley–Godwin circle

British Museum – Manuscripts held at the British Museum, now the British Library, London. These include: The Gutch Memorandum Book, Add. Mss. 27901; Coleridge's original Notebooks, Nos 1–50, Add. Mss. 47,496–47,545; Tom Poole's papers, Add. Mss. 35,343–5; Daniel Stuart's papers, Add. Mss. 34,046; and miscellaneous Coleridge papers, Egerton 2800–1

(3) Secondary Works

Campbell – *Samuel Taylor Coleridge: A Narrative of the Events of his Life*, by James Dykes Campbell, 1894; Basil Savage, Highgate, London, 1970

Chambers – *Samuel Taylor Coleridge: A Biographical Study*, by E. K. Chambers, Oxford, 1938

Cottle – *Early Recollections; chiefly relating to the late Samuel Taylor Coleridge*, 2 vols, by Joseph Cottle, 1837

Devonshire – *The Story of a Devonshire House*, by Lord Coleridge, K. C., Fisher Unwin, 1905

Dorothy – *The Journals of Dorothy Wordsworth*, edited by Mary Moorman, Oxford, 1971

Fruman – *Coleridge, the Damaged Archangel*, by Norman Fruman, Braziller, 1971

Gillman – *The Life of Samuel Taylor Coleridge*, by James Gillman, 1838

Hazlitt – *William Hazlitt: Selected Writings*, edited by Ronald Blythe, Penguin Classics, 1987

Heritage – *Coleridge: the Critical Heritage*, edited by J. R. de J. Jackson, Routledge, 1970

Lamb – *The Letters of Charles and Mary Lamb*, 3 vols, edited by Edwin J. Marrs, Jr, Cornell University Press, 1975

Lefebure – *Samuel Taylor Coleridge: A Bondage of Opium*, by Molly Lefebure, Gollancz, 1974; Quartet, 1977

Lowes – *The Road to Xanadu*, by John Livingston Lowes, 1927; Picador, 1978.

Moorman – *William Wordsworth, A Biography*, 2 vols, by Mary Moorman, Oxford, 1957–65

Poole – *Thomas Poole and his Friends*, 2 vols, by Mrs Henry Sandford, 1888

Southey – *New Letters of Robert Southey*, 2 vols, edited by Kenneth Curry, New York, 1965

Wordsworth – *The Early Letters of William and Dorothy Wordsworth*, edited by E. de Selincourt, Oxford, 1935; revised 1970

Reference Notes

Preface

I For example, opium addiction in Lefebure; plagiarism in Fruman; apostacy in Hazlitt, *passim*, and Nicolas Roe, *Wordsworth and Coleridge: the Radical Years*, Oxford, 1988; sexual fantasies in Lefebure, Fruman, and Geoffrey Yarlott, *Coleridge and the Abyssinian Maid*, London, 1967; and Coleridge's unsatisfactory marriage in Molly Lefebure, *The Bondage of Love: a Life of Mrs Samuel Taylor Coleridge*, Gollancz, 1986. It should be emphasised that many of the best writers on Coleridge are to some degree hostile towards him, a necessary abrasion perhaps. See my later remarks on Hazlitt.

Chapter 1: Child of Nature

1 *P.W.*, p. 174
2 Gillman, p. 12
3 *Letters*, I, p. 347
4 *P.W.*, p. 324
5 *Letters*, I, p. 179
6 *Devonshire*, p. 11
7 *Letters*, I, p. 303
8 Bodleian MS Abinger C604/3
9 Gillman, p. 2
10 Chambers, p. 4
11 *Letters*, I, p. 310
12 Ibid, p. 311
13 *Philip Quarll, The English Hermit*, 1724, p. 157
14 *P.W.*, p. 325
15 *Letters*, I, p. 347
16 *P.W.*, p. 197
17 Ibid, p. 241
18 *Letters*, I, p. 347
19 *Devonshire*, p. 62
20 *Letters*, I, p. 310
21 Ibid, p. 354
22 Campbell, p. 10
23 Gillman, p. 28
24 *Letters*, II, p. 758
25 Ibid, III, p. 31
26 Southey, I, p. 195
27 *Devonshire*, p. 25
28 Ibid, p. 44
29 *Letters*, I, p. 347
30 *Friend*, I, p. 148n
31 *Letters*, I, pp. 347–8
32 Bodleian MS Abinger C604/3
33 *Letters*, I, p. 348
34 *P.W.*, pp. 413–4
35 *Friend*, I, pp. 148–9
36 *P.W.*, p. 54
37 Ibid, p. 48
38 *Letters*, I, p. 348
39 *P.W.*, p. 173
40 *Letters*, I, p. 311
41 *P.W.*, p. 78
42 *Devonshire*, p. 46
43 Ibid, p. 47
44 *Letters*, I, p. 353
45 Ibid, pp. 353–4
46 *Notebooks*, I, 1416
47 *P.W.*, p. 287
48 *Letters*, I, p. 53
49 Ibid, p. 354
50 Ibid, pp. 354–5
51 Ibid, II, p. 1053
52 Gillman, p. 10

Chapter 2: Orphan of the Storm

1 *Letters*, I, p. 355
2 Ibid, p. 388

3 Church Archives, St Mary Ottery
4 *Devonshire*, p. 29
5 Ibid, p. 40
6 *P.W.*, p. 184
7 Ibid, p. 29
8 *Letters*, I, p. 388
9 Gillman, p. 12
10 Bodleian MS Abinger C604/3
11 *Letters*, I, p. 1
12 Gillman, p. 17
13 Ibid, p. 20
14 Ibid, p. 188; *Table Talk*, p. 134
15 Ibid, p. 20
16 *Biographia*, I, p. 8
17 Gillman, p. 23
18 Ibid, pp. 21–2
19 Ibid, p. 24
20 Leigh Hunt, *Autobiography*, 1850, edited by Edmund Blunden, Oxford, 1928
21 e.g. *Notebooks*, I, 1176
22 *P.W.*, p. 4
23 *Letters*, I, pp. 2–3
24 *Letters*, II, p. 791
25 *The Prelude*, 1805, Bk VI, lines 274–6
26 Campbell, p. 14; Charles Lamb, "Christ's Hospital Five-and-Thirty Years Ago", 1820, *Essays of Elia: First Series*, Moxon, 1840, p. 13
27 *P.W.*, p. 11
28 Ibid, p. 11
29 *Biographia*, I, p. 9
30 Ibid, p. 7
31 Ibid, pp. 13–14
32 Ibid, p. 10
33 Gillman, p. 28; *Letters*, V, p. 218
34 *Biographia*, I, p. 4
35 Ibid, p. 5
36 *Letters*, I, p. 7. *P.W.*, p. 18
37 *P.W.*, p. 17
38 Ibid, p. 20
39 Ibid, p. 20
40 Ibid, p. 29

Chapter 3: Prodigal Son

1 Gillman, p. 21
2 *Letters*, I, pp. 21–2
3 Ibid, p. 15
4 Ibid, p. 18
5 Ibid, pp. 16–17
6 Ibid, p. 18
7 Ibid, p. 18
8 Ibid, p. 22
9 Ibid, p. 31
10 Ibid, pp. 27–8
11 Ibid, p. 30
12 Ibid, p. 26
13 Ibid, p. 35
14 Ibid, p. 34
15 Ibid, p. 35
16 Campbell, pp. 653–4
17 *Letters*, I, p. 40
18 Ibid, p. 54
19 Ibid, p. 41
20 Ibid, p. 41
21 Ibid, p. 67
22 Chambers, p. 20
23 *Letters*, I, pp. 49–50
24 Ibid, p. 52
25 Gillman, p. 54n
26 Henry Gunning, *Reminiscences of the University, Town, and County of Cambridge*, vol. I, 1855, p. 279
27 Ibid, p. 308
28 Chambers, p. 20
29 Henry Gunning, op. cit., p. 297
30 Ibid, pp. 297–8
31 Daniel Stuart, *Gentleman's Magazine*, vol. 10, July 1838, pp. 124–8
32 Gillman, p. 55
33 Henry Gunning, op. cit., pp. 299–301
34 *Letters*, I, p. 53
35 Ibid, p. 46
36 Ibid, p. 51
37 Ibid, p. 59
38 Christopher Wordsworth, *Social Life at the English Universities*, 1874, pp. 587–90
39 *Letters*, I, p. 60
40 Ibid, p. 130
41 *P.W.*, p. 42
42 Ibid, p. 40n
43 *Letters*, I, p. 68
44 Ibid, p. 68
45 *P.W.*, p. 55
46 Christopher Wordsworth, op. cit., pp. 587–92
47 *Letters*, I, p. 67

48 Ibid, p. 66
49 Ibid, p. 62
50 Chambers, p. 23
51 *Letters*, I, p. 65
52 Ibid, p. 63
53 Ibid, p. 64n
54 Ibid, p. 65
55 Ibid, pp. 67–8
56 Ibid, p. 71
57 Ibid, p. 71
58 Ibid, p. 73
59 Ibid, p. 72n
60 *Letters*, I, p. 78
61 Ibid, p. 79
62 Ibid, p. 76n

Chapter 4: Pantisocrat

1 *Letters*, I, pp. 80–1
2 Ibid, p. 80
3 Ibid, p. 82
4 Ibid, p. 93
5 Ibid, p. 84
6 *Southey*, I, p. 56
7 *Lamb*, I, p. 196
8 *Southey*, I, p. 58
9 Ibid, pp. 74–5
10 *Letters*, I, p. 152 and Bodleian MS Abinger C604/3
11 Ibid, pp. 84–5
12 Ibid, pp. 89–91
13 Joseph Hucks, *A Pedestrian Tour Through North Wales*, 1795, p. 26
14 *Notebooks*, II, 2398
15 *Friend*, II, pp. 146–7
16 *Letters*, I, pp. 88–9
17 *Table Talk*, p. 107
18 Joseph Hucks, op. cit., p. 110
19 *Letters*, I, p. 92
20 Ibid, p. 88
21 Ibid, p. 92
22 *P.W.*, p. 63
23 *Letters*, I, p. 96
24 *Southey*, I, pp. 67–8
25 Cottle, I, p. 7
26 *Letters*, I, p. 132
27 Molly Lefebure, *The Bondage of Love: A Life of Mrs Samuel Taylor Coleridge*, Gollancz, 1986, p. 31–2
28 *Southey*, I, p. 68
29 Ibid, p. 68
30 *P.W.*, pp. 58–9
31 *Poole*, I, p. 101
32 Ibid, p. 103
33 Ibid, pp. 98–9
34 Ibid, p. 98
35 Ibid, pp. 96–7
36 *Complete Poetical Works*, II, p. 502
37 *P.W.*, p. 71
38 *Southey*, I, p. 70
39 Ibid, p. 71
40 Ibid, p. 72
41 *Letters*, I, p. 103
42 *P.W.*, p. 69; *Letters*, I, p. 104
43 Ibid, pp. 68–9
44 *Letters*, I, p. 98
45 Thomas Cooper, *Some Information Respecting America*, 1794, p. 105; and Sister E. Logan, "Pantisocracy" in PMLA, vol. 45, 1930
46 *Letters*, I, p. 99
47 Ibid, p. 97
48 Ibid, p. 103
49 Ibid, p. 119
50 Ibid, p. 117
51 Ibid, pp. 114–15
52 Ibid, p. 115
53 Ibid, pp. 112–13
54 Ibid, p. 116
55 Ibid, p. 116
56 Ibid, p. 122
57 Ibid, p. 127
58 Ibid, p. 130
59 Ibid, p. 137
60 *Friend*, II, p. 146
61 *Letters*, I, p. 121
62 *P.W.*, p. 75; *Letters*, I, p. 143
63 *Letters*, I, p. 119
64 Ibid, p. 154
65 Ibid, p. 132
66 *Southey*, I, pp. 89–90
67 *Letters*, I, p. 138
68 Ibid, p. 151
69 Ibid, p. 102
70 Ibid, p. 147; with alterations in *P.W.*, pp. 78–9
71 Ibid, p. 144
72 Ibid, p. 145
73 Ibid, p. 148
74 *Southey*, I, p. 91

Chapter 5: Watchman

1 *Letters*, I, p. 165
2 *Gentleman's Magazine*, April 1796
3 Joseph Priestley, *Memoirs*, 1806, vol. I, p. 126
4 Ibid, p. 165
5 "Thomas Cooper M.D., 1759–1840", in *The Dictionary of National Biography*
6 Gillman, p. 69
7 *Letters*, I, p. 150
8 Richard Holmes, "Chatterton", *Cornhill Magazine*, No. 1065, Autumn 1970
9 *Monthly Magazine*, Oct. 1819, p. 204
10 *Lectures*, p. 5
11 Cottle, I, p. 178n
12 *Lectures*, p. 5
13 *Monthly Magazine*, Oct. 1819, pp. 203–5
14 *Letters*, I, p. 152
15 *Notebooks*, I, p. 42
16 *Letters*, I, p. 151
17 Ibid, p. 164
18 *P.W.*, p. 101
19 *Southey*, I, p. 93
20 *Lectures*, p. 215
21 Ibid, p. 108
22 Ibid, p. 2
23 *Letters*, I, pp. 164–5
24 British Museum Adds MS 47, 530 v 35
25 *Letters*, I, p. 165
26 Ibid, p. 165
27 Ibid, p. 173
28 Moorman, I, p. 271
29 *Poole*, I, pp. 124–6
30 *P.W.*, p. 97
31 Ibid, p. 97n
32 *Letters*, I, p. 160
33 Ibid, p. 160
34 *Poole*, I, p. 122
35 *P.W.*, p. 102
36 *Lamb*, I, p. 12
37 *Notebooks*, I, 54, 73
38 *P.W.*, p. 108
39 *Lectures*, p. 70 and n
40 Ibid, p. 43
41 Ibid, p. 29
42 *Poole*, I, p. 123
43 *Lectures*, p. 361
44 *Letters*, I, p. 174
45 Ibid, p. 161
46 *Biographia*, I, pp. 115–16
47 *Letters*, I, p. 182
48 Ibid, p. 176
49 Ibid, p. 177
50 Ibid, p. 180
51 Ibid, p. 185
52 Ibid, p. 197
53 *P.W.*, p. 66
54 *Letters*, I, p. 192
55 Ibid, p. 192
56 Ibid, p. 192
57 Ibid, p. 195
58 Ibid, p. 195n
59 Ibid, p. 205
60 *P.W.*, p. 101
61 *Letters*, I, p. 227
62 *P.W.*, p. 108n
63 *Lamb*, I, p. 19
64 Ibid, p. 18
65 Ibid, p. 61
66 *Letters*, I, p. 207
67 Ibid, p. 208
68 Ibid, p. 208
69 Ibid, p. 240
70 Ibid, p. 212

Chapter 6: Prodigal Father

1 *Letters*, I, pp. 209–10
2 Ibid, p. 209
3 *Friend*, II, p. 26n
4 Ibid, p. 25n
5 *Letters*, I, p. 217
6 *Notebooks*, I, 176
7 *Letters*, I, p. 218
8 Ibid, p. 223
9 *Notebooks*, I, 161, 174
10 Ibid, 174
11 Moorman, I, p. 291
12 *P.W.*, p. 122
13 *Letters*, I, pp. 216–17
14 Ibid, p. 227; and *Lamb*, I, p. 23
15 *Letters*, I, p. 232
16 Ibid, p. 231
17 Ibid, p. 231
18 Ibid, p. 236
19 Ibid, p. 236
20 *P.W.*, p. 154
21 *Letters*, I, p. 240

22 Ibid, p. 242
23 Ibid, p. 237
24 Ibid, p. 238
25 Ibid, p. 252
26 The Preface is reprinted in *Complete Poetical Works*, II, p. 1139
27 *Letters*, I, p. 239; and *Lamb*, I, pp. 44–5; 51
28 *Lamb*, I, p. 52
29 *Letters*, I, pp. 249–50
30 Ibid, p. 257
31 Ibid, p. 250
32 Ibid, p. 249
33 *Lamb*, I, p. 58
34 *Letters*, I, p. 251
35 Ibid, p. 259
36 Ibid, p. 277
37 Ibid, pp. 259–60
38 Ibid, pp. 259–60
39 Ibid, p. 282
40 Ibid, p. 278
41 Ibid, pp. 278–9
42 Ibid, p. 295
43 Ibid, p. 253
44 Ibid, p. 262
45 Ibid, p. 284
46 Ibid, p. 264
47 Ibid, p. 270
48 Ibid, p. 266
49 *P.W.*, p. 168
50 *Letters*, I, p. 271
51 Ibid, pp. 274–6
52 Ibid, p. 287
53 Ibid, p. 288
54 *Notebooks*, I, 213, 217
55 *Letters*, I, p. 296

Chapter 7: Kubla Coleridge

1 *Biographia*, I, p. 121
2 *Letters*, I, p. 302
3 Ibid, p. 308
4 Ibid, p. 308
5 *Biographia*, I, p. 121
6 *Letters*, I, p. 297
7 Ibid, p. 273
8 *Biographia*, I, pp. 132–3
9 *Letters*, I, p. 301
10 Ibid, p. 322
11 Second edition 1800, in *P.W.*, p. 186
12 *Lamb*, I, pp. 95–7
13 *Letters*, I, p. 309
14 *P.W.*, p. 134
15 Ibid, p. 148
16 Ibid, p. 135n
17 Ibid, p. 197
18 Ibid, p. 140
19 Ibid, p. 140n
20 *Letters*, I, p. 313
21 Ibid, p. 316
22 Ibid, p. 318
23 Ibid, p. 316
24 Ibid, p. 318
25 Ibid, p. 318
26 Ibid, p. 321
27 Ibid, p. 320
28 Ibid, p. 319; and *Biographia*, I, pp. 58–9
29 Ibid, p. 324
30 Ibid, pp. 320–1
31 Ibid, p. 323
32 *Lamb*, I, p. 109
33 Cottle, I, pp. 146–7
34 *P.W.*, p. 175
35 Ibid, p. 174
36 Ibid, p. 175
37 MS note in *P.W.*, I, p. 173n
38 *Letters*, I, p. 330; and *Heritage* p. 42
39 Moorman, I, p. 317
40 *Letters*, I, p. 325
41 *Wordsworth*, I, p. 168
42 *Letters*, I, p. 327
43 Ibid, p. 336
44 Ibid, p. 336
45 Ibid, p. 334
46 Moorman, I, p. 326
47 *Letters*, I, p. 339
48 MS note in *P.W.*, pp. 179 and 181
49 *Letters*, I, pp. 330–1
50 *Lamb*, I, p. 224
51 *P.W.*, p. 181
52 *Letters*, I, p. 334
53 *Poole*, I, p. 235
54 Ibid, p. 233
55 Ibid, p. 233
56 Edmund Blunden and E. L. Griggs, *Coleridge: Studies by Several Hands*, Constable, 1934, p. 83
57 *Letters*, I, pp. 339–40
58 *Poole*, I, p. 233

59 John Thelwall, *Poems Written Chiefly in Retirement*, 1805, pp. 129–31
60 *Table Talk*, July 1830, p. 105
61 Moorman, I, p. 328
62 *Table Talk*, July 1830, p. 105
63 *Letters*, I, p. 342
64 Ibid, pp. 343–4
65 Blunden and Griggs, op. cit., p. 82
66 *Letters*, I, p. 344
67 *Dorothy*, p. 1. All further citations are simply dated in my text, without additional references, as many modern editions (several illustrated) are available to the reader.
68 Blunden and Griggs, op. cit., p. 80
69 *Biographia*, I, p. 128
70 Ibid, p. 129
71 *Biographia*, I, p. 129
72 Letters, I, p. 355
73 Ibid, p. 355
74 *Complete Poetical Works*, II, p. 584
75 *Notebooks*, I, 1840
76 Samuel Purchas, *Purchas his Pilgrimage*, 1614, Bk 4 Chapter 13, p. 415
77 *Notebooks*, III, 4006
78 Lowes, p. 323
79 *Complete Poetical Works*, II, p. 552
80 *Notebooks*, I, 240–1
81 *Letters*, I, p. 350
82 Ibid, p. 349
83 *P.W.*, p. 298
84 *Letters*, I, p. 539
85 *P.W.*, p. 325n

Chapter 8: Mariner

1 *P.W.*, pp. 267–84
2 Ibid, pp. 286–7
3 Moorman, I, p. 345
4 *P.W.*, p. 287
5 Moorman, I, p. 347
6 Ibid, p. 347
7 Ibid, p. 348
8 *Letters*, I, p. 357
9 *P.W.*, p. 190
10 *Letters*, I, p. 357
11 Ibid, p. 357
12 Barbara and Hensleigh Wedgwood, *The Wedgwood Circle 1730–1897*, Studio Vista, 1980, pp. 110–11
13 *Letters*, p. 360n
14 *P.W.*, p. 237
15 *Letters*, I, p. 360n
16 Ibid, p. 365
17 William St Clair, unpublished paper given at the Royal Institution, London, 1988, based on Treasury Tax Returns c.1800–15. Other indicative figures include pension for an Admiral's wife set at £120 p.a.
18 Moorman, I, pp. 269–70
19 *Letters*, I, pp. 365–7
20 Ibid, p. 367
21 *Hazlitt*, p. 45
22 *Letters*, I, p. 374
23 *Hazlitt*, pp. 46–55
24 *Letters*, I, p. 394
25 Ibid, p. 374
26 Ibid, p. 383n
27 Ibid, p. 375
28 Ibid, p. 383
29 Ibid, p. 372
30 Ibid, pp. 377–9
31 *Wordsworth*, I, p. 188
32 *Letters*, I, p. 387
33 *Notebooks*, I, 330
34 *P.W.*, p. 242
35 Ibid, p. 242
36 *Notebooks*, I, 329
37 Ibid, p. 209
38 *Biographia*, I, p. 167
39 John Beer, *Coleridge's Poetic Intelligence*, Macmillan, 1977, pp. 142–3
40 *P.W.*, pp. 242n–3n
41 *Letters*, I, pp. 394–5
42 Ibid, p. 397
43 *The Prelude*, 1850, Bk XIV, line 395ff
44 *Letters*, I, p. 411n
45 Ibid, pp. 391, 399
46 Ibid, p. 391
47 Ibid, p. 399
48 Ibid, p. 400
49 Ibid, p. 403
50 Moorman, I, p. 372
51 *Letters*, I, p. 412
52 *Letters*, I, p. 412

53 *Lyrical Ballads*, 1798, p. ii
54 *Biographia*, II, p. 6
55 Ibid, p. 5
56 Ibid, p. 6
57 Moorman, I, p. 382
58 *P.W.*, p. 185
59 *Letters*, I, p. 391
60 Ibid, p. 410
61 *P.W.*, p. 265
62 Ibid, p. 266
63 *Notebooks*, I, 219
64 *P.W.*, pp. 266–7
65 *Hazlitt*, pp. 57–64
66 Ibid, pp. 59–60
67 *Biographia*, I, p. 137
68 *Letters*, I, p. 403
69 *P.W.*, I, p. 243
70 *Letters*, I, pp. 413–14
71 Ibid, p. 414
72 Ibid, p. 441
73 *Lamb*, I, p. 128
74 Ibid, p. 128
75 *Heritage*, p. 53
76 *Lamb*, I, pp. 142–3
77 *Letters*, I, p. 432
78 Molly Lefebure, *Mrs Samuel Taylor Coleridge*, op. cit., p. 109
79 *Heritage*, pp. 48–9
80 *Letters*, I, p. 420
81 *P.W.*, I, p. 262
82 Ibid, p. 245
83 Ibid, p. 245
84 Ibid, p. 246
85 Ibid, p. 247
86 *Letters*, I, p. 425
87 Ibid, p. 415
88 Ibid, p. 416
89 Ibid, p. 416

Chap :r 9: Der Wanderer
1 *Letters*, I, pp. 425–6
2 Ibid, p. 416
3 Ibid, p. 426
4 Ibid, pp. 415–17
5 Ibid, p. 443
6 Ibid, p. 443
7 Ibid, p. 435
8 Ibid, p. 433
9 *Notebooks*, I, 340
10 Ibid, I, 342
11 *Letters*, I, p. 460; *Notebooks*, I, 360
12 *Notebooks*, I, 346
13 *Letters*, I, p. 445
14 Ibid, p. 445
15 *Poole*, I, pp. 279–80
16 *Letters*, I, p. 445
17 Ibid, p. 449
18 *Biographia*, I, pp. 137–8n
19 *Letters*, p. 461
20 Ibid, p. 461
21 Ibid, p. 462
22 *The Prelude*, 1805, Bk I, lines 467–72
23 *Wordsworth*, I, p. 105
24 *Letters*, I, p. 451
25 Ibid, p. 452
26 Ibid, pp. 452–3
27 Ibid, p. 454
28 Ibid, p. 449
29 Ibid, p. 485
30 Ibid, p. 485
31 Ibid, p. 486
32 Ibid, p. 457
33 Ibid, pp. 454–5
34 Ibid, pp. 454–5
35 Ibid, p. 455
36 Ibid, p. 459
37 *Notebooks*, I, 377
38 Ibid, 383
39 Coleridge, *Shakespearean Criticism*, 2 vols, edited by T. M. Raysor, 1907, 1962; II, p. 103
40 *Letters*, I, p. 472
41 Ibid, p. 473
42 *Notebooks*, I, 399
43 *Letters*, I, p. 475
44 Ibid, p. 475
45 Ibid, p. 518
46 Ibid, p. 476
47 Ibid, p. 476
48 Ibid, p. 519
49 Ibid, p. 477
50 Ibid, p. 470
51 Ibid, pp. 470–1
52 Lefebure, p. 113
53 *Poole*, I, pp. 290–4
54 Molly Lefebure, *Mrs Samuel Taylor Coleridge*, op. cit., p. 117
55 *Letters*, I, p. 478
56 Ibid, p. 479
57 Ibid, p. 479
58 Ibid, p. 480

59 Ibid, p. 483
60 Ibid, p. 483
61 Clement Carlyon, MD, *Early Years and Late Reflections*, 2 vols, 1836; I, p. 90
62 *Letters*, I, p. 490
63 Ibid, p. 484
64 Ibid, p. 488
65 Ibid, p. 490
66 Ibid, p. 494
67 Ibid, p. 494
68 Ibid, p. 494
69 Clement Carlyon, op. cit, I, pp. 50–1
70 Ibid, pp. 29–30
71 Ibid, pp. 100–1n
72 *Letters*, I, p. 496
73 Clement Carlyon, op. cit., I, p. 51
74 *Friend*, II, Dec. 1809
75 *P.W.*, p. 189
76 *Letters*, I, p. 512
77 Ibid, p. 498
78 Ibid, p. 505
79 Ibid, p. 493
80 *P.W.*, pp. 315–16
81 Ibid, p. 328
82 Ibid, p. 311
83 *Letters*, I, p. 51
84 Ibid, p. 501
85 Clement Carlyon, op. cit., I, p. 127
86 *Letters*, I, p. 510
87 Ibid, p. 519
88 Ibid, p. 518
89 Ibid, p. 519
90 Ibid, p. 519
91 Clement Carlyon, op. cit., I, pp. 161–2
92 *Letters*, I, p. 520
93 Clement Carlyon, op. cit., I, p. 179
94 *Letters*, I, pp. 522–3
95 *Notebooks*, I, 452

Chapter 10: Journeyman

1 *Letters*, I, p. 484
2 Ibid, p. 525
3 Ibid, p. 523
4 *Southey*, I, p. 191
5 *Poole*, I, p. 301
6 *Letters*, I, p. 523
7 Ibid, p. 524
8 Ibid, p. 528
9 *P.W.*, pp. 319–23
10 *Notes and Queries*, August 1889, 7th series, vol. 8, p. 161
11 *P.W.*, p. 320
12 *Letters*, I, p. 540
13 Ibid, p. 528
14 Ibid, p. 526
15 Ibid, p. 527
16 Ibid, pp. 533–4
17 Ibid, p. 534
18 Ibid, p. 535
19 Ibid, p. 538
20 *Notebooks*, I, 556
21 *Letters*, I, p. 540
22 Ibid, p. 538
23 *Notebooks*, I, 490
24 Ibid, 493
25 Ibid, 496
26 Ibid, 523 -
27 Ibid, 528
28 Ibid, 549
29 Ibid, 551
30 Ibid, 540
31 *Letters*, I, pp. 544–5
32 Ibid, p. 544
33 Ibid, p. 543
34 Moorman, I, p. 440
35 *Letters*, I, p. 545
36 *Notebooks*, I, 555
37 Ibid, 578
38 *P.W.*, p. 346
39 *Notebooks*, I, 1575
40 Ibid, 1575
41 *P.W.*, pp. 330–2
42 Campbell, p. 613
43 *Notebooks*, I, 579
44 *P.W.*, p. 334
45 *Letters*, I, p. 551
46 *Notebooks*, I, 582, compare I, 1589 written October 1803
47 *Letters*, II, p. 842; *Notebooks*, I, 1589; 1779
48 *Notebooks*, I, 1592
49 *Biographia*, I, p. 141
50 Ibid, p. 142
51 *Essays*, I, pp. 39–40
52 *Letters*, I, p. 552
53 Ibid, p. 568
54 Ibid, p. 569
55 Ibid, p. 552n
56 *Essays*, I, p. lxvii

57 *Letters*, I, pp. 562–3
58 Ibid, p. 553
59 Ibid, p. 549
60 Don Locke, *A Fantasy of Reason: The Life and Thought of William Godwin*, Routledge, 1980, pp. 181–2
61 Bodleian MS Abinger C604/3
62 *Letters*, I, p. 549
63 Ibid, p. 588
64 Ibid, p. 557
65 Ibid, p. 553
66 Ibid, p. 556
67 Ibid, p. 562
68 Ibid, pp. 570–1
69 Ibid, p. 588
70 Ibid, p. 572
71 Ibid, p. 582
72 Ibid, p. 584
73 Ibid, p. 585
74 Ibid, p. 582
75 Ibid, pp. 582–3
76 Ibid, p. 571
77 *Lamb*, I, p. 217
78 Ibid, p. 189
79 *Letters*, I, p. 581
80 Ibid, pp. 579–80
81 *Essays*, I, p. 114
82 *Lamb*, I, p. 168
83 *Essays*, I, p. 131
84 Ibid, p. 162
85 Ibid, p. 219
86 Ibid, p. 220
87 Ibid, p. 223
88 Ibid, p. 221
89 John Colmer, *Coleridge: Critic of Society*, Oxford, 1959, p. 79
90 *Essays*, I, p. 226
91 *Lamb*, I, p. 189
92 *Letters*, I, p. 587
93 Ibid, p. 579
94 Chambers, p. 125
95 *Complete Poetical Works*, II, pp. 598–9
96 *Table Talk*, p. 425
97 Ibid, p. 210
98 *Complete Poetical Works*, II, p. 649
99 *Essays*, I, p. 226n
100 Ibid, p. 238
101 *Lamb*, I, p. 191
102 *Notebooks*, I, 720
103 Ibid, 718
104 Moorman, I, p. 476
105 *Letters*, I, p. 587
106 Ibid, pp. 585–6
107 *Southey*, I, pp. 220, 210
108 Moorman, I, p. 487

Chapter 11: Laker

1 *Letters*, I, p. 588
2 Ibid, p. 590
3 *Notebooks*, I, 760
4 Ibid, 753
5 *Letters* I, pp. 593–602
6 Ibid, p. 603
7 Ibid, p. 605
8 Ibid, p. 612
9 Ibid, pp. 611–12
10 Ibid, p. 612
11 Ibid, p. 612
12 Ibid, p. 618
13 Ibid, p. 620
14 Ibid, p. 644
15 Ibid, p. 658
16 *P.W.*, pp. 347–8. For a scholarly dispute over Wordsworth's possible authorship of part of this poem, see Stephen Parrish and David Erdman, *Bulletin of the New York Public Library*, LXIV, (1960), pp. 209–37. But "The Mad Monk" was first published under Coleridge's name in an anthology in 1804, and Wordsworth never reclaimed it. The beautiful "Sicilian" opening is clearly Coleridge's, yet perhaps the "voice" is partly based on Wordsworth. See my footnote, p. 43
17 *Letters*, I, pp. 618–19
18 Ibid, p. 643
19 *Notebooks*, I, 798
20 Ibid, 799; and *Dorothy*, p. 37 (29 August 1800). See Chapter 7, note 67.
21 Ibid, 808
22 Ibid, 834
23 Ibid, 835
24 Ibid, 785–7
25 Campbell, p. 117
26 *Letters*, I, p. 627

27 *Notebooks*, I, 828
28 Moorman, I, p. 490
29 *Letters*, I, p. 643
30 Ibid, p. 631
31 Moorman, I, p. 491
32 *Letters*, I, p. 658
33 Ibid, pp. 631, 634
34 *Wordsworth*, I, p. 267
35 *Letters*, I, p. 643
36 *P.W.*, p. 226
37 *Table Talk*, p. 441
38 *P.W.*, p. 235
39 Ibid, p. 232
40 *Letters*, I, p. 634
41 *Notebooks*, I, 830
42 *Letters*, I, p. 638
43 *Notebooks*, I, 828
44 *Letters*, I, p. 638
45 Ibid, pp. 638–9
46 Ibid, pp. 647–9
47 Lefebure, Appendix I
48 *Notebooks*, I, 832; compare with *P.W.*, I, pp. 367–8 lines 110–13
49 Ibid, 848
50 *Letters*, I, pp. 643–4
51 *Notebooks*, I, 869
52 *Letters*, I, p. 651
53 Ibid, p. 648
54 Ibid, p. 652
55 *Notebooks*, I, 863
56 *Letters*, I, pp. 649–50
57 *P.W.*, p. 378
58 *Letters*, I, p. 654
59 Ibid, p. 656

Chapter 12: Lover

1 *Letters*, II, p. 668–9
2 *P.W.*, p. 368
3 *Letters*, II, p. 731
4 Ibid, p. 668
5 *Notebooks*, I, 918
6 Ibid, 923
7 Ibid, 925
8 Ibid, 926
9 *Biographia*, II, pp. 128–9
10 *Letters*, II, pp. 677–703
11 *Notebooks*, I, 887
12 *Letters*, II, pp. 677–703
13 Ibid, p. 706
14 *Notebooks*, I, 932
15 *Letters*, II, pp. 713–14
16 Ibid, p. 709
17 Ibid, p. 719
18 *Wordsworth*, I, p. 273
19 *Letters*, II, pp. 732–3
20 Ibid, p. 727
21 Ibid, p. 717
22 Ibid, p. 710
23 *Wordsworth*, I, p. 281
24 *Letters*, II, p. 755
25 Ibid, p. 745
26 *Notebooks*, I, 959
27 Ibid, 948
28 Ibid, 949
29 *Letters*, II, p. 736
30 Ibid, p. 739
31 Ibid, p. 747
32 *Notebooks*, I, 970
33 *Letters*, II, p. 751
34 *Notebooks*, I, 979
35 *P.W.*, p. 359
36 Ibid, p. 387
37 *Notebooks*, I, 985
38 Ibid, 984
39 *Notebooks*, III, 3708
40 *Letters*, II, pp. 792–3
41 *Notebooks*, I, 980
42 *P.W.*, p. 382
43 *Letters*, II, p. 759
44 Ibid, p. 760
45 Ibid, p. 762
46 Ibid, p. 766
47 Ibid, pp. 766–7
48 *P.W.*, pp. 360–1
49 *Letters*, II, pp. 774–5
50 Ibid, p. 775
51 Ibid, p. 777
52 *Notebooks*, I, 1098
53 *Letters*, II, p. 780
54 Ibid, p. 786
55 Ibid, p. 789
56 *Notebooks*, I, 1065
57 Ibid, 1072
58 Ibid, 1062
59 Ibid, 1064
60 *Letters*, II, pp. 782–4
61 Bodleian MS Abinger B229/4 (A)
62 *Letters*, II, p. 800
63 Ibid, p. 793
64 *Notebooks*, I, 1151
65 *Letters*, II, p. 798
66 Ibid, p. 794

67 *Notebooks*, I, 1151
68 Ibid, 1153, 1156, 1157, 1158, 1159
69 Dove Cottage MS of "Dejection"; a few lines, with Coleridge's comments in prose, are also preserved at British Museum Add. MS 27,902 f. 12
70 *Notebooks*, I, 1134
71 *P.W.*, p. 365
72 *Letters*, II, p. 797

Chapter 13: Metaphysical Mountaineer
1 *Letters*, II, p. 875
2 Ibid, pp. 832–3
3 *Wordsworth*, I, p. 303
4 Ibid, p. 302
5 Wordsworth, *Poems*, edited by John O. Hayden, Penguin 1982, vol. I, pp. 557–8
6 *P.W.*, pp. 369–70
7 *Letters*, II, p. 804
8 Ibid, p. 802
9 Ibid, p. 808
10 Ibid, p. 812
11 Ibid, p. 810
12 *Notebooks*, I, 1244
13 Ibid, 1220
14 *Letters*, II, pp. 865–6
15 Ibid, p. 864
16 Ibid, p. 814
17 Ibid, p. 869
18 Ibid, pp. 826–7
19 Ibid, p. 825
20 Ibid, p. 828
21 *Notebooks*, I, 1206
22 *Letters*, II, pp. 834–5
23 *Essays*, I, p. 357
24 *Letters*, II, pp. 835–6
25 Ibid, p. 839
26 Ibid, pp. 840–1
27 Ibid, p. 842
28 Ibid, p. 844
29 *Notebooks*, I, 1214
30 *Letters*, II, pp. 846, 850
31 *Lamb*, II, p. 65
32 Ibid, p. 69
33 Ibid, p. 70
34 *Letters*, II, p. 854
35 Ibid, p. 853
36 Ibid, pp. 853–4
37 Ibid, p. 876
38 *P.W.*, pp. 378–9
39 *Lamb*, II, p. 75
40 *P.W.*, p. 357
41 *Letters*, II, pp. 864–5
42 Ibid, p. 865
43 Ibid, p. 876
44 *Notebooks*, I, 1250
45 Ibid, 1253
46 Campbell, p. 134
47 *Notebooks*, I, 1248
48 *Letters*, II, p. 878
49 Ibid, p. 888
50 Ibid, p. 894
51 Ibid, p. 884
52 *Essays*, I, pp. 372–3
53 *Lamb*, II, p. 81
54 *Essays*, I, pp. 403–4
55 Ibid, p. 414
56 *Notebooks*, I, 1432
57 Ibid, 1395
58 *Essays*, I, p. 408
59 *Notebooks*, I, 1432
60 Ibid, 1267
61 *Letters*, II, p. 890
62 Ibid, p. 889
63 Ibid, p. 891
64 Ibid, p. 902
65 Ibid, p. 914

Chapter 14: Exile
1 *Letters*, II, p. 912
2 Ibid, pp. 913–14
3 Ibid, p. 909
4 Ibid, p. 909
5 *Notebooks*, I, 1273
6 *Letters*, II, p. 914
7 Ibid, p. 916
8 Ibid, pp. 918–19
9 Ibid, p. 933
10 Ibid, p. 934
11 Ibid, p. 938
12 Chambers, p. 167
13 *Letters*, II, p. 913
14 Ibid, p. 929
15 Ibid, p. 929
16 Ibid, p. 941
17 Ibid, p. 926
18 Chambers, p. 166
19 *Letters*, II, p. 941
20 Chambers, p. 169
21 *Notebooks*, I, 1378

22 *Letters*, II, p. 941
23 *Lamb*, II, p. 111
24 Ibid, p. 109
25 *Letters*, II, pp. 944–5
26 Ibid, p. 947
27 Ibid, pp. 955–6
28 *Essays*, I, pp. 434–5
29 *Notebooks*, I, 1411, 1415, 1412, 1428, 1401
30 Ibid, 1416, 1390
31 *Letters*, II, p. 960
32 *Notebooks*, I, 1616
33 *Letters*, II, pp. 990–1
34 Henry Crabb Robinson, *On Books and their Writers*, 3 vols, edited by Edith J. Morley, Dent, 1938; I, p. 169
35 *Letters*, II, pp. 1024–5
36 Ibid, p. 958
37 Ibid, p. 973
38 Ibid, pp. 966–73
39 Ibid, pp. 1000–1
40 Ibid, pp. 1001–2
41 Ibid, p. 965
42 Ibid, p. 975n
43 Ibid, p. 975
44 *Notebooks*, I, 1451
45 Ibid, 1406
46 Ibid, 1460
47 Moorman, I, p. 591
48 *Letters*, II, p. 1010
49 *Notebooks*, I, 1471
50 Moorman, I, p. 592
51 *Notebooks*, I, 1490
52 *Letters*, II, p. 994
53 Ibid, p. 986
54 *Notebooks*, I, 1504
55 Ibid, 1515
56 *Letters*, II, p. 982
57 Ibid, p. 983; *P.W.*, pp. 389–90
58 Ibid, pp. 988–9
59 Ibid, p. 990
60 *Notebooks*, I, 1681
61 Ibid, 1577
62 *Letters*, II, p. 1013
63 Ibid, p. 1013
64 Ibid, p. 1059
65 *Notebooks*, I, 1801
66 Ibid, 1798
67 *Letters*, II, p. 1035
68 Ibid, p. 1049
69 Ibid, p. 1109
70 Ibid, p. 1106
71 Ibid, p. 1083
72 Ibid, pp. 1115–16
73 Ibid, p. 1161
74 Ibid, p. 1072; and Bodleian MS Abinger B229/2(A)
75 Ibid, p. 1074
76 Ibid, p. 1095
77 Ibid, p. 1103n
78 Ibid, p. 1104
79 Ibid, p. 1115
80 Ibid, p. 1112
81 Ibid, p. 1122–3
82 Ibid, p. 1128

Acknowledgments

For the use of copyright materials, and kind permission to consult and refer to manuscripts and archives, my most grateful acknowledgments are due to the British Library, London; Lord Abinger; the Bodleian Library, Oxford; the Highgate Literary and Scientific Institution; the Wordsworth Library, Grasmere; the National Trust, Nether Stowey; the Staatsbibliothek, Göttingen; the Royal Library, Valetta, Malta; the Museo Archelogo, Syracusa, Sicily; the London Library; the New York Public Library; the Church Archive, Ottery St Mary; the Bristol County Library; Oxford University Press for permission to quote from the *Collected Letters of Samuel Taylor Coleridge*, edited by E. L. Griggs, and the *Complete Poetical Works of Samuel Taylor Coleridge*, edited by E. H. Coleridge; Routledge for permission to quote from the *Notebooks of Samuel Taylor Coleridge*, edited by Kathleen Coburn; the Public Records Office, Kew; the Ordnance Survey, Southampton; Aerofilms Ltd; and the Westmorland Gazette, Kendal.

My warmest personal thanks are due to Lady Rosamund Coleridge, at Ottery St Mary; Godfrey King and Mervyn Todd at Nether Stowey; Gwynydd Gosling at Highgate; Jeff Cowton, the Librarian, at the Dove Cottage Library, Grasmere; Barbara Harvey, who helped me climb on to the roof at Greta Hall, Keswick; William St Clair who advised me about Bodleian manuscripts; James MacGibbon, skipper of the *Pentoma*, who taught me the ropes; Rupert Christiansen who read and raised questions; Alan Judd who advised on British Foreign policy at Anchor; Chris Bentley of ML Design who drew the maps; Professor Magdalene Heuser, and Dr John Coates, at Göttingen; Professor John Beer at Cambridge; Professor Heather Jackson at Toronto; Professor Tom McFarland at Princeton; Dr Peter Vassallo at Malta; Catherine Carver in Paris; the family Archimede at Syracusa; and once again, those Quantock farmers.

For support and encouragement, my gratitude goes to the Society of Authors, Ismena Holland, Philip Howard of *The Times*, and as ever to my old friend and advisor Peter Janson-Smith.

My best thanks also to my wonderful editors Ion Trewin and Simone Mauger in London; and Christine Pevitt and Dan Frank in New York.

To those who have so far withstood the flapping of the Great Albatross, at Bridge House, and at Brixton, my love.

Index

NOTE: An asterisk * indicates those named in "Coleridge's Circle" (pp. 365–371)